A HISTORY OF THE ANCIENT WORLD

VOLUME I
THE ORIENT AND GREECE

OXFORD UNIVERSITY PRESS
AMEN HOUSE, E.C. 4
LONDON EDINBURGH GLASGOW
LEIPZIG NEW YORK TORONTO
MELBOURNE CAPETOWN BOMBAY
CALCUTTA MADRAS SHANGHAI
HUMPHREY MILFORD
PUBLISHER TO THE
UNIVERSITY

First edition, 1926
Reprinted, 1928
Second edition, 1930

RELIEF OF ARCHELAUS OF PRIENE

APOTHEOSIS OF HOMER

APOTHEOSIS OF HOMER

Zeus and the Muses are shown in the upper part of the relief upon a mountain side, and Apollo stands in a cave. Beside him is the *omphalos* or sacred stone of Delphi. On the right is a statue of a poet with a tripod. In the lowest row Homer is enthroned between figures of Iliad and Odyssey. He is crowned by Time and the World; figures of Myth, History, Poetry, Tragedy, Comedy, and other personifications are making an offering.

The relief was probably dedicated by a poet who had won a tripod in a contest, and had derived his inspiration from Homer. It is inscribed with the names of the sculptor Archelaus, son of Apollonios of Priene. 3rd cent. B.C. British Museum.

A HISTORY OF THE ANCIENT WORLD

BY

M. ROSTOVTZEFF

HON. D.LITT. (OXON.)
HON. D.LITT. (WISCONSIN)
PROFESSOR OF ANCIENT HISTORY
IN YALE UNIVERSITY

VOLUME I
THE ORIENT AND GREECE

Translated from the Russian by
J. D. DUFF

SECOND EDITION

OXFORD
AT THE CLARENDON PRESS
1930

Printed in Great Britain

TO
THE UNIVERSITY
OF
WISCONSIN

PREFACE

THIS book was planned and written between 1921 and 1923 at Madison (Wisconsin). It is a course of lectures on Ancient History which I gave yearly for nearly five years to the Freshmen of Wisconsin University, and which I am now giving, in a slightly altered form, to the Sophomores of Yale University. For publication in the shape of a book, these lectures of course have been revised, corrected, and supplemented.

My 'Outline of Ancient History' was not written merely as a text-book for the use of students. My chief object was to collect therein those fundamental ideas and views, concerning the main problems of ancient history, which I had gained from long years spent on the study of the subject. To give to this work a strictly scientific form would have required too much time, and also too great sacrifices on the part of the publishers. And further, it is too late for me to think now of a large and complicated work of the kind. I consider it more useful to devote what remains to me of life to work of a more specialist nature. For this reason I publish my book without scientific apparatus, endeavouring merely to make the exposition as simple and clear as possible. Published in such a shape, my book may serve as a text-book for students beginning the subject, and also may be read by those who wish to acquaint themselves with the general course of development in the ancient world.

In composing a brief outline of the subject, the chief difficulty was the selection and distribution of the matter. We know, of course, much more about the ancient world than is here set forth. It was difficult, also, to assign the right space to each epoch in the development of antiquity, and to each aspect of that development. My own interests and studies have been directed, and are still directed, to certain subjects in particular—the East, the Hellenistic Age, and the Roman Empire—and to the problems connected with the history of those periods, whether economic or social or cultural. But I have done all I could to prevent the matters in which I am specially interested from being too prominent, and have tried to allot due space to the history of the Greek cities and republican Rome, as also to the political and military history of the ancient world in general. How far I have been successful in this attempt, it is not for me to judge.

This 'Outline', as has been said already, does not contain references either to the ancient sources or to the works of modern scholars. This limitation was made necessary for me by the nature of my book. In general, I only refer to sources where the course of my narrative seems to require it. The most important modern works on the subject are enumerated in a short bibliography appended to the book; and there I mention also such English books as give a good summary of our knowledge in an easily accessible form. I have given this preference to English books, because my own book, in its English version, is intended mainly for English and American readers and students.

I recognize the very great importance of good maps for historical works. But unfortunately I am not a specialist in historical cartography or cartography generally, and I cannot myself make maps. I have been obliged therefore to be content with certain maps borrowed from other works—such maps as I considered most necessary to explain the narrative.

An archaeologist myself, I recognize the immense power of archaeological material to throw light upon antiquity. I have therefore devoted much time and pains to the selection of such material for the illustration of my book. I have been much helped in this matter by my friends Mr. B. Ashmole, Mr. J. D. Beazley, and Mr. H. Mattingly; the last has helped me specially with coins. In the choice of these illustrations, my object has not been merely to amuse and entertain my readers.

The soul of a people is just as clearly reflected in its literature as in its art. I have endeavoured to make due use of ancient literature in the course of my text; but extracts can give no idea of its real character and real greatness. Mere quotations from any great literary work are lifeless things, and therefore I abstain from them. If any reader of my book wishes to understand the soul of the ancient world, he must read at the same time the great works of ancient literature either in the originals or in translations. If other teachers do me the honour of recommending my work as a text-book to their students, they must insist on this point—that the chief monuments of the literature, Eastern, Greek, and Roman, be read, in their entirety and not in extracts, at the same time.

With regard to the plastic arts my position was different. In this case it is possible to give a selection of the noblest productions of ancient art, and to give it in the same book in which this material is used by the historian. Moreover, each of these monuments not only throws light upon various aspects of the ancient mind, but brings before the eyes either the great characters of the age in portraits which are often remarkable, or separate scenes from life, as they were represented in the fancy of the ancient sculptors and painters. These considerations account for the large space allotted in my book to the monuments of ancient art. For the benefit of the reader I have given short descriptions of the separate monuments, but without references to modern publications of them. Some such references the reader will find in the bibliography.

Lastly, an immemorial custom allows an author, when concluding his preface, to thank those whose assistance has lightened the composition and publication of his book. Unfortunately, I cannot enumerate all those who have contributed to the illustration by sending me photographs or permitting me to use monuments already published: a list of the names would probably fill more than one page. One acknowledgement, however, must not be omitted. My requests, which were often not too modest, did not meet with a single refusal from any European country or any institution in the United States. This is one more proof of the rapid restoration of international scientific relations, which the war seemed at one time to have shattered irrevocably. I must make a further exception and record the friendly assistance of my pupil, Miss T. S. Varsher, who spent much trouble and time in collecting photographs for my use in Rome and Italy.

My book appeared first at Berlin in the Russian language. I had not myself the time to make an English version of it; but fortune sent me an ideal translator in the person of Mr. J. D. Duff. Mr. Duff, who combines an exact knowledge of Russian with the training of a classical scholar, did not decline the thankless task of translating the work of an author who was too modest to translate it himself. I permit myself to offer him here my sincere and warm acknowledgements.

I must also mention here, not for the first time, my great obligations to the Clarendon Press and its conductors. It is due entirely to their courtesy that the book is provided with so large a number of excellent illustrations; and, further, I feel bound to acknowledge the assistance of the Oxford Press, both in the choice of a translator, and in procuring originals for illustration, and in the distribution of these illustrations upon the plates. A better publisher for my book I could not possibly have found.

I dedicate the book to the University of Wisconsin. In the darkest hour of my life the University of Wisconsin made it possible for me to resume my learned studies and carry them on without interruption. During five years which I spent there I met with constant kindness from my colleagues, and unvarying consideration, on the part of the University authorities, for my requests and my scientific occupations. Nor can I recall without a feeling of gratitude the sympathy of the students. Such an atmosphere lightened the toil of writing this book; and it was addressed in the first instance to the students of Wisconsin.

Vade felix libelle.

M. R.

NEW HAVEN (CONN.),
Sept. 25, 1925.

PREFACE TO THE SECOND EDITION

SINCE the publication of the first edition of this book four years ago a great deal of work has been done in the field of ancient history. Especially important are the new discoveries in the history of the Orient. Excavations in Egypt, in Mesopotamia, in Syria, and in Asia Minor have brought to light so much new material that it was impossible to leave the text and plates which deal with this period as they were compiled in 1925. The new edition, however, has been mainly printed from the stereo plates of the first edition (corrected for the purpose), and for that reason, and also because my publisher was obliged to call upon me for my corrections at short notice, I have been able to make fewer changes than I should have wished. In the sections dealing with Greece no changes have been made. To the plates of this section two new plates have been added, reproducing some archaic and hellenistic terra-cottas which bear on Greek life in the corresponding periods. The bibliography has been revised as far as it was possible in the short time at my disposal.

M. R.

OXFORD,
October, 1929.

CONTENTS

INTRODUCTORY

I. History: its Aims and Methods . . . 1

II. Ancient History: its Problems and Importance . 8

THE ORIENT

III. Earliest History of Mesopotamia and Egypt . 13

IV. Political History of Mesopotamia and Egypt in the Fourth and Third Millenniums B.C. . . 22

V. Government and Civilization of Egypt and Babylonia in the Third Millennium B.C. . . 40

VI. Political History of the Ancient East in the Second Millennium B.C. 65

VII. Political Development and Culture of the Ancient East in the Second Millennium B.C. . . 79

VIII. Political History of the East at the end of the Second and during the First Millennium B.C. . 105

IX. Culture and Art in the East during the First Millennium B.C. 127

X. Political, Social, and Economic Organization of the World-Empires of the East . . . 143

XI. Religious Development in the Eastern World . 157

GREECE

XII.	Greece and the Aegean Kingdoms	177
XIII.	Anatolian Greece. Economic Revolution in Greece in Centuries VIII–VI B.C.	189
XIV.	Sparta: her Social, Economic, and Political System	205
XV.	Athens and Attica from 800 to 600 B.C.	213
XVI.	Civilization of Greece in the Seventh and Sixth Centuries B.C.	229
XVII.	The Persian Wars	249
XVIII.	The Athenian Empire	262
XIX.	The Peloponnesian War	273
XX.	Greek Civilization and Social Development from 500 to 400 B.C.	282
XXI.	Greece in the Fourth Century B.C.	311
XXII.	Macedonia and her Struggle with Persia	322
XXIII.	Greek Civilization in the Fourth Century B.C.	333

THE HELLENISTIC PERIOD

XXIV.	The World-Monarchy of Alexander the Great, and the Political History of the Graeco-Oriental World in the Third Century B.C.	349
XXV.	The Greek World after Alexander: Politics, Society, and Economics	364
XXVI.	Greek Civilization in the Third and Second Centuries B.C.	378
Chronology		397
Bibliography		401
Index		407

LIST OF PLATES

Relief of Archelaus of Priene: The Apotheosis of Homer. Photo Mansell . . . . . . *frontispiece*

THE ORIENT

I. The Early Sumerians: 1, A Sumerian (British Museum); 2, King Gudea of Lagash (Photo Giraudon); 3, The Tablet of Lagash (E. de Sarzec, *Découvertes en Chaldée*) . *facing page* 24

II. A Military Expedition of Eannatum, King of Lagash: The so-called Stele of the Vultures (Photos Giraudon) . . 26

III. Naram-Sin and Hammurabi: 1, The Stele of Naram-Sin (Photo Giraudon); 2, The Code of Hammurabi (Photo British Museum); 3, Head of Hammurabi . . . 28

IV. The Early Kings of Egypt: 1 and 3, The Palette of King Narmer (Photos British Museum); 2, An early King of Egypt (Ashmolean Museum, Oxford) 30

V. Kings and Dignitaries of the IVth–VIth Dynasties of Egypt: 1, King Khafre (Khefren) (Cairo Museum); 2, A dignitary of the Old Kingdom (Metropolitan Museum of Art, New York); 3, Prince Montesupis (Cairo Museum) . . . 34

VI. Kings of Egypt of the Middle Kingdom: 1, King Senusret I (Photo Metropolitan Museum of Art, New York); 2, Sphinx of Amenemhet III (Cairo Museum) 38

VII. 1, The Palace of Kish (Photograph, Professor Langdon); 2 and 3, The 'Standard' of Ur (Photograph British Museum) . . 42

VIII. The Economic Life of Sumer: Frieze of the sanctuary near the city of Ur at Tell-el-Obeid (Photos British Museum) . . 44

IX. The Activity of the Early Kings of Egypt: 1, Ivory plaque from the tomb of King Semti (British Museum); 2, Mace-head of King Scorpion (Ashmolean Museum, Oxford) . . 46

X. The Pyramids: 1, The Sphinx and Pyramids of Gizeh (C. Jéquier, *Les Temples Memphites et Thébains*); 2, Restoration of the Pyramids of Gizeh (L. Borchardt and G. Steindorf, *Das Grabdenkmal des Königs Chephren*); 3, Reconstruction of the Pyramids of Abusir (after L. Borchardt) . . . 48

XI. Egyptian Life in the time of the Early Kingdom: 1, The Desert and the Nile. Tomb of Ptahotep; 2, Cattle Breeding. Tomb of Ti; 3, Ploughing, hoeing, sowing and stamping the seed into the earth. Tomb of Ti. (Photographs Lehnert and Landrock, Cairo) 50

List of Plates

XII. Egyptian Life in the time of the XIth Dynasty: Models of, 1, A Cabin-boat; 2, Inspection of cattle; 3, Cabin-chair, couch, and trunks (Photos Metropolitan Museum of Art, New York, and Cairo Museum) . . . *facing page* 52

XIII. Egyptian jewellery of the Middle Kingdom: 1, Pectoral of the XIIth Dynasty (Metropolitan Museum of Art, New York); 2 and 3, A necklace and mirror . . . 54

XIV. Writing in Egypt: 1, Scribe of the Old Kingdom (Photo Giraudon); 2, Inkpot and pens; 3, Papyrus roll (British Museum) 56

XV. Egyptian letters: 1, Hieroglyphic script; 2, Demotic script (British Museum) 58

XVI. Sumerian Art: 1, Statuette of the time of Gudea (Photographs, Les Archives photographiques d'Art et d'Histoire); 2, Harp of Queen Shub-ad (British Museum); 3, Shell plaque (University Museum, Philadelphia) . . . 60

XVII. Sumerian writing: 1, Stylus; 2, Pictographic tablet from Kish; 3, Sumerian seal cylinder from Kish; 4, Assyrian seal cylinder (Ashmolean Museum, Oxford) . . . 62

XVIII. Life in Minoan Crete: 1 and 3, Steatite vases from Hagia Triada (Photos Ashmolean Museum); 2, Gold ring-bezel (National Museum, Athens) 68

XIX. A city on the mainland attacked by enemies who come from the sea. (By the courtesy of Sir Arthur Evans) . . 72

XX. The Hittite Empire: 1, Ruins of the lower palace of Carchemish (Photo D. G. Hogarth); 2, Soldiers of Carchemish (Photo D. G. Hogarth); 3, Hittite soldier or god; 4, Soldier of Zenjirli. 74

XXI. War and Peace in Egypt in the time of the XVIIIth Dynasty: 1, The Queen of Punt (Cairo Museum); 2, Horemheb and the ambassadors from the Syrian lands (Museums of Vienna, Leyden and Berlin) 76

XXII. Thutmose III and the might of Egypt: 1, Thutmose III (Cairo Museum); 2, A Syrian Embassy to Pharaoh (Photograph British Museum) 80

XXIII. The Hittite King and the Hittite Priests (Photographs D. G. Hogarth) 82

XXIV. The Palace of Cnossus: 1, Store-rooms; 2, A state room; 3, The throne room (Photos Mr. Percival Hart) . . 84

XXV. Minoan Pottery: 1, Stone vessel from Isopata; 2, Pot of Kamares style (Candia Museum); 3 and 5, Minoan jugs; 4, Minoan amphora (Ashmolean Museum, Oxford) . . 86

XXVI. Minoan painting; part of a mural decoration of the Palace of Cnossus (Museum at Candia) 90

XXVII. The Temples of Luxor and Karnak (Photos Sir Alan Cobham) 92

List of Plates

XXVIII. The temples of Deir-el-Bahari (Photo Metropolitan Museum of Art, New York) . . . . . *facing page* 94

XXIX. Ikhnaton and his wife: 1, Queen Nefertiti; 2, King Ikhnaton (Photos Prof. Zahn) 96

XXX. Horemheb and the family of Ikhnaton: 1, Statue of Horemheb (Metropolitan Museum of Art, New York); 2, Queen Tiy (Photo British Museum); 3, A daughter of Ikhnaton (Photo British Museum) . . . 100

XXXI. Tutankhamen fighting and hunting (H. Carter and A. Mace, *The Tomb of Tutankhamen*) . . . 102

XXXII. Tutankhamen and his wife (H. Carter and A. Mace, *The Tomb of Tutankhamen*) 103

XXXIII. Life of the Egyptian nobles of the New Kingdom: 1 and 2, Parts of a fresco from a Theban grave (British Museum) 106

XXXIV. Assyrian warfare: 1, Bas-relief from the palace of Ashur-nazir-pal III; 2, Bas-relief from the palace of Tiglath-pileser IV (Photos Mansell) 108

XXXV. The Assyrian King and his army: 1, Stele of Esarhaddon; 2, Mounted soldier; 3, A war-chariot (Photos Giraudon) 112

XXXVI. The Persian Kings: 1, Darius and a lion (Photo Dr. Sarre); 2, Head of King Darius (Photo R. Campbell Thompson); 3, The Bodyguard of King Darius (Louvre, Paris); 4, King Darius fighting his enemies (British Museum) . 116

XXXVII. King Darius and the Rebels: 1-3, Rock bas-relief at Behistun (Photos R. Campbell Thompson) . . . 118

XXXVIII. Sculptures of the Persian period: 1, Tribute bearers; 2, Persian ladies on horseback (Photos Dr. Sarre) . 120

XXXIX. Late Egyptian Sculpture: 1, Queen Karomama; 2, Queen Amenirtis (Photos Giraudon) 122

XL. The Art of Neo-Babylonia: 1, A bull; 2, A snake-dragon (R. Koldewey, *Das wiedererstehende Babylon*, 4th edition, published by J. C. Hinrichs, Bookseller, Leipzig, 1925) 124

XLI. Art of Cyprus, Asia Minor, and Phoenicia: 1, 2, Sarcophagus of King Ahiram of Byblus (By permission of M. Pierre Montet); 3, Entrance to a grave-chamber in a rock at Paphlagonia (R. Leonhard, *Paphlagonia*); 4, A Cyprian sarcophagus (Metropolitan Museum of Art, New York) . 130

XLII. Assyrian Art: Part of the bas-reliefs from the palace of King Ashur-bani-pal at Nineveh (Photo Mansell) . 132

XLIII. The Palaces of Persian Kings: 1, Palace of King Cyrus at Pasargadae (J. Strzygowski, *Studien zur Kunst des Ostens*); 2, Palace of King Darius at Persepolis (J. Strzygowski, *ib.*); 3, Staircase of the hall of King Xerxes at Persepolis (Photo Dr. Sarre) . . . 134

List of Plates

XLIV. Persian Ornamental Art: 1, Winged 'genii' (Photo Les Archives Photographiques d'Art et d'Histoire); 2, Horned and winged lion-griffin (Photo Alinari) . . *facing page* 136

XLV. Agricultural Life in Egypt of the New Kingdom: 1, Fresco from a Theban grave (Photo Giraudon); 2, Mural decoration from the grave of Nakht (Photo Metropolitan Museum of Art, New York) 140

XLVI. Agricultural Life in Egypt of the New Kingdom: 1 and 2, Mural decoration from the grave of Nakht (Photos Metropolitan Museum of Art, New York) . . . 141

XLVII. Industry in Egypt of the New Kingdom: 1 and 2, Decorations from the tomb of Apuki and Nebamun (Photos Metropolitan Museum of Art, New York) 146

XLVIII. The Earliest Temples of Egypt: 1, Clerestory hall in the temple of Khafre at Gizeh (L. Borchardt and G. Steindorf, *Das Grabdenkmal des Königs Chephren*); 2, Restoration of the sun temple of King Ne-ouser-ra (L. Borchardt, *Das Re-Heiligtum des Königs Ne-Woser-re*) 150

XLIX. The Rock Temples of Abu-simbel (Photos Metropolitan Museum of Art, New York) 152

L. Egyptian Religion: 1, Seti in adoration before Osiris (Metropolitan Museum of Fine Art, New York); 2, Ra-Amon; 3, Isis, wife of Osiris; 4, Osiris (2 and 4, British Museum) 154

LI. Sumerian, Babylonian, and Assyrian Religion: 1, Restoration of entrance to the temple of Tell-el-Obeid (C. L. Woolley); 2, Stele with figure of Babylonian gods, &c. (Photo Mansell); 3, Bas-relief with figures of Assyrian demons (Photo Mansell) 158

LII. Minoan Religion: 1 and 2, Bezels of gold rings from Mycenae (National Museum, Athens); 3, Painted faience statuette (by courtesy of Sir Arthur Evans); 4, Painted sarcophagus from Hagia Triada (Photo Ashmolean Museum) 160

LIII. Hittite Religion: 1, Statue of the god Hadad; 2, The great god of the Hittites and his priest (Photos D. G. Hogarth) 164

LIV. Phoenician Religion: 1 and 3, Phoenician gods (Photos Les Archives Photographiques d'Art et d'Histoire); 2, One of the Semitic Baals (de Clercq and J. Menant, *Catalogue méthodique et raisonné*); 4, Side of sarcophagus of Amathus (Metropolitan Museum of Art, New York) . . . 168

LV. Persian Religion: 1, Bas-relief from palace of Xerxes at Persepolis; 2, Persian altars of fire-worshippers; 3, Rock-grave behind the palace terrace at Persepolis (Photos Dr. F. Sarre) 170

List of Plates

GREECE

LVI. Mycenean Greece: 1, Tiryns (Photo E. Norman Gardiner); 2, Vaulted corridor at Tiryns (Photo Mansell); 3, Reconstruction of a fresco-frieze in the palace of Mycenae, showing warrior, grooms, and horses (National Museum, Athens) . . . . *facing page* 178

LVII. Early Greek pottery: 1, Late Mycenean vase (British Museum); 2, Colossal Athenian vase (Metropolitan Museum of Art, New York); 3, Attic vase (Berlin Museum); 4, Rhodian jug; 5, Corinthian pot (Metropolitan Museum of Art, New York) . . . 186

LVIII. Greece under Oriental influence: 1, Ivory relief from Sparta—Spartan ship (Sparta Museum); 2 and 3, Ivory statuettes from Ephesus—a high priest and a priestess (Constantinople Museum) 192

LIX. Oriental and Greek Coins 196

LIXA. Greek Life in the VIth and Vth cent. B.C.: 1, 2, Clay statuettes found at Tanagra in Boeotia (from *Bull. de corres. hell.* xvii, 1893); 3, 4, Two clay statuettes found at Thebes in Boeotia (Photographs Giraudon) 197

LX. Greek vases, VIIth to VIth cent. B.C.: 1, Proto-Corinthian jug—Greek warriors (after *Antike Denkmäler*); 2, Archaic 'hydria' from Caere—Heracles and Busiris (after Fürtwangler-Reichhold) 202

LXI. Early Greek architecture: 1, Restoration of an archaic temple at Prinias (*Fouilles de Delphes*); 2, Door-posts and frieze of the temple at Prinias (*Ann. d. R. Scuola Arch. di Atene e d. Missione italiana in Oriente*); 3, Reconstruction of the Temple of Apollo at Delphi (after Replat) . 230

LXII. Greek architecture in Italy and Sicily: 1, Two of the temples of the Greek city Poseidonia (Photo Alinari); 2, The most ancient temple of the acropolis of Selinus; 3, Reconstruction of the city of Selinus (after Hulot-Fougères) . . 234

LXIII. Early Greek sculpture: 1, Marble statue of Cleobis or Biton (Delphi Museum); 2, Marble statue of a goddess or priestess (Berlin Museum); 3, Marble statue of a seated goddess (Photo Julius Bard); 4, Marble statue of Apollo (Museum, Olympia) 236

LXIV. Early Greek sculpture: 1, Attic grave-stele (Metropolitan Museum of Art, New York); 2, Marble grave-stele from Chrysafa (Berlin Museum); 3 and 4, Two sides of a base found in the wall of Athens—wrestling and a cat and dog fight (National Museum, Athens) . . . 244

List of Plates

LXV. Greek pottery of the VIth cent. B.C.: 1, Spartan kylix—King Arcesilas of Cyrene (Photo Giraudon); 2, Attic amphora—wedding (Metropolitan Museum of Art, New York); 3, Athenian kylix—Athenian ships (Photo Giraudon); 4, Attic amphora—Eos and Memnon (Photo Alinari) . 246

LXVI. Greek pottery of the Vth and IVth cent. B.C.: 1, Red-figured crater—King Darius (Furtwängler and Reichhold, *Griechische Vasenmalerei*); 2, Red-figured amphora—death of Croesus (*ib.*); 3, Red-figured cup—Greeks and Amazons (*ib.*) . . . . . *facing page* 254

LXVII. Greek pottery of the Vth cent. B.C.: 1, Red-figured Attic cup—Theseus (Photo Giraudon); 2, Red-figured Attic cup—Athenian warrior and his father (Photo Alinari); 3 and 4, Attic cups—Oedipus and the Sphinx, Jason and the Dragon (Photos Alinari); 5, A Greco-Persian gem—Persian king and Greek warrior (after W. Weber) . . 264

LXVIII. War in the Art of the Vth cent. B.C.: 1, Red-figured cup—capture of Troy (Furtwängler and Reichhold, *loc. cit.*); 2, Red-figured wine-cup—Heracles and the Amazons (*ib.*) 274

LXIX. Athens of the Vth cent. B.C.: 1, Restoration of the Acropolis (British Museum); 2, Ruins of the Parthenon (Photo Alinari); 3, The so-called temple of Theseus (Photo Kunsthist. Seminar, Marburg) 284

LXX. Greek sculpture of the Vth cent. B.C.: 1, Part of the marble frieze of the Parthenon (Photo Mansell); 2, Marble head of Zeus (Museum of Fine Arts, Boston); 3, Marble relief from Athens—Athena leaning on her spear (National Museum, Athens) 286

LXXI. The frieze of the Parthenon (Photos British Museum and Prof. Baur) 288

LXXII. Mystic elements in Greek religion: 1, Relief from Eleusis—Demeter, Kore, Triptolemus (National Museum, Athens); 2, Relief found in Italy—Orpheus and Eurydice (Naples Museum) 290

LXXIII. The great Athenian dramatists: 1, (?) Aeschylus (Photo Anderson); 2, Euripides; 3, Sophocles (Photo Anderson) 292

LXXIV. The great men of Greece in the Vth cent. B.C.: 1, Pericles (British Museum); 2, Herodotus (Metropolitan Museum of Art, New York); 3, Thucydides (Holkham Hall); 4, Socrates (British Museum) 298

LXXV. Greek sculpture of the Vth cent. B.C.: 1, Charioteer (Museum, Delphi); 2, Goddess—(?) Demeter (Museum, Cherchel); 3, Discus-thrower (*Denkmäler griechischer und römischer Sculptur*); 4, 'Idolino' (Photo Alinari) . . . 300

List of Plates

LXXVI. Greek sculpture of the Vth cent. B.C.: Reliefs from the
Villa Ludovisi (Photos Anderson) 302

LXXVII. Pottery of the Vth cent. B.C.: 1, Red-figured cup by
Duris—Athenian school (Furtwängler and Reichhold,
loc. cit.); 2, Red-figured cup—Heracles and Dionysus (*ib.*) 306

LXXVIII. Greek painting: 1, Polychrome Attic lekythos—grave of
an ephebe (W. Reizler, *Weissgrundige attische Lekythen*); 2, Athenian lekythos—Charon, Hermes, and
the soul (*ib.*); 3, Red-figured vase—decking of the
bride (Furtwängler and Reichhold, *loc. cit.*) *facing page* 308

LXXIX. The great men of Greece of the IVth cent. B.C.: 1, Plato
(Holkham Hall); 2, Aristotle (Vienna Museum); 3,
Demosthenes (Ashmolean Museum, Oxford) . . 336

LXXX. Greek sculptures of the IVth cent. B.C.: 1, Hermes
(Photo Alinari); 2, Demeter (British Museum); 3,
Athlete (Lansdowne House); 4, Sea-goddess (Ostia
Museum) 340

LXXXI. Greek sculpture of the late Vth and the IVth cent. B.C.:
1, Fight between Amazons and Greeks (Photo Mansell); 2, Grave-stele of an athlete (National Museum,
Athens); 3, Grave-stele of an Athenian lady (Cemetery
of the Ceramicus, Athens) 342

THE HELLENISTIC PERIOD

LXXXII. Alexander and his successors: 1, Alexander (Photo
Sebah); 2, Hellenistic ruler (Photo Alinari); 3, Attalus I (Photo Julius Bard); 4, (?) Alexander and
Olympias (Vienna Museum) 350

LXXXIII. Hellenistic sculpture: 1, Tyche of Antioch (Vatican);
2, Restoration of Nike of Samothrace (after Falize
and Cordonnier); 3, Nike of Samothrace (Photo
Giraudon) 354

LXXXIV. Coins of the Hellenistic period 360

LXXXV. The Hellenistic cities: 1, Priene (after Zippelius);
2, Pergamum (after Thiersch and Blaum) . . 366

LXXXVI. Hellenistic architecture: 1, Restoration of the tomb of
Mausolus (*Monuments antiques*); 2, Restoration of the
banquet-tent of Ptolemy Philadelphus (F. Studniczka,
Das Symposion Ptolemaios II; in *Abhandl. der Sächs.
Gesellschaft der Wissenschaften*, 1913–14) . . . 372

LXXXVII. Hellenistic painting and relief: 1, Mendicant musicians
(Naples Museum); 2, Comic poet at work (Photos
Anderson) 380

LXXXVIII. Hellenistic sculpture: 1, The dying Galatian (Photo Anderson); 2, Peasant woman (Metropolitan Museum of Art, New York); 3, Hellenistic ruler (Photo Anderson); 4, Nubian boy (Photo Giraudon) . . . 384

LXXXIX. Painting and sculpture. IVth cent. B. C. to 1st cent. A. D.: 1, Wall-painting in a chapel at Doura (*Syria*, 1922); 2, Funeral stele of a Phoenician priest Ba' Alyation (Photograph Sophus Bengtsson); 3, Relief from the tomb of Petosiris (Photograph F. Lefebvre) . . 390

XC. Greek life in Hellenistic times: 1, Figurine found in Egypt; 2, Statuette from Alexandria; 3, 4, and 5, Statuettes from Asia Minor (Photographs Giraudon) . 396

FIGURES IN THE TEXT

1. Seal impression of a clay tablet of the Kassite period found at Nippur (L. W. King, *History of Babylon*) 55
2. Section of the bas-reliefs of the rock-sanctuary of Yasili-Kaia (G. Perrot and C. Chipiez, *History of Art in Sardinia*) . . 83
3. Plan of the Minoan city of Gournia (American Exploration Society) 89
4. Plan of the Minoan palace at Phaestus (after L. Pernier) . . 91
5. Plan of the great temple of Amon at Karnak (G. Perrot and C. Chipiez, *Art in Ancient Egypt*) 98
6. Restoration of the hypostyle central hall of the temple of Karnak (*ib.*) 99
7. Restoration of the Ishtar gate of the temple of Marduk at Babylon (Koldewey, *loc. cit.*) 128
8. The Phoenician inscription on the sarcophagus of Ahiram, King of Byblus 129
9. Plan of the palace of King Sargon at Khorsabad . . . 133
10. Plan of the palaces of the Persian kings at Persepolis . . 139
11. Restoration of the buildings on the palace terrace at Persepolis (G. Perrot and C. Chipiez, *Histoire de l'Art dans l'Antiquité*) . 142
12. Restoration of the 'Ziggurat' of the tower-temple of Marduk in the Esagilla sanctuary of Babylon (*Jahrbuch des Deutschen Archäologischen Instituts*) 166
13. Restoration of the temple of Anu-Adad at Ashur (W. Andrae, *Der Anu-adad-Tempel in Assur*) 167
14. Upper part of the stele of King Esarhaddon of Assyria . . 169
15. Reconstruction of the north-western angle of the courtyard of the palace of Mycenae 180
16. Plan of the fortified palace of Tiryns 181
17. Restoration of the sixth-century temple of Artemis at Ephesus . 191
18. Painting of a black-figured cup showing scenes of rustic life (G. Perrot and C. Chipiez, *Histoire de l'Art dans l'Antiquité*) . 198
19. Black-figured cup showing a herd of goats with shepherd and dogs (G. Perrot and C. Chipiez, *ib.*) 199
20. A votive plaque from a sanctuary of Poseidon, near Corinth . 200
21. Votive plaque from Corinth 201
22. Laconian black-figured cup (*Jahrb. des Deutsch. Arch. Inst.*, 1901) . 209
23. The palace of Thetis from the so-called François vase . . 215

24. Black-figured water-pot (hydria): Athenian women at a public fountain (G. Perrot and C. Chipiez, *Histoire de l'Art dans l'Antiquité*) 217
25. Red-figured vase: Odysseus and the Sirens (Furtwängler and Reichhold, *Griechische Vasenmalerei*) 223
26. Reconstruction of the throne of Amyclae, near Sparta . . 227
27. Red-figured cup: Apollo killing the Titan Tityos (Furtwängler and Reichhold, *loc. cit.*) 231
28. Reconstruction of part of the 'Altis' of Olympia (Curtius and Adler, *Olympia*) 238
29. Reconstruction of part of the 'Altis' of Olympia (*ib.*) . . 239
30. Red-figured pot: Sappho and Alcaeus (Furtwängler and Reichhold, *loc. cit.*) 241
31. Red-figured cup: a pack donkey (G. Perrot and C. Chipiez, *Histoire de l'Art dans l'Antiquité*) 267
32. Red-figured cup: an Athenian foundry (Furtwängler and Reichhold, *loc. cit.*) 305
33. Red-figured water-pot: a potter's workshop (G. Perrot and C. Chipiez, *Histoire de l'Art dans l'Antiquité*) 309
34. Restoration of the temple of Artemis at Ephesus after the fire of Herostratus 335
35. Restoration of the Pharos of Alexandria (H. Thiersch, *Pharos, Ant. Islam und Orient*, 1909) 369
36. Restoration of the pleasure-ship of Ptolemy IV (*Jahrb. des Deutsch. Arch. Inst.*, 1916) 393

LIST OF MAPS

(*At end*)

1. The Orient.
2. Babylonia.
3. The Assyrian Empire.
4. Greece and Asia Minor.
5. The Persian Empire and the Empire of Alexander the Great.

Maps 1, 4, and 5 are based on maps in Robinson and Breasted's *Outlines of European History*. (Ginn & Co., Ltd.)

INTRODUCTORY

I

HISTORY. ITS AIMS AND METHODS

THERE are many different theories concerning the business of history as a science, but on one main point they all agree: it is evidently the business of the historian to reveal the past of humanity, and to reproduce the life of mankind in all its variety and trace its development from the most ancient times down to our own day.

History owes its origin to the same characteristic of man's nature which has created the other departments of learning: I mean the desire for knowledge innate in humanity. The object of this knowledge is the world in its entirety and, above all, man himself. In this desire to learn about the world and mankind and those powers which work in nature and human life, an important part is played by our inborn desire to know about our own past and the past of the world. From the earliest times man has endeavoured to record the prominent incidents of his own personal life, of the life of his family, clan, and country, and, eventually, of the life of humanity as a whole.

In this, as in other departments of knowledge, practical problems have moved side by side with this innate desire. Man learns by experience, and experience lies in the past. Many of our rights and claims are founded on incidents which took place in past times; and hence the desire to record these incidents and to preserve them from the possibility of being at any time forgotten.

But the memory of man is short, and his imagination is fertile. Facts in their actual form are easily forgotten and soon covered over by the accretions of imagination. Religion and reality overlap in human life; and therefore historical incidents easily assume the form of fairy-tales and legends, and are mixed up with man's belief in higher powers which direct his life. For this reason many historical facts, in the course of oral or even of written transmission, assume the form of myths, or tales which describe the interference in human life of divine and superhuman powers.

As soon as man devised the means of perpetuating the

incidents of his life in writing, it became possible for the first time to record exactly what had happened, and written historical tradition began. With the development of civilization man's interest in his own past increased, a number of facts known to him concerning that past were accumulated, and methods were contrived for putting these facts together and combining them into a connected narrative dealing with the past of this or that group of men or of all mankind in general. Just as in other fields of knowledge, a disorderly accumulation of separate observations was followed by a period when these observations were reduced to order and system, and this again by a period when they were utilized by means of a series of methods intended to clear up these two questions : What are the laws which operate in man's life and control him ? Is it possible to learn these laws from the facts of history and, having learnt them, not only to understand the past but to foretell the future ?

Different methods have been invented by man in order to learn about his own past. The first duty of history is to collect facts about that past. Incidents which aroused the interest of men were sometimes recorded by them immediately, at the moment of their occurrence, and sometimes, in a less exact form, later and from memory. But much was never recorded at all, and merely reflected in this or that form assumed by the outward and inward life of man ; and therefore it is obviously the business of the historian to collect not only the written records of man's past but also the material relics of his existence at different periods of his development. For the former purpose all written memorials of the past are collected in archives, libraries, and museums ; these are read, and the most important are published, and thus there is created the skeleton of history—a series of facts recorded by man in writing. To accomplish this task, the historian must be a philologer : in other words, he must know the languages in which historical documents are written, and also the gradual development of those languages, that is, the form which they possessed at different periods in the existence of this or that nation. Again, since the symbols which were and are used by man to denote the sounds, syllables, and words of language are unlike, and since this has given rise to an infinite variety in systems of writing, therefore the historian must be a palaeographer ; that is, he must know the development of these systems and their peculiarities.

The unwritten monuments of man's history which bear witness to his gradual advance in civilization are studied by specialists known as archaeologists. The results and methods of this specialist study must be completely known by the historian, because many eras of human life have left no written monuments. For it must be remembered that the first written symbols were invented not earlier than the fourth millennium B.C., and therefore have not existed more than 6,000 years, whereas the years of man's life on earth are reckoned by tens of thousands. It must also be remembered that the peoples of Europe, for the most part, were decidedly later than the peoples of the East in making use of written symbols—later by some millenniums—and that the earliest written monuments left by the Greeks, the pioneers of European civilization, are not older than the eighth century B.C. For the period that precedes writing, the material and, in part, the spiritual life of man must be ascertained almost wholly by a single method—by collecting and studying the records of his life left by him in the ruins of his dwellings and in his tombs. This period in the life of man in general and in the life of separate nations in particular is commonly called the prehistoric period.

When the historian has collected facts concerning the life of this or that nation, and wishes to make use of them to reproduce the past, he must, first of all, settle the sequence of these incidents and define which was earlier and which later; he must, that is, make clear their relative chronology. His next business is to define more precisely the time when this or that incident took place, and the interval that divides it from his own age; this we call the determination of absolute chronology. For this purpose, the historian must study and master the different methods of reckoning time which were devised by man in different places and at different epochs. These methods are infinitely different and very complicated; and all of them, including those which we now use, are exceedingly imperfect. We must not forget that our year is shorter than the astronomical year, and that our reckoning from the Birth of Christ is merely provisional, because we do not know the year in which Christ was born. Hence it is one of the fundamental problems of the historian to be able to calculate, precisely or approximately, by means of a series of observations and comparisons, the date of a given event or epoch in the life of a people.

In order to understand the events of history and estimate them aright, it is not enough to know what happened and when it happened: we must know also where it happened; that is, we must be able to connect the event with a definite place and have exact knowledge of the peculiarities of that place. Not only must man and his manner of life be known but also the sphere of his activity—the earth, with its different parts, with their geological and climatic differences, with their flora and fauna. In short, it is necessary to know the conditions of man's life in different places and at different epochs of his existence. The study of the earth is the business of the geographer. But this is not enough for the historian: he must know not merely the present appearance of the earth but also its changes and its history. He must know, too, the changes that have taken place in the distribution of mankind upon the globe, the location of this or that people, and the main centres of the life of separate nations and of the different kingdoms and empires. The history of the earth is taught us by physical geography, while historical geography deals with the relations of man to the earth which he inhabits.

The fact that a man belongs to this or that clan, to this or that race, is of vast importance in human history. Clans and races differ from one another in physical peculiarities, and in peculiarities of habit and language. To explain these differences is the business of anthropology, which studies man, as a part of the animal world, in his historical development. Closely connected with this are two other sciences—ethnography, which studies the peculiarities of separate nations, and comparative philology. The historian must be acquainted with the methods and conclusions of all these sciences.

The facts collected by the historian, when arranged in order of time and definitely assigned to the places and peoples concerned, form only the skeleton of history. These facts, especially such as are recorded in written and oral tradition, require verification. I have said already that man has not only a strong impulse to learn truth but an equally strong impulse to mutilate it, consciously and unconsciously. Man's tendency to poetic creation and the fertility of his imagination cause him often to restate facts till they are unrecognizable; he fills up gaps where he is ignorant and alters what he knows; he mixes up the region of religious and fabulous conceptions with the sphere of actual events. Myth and legend are inseparable from history, and even in our own time grow up round great historical events and, even more, round great historical persons. Together with this process, facts are also deliberately distorted under the influence of various motives—material advantage, or the endeavour to defend the reputation of the narrator or his friend, or the tendency to support a particular point of view or political theory. The influence of patriotism is active here: the writer wishes to prove that the nation to which he belongs is superior to all others, that it is always in the right and its adversaries always in the wrong. We must never forget that historical events were not recorded by machinery but by men, distinct personalities with definite characteristics of their own. Few of them have kept free from prejudice while recording historical events which, in one way or another, touched themselves nearly. Hence the historian, while collecting facts, must at the same time verify them and convince himself that they correspond with the reality. This is a complicated and difficult problem: it requires great caution and familiarity with various methods of verification. This part of the historian's work we call historical criticism.

When the historian has collected and verified his facts, he then proceeds to set them forth. But, while methods have been developed and perfected for dealing with facts, in order to collect and comprehend them, to date them and arrive at a critical estimate of them, there has arisen at the same time a different view of the historian's task, that is, of the immediate object of his labours. The number of historical facts is infinite, and they bear reference to different sides of the infinite variety of human life. Which among this multitude of facts are most valuable and important? What sides of life deserve study more than others? For long, history was mainly political history, and historical narrative was confined to an account of the most important crises in political life, or to an account of wars and great generals. But even the Greeks realized that if these facts, the incidents of man's history in politics and war, are important, it is still more important to ascertain the causes of these incidents and their connexion with one another and with the other phenomena of the life of communities. It has become clear that war, in spite of the profound impression it produces, is only one phase of man's life, and not the most important phase, and that the origin and course of wars are closely connected with the development of economic, social, and religious life and civilization. From this point of view politics and war have not become less interesting and important in the history of the separate groups of mankind; but men's eyes have been opened to the immense importance of studying the conditions of human development during periods that were not disturbed by war. From another side, a more thoughtful attitude to historical events has shown the very great importance of personality in the history of man's development; hence the historian endeavours to explain the psychology of the most prominent individuals in history, and to throw light on their character and the conditions which created it. And gradually another fact has come to light—that, if the psychology of individuals has an important influence upon the course of historical development, history is affected not less, and perhaps even more, by the psychology of separate groups of men, the ' psychology of the herd ', which finds its expression both in the organization of small groups of men, the family, for instance, and in the peculiar ordering of larger units—the clan, country, and nation. Lastly, it became clear how strongly this ' psychology of the herd ' has affected acute crises in the life of the community, such as find expression in wars and revolutions.

In the endeavour to comprehend the complicated structure of man's social life, history works hand in hand with the departments of scientific inquiry which have gradually become separate both from history and from philosophy: these are the economic sciences, sociology, political and juristic science, psychology, and such branches of knowledge as literature and art, which bear upon man's spiritual life and the special products of his civilization.

In close connexion with other departments of human knowledge, history tends to become more and more a science, whose end is to define the laws under which the life of man develops, and the regular process by which one type of communal life is displaced by another. Nevertheless, history still remains a branch of literature, because the narrative of events and the lively and picturesque transmission of them, together with the truthful and artistic delineation of important historical characters, will always remain one of the historian's chief tasks, a task of a purely literary and artistic nature. While becoming more and more a department of exact science, history cannot and must not lose its literary, and therefore individual, character.

II

ANCIENT HISTORY: ITS PROBLEMS AND IMPORTANCE

ANCIENT history is the history of man's development in the earliest period of his existence: it tells how at that period he created and developed the civilization from which the culture of all nations now existing is derived. By civilization I understand the creation of those forms of political, communal, economic, and cultural life which distinguish us from the savage. The savage continues to live in those primitive conditions which assimilate his life to that of the animal and distinguish it from the life of civilized man.

This ancient civilization, which spread by degrees over the world, was first developed in the Near East, and chiefly in Egypt, Mesopotamia, and Central Asia, in the islands of the Aegean Sea, and in the Balkan peninsula. From the Near East it passed into the West, beginning with Italy; and from Italy it conquered all western Europe and some regions in the centre of that continent. In this civilization there were successive epochs of high development—a series of creative periods which produced inestimable treasures not only of a material kind but also in the intellectual region of culture; and there were also periods of temporary stagnation and decline, when the creative powers of this or that part of the ancient world were for the time enfeebled. The zenith of cultural creation was attained by Egypt and Babylonia in the third millennium B.C.; by Egypt again in the second millennium and, at the same time, by Asia Minor and part of Greece; by Assyria, Babylonia, and Persia in the eighth, seventh, and sixth centuries B.C.; next by Greece from the sixth century B.C. to the second, and by Italy in the first century B.C. and the first century A.D. From the second century A.D. a general stagnation in creative power is observable in the whole of the ancient world; and from the third century an almost complete cessation of this power and a gradual reversion to more and more primitive conditions of life. But the foundations of culture still survived and were maintained—in the West by Italy and the provinces of the Roman Empire in western Europe, in the East by the Byzantine Empire, i. e. in the Balkan peninsula and Asia Minor. These foundations were taken over by new centres of government, which arose in the West in consequence of the conquest by German tribes of successive parts of the western Roman Empire, and in the East by the Slavonic kingdoms in the Balkan peninsula and in Russia, and by the great Mussulman powers, first Arabian and then Turkish. Thus taken over, they served as a basis of culture and enabled the peoples of Europe to start their creative civilization, not from the lowest stratum of prehistoric life but from the comparatively high level bequeathed to posterity by the ancient world.

Therefore it cannot be said that ancient civilization finally disappeared at any time: it still lives, as the foundation of all the chief manifestations of modern culture; but its creative period lasted, approximately, from the beginning of the third millennium B. C. to the second century A. D., or more than three thousand years, a period twice as long as that during which contemporary European culture has been developed.

From a geographical point of view, ancient civilization belongs to a single part of the world and not a large part: it was confined to a small part of Western and Central Asia and of the Mediterranean coast. It reached its highest development on the shores of the Mediterranean and may therefore be called 'Mediterranean civilization'. It was not confined to one people or one race: a series of nations took an active part in creating it. The first pioneers were the Sumerians in Babylonia and the earliest inhabitants of Egypt, probably of African descent; next came the Semites of Western Asia and the Aryans originally of Central Asia; the natives of the Caucasus and Asia Minor; the Iranians in Persia and Central Asia; and, finally, the Greeks in Asia Minor and the Balkans, and the Italians and Celts in Italy. Among all these nations the Greeks were especially remarkable for the power of their creative spirit, and to them we are principally indebted for the foundations of our civilized life.

But it must be remembered that the lofty creation of Greece was developed from the culture attained by the ancient

East; that Greek civilization only became world-wide as the result of a fresh and prolonged contact with the Eastern cultures, after the conquest of the East by Alexander the Great; and that it became the property of the West, that is, of modern Europe, simply because it was taken over in its entirety by Italy. We must also remember that Italy alone made it accessible, in its Roman form, to all those parts of the ancient world which Italy united for the purpose of civilized life. If the civilization of the East and of Greece was not confined to the eastern part of the ancient world but became the foundation of culture for the West and for modern Europe, for this Europe is indebted to Italy and to Rome. Hence, if ancient civilization is to have any ethnographical label, it should properly be called Graeco-Roman.

The study of this ancient Graeco-Roman civilization is of immense importance to every intelligent sharer in modern culture, and ought to form one of the main subjects of higher education.

The creation of a uniform world-wide civilization and of similar social and economic conditions is now going on before our eyes over the whole expanse of the civilized world. This process is complicated, and it is often difficult to clear up our minds about it. We ought therefore to keep in view that this condition in which we are living is not new, and that the ancient world also lived, for a series of centuries, a life which was uniform in culture and politics, in social and economic conditions. The modern development, in this sense, differs from the ancient only in quantity and not in quality. The ancient world witnessed the creation of a world-wide trade and the growth of industry on a large scale; it lived through a period of scientific agriculture and through the development of strife between the different classes of the population, between capital and labour. It also witnessed a period, when each discovery became at once the property of all civilized humanity, when the nations and peoples, over the enormous expanse embraced by the Roman Empire, came into daily and constant contact, and when men began to realize that there is something higher than local and national interests, namely, the interest of all mankind.

In a word, the ancient world experienced, on a smaller scale, the same process of development which we are experiencing now. If we study the successive stages of that development, we shall realize how nearly and closely we are connected with that world. For instance, the ancient world created the three main forms of government which are still preserved in our own political life. These are, first, the monarchical form, where the country is ruled by a central bureaucracy and all the threads of government are united in the hands of the monarch alone; secondly, the self-ruling free state, where all are politically equal and power resides in the sovereign people and its chosen representatives; and, lastly, the federal system, which combines in one political alliance a number of free and self-governing political units. To this day we have never got beyond these three fundamental forms of government; to this day we are struggling with the master problem of political organization—how to combine personal freedom and self-government of the separate parts with a single strong and intelligent controlling power.

Our dependence on antiquity is just as great in the sphere of science and art. Modern exact science has been built up entirely on the method of experiment, and this was first applied to the natural sciences by the Greek thinkers of the fourth and third centuries B. C. Our philosophy and morals are still founded on the scientific methods of abstract thought first hammered out by the ancient philosophers, and especially by Plato and Aristotle. In literature and the plastic arts we merely build on foundations laid by the genius of the ancient writers and artists; we re-fashion the same literary ideas and the same artistic themes which they originally created. Finally, in the sphere of religion, a great part, if not the whole, of modern mankind lives by virtue of beliefs which were first made their own by men of the East and of the West in the age of classical antiquity. We must not forget that Christ lived in the time of Augustus and Tiberius; that the Jewish religion is one of the religions of the Semitic East; and that the Mussulman creed grew up among the Arabian Semites who were strongly influenced by Greek civilization. These few indications are sufficient to prove that the study of antiquity is of immense importance to ourselves; for no one can understand the present, unless he has a clear conception of the evolution of government and civilization in the ancient world.

THE ORIENT

III

EARLIEST HISTORY OF MESOPOTAMIA AND EGYPT

FOR tens of thousands of years mankind over the whole earth lived in conditions akin to the manner of life among animals. Man, like the animals, used as food the flesh of the wild beasts he killed, together with wild plants and fruits; he, too, found shelter from heat, cold, and foul weather in natural caves; he, too, lived in separate families or in small groups. But as soon as he began to fashion his first weapon out of chipped stone and learned to use fire, the level of his life quickly rose above that of the beasts. Out of stone, wood, and bone he began to fashion not only continually improved weapons but various implements for domestic use, corresponding to his needs; he began to construct, with branches, earth, and stone, subterranean dwellings, which were half-cave and half-house. The earliest rudiments of art appeared: on their utensils and on the walls of their dwellings men began to scratch or draw in colour the figures of beasts and men; and they carved on wood or bone the first representations in relief of the living creatures round them. Finally, it was one of man's greatest conquests when, at the very end of this period of his existence, he forced certain animals to serve him, and learned not only to pick wild fruits and herbs but also to grow them. The long millenniums of this slow development we are accustomed to call the palaeolithic or Old Stone Age, because for his weapons and domestic utensils man used stone exclusively (apart from wood and bone), and stone in its most primitive form, merely chipped and not smoothed.

An immense forward stride was taken when men learned not merely to chip stone but, by means of strong pressure and friction, to smooth it and to give to stone implements whatever shape was desired and suited to man's needs. The age of these smoothed stone implements we call the neolithic or New Stone Age. Man's life and man's outlook on life both underwent a radical change in this era. It is possible that this change is connected with the appearance of a new race in Europe, Hither Asia, and North Africa—a race that had adapted itself to the new climatic conditions, new vegetation, and new animals of the post-glacial period, and also to the distribution, permanently established in the so-called quaternary epoch, of forests, rivers, lakes, steppes, and deserts over the surface of the earth.

Man's life, as I have said, became different. The introduction of polished stone weapons was only one innovation and not the most important. The fact that man, in the new conditions of climate, ceased to be merely a hunter, is much more significant. The larger animals which had been used for food had gradually disappeared from the forests and steppes, so that hunting became a more and more difficult business. New resources had to be devised. Agriculture, or the artificial growth of certain plants, and stock-breeding, or the raising of domestic animals, became the chief occupations of mankind. The animals were goats, sheep, cattle, asses, camels, and horses; they supplied milk, butter, cheese, and meat for man's food, and skins and wool for his clothing; the wild animals were no longer needed.

A further advance of immense importance was made by man in this age, when he first learned to mould pots out of clay and bake them, and when earthenware vessels took the place of the gourds, skins, basketry of various kinds, and hollowed-out pieces of wood, which had previously served his needs. This addition to his household goods has done remarkable service not to himself alone, for it enables us to trace his advance in civilization. Clay vessels are cheap and handy but exceedingly fragile. Hence a number of broken vessels are found wherever men have lived even for a short time; and in places that have been long inhabited, they have left behind them one layer of potsherds on the top of another. These potsherds are immortal. Wood, leather, and cloth rot in the ground; metal is eaten up by rust; but baked clay lasts for ever, unaffected by damp and proof even against fire. Thus it is comparatively easy, by studying the potsherds from an inhabited site and the whole pots placed by the living in the graves of the dead, to trace the steady advance of culture either in the altered shape of the vessels, or in the introduction of new patterns in the ornamentation, or in improved technical skill, due, for instance, to the invention of the potter's wheel. By the same method we can trace peculiarities in the life of separate groups of men, and the influence of one group upon another.

The change in the conditions of man's life which took place in the New Stone Age brought with it a corresponding change in his habits. In the earliest period of his existence he was a nomad or a semi-nomad. He lived on vast grass-covered prairies or on plains intersected here and there by copses; and he moved constantly from place to place, in pursuit of the wild birds and animals of the steppes. But when he had succeeded in taming certain animals, his manner of life, though still that of a wanderer, became different. His movements were no longer dictated by those of the wild beasts which he hunted. Now he drove his flocks and herds of tamed animals from place to place, wherever there was most grass, and where there was a spring of fresh water, a lake, or a river. The flocks were followed by their owners, riding on asses and camels, which man had trained to carry him, his family, his tent or movable house made of skins or felt, and his goods and chattels. It is probable that this movable house, half-cart and half-tent, was originally invented by these nomads.

A similar wandering life was led by primitive man also in mountainous and wooded districts. The winter he tried to spend with his animals in warm valleys protected from snow; in summer, when the valleys were infested by mosquitoes which spread the plague of malaria, he moved off to the mountains and climbed higher and higher. In the forests he sought for open glades which provided fodder for his cattle and enabled him to defend himself, his family, and his stock against the attacks of wild animals.

But as soon as man attained more agreeable conditions of life, as soon as he found perpetual pastures and places suitable for the sowing and reaping of crops, he naturally remained the year through in such places, converting his wagon or tent into a house, and defending this house, together with his flocks and fields, from wanderers like himself, who sought, as he did, convenient spots for permanent habitation. In such places, and especially at the mouths of great rivers, where the annual floods created splendid pasturage and made fields fit for cultivation, and also on the banks of great lakes, or along the course of great rivers, or as near as possible to some abundant spring, man naturally tried to settle, permanently if possible, to secure for himself, and himself alone, these pastures and fields, and to protect them from rivals who sought to share in his advantages. And so by degrees the nomadic life of the hunter and herdsman became the life of the landowner, the lord of fields and pastures.

Such were the conditions in which the original forms of social life were developed. Even in the nomad state men felt themselves stronger when collected in groups: it was easier for a group to lay low a great wild beast or to defend themselves from the attacks of robbers. And the necessity of unity within the group was felt still more acutely by the nomads who reared cattle: a single man or a single family was powerless to struggle against the elements, or fierce packs of wolves or hyenas or lions, or against neighbours who wished to make use of the same pasture. But the need of unity was greater still for permanent settlers. For continuous residence on one patch of ground increased the danger from wild beasts and from neighbours who were still in the nomad state: these neighbours, whether beasts or men, knew where to find tempting prey in abundance. Thus permanent habitation naturally led to unity—to a settlement of families in groups or clans, who spoke the same language and worshipped the same gods. This group tries, as far as possible, to protect its settlements by making them inaccessible. They build their villages on lakes or marshes, and place their houses and cattle-sheds on platforms, supported on piles and surrounded by water or quagmires. In hilly districts they settle on precipitous heights, surrounding their settlements with a rampart of earth or stone or felled trees. Some of these fortresses are not used to live in but merely as a refuge in time of danger for the members of a single group, whose houses are scattered over the district near the fields owned by the community. Living in groups and learning from one another, men naturally create a definite organization, submit to a definite discipline, and also continually improve the conditions of their life— clothing, implements, and domestic utensils becoming more useful and more artistic. Under these or similar conditions men lived for thousands of years in Europe, Asia, Africa, America, and Australia, the difference in different places depending on the climate, the nature of the country, and its peculiar powers of production. And under these conditions men still live in some parts of the earth to this day.

Two discoveries, which were probably made simultaneously in two centres of the life of neolithic man—in Mesopotamia (or Central Asia) and in Egypt—were of capital importance for the further elaboration and perfection of the conditions of life, and enabled men at once to take a long stride along the path of progress—I refer to the discovery of metals and the use of writing. The first discovery enabled man to make endless improvements in his material condition, while the second advanced his intellectual development and, in a wonderful degree, widened and deepened his ideas, religious and social, and, by this time, political also.

Let us examine more closely the conditions of life which obtained among those men who first discovered and utilized the metals, beginning with copper, and the art of writing.

Mesopotamia is our name for the country which lies between two great rivers of Hither Asia—the Tigris and the Euphrates. Both rivers rise in the mountains of Armenia, flow southward, and pour their waters into the Persian Gulf close to one another. The soil carried down to the mouths of these rivers gradually projected farther and farther into the sea, and created by degrees a level plain pierced here and there by the mouths of the Euphrates. Near the sea this plain was marshy and overgrown with reeds and bushes, and abounded with game and fish; but it grew drier in proportion to its distance from the sea and became more suitable, not only for hunting and fishing, but also for agriculture and cattle-breeding; and by all these qualities it attracted the neighbouring peoples who inhabited the mountains to the north and east and the deserts to the west.

Every year the melting snow upon the mountains produced great floods in the rivers; and these, overrunning their banks, inundated great stretches of the plain. The alluvial soil, very rich itself, was saturated by the floods, which left behind a coating of mud of extraordinary fertility; and the grain, sown in this mud, soon sprouted under the influence of the hot sun and gave fabulous harvests.

These inundations and the properties of this alluvial soil were, of course, observed at once by the first inhabitants of the plain, and at once utilized by them for intensive tilling of the soil, breeding of cattle, and culture of certain kinds of trees, especially the date-palm. But the climate of southern Mesopotamia is such that the harvest is insecure unless it is possible to retain the flood-water on the land longer than the flood itself lasts; and the harvest is especially abundant if the fields are watered at regular intervals after being flooded, so that the soil is not allowed to harden under the rays of the burning southern sun. Therefore, in order to make use of the infinite fertility of this plain, it was necessary to create a network of pools by means of dikes and dams, to regulate the flow of water, and also to make artificial irrigation possible by means of canals. Such was the manner of life contrived by the dwellers at the mouths of the Euphrates and Tigris. It certainly cannot be called an easy and careless life, and it became by degrees more and more complicated. Their fields yielded rich harvests; but the harvest depended entirely on the increasing and systematic labour devoted to the dikes and canals. Their flocks increased in numbers; but they might be utterly lost, unless the requisite attention was given to the pastures. Men themselves grew and multiplied, unless they were carried off by fevers and epidemics, by flood and famine. And there was a worse danger still. Life on the plain was jealously and greedily watched by the nomads in the neighbouring mountains and prairies, who were ready every moment to fall upon the flocks, fields, gardens, and houses of their richer neighbours. It was difficult even to keep the peace with their own clansmen who dwelt on the far side of a canal or branch of the river and owned the nearest gardens and fields.

An existence of this fashion imperatively demanded organization and long-sighted guidance, with power, intelligence, and experience in its leaders. They alone could assure the group of victory in the struggle with neighbours; they alone knew where to dig a canal and how to prevent it from silting up; they alone had skill to cure diseases and guard against them; and they also taught men to make use of metals and of writing, improved their weapons and implements, and taught them to reckon and measure, and to observe the heavenly bodies. From the very beginning of civilized existence, men were convinced that their life was directed by higher powers in the shape of gods and goddesses, who monopolized supreme knowledge, and without whose aid man was powerless. It was therefore natural that the strongest and wisest members of the community, who showed others how to live and labour and led them in battle, should pass for beings of a higher order, a special and exceptional class which stood in close relation to the god and received revelations from him. These men naturally became leaders of the people, guiding them in the struggle against nature and their enemies, and interceding for them with the gods; the bearers of experience and knowledge, they were kings, priests, and judges. They alone knew how to address the gods, to propitiate and please them; how to perform certain ceremonies and offerings, and in this way to secure that the floods should bring fertility and not destruction, that men and animals should recover from their sicknesses or escape them altogether, that their enemies should be defeated, and that their neighbours should forfeit to them fields and flocks.

Thus a communal life began and was developed at the mouths of the Tigris and Euphrates. Separate groups of men found priest-kings to guide them and rallied round them, settling in close proximity to the temple of their god and the dwelling of their king, the god's earthly representative; both temple and palace were fortified with strong walls and ditches. In short, these men first created a more or less ordered kingdom, concentrated round a single fortified town and ruled by one man, the strongest and wisest of their number; and round him were ranged his family and his chief assistants.

We do not know precisely who these settlers were who first created a form of ordered government at the mouths of the Tigris and Euphrates. They called themselves Sumerians. There are good reasons for supposing that they were not the original inhabitants of the country but came there from the mountainous districts to the north and east. The earlier inhabitants whom they conquered were perhaps themselves immigrants from the deserts of Arabia. In any case it is certain that the Sumerians did not belong to the same race as the inhabitants of the desert, whom we commonly call Semites, and who still form the larger part of the population in the Near East. But it is equally certain that the Sumerians, from the beginning of their residence in Mesopotamia, were mixed up with Semites and were always surrounded, on almost all sides, by neighbours of Semitic origin who were gradually abandoning a nomadic life and settling down. It is possible that the Sumerians were familiar with the use of metals and writing and with the rudiments of political life and agriculture even before their migration to Mesopotamia. All this, however, is not more than guesswork.

A similar life was developed at nearly the same time on the banks of the Nile in Egypt. Here, too, there was a mighty river, flowing from the mountains and swamps of Central Africa and carrying down its waters to the sea; and here, too, a rich and fertile alluvial soil was created by the annual floods. In Egypt this alluvial soil extends in a narrow strip from south to north between two rocky precipices of the desert which hems in the Nile on the east and west. Towards the north this strip grows wider and wider, and at the outflow of the river takes the shape of a triangle, which is called the Delta, from the shape of the fourth letter of the Greek alphabet. The Delta is pierced in all directions, but especially from south to north, by arms of the river spreading like a fan. Here, finally, there are annual floods, which demand the same attention and the same regular labour as the floods of Mesopotamia.

But all the conditions of life were not identical in the two countries. Mesopotamia was open and unprotected on all sides. It was surrounded by districts, mountainous or flat, which were comparatively thickly populated. The neighbouring plain did not at once take the form of a desert. Owing to the spring rains, considerable parts of it, bounded on the north by mountains, on the east by the estuaries of the Tigris and Euphrates, and on the west by the Mediterranean, are suitable for agriculture and cattle-breeding; such is the origin of that 'fertile crescent' which has played a considerable part in the destiny of Hither Asia. In Egypt things are different. Outside the Nile valley and its narrow strip of fertile land, to the east and to the west at once begins the desert, limitless, burning, and barren, and containing very few oases. It had hardly any population, and certainly no considerable number of inhabitants living in large groups. Egypt is therefore exposed on two sides only, the south and north. It is bounded on the south by Nubia, the region of the Upper Nile with a comparatively dense population; and next to Nubia comes the rich coast of the Red Sea, formerly known as Punt and now Somaliland. But the Upper Nile is not easily navigable, because its course is broken at several points by the cataracts. Hence the defence of Egypt on the south was a comparatively simple problem. In the north the position was more complicated. Here the Nile valley grows wider and is bordered on both sides by the rocky desert, which runs, on the west, far into the depths of Africa, and, on the east, connects Egypt with Hither Asia. The district which fringes lower Egypt on the west—the so-called Libyan coast of the Mediterranean—is less forbidding and barren than farther south; but even here climatic conditions and the lie of the land prevented any considerable numbers from settling; so that the dense population of the Delta, pierced by canals and branches of the Nile, could easily protect themselves against attacks from their western neighbours. The chief danger that threatened Egypt came from the north-east. The peninsula of Sinai, which borders the Delta on the east, is forbidding, barren, and waterless; but the journey across it from Arabia or Palestine is short. Hence it was not difficult for inhabitants of Hither Asia, who were familiar with the desert, to make their way from time to time, even in great numbers, into Egypt. Finally, Egypt was continually threatened by danger from the north, from the sea. On this side she is defenceless; and it was never difficult for a strong maritime power to penetrate with a fleet along the branches of the Nile far into the rich Delta.

Still, thanks to her geographical position, Egypt was less exposed to attacks from neighbours than Mesopotamia, though less accessible to a large and active international commerce. She was more self-contained, more isolated; it was easier for her, with appropriate organization, to resist would-be conquerors. It is therefore natural that life in Egypt was of a more peaceful and less military type. But Egypt, too, was forced to keep constant guard, and therefore the king's power is of the same military-religious kind as in Mesopotamia, but with a greater predominance, perhaps, of the economic element. But with this comparatively trifling difference life was almost identical in both these cradles of human civilization. In both countries it was the creation of a river; in both it demanded strict organization, unity, and skilled direction; it forced men to labour and to think; it made them subordinate themselves deliberately to directors and organizers. Both in Egypt and Mesopotamia, nature had created exceptionally favourable conditions for developing an ordered life of effort—the only kind of life capable of creating a real culture.

IV

POLITICAL HISTORY OF MESOPOTAMIA AND EGYPT IN THE FOURTH AND THIRD MILLENNIUMS B.C.

THE brilliant development of civilization in Mesopotamia and Egypt which followed the discovery of the metals and the invention of writing (see Chapter V), together with their advance in economic life and commercial relations with their neighbours, had political results which are important for the history of both countries. Babylonia and Egypt became by degrees densely populated and completely cultivated countries, consisting of fields, gardens, and rich pastures; here and there on high artificial hills there rose temples and palaces, surrounded by walls; and these were the first cities of the new civilization. The neighbours, whether semi-nomads of the mountains or real nomads of the desert, looked with envy at the wealth and culture of these two countries; they were eager to barter their own produce—cattle, ivory, rare kinds of wood and stone, spices, precious stones, and probably gold and silver; and they received in exchange corn, fruit and vegetables, garments of wool and flax, and especially various metal products. The manufacture of copper and bronze was steadily developed in Babylonia and Egypt; the former brought the ore or partly refined ingots down the Euphrates from the Transcaucasian mountains and the shores of the Black Sea, while the latter drew their supplies from the peninsula of Sinai. Constant communication made their neighbours familiar with the technical skill acquired by Babylonia and Egypt, till they began, not merely to buy metal tools and weapons, but to make them for themselves. The nearer they lived to the civilized centres, the more they improved their technical skill and organization, especially with a view to war, and the more dangerous they became to the dwellers in the rich valleys of the Euphrates and the Nile.

Attacks from neighbours were the natural consequence of the influence exercised upon them by the civilization of

Babylonia and Egypt, and forced both these countries to strive for concentration and for the coalition of small kingdoms with a trifling extent of territory. This kind of combination, apart from its obvious military advantages, was also highly important for the further development of economic life. The network of dikes and canals was developed with greater foresight; the exchange of products between different parts of the country became easier and more convenient, owing to these dikes and canals; and relations with neighbouring peoples became less difficult. But this unity could not be brought about by peaceful methods, because each city reckoned that its god was the best god, and that all its neighbours should submit to it. Disputes about boundaries or pasture or irrigation led to collisions, and collisions gave birth to wars; wars were followed by conquests and by the temporary rule of this or that city over its neighbours and over the whole fertile plain. But as soon as the strength of a ruling city began to fail, its neighbours—the priest-kings of the cities nearest it—became rivals for its position; and this led over again to wars and mutual extermination, until the dwellers in the plain, weakened by internal strife, became an easy prey to neighbouring peoples. These invaders conquer separate cities and dominate the original inhabitants; and then a time comes when the oppressed arise in their turn and attempt, sometimes successfully, to shake off the yoke of the oppressor.

This process can be observed more clearly in Babylonia than in Egypt. For, as has been said already, Egypt was less in danger of conquest from without, and therefore the unification of the country was accomplished more quietly, without constant disturbances and the substitution of one foreign conqueror for another. How the process described above gradually came about in Babylonia we do not yet know with any completeness. We possess only casual records, found during the excavation of the few Babylonian cities which have so far been examined. They consist mainly of narratives by individual priest-kings (*patesis*), preserved in their temple-archives, and telling of their victories over their enemies. We have also some later documents, not contemporary with the events they describe, which try to give a connected history of an early period.

These latter Babylonian records are of a comparatively

PLATE I

THE EARLY SUMERIANS

1. STATUETTE OF A SUMERIAN, probably of a ' patesi '. He is seated in the attitude of prayer. Note the primitive workmanship and the rude attempt at a portrait. About 3000 B.C. British Museum.

2. BASALT STATUE OF KING GUDEA OF LAGASH. Found at Lagash. Note the rapid advance of sculpture in Sumer. About 2600 B.C. Paris, Louvre.

3. SCULPTURED AND INSCRIBED STONE PLAQUE, probably a votive offering. Found at Lagash. The king Ur-Nina is represented twice. On the upper part of the tablet he is carrying a mason's basket on his head. The ceremony is the foundation of a temple. The inscription, in archaic cuneiform characters and in Sumerian language, says that the king has built a temple to the god Ningirsu, with a great basin and a temple to the goddess Nina. The king looks at the members of his family whose names are inscribed on their figures. Near him is his cup-bearer. On the lower half of the plaque the king is pouring a libation. The inscription says that he brought wood from the mountains, probably for building the temples. Behind the throne is the cup-bearer. Of the figures facing the king the first is his prime minister Dudu, while the other three are his sons. About 3100 B.C. Paris, Louvre.

1. STATUETTE OF A SUMERIAN   2. KING GUDEA OF LAGASH

3. THE TABLET OF LAGASH

I. THE EARLY SUMERIANS

late period—the earliest of them belong to the twenty-third century B.C.—and cannot lay claim to historical authenticity. They mix up legend with history; and the chronology of the earliest dynasties, which may be placed before the middle of the fourth millennium, is fanciful and obviously invented. But excavation is still going on in Babylonia and each new campaign of the explorers reveals new documents; and we may believe that in the near future we shall know much more than is possible at this moment of the early history of Mesopotamia. Out of scores of ancient cities of Sumer very few have as yet been examined in detail; of these the chief are Kish, Ur, and Eridu with their splendid monuments recently discovered, and also Lagash and Nippur, which first revealed to us the secret of the Sumerian language and culture.

From the evidence which lies before us at present we may conclude that at the end of the fifth millennium B.C. the process above mentioned was going on in the southern part of Mesopotamia—the process by which the territories of separate Sumerian and Semitic cities were united to form larger kingdoms under the headship of a single city, either Sumerian or Semitic. The earliest rulers of the south and north—of Sumer and Akkad—were successively, and perhaps to some extent contemporarily, dynasties of Kish, Uruk, Ur, and a series of other cities. The Third Dynasty of Kish, about the end of the fourth millennium, is entirely authentic, and one of its most eminent kings was Mesilim. About 3000 B.C. an important part in the history of Babylonia was played by the Sumerian dynasty of kings who reigned in Lagash. Though the city of Lagash never united the whole of Sumer and Akkad round itself, yet it was one of the strongest powers tributary to the cities which aspired to sovereignty in both countries. The most famous kings of Lagash were Ur-Nina and, especially, his grandson Eannatum (about 3000 B.C.), and the immediate successors of the latter. The power of Lagash was finally destroyed by the first great Sumerian conqueror about whom we are well informed. This is Lugal-zaggizi, King of Umma and Uruk, who was able not only to subdue the cities of Sumer but also to undertake foreign campaigns, from the Persian Gulf to the shores of the Mediterranean; the date is after 2900 B.C.

His rival was Sargon I, King of the Semitic city of Akkad on the northern part of the lower Euphrates. About 2800 B.C.

PLATE II

A MILITARY EXPEDITION OF EANNATUM THE KING OF LAGASH

THE SO-CALLED STELE OF THE VULTURES OR EAGLES. Found at Lagash. Only seven sculptured fragments of the stele are preserved. The bas-reliefs of the front and back, and the inscription which covers both the front, back, and edges of the stele, tell the story of Eannatum, king of Lagash and especially of his great victory over the rival city of Umma. On the front we see the god Ningirsu with the arms of the city of Lagash (the lion-headed eagle with two lions in his claws) in his left hand and the mace in his right. He has caught in his net the enemies of Lagash and kills them with his mace one after the other. The other fragments of this side show that the colossal figure of the god was surrounded by the smaller figures of the king and his victorious soldiers. On the back of the stele the great battle is depicted. The top represents the sky where eagles are carrying away in their claws the limbs of the conquered enemies. In the first panel from the top the king on foot is leading his army. He is armed with the peculiar Sumerian sword (the 'boomerang'). The soldiers with their large shields and spears form a real 'phalanx'. They march over the bodies of slain enemies. Before the army are heaped bodies of the slain. In the second panel the king in a chariot leads his soldiers. The next panel is occupied by a religious ceremony performed by the king before a heap of bodies. Further below the king is represented killing his rival with his spear. This stele is the first artistic attempt to give the full story of an event in pictures. The art though primitive is pathetic and tragic. Early third millennium B.C. Paris, Louvre.

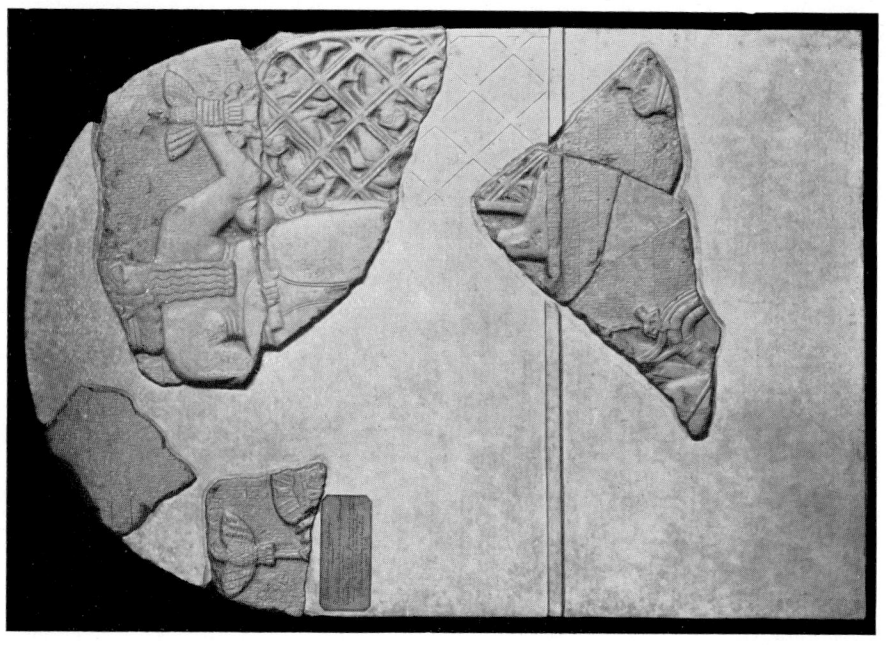
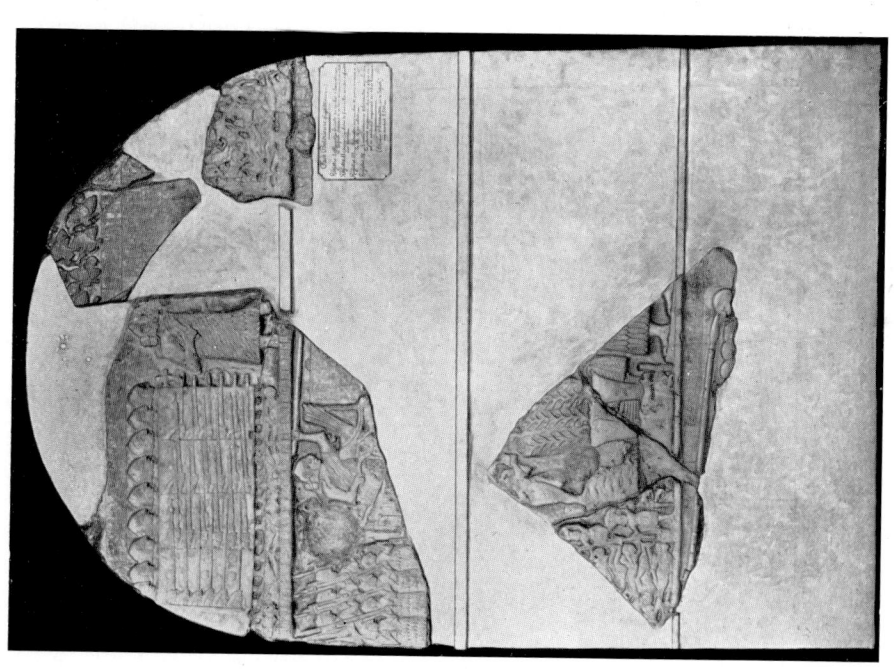

II. A MILITARY EXPEDITION OF EANNATUM THE KING OF LAGASH

Sargon conquered Lugal-zaggizi and laid the foundation of a comparatively substantial and prolonged union of all the territories along the lower Tigris and Euphrates under the rule of the kings of Akkad; of this region the northern part was inhabited by Semites and the southern by Sumerians. He is remarkable partly for his conquests over neighbouring races and countries and partly as the creator of an empire including different nations. Abandoning a policy of passive defence, Sargon and his successors, of whom King Naram-Sin is the most conspicuous, adopted, for the protection of their kingdom, a policy of active defence: they waged repeated campaigns in the territory of their neighbours, especially the mountaineers of Elam in the east, the Semites in the west, and the various tribes who lived on the upper Euphrates and on the north-eastern plateau of Asia Minor. From Sargon's time this policy became traditional with all powerful eastern kings.

These conquests were not followed by the creation of one great empire, governed from one centre and including various nations. The conquering kings were content if their neighbours merely confessed themselves defeated, the sign of defeat being a yearly tribute and also (probably) an engagement not to interfere with the commercial caravans sent by the victors through the territory of the vanquished and with the settlement of colonists in the conquered lands. Otherwise the life and government of the defeated countries remained unchanged. Even in Sumer and Akkad Sargon and his successors did not create a centralized government: each separate city still kept its own *patesi* or priest-king; and the kingdom of Sumer and Akkad was always a union of petty kingdoms controlled by the kings of the ruling race, never a centralized kingdom ruled by a single king and his officials.

The vigorous foreign policy of Sargon and Naram-Sin led them and their armies far beyond the limits of the Tigris and Euphrates—all the way to the shores of the Mediterranean and the Black Sea, and perhaps as far as Cyprus. This was of great importance for the future, because in this way the culture acquired by Sumer was first made accessible to a series of races and peoples in Hither Asia, and laid the foundations for an independent culture, developed later in the north and north-west by Asia Minor, Syria, and Transcaucasia, and in the east by Elam and Persia. It should also be noted that

PLATE III

NARAM-SIN AND HAMMURABI

1. STELE OF NARAM-SIN KING OF SUMER AND AKKAD. Found at Susa, whither it had been carried as a part of war booty by one of the later Elamite kings. The few remains of the inscription show that in the bas-relief of this stele Naram-Sin celebrated his victory over some peoples who dwelt to the east of the Tigris in the Zagros mountains. The king is represented in his military dress with bow and arrow in his hands ascending a mountain. He is followed by his soldiers with standards and spears. His enemies are killed in masses and their bodies slide down the wooded slopes of the mountain. Some (one with a broken spear) are begging for mercy. In the sky are the two stars of Ishtar, the protectress of Akkad and the goddess of war. The stele shows the same tragic conception of the subject as the stele of the eagles, but art has advanced enormously. The monument is full of life and movement, and the composition skilful; the first attempt at reproducing a landscape is here made. 28th cent. B.C. Paris, Louvre.

2. STELE OF HAMMURABI WITH A COPY OF HIS FAMOUS CODE OF LAWS. Found at Susa, whither it had been carried by an Elamite king as war booty. The stele is about 8 ft. high. The copy of the code extends right round the shaft and consists of over 3,600 lines. The top of the front is occupied by an excellent bas-relief showing King Hammurabi in adoration before the great Sun-god of Babylon (Marduk) who is handing him over the code of laws. Thus the divine origin of the laws is emphasized. The rays behind the shoulders of the god show that he is a sun-god. About 2100 B.C. Paris, Louvre.

3. HEAD OF HAMMURABI. Detail of fig. 2.

1. THE STELE OF NARAM-SIN

2. THE CODE OF HAMMURABI

3. HEAD OF HAMMURABI

III. NARAM-SIN AND HAMMURABI

the power of Sumer and Akkad had a favourable influence on the development of the Sumerian cities. Gudea, the famous *patesi* of Lagash (about 2600 B.C.), was a contemporary of the kings of Uruk who followed Sargon's dynasty; and the French excavations already mentioned show that Lagash reached its highest point of civilization under Gudea.

Sargon's kingdom lasted for about two centuries, approximately till 2625 B.C. Gradually, however, the centrifugal forces of the kingdom outweighed the centripetal, and decomposition and feebleness set in. It was a great disaster when successive parts of the country were seized by savage mountain tribes from Gutium, laid waste the land, and destroyed and burned down cities, palaces, and temples. The rule of the Gutian dynasty lasted about a century. The civilized inhabitants of Sumer and Akkad—Sumerians and Semites—recognized by degrees the necessity of union; and their united forces, under the command of Utukhegal, King of Uruk, defeated and expelled the Gutian invaders. This liberation was followed by an outburst of national and cultural regeneration. The Sumerians come again to the front of the stage. After 2465 B.C. the Kings Ur-engur and Dungi form a lasting union of all Sumer and Akkad under the control of Ur, and even restore, almost entirely, the empire of Sargon and Naram-Sin: northern Mesopotamia, including Assyria and even Cappadocia, Elam, and the mountain districts to the east of the middle Tigris, were all provinces of this empire: one of the many business documents in cuneiform found in Cappadocia bears the seal of Ibi-sin King of Ur. The reign of Dungi witnessed also a marked advance in the art, religion, and culture of the Sumerians. The first attempt to codify civil and criminal law is connected with his name, and also the first organized worship of the king, in his lifetime and after his death. The powerful dynasty of Ur was overthrown by a revolt of the Elamites, and its place was taken by the Semitic dynasties of Larsa, Isin, and, after 2129 B.C., of Babylon. During this period the chief rivals of the Sumerians and Semites in Mesopotamia were the Elamites, their most enlightened neighbours, whose civilization was just as old and just as remarkable as that of Sumer. This has been proved by the French archaeologists who have excavated their chief city, Elam, later known as Susa.

Babylon, under its able ruler, the Amorite Hammurabi (2123–2081 B.C.), united Mesopotamia once more and inflicted

PLATE IV

THE EARLY KINGS OF EGYPT

1 & 3. THE PALETTE OF KING NARMER (Ist DYNASTY). Palettes of the same form are regularly found in prehistoric graves of Egypt; they were used for mixing paint. This palette was found at Hieraconpolis with a mace-head of the same king. The bas-reliefs represent the great victories of the king over his Northern foes. On one side he is represented wearing the Northern crown and smiting a Northerner with his mace. Behind him is the bearer of his cup and sandals; before him is the god Horus (the falcon) holding by a string a head of a Northerner and seated on six papyrus-plants which symbolize the ' North '. Below are two Northerners in wild flight. On the other side the king, wearing the Southern crown, is inspecting a heap of decapitated bodies of Northerners. Before him go his ' vizier ' and four bearers of standards with the symbols of Egyptian gods; behind him is the cup- and sandal-bearer. The lower part of this side of the palette is occupied by the figure of a bull (i. e. the king) destroying the fortress of the enemies and trampling upon a vanquished foe. The centre of the palette represents two fantastic animals (i. e. the primeval forces of nature) mastered by two men. On the top of the palette on both sides are four horned heads of the goddess Hathor. Scattered over the field are signs belonging to the early pictorial script. Note many similarities with Sumerian monuments of the same time. According to a recent theory the palettes do not belong to the protohistoric period of Egypt but to the obscure period of foreign conquest after the end of the VIth Dynasty. Fourth millennium B. C. Cairo Museum.

2. STATUETTE OF AN EARLY KING OF EGYPT. The head is clean-shaven; the beard is artificial. On the belt there is a quiver. The feet are broken off. The sculpture is very primitive. Fourth millennium B. C. Ashmolean Museum, Oxford.

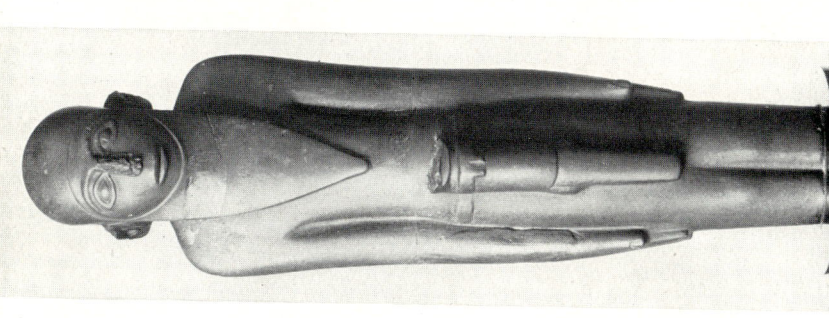
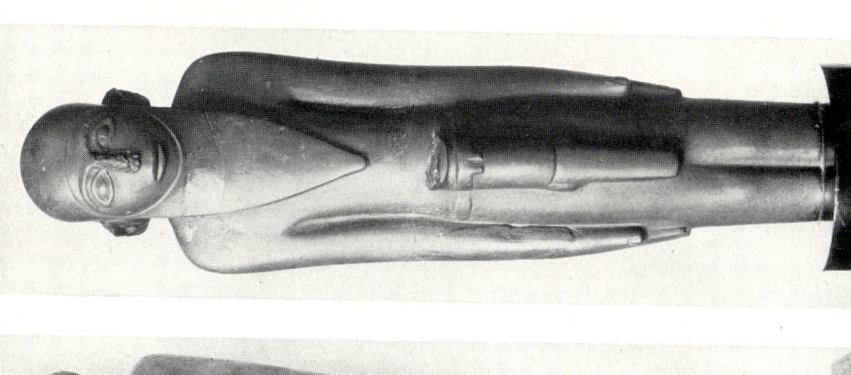

1. THE PALETTE OF KING NARMER   2. AN EARLY KING OF EGYPT   3. THE PALETTE OF KING NARMER

IV. THE EARLY KINGS OF EGYPT

decisive blows upon the Elamites. From this date the government of the country passes finally into the hands of Semitic races, and the Sumerians, as a nation, disappear below the horizon of history. The name of Hammurabi, the most famous king of Babylon, is closely connected with a code of civil and criminal law, defining the relations between the inhabitants of a single kingdom. This code is the earliest in the history of mankind, and it has been preserved almost entire. Another feat of Hammurabi's was to restore the Sumerian Empire and to create in his own land a centralized government in the hands of the King of Babylon, which almost entirely destroyed the independence of the cities composing the kingdom.

The union of the country under the rule of Babylon did not last long. Even in the reign of Hammurabi's successor internal disorder and foreign invasion began ; and these went on without interruption until the fall of the dynasty. The southern districts on the coast seceded from Babylon and constant attacks from north, east, and west undermined the prosperity of the country. Her northern neighbours were especially dangerous : at the beginning of the second millennium B.C. Babylonia was seized for a time by the Hittites, a people who were at that time ruling in Asia Minor. At the same time the Kassites, eastern neighbours of Babylon, never ceased from their incursions, until finally, about 1746 B.C., they were able to establish themselves permanently in Babylonia. The dynasty of Kassite kings, with Babylonia for their centre, continued to reign without a break for 576 years from this time ; but the country was enfeebled and had reverted to a feudal condition, in which independent cities and large landowners professed to acknowledge the superior power of the Babylonian king.

The political development of Egypt in the earliest period of its historical existence closely resembles, in general, the political development of Babylonia. Here also we find a comparatively sharp division of the country into two parts, of which the northern corresponds to Akkad and the southern to Sumer. It appears that these two parts were inhabited by races of different origin. The southern race was probably connected ethnographically with the Nubians of the Upper Nile, and the northerners with the aboriginal population of the north coast of Africa. It is, however, possible—and this is indicated by the examination of many prehistoric graves in southern and central Egypt—that the population of Egypt was all of one blood, and that the differences observed were due to the appearance of foreign conquerors from both north and south.

The historical epoch in Egypt, when the names of kings were first recorded on their monuments in their own lifetime, begins in the fifth millennium B.C.; it probably dates from the introduction of a correct calendar in 4241 or 4238 B.C., and from the time when the art of writing was perfected. At a later date—the earliest list of kings which has come down to us belongs to the time of the Third Dynasty—attempts were made to combine all the existent data and to make continuous lists of all the kings, called Pharaohs, who ruled Egypt before it was united into one kingdom, and while both parts of the country contained a number of kingdoms, each ruled by a monarch of its own. These lists have become the foundation of Egyptian history and chronology. They were continued and supplemented by the later kings. They were edited afresh at the time of the Nineteenth Dynasty, when the kings of that dynasty discovered the tombs of the early Pharaohs at Abydos and used the new data to supplement and correct the lists which they already possessed. That they used accurate and correct methods was proved by those modern investigators who were successful not long ago in discovering some of the tombs at Abydos in which the earliest kings were buried.

Our knowledge of the earliest Egyptian history is, no doubt, imperfect and inexact. But the fundamental facts are beyond doubt. The first decisive steps along the path of political development and culture were taken in the southern district. It was here that the first cities grew up; it was here that the first kingdoms, later called 'Nomes', grew up round these cities; here, too, we first observe the impulse of several cities to coalesce into one kingdom under the direction of the ruler of one city. In the second half of the fifth millennium B.C.—the so-called predynastic period—the ruling part in southern Egypt was played by the dynasty which reigned over the 'falcon-city', called Hieraconpolis in Greek. These kings were descended from the falcon-god, Horus, whose worship was centred at the city of Edfu. The attempts of these kings at unification and conquest brought them into collision not only with the northern part of the Egyptian valley—the 'lower' kingdom, whose chief centres, for some time at least, were the cities of Buto and Sais under the protection of the serpent-goddess—but also with the northern and southern neighbours of Egypt.

The struggle between south and north is the chief episode in the history of the first three dynasties; these kings unified Egypt and played there the same part that Lugal-zaggizi and Sargon had played in Babylonia. Very late tradition assigns the name of Menes to the king who effected the union. But though this name is attested by ancient Egyptian monuments, it is probable that the exploits of this monarch, as reported in our tradition, merely reflect the main incidents of the era when Upper and Lower Egypt were united into a single kingdom. The Pharaohs who brought about the union had probably left Hieraconpolis and moved northward to Thinis, as their place of residence. The cemetery of these kings, excavated by an American archaeological expedition, was found near that city. Another cemetery, at Abdu (Abydos) and not far from Thinis, was under the protection of the jackal-god Anubis; and this became by degrees pre-eminently a city of the dead, where all the Pharaohs desired to have their tomb and mortuary temple, even those who were actually buried elsewhere. The struggle for unity probably went on throughout all the reigns of the First Dynasty. An important event belonging to this period was the foundation by Merpeba, a king belonging to the First Dynasty, of Memphis, a famous city in later times and the political centre of Lower Egypt. Its chief god was Ptah ('revealer'); near by, at Heliopolis (a late Greek name for the city), stood the ancient shrine of Ra, the great sun-god.

During the Second Dynasty it appears that Northern Egypt ruled over Southern. Perhaps the centre of government was transferred at this time to Memphis. The success of the south which followed marks the beginning of a new dynasty known as the Third; these kings were energetic warriors who secured the political acquisitions of the First Dynasty. Though the victory of the south was complete, Memphis still remained the capital of the united kingdom, even under the first king of the Third Dynasty, and from that time played the same part in Egyptian history that Babylon played in the history of Mesopotamia. To the period of this struggle for unity we must probably refer also the

PLATE V

KINGS AND DIGNITARIES OF THE IVth–VIth DYNASTIES OF EGYPT

1. PORTRAIT OF KING KHAFRE (KHEFREN) OF THE IVth DYNASTY, builder of the Second Pyramid of Gizeh (see pl. X). Found in the temple in front of the pyramid. Part of a seated statue. Behind the head is the god Horus protecting the king with his wings. A marvellous piece of portrait sculpture. After 3100 B.C. Cairo Museum.

2. FRAGMENT OF A PORTRAIT STATUETTE OF A DIGNITARY OF THE OLD KINGDOM (Vth–VIth Dynasties). Found in Egypt. About 2700. Metropolitan Museum of Art, New York.

3. PART OF A COPPER STATUETTE OF PRINCE MONTESUPIS, son of King Pepi I (about 2700 B.C.). Found at Hieraconpolis. The statue was hammered into shape over a wooden block. The eyes, made of rock-crystal, are inlaid. Another remarkable piece of early portrait sculpture. The portrait is more individual, less typical and idealized, than that of Khafre. Cairo Museum.

1. KING KAFRE

2. A DIGNITARY OF THE OLD KINGDOM

3. PRINCE MONTESUPIS

V. KINGS AND DIGNITARIES OF THE IVth–VIth
DYNASTIES OF EGYPT

first foreign expeditions of the Pharaohs, which were directed mainly to the peninsula of Sinai and probably extended to the coasts of Palestine, Phoenicia, and Syria, in quest of metals and timber for building. The latest excavations in Phoenicia by French archaeologists show that even the kings of the earliest dynasties had a firm footing in Phoenicia and built temples to their gods there.

The kings of the Fourth, Fifth, and Sixth Dynasties (approximately 3100–2700 B.C.) are contemporary, more or less, with Sargon and Naram-Sin. These are the so-called 'builders of pyramids', and their era must be reckoned as the palmy days of ancient Egypt. To the importance of this epoch witness is borne at the present day by the splendid tombs of the kings which cluster about Memphis, and by their magnificent pyramids and the mortuary temples, growing ever more elaborate, which were connected with the pyramids. These temples and the tombs of royal personages which surround the pyramids display on their walls a series of long inscriptions, which tell us of the titles borne by the kings and their favourites, of their lineage and conquests and journeys; they tell also of the religious beliefs of the age. The pyramids, especially the most colossal of them, made a profound impression upon contemporaries and upon succeeding generations. The names of their builders, the great Pharaohs of the Fourth Dynasty—Khufu (the Kheops of the Greeks), Khafre (or Khefren), and Menkaure (or Mycerinus)—remained for ever connected with their tombs. The very features of some kings of this dynasty are known to us, having been perpetuated in their statues; for example, there is a famous statue of Khafre at Cairo and a series of statues of Menkaure in Boston, U.S.A. The glory of Egypt under the Fourth Dynasty was maintained by their successors, the kings of the Fifth Dynasty; they were worshippers and priests of Ra, the great sun-god, who gradually became identified with Horus, the mighty protector of the first four dynasties of Pharaohs. In honour of Ra these Pharaohs first built temples with conical pillars of stone in their centre —those graceful obelisks which, like the pyramids, have become, to some extent, symbolic of Egypt. The Sixth Dynasty begins with Pepi I; his features are preserved in the first portrait-statue of bronze that has come down to us; but after his death the united kingdom of Upper and Lower

Egypt is beginning to dissolve, and the power of the Pharaohs becomes steadily less and less of a reality.

The great period of a united Egypt (Dynasties I–VI) falls in the second half of the fourth millennium B.C. and the beginning of the third. The kings of that period seem to us to have been employed mainly in peaceful pursuits—constructing great monuments and consolidating the principles of national administration and finance. Yet, in all probability, that age witnessed also a mighty outward expansion, when the bounds of Egypt were extended southwards to Nubia and eastwards to Sinai and the coasts of Palestine, Phoenicia, and Syria. It is certain that under the first dynasties Egypt ceases to be merely a land-empire and begins to lay the foundations of sea-power also.

The separate parts or 'nomes' of Egypt, which had once been independent kingdoms, still remembered their former status; and it was the separatist tendency of their governors that brought about the disruption of the united kingdom. The royal officers, called by the Greeks *nomarchi*, who ruled these districts in the name of the kings, gradually consolidate their power, relying on their acquired riches and the goodwill of the population; they create an army of their own and insist on the merely nominal nature of their dependence upon the kings who exercise the central power. The success of the subordinates in this struggle ends in the splitting up of Egypt into a number of almost independent petty kingdoms, and brings about conditions which we may call 'feudal', from their likeness to the conditions prevalent in Europe during the Middle Ages. This feudal period of Egyptian history, the period of the shadowy dynasties from the Seventh to the Eleventh, was a time of trouble and disorder: it witnessed a great foreign invasion from Asia, constant internal wars, and a marked decline in creative genius. This state of things is deplored with pathetic eloquence and profound pessimism by Ipuwer in his *Admonitions*; by the prophet Neferrohu in that gloomy picture of the future which he professes to display to King Snefru, who preceded Khufu; and in the famous *Dialogue with his Soul by the Man weary of Life*. The first two of these writers foresee a bright future and the advent of a Messiah, but the last sees no consolation except in death.

Even at this time, however, the centralizing impulse is not extinct. Individual Pharaohs attempt, generally without success, to unify the kingdom once more ; and this leads to ever fresh wars and ever fresh confusion. The central power begins again to change its seat : from Memphis it moves to the city called in Greek Heracleopolis ; later it was monopolized by the local rulers of Southern Egypt. These rulers resided in Thebes ; and Thebes now became, and remained for many centuries, the religious and political centre of the whole country.

At the end of the third millennium B. C. the Theban dynasty succeeded to some extent in reuniting feudal Egypt under their sceptre, and in regenerating the political life and culture of the country. These kings belong to the Eleventh and Twelfth Dynasties and bear one of two names—Amenemhet and Senusret ('Sesostris' in Greek). They were able and enterprising rulers, especially Senusret III (2099–2061 B.C.) and Amenemhet III (2061–2013 B.C.), who succeeded in compelling their vassals, the governors of separate nomes, to obey them, and also concentrated their activity upon a series of large enterprises both within and without Egypt. Their chief internal success was the creation of a new fertile province, the present Fayum, on the banks of Lake Moeris, by constructing extensive works for irrigation and reclamation. The chief city of this province they adopted as their second capital ; and the chief god of the city—the 'crocodile-god'—was made the divine consort of the Theban god Amon, who had become identified with Ra, the god of Heliopolis. Their foreign policy carried out aims which had been originated by their predecessors of the Fourth and Fifth Dynasties. Under their reign Egypt emerges more and more from its isolated position. Active commercial intercourse was developed with the African coast, South Palestine, Syria, and the rich islands of Cyprus and Crete. Trading fleets from Egypt became constant visitors in the harbours of the Red Sea and part of the Mediterranean. With their commercial enterprises these monarchs combine a series of campaigns in Nubia and Palestine ; it is possible that their arms penetrated into Phoenicia, Syria, Cyprus, and Crete. In Hither Asia the fame of Senusret rivals that of Sargon, and his name becomes typical of a victorious monarch.

But even the Theban Pharaohs were unable to check the tendency to disruption. During the Thirteenth and Fourteenth Dynasties their empire grows weaker and less united.

PLATE VI

KINGS OF EGYPT OF THE MIDDLE KINGDOM

1. PART OF ONE OF THE MANY SEATED STATUES OF KING SENUSRET I (XIIth Dynasty) found in the funerary temple of his pyramid at Lisht.   22nd cent. B.C. Cairo Museum.

2. ONE OF THE SPHINXES (HUMAN HEAD AND LION'S BODY) FOUND IN A TEMPLE AT TANIS. It probably represents King Amenemhet III the great successor of Senusret III, as prominent in peace as Senusret III in war. His statues were probably dedicated by him in his funerary temple at Hawara (the so-called 'Labyrinth') in the district near Lake Moeris, which he had reclaimed for cultivation by means of his famous barrage at Lahun. The statues were probably carried later by the Hyksos kings to their capital at Tanis. Cairo Museum.

2. SPHINX OF AMENEMHET III

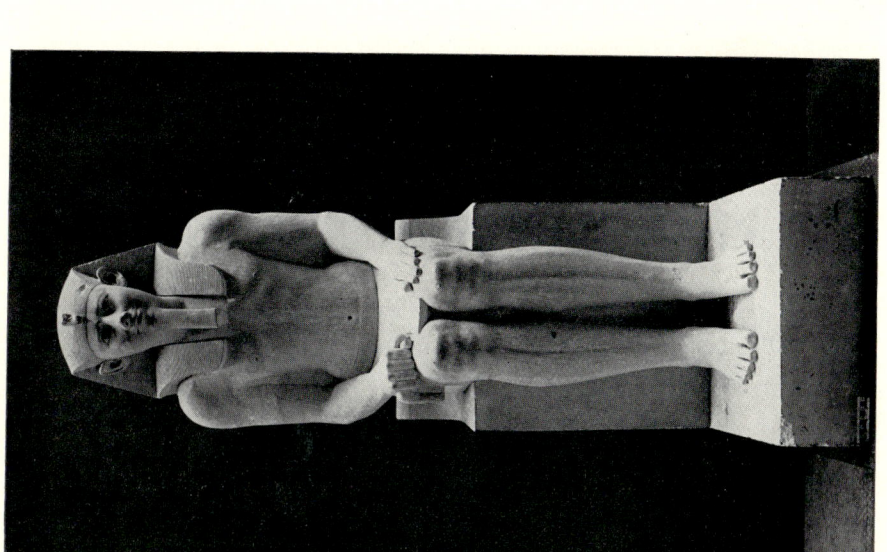

1. SENUSRET I

VI. KINGS OF EGYPT OF THE MIDDLE KINGDOM

Disaster follows, just as it did in Mesopotamia about the same time. It is probable that the great movement of Aryans which began as early as in the third millennium B.C., and of which various successive waves created ever larger and more civilized states in Asia Minor and on the upper Euphrates (the empire of the Hittites in the former and the Mitanni or Hanigalhat on the latter, to name the more important), drove the Kassites to Babylon and a conglomerate of tribes which the Egyptians call the Hyksos and which consisted probably of men of various races (the Aryans prevailing ?) to Egypt. The Hyksos penetrated into Egypt about 1800 B.C., and consolidated their rule there for many centuries.

V

GOVERNMENT AND CIVILIZATION OF EGYPT AND BABYLONIA IN THE THIRD MILLENNIUM B.C.

ON the banks of the Nile, and also on the banks of the Tigris and Euphrates, the third millennium B.C. was a great creative epoch of progress, both material and intellectual. During this period both countries created and worked out in detail a system, peculiar to themselves, of government and of society—a system which lies at the root of all progress in the East even to our own time and has affected the life of Europe, Eastern and Western. The form assumed originally by this system was identical in Egypt and Babylonia, though it presents a few characteristic differences.

In Egypt the system rested upon a close alliance between religious and civil life. At the head of the government stood the king, who was believed to be the son of a god and was himself, in the eyes of the people, divine. His power was unlimited. He ruled the country in the god's name, as its sole master and lord; he commanded his armed subjects in war, directed their industry, prescribed the course of labour necessary for irrigation, and disposed of all the resources of the country at his own discretion.

In religious matters he was assisted by the priests, who lived in the temples and helped the king to propitiate the gods with victims, solemn rites, hymns, and liturgies. The priests also assured to believers the possibility of a life beyond the grave, embalming the bodies of the dead and pointing out what must be done in order to secure for the departed a favourable result of the last judgement held upon their souls.

In secular affairs the king was assisted by officials, who carried out his commands and directed the people in their occupations of peace or war. Some of them commanded the army and the fleet; others collected from the people those products of their labour which the king found it necessary to spend on the requirements of the temples, the government, and his own private life; others directed public works and portioned out the labour among the people; others administered justice and maintained order; while others gave personal service to the king and the royal family. Some of these officials discharged single-handed many different duties. They had no independence or power of initiative: they, like the priests, were merely personal servants and agents of the king and the god. Side by side with the priests and high officials an army of scribes, overseers, artisans, and policemen was employed. They all received maintenance from the king, and all, from the highest to the lowest, were, in theory, appointed by him, though in fact he only nominated the chiefs and they appointed their subordinates; and, lastly, they were all accountable to the king, who disposed of their lives and property as he thought fit.

The population was absolutely at the mercy of the king and his officials. In the political life of the country they took no share whatever; they had no right of private property, especially in land. Their lives, their goods, and their labour were in the king's hands, and he might dispose of them as he thought fit. He laid down what fields were to be sown in any year, what seed should be sown, and who should sow it; he settled what share of the harvest must be surrendered by the husbandman to the government. He named particular persons to perform particular public services —to dig canals, to build dikes or temples or tombs or palaces or ships, to quarry stone, to hunt wild animals, to mine for salt or metals. He appointed the exact number of men for service in the army or the police, or in the fleet as rowers or marines. He settled also what part of the produce of his labour the artisan must surrender to the state, and which artisans must work exclusively for the king and the temples. It is certain that the merchants also gave up to the state a certain part of their gains prescribed by the king. Thus the system of government was strictly autocratic and bureaucratic. Ideas of political freedom and self-government were foreign to Egypt, and have remained foreign to all the East until very recent times.

This state of things was unaltered even when Egypt exchanged a central government for feudal institutions, under which she was split up into several parts, each governed by its own independent ruler who acknowledged a merely nominal sovereignty belonging to one king. The country was divided into several almost independent kingdoms; but the mutual

PLATE VII
THE PALACE OF KISH

1. THE ROYAL PALACE OF THE SUMERIAN CAPITAL KISH as excavated recently by an Anglo-American expedition. A similar palace has been excavated at Lagash. The view shows a portico of four columns, probably the place where the king administered justice. Before the discoveries at Lagash and Kish it was generally supposed that the Sumerians never used the column in their architecture. Before 3000 B.C.

2. THE 'STANDARD' OF UR (0.42 m. long, 0.22 m. high), found at Ur in grave PG.-229. The so-called standard is a mosaic shaped like a house-roof. The mosaic consists of shell and red paste or red stone against a lapis lazuli background, the tesserae being set on wood overlaid with bitumen. One side of this standard represents the Sumerian king in battle. The upper register is occupied by the king, represented taller than his soldiers and enemies. He is carrying an axe and a broad-bladed spear. Behind him are three armed men, and a small boy, also armed, probably the sons of the king. In the corner is the empty war-chariot of the king, drawn by four asses (their heads have recently been found). Behind the chariot stands the driver. In front of the king naked prisoners of the same racial type as the soldiers, their arms bound behind their backs, are brought in under guard. In the second and third rows a victorious battle is represented, the results of which are illustrated in the first register. On the left we see the heavy infantry of the king marching in single file (the artist was not able to represent a phalanx). The soldiers wear copper helmets, heavy cloaks, and short pointed kilts, probably of leather, hanging from a belt. They are armed with short spears. In front of them light infantry is engaged with the enemy, as are also the war chariots of the third row. The chariots are like the king's, heavy cars of wood and metal with solid wheels, drawn by four asses. In each chariot are a driver and an armed man. To the front of each chariot is fixed a quiver containing four spears. Third millennium B.C. London, British Museum.

3. THE 'STANDARD' OF UR. Feast after victory. After the victorious battle the king is feasting. He is seated in a chair and receives wine or beer from the hands of a servant. Another servant is ministering to the six other participants of the banquet: the king's family or his generals. To the right a musician is playing the harp and behind him a woman is singing or dancing. The second and third row are occupied by tribute-bearers, probably the conquered foemen, paying their tribute to the king. Some of them are of Semitic type and dress, with black beards and long hair, others are good Sumerians. They bring cattle, sheep, goats, fish, wild asses, and loads attached to frameworks of wood.

1. THE PALACE OF KISH

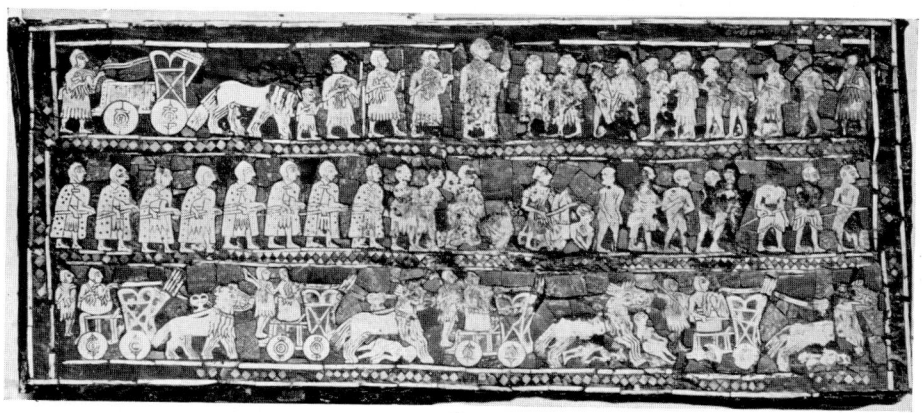

2 AND 3. THE 'STANDARD' OF UR

VII. THE PALACE OF KISH AND THE 'STANDARD' OF UR

relations between each king and his subjects remained exactly what they had been in a united Egypt.

A similar system, political, economic, and social, was developed in the kingdoms of Sumerians and Semites, situated in the plain of the Tigris and Euphrates. Here also government and religion were inseparable. Here too the king's power is divine, though this conception finds a slightly different expression in Babylonia. Some of their kings, including Sargon, Dungi, and Dungi's successors, claimed to be the sons of gods; but the majority were content to be considered the high priests and servants of the deities, receiving their power directly from them and anointed by them. In Babylonia also the king is an autocrat, who rules the kingdom, absolutely and at his own discretion, by means of a host of officials, appointed by him and entirely dependent upon him. Lastly, here also the king keeps in his own hands all the threads of the religious, financial, and military life of the country; and in case of need, he disposes, at his own discretion, of the life, labour, and property of his subjects. In some respects the kings of Babylonia, and later of Assyria, go even further. The extensive development of commerce in Hither Asia, and the part played by retail trade in the life of the people, induced the kings to interfere in this department. Tariffs were published from time to time, fixing a maximum price for commodities; and we know of such tariffs in Babylonia and Assyria at the beginning of the second millennium B.C.

In Sumer and Babylonia, however, owing mainly to their peculiar political development, constant military effort, and the early and rapid growth of foreign commerce, it happened that industrial life and, in connexion with it, the relations of government to individuals, took a shape unlike that in Egypt. The king was not the sole owner of all the property and all the land of the country. His subjects, and especially the highest class of the population—the priests and the steady supporters of the throne, the Sumerian and Semitic inhabitants of the fortified cities—ranked with the king and the temples in this respect: they could own land, cattle, and personal property. Like the king's right to dispose of the lives of his subjects and the wealth of the land, their rights also were consecrated by religion and protected by the god and the god's earthly representative—the king. Hence there was a rapid and powerful development of law, especially

PLATE VIII

THE ECONOMIC LIFE OF SUMER

1, 2. FRIEZE OF THE SANCTUARY RECENTLY EXCAVATED NEAR THE CITY OF UR AT TELL-EL-OBEID (modern name). The location of the frieze on the outer wall of the platform on which the sanctuary was built is shown on pl. LI. The frieze consisted of a wooden frame, the inside of the frame being filled with a thick layer of bitumen and the outstanding borders being covered with copper. In the bitumen were inlaid charming figures of men and animals cut in white limestone or in shell. What is represented is the entrance to the temple-precinct. The Oriental temples were not only places for worship but also important centres of business operations. On the right of the entrance men are milking cows in the presence of the calves. On the left the milk is being poured into big jars, strained, and worked into butter or cheese. Farther to the right and left, or over this frieze, was another frieze or friezes showing a herd of cows and a flock of geese. The main income of the temple consisted probably of revenues from large herds and flocks. Similar scenes are often reproduced on Sumerian seals. About 3000 B.C. British Museum, London, and Museum of the University of Pennsylvania, Philadelphia.

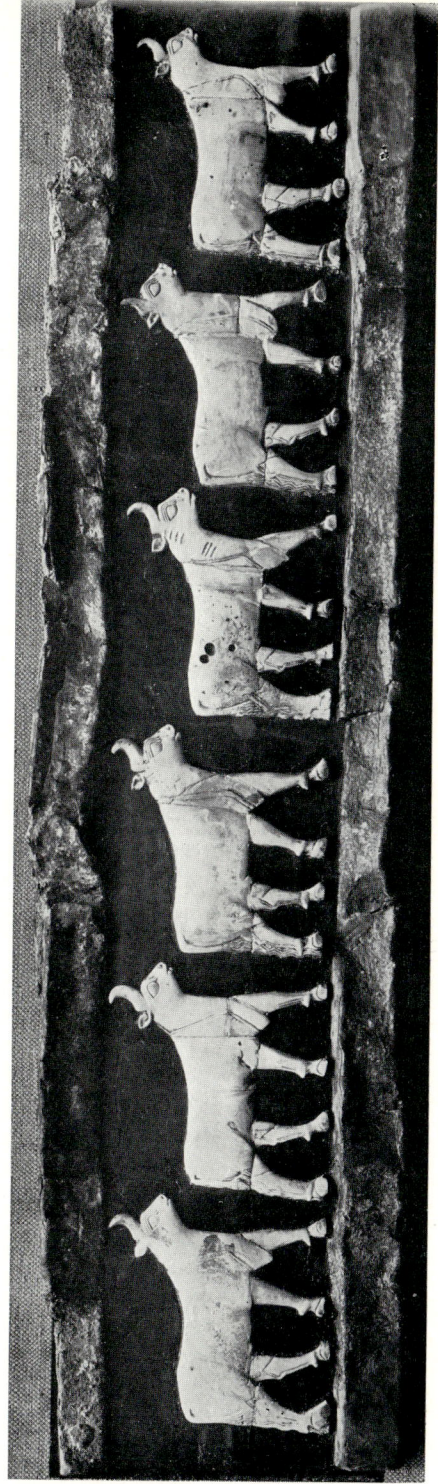

VIII. THE ECONOMIC LIFE OF SUMER

written law. Contracts of various forms make their appearance, and laws of a general type are passed to regulate these contracts, while the king issues notices and decrees, showing how far he will protect their sanctity. He begins also to publish laws, which, until he alters them, bind himself and his successors and serve as indications of his attitude towards his subjects. I have already pointed out how laws gradually accumulate and are connected with one another, until they compose a complete code which becomes familiar to the public and directs their actions. Owing to this development Sumer and Babylonia became the cradle of civil law which spread far and wide all over the huge Sumero-Babylonian Empire into Assyria, N. Syria, Eastern Asia Minor, and Cyprus. The development of commerce and industry gave rise to another very important invention: the use of metal currency in silver, which also spread all over Hither Asia.

The institution of private property securely held is effective in dividing the population into different classes enjoying different rights. In Egypt all men are equal before the king and the god, all alike serve them. It is true that there is inequality in a social and economic sense: there are separate groups, one of priests, another of royal officials higher and lower, another of peasants and artisans; but there is no sharp division between these groups—it is possible to pass from one to another; and they are all alike in one main point—that no member of any group has full ownership of his property, especially landed property. There are only two proprietors—the god and the king; and they surrender a larger or smaller share of their property for the use of members of their family, their friends, officials, and servants.

In Babylonia it was not so. Here too, there is of course inequality of wealth, in the same degree and for the same reasons as in Egypt; but it was early recognized as a normal thing and then confirmed and consecrated by religion and law. On this principle of inequality, different classes take rise among the population—a class of rich landowners and merchants, a class of priests, a class of petty landowners, a class of soldiers (whom the king allows to occupy part of the royal demesne), a class of tenants bound to the soil, and an extensive class of persons engaged in agriculture, manufacture, and trade. Some of these classes get by degrees special rights of inheritance, and government comes forward

PLATE IX

THE ACTIVITY OF THE EARLY KINGS OF EGYPT

1. ONE OF THE IVORY PLAQUES FOUND IN THE TOMB OF KING SEMTI OR DEN (Ist DYNASTY) AT ABYDOS. Plaques of the same type were found in many tombs of the kings of the Ist Dynasty. Each contains official records of the events of a single year in primitive hieroglyphic script and in engraved figures. Our tablet represents the Pharaoh smiting a Libyan with his mace. These tablets show the beginning of historical records in Egypt. They formed later the basis of regular annals. Fourth millennium B.C. British Museum.

2. FRAGMENTS OF A CEREMONIAL MACE-HEAD OF A KING OF THE Ist DYNASTY CALLED USUALLY KING SCORPION (see the scorpion represented near his figure). Found at Hieraconpolis. The upper row shows the victorious standards of the Southerners on which birds, as symbols of the vanquished foes, are hung. Beneath, the Pharaoh himself, after his victory over the North (he wears the Northern crown on his head), is directing the construction of dikes and canals. He is shown with a hoe in his hands. Behind him stand his fan-bearers and before him his standard-bearers. Under his feet is the Nile and the canals with men working on them. The work is probably being done in Northern Egypt by the conquered Northerners. Fourth millennium B.C. Ashmolean Museum, Oxford.

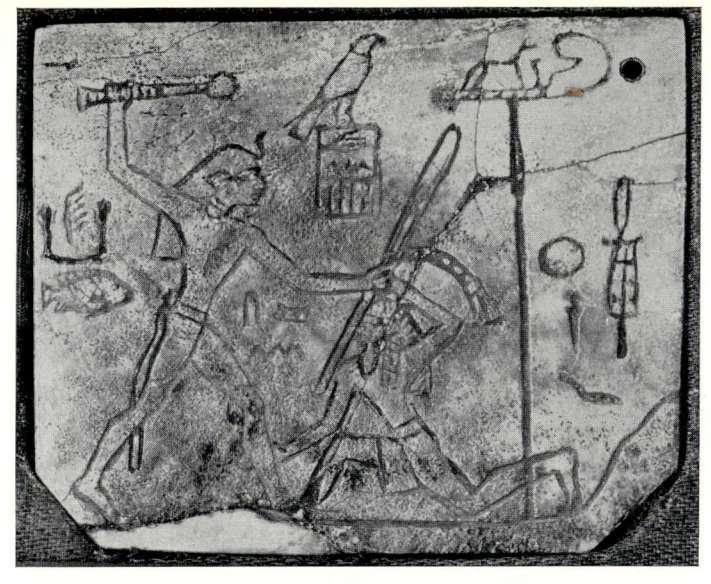

1. IVORY PLAQUE FROM THE TOMB OF KING SEMTI

2. MACE-HEAD OF KING SCORPION

IX. THE ACTIVITY OF THE EARLY KINGS OF EGYPT

to protect these rights. Crimes affecting the life and property of persons belonging to the higher classes are punished more severely than similar offences against obscurer persons. Inequality before the law, once started, soon grows till it leads to crying abuses; then the highest power, the king himself, is forced to come forward and defend the oppressed. Urukagina, the last king of an ancient dynasty of Lagash, appears in this character. It becomes a commonplace, often quite meaningless, for kings to say that they represent the interests of the poor against the rich, of the humble against the mighty; indeed this claim was not unknown to the kings and ministers of Egypt also.

Connected with this development of classes there is another feature which distinguishes Babylonia from Egypt. This is the acquirement by the highest class of a certain measure of political rights, especially in the way of self-government for the cities. These germs, however, never developed very far. With this phenomenon we may connect the growth of priestly influence upon politics. This happened in Egypt also, but is most apparent in the political life of Babylonia.

The monarchical system of Egypt and Babylonia, with these political, economic, and social features, left its impress upon the material and intellectual culture of the two kingdoms. Here too we notice many resemblances but also important and characteristic differences. Let us take Egypt first. I have pointed out already how the country prospered owing to orderly government and the centralized control of its resources. The network of canals and dikes was extended and improved, as accumulated observations served to develop hydraulic skill; and together with improved irrigation, the area of cultivated land was enlarged and greater skill in agriculture attained. Better implements were made, new methods of cultivation were introduced, a fixed rotation of crops was practised, new breeds of domestic animals made their appearance. And, because the direction of agriculture belonged to the king alone, each fresh discovery and improvement became at once the property of the whole country.

As the economic life of the land grew more complicated, its growing wealth and the increasing demands of the higher classes brought about a high degree of specialization in industry and art. There were sculptors, painters, jewellers, potters, and others, who confined themselves exclusively to

PLATE X

THE PYRAMIDS

1. TWO OF THE THREE FAMOUS PYRAMIDS OF GIZEH NEAR CAIRO. Before them is the gigantic Sphinx of Gizeh. The head of the Sphinx represents King Khafre of the IVth Dynasty. The body of the Sphinx is 187 ft. long and the head is 66 ft. high.

2. RESTORATION OF THE GREAT PYRAMIDS OF GIZEH. One of the pyramids (that on the right) was the funeral monument of King Khufu (Kheops), the other (on the left) of King Khafre (Khefren). The pyramids of the kings were surrounded by funeral monuments of the queens and great officers of their courts. In front of the entrance to the pyramid stood the mortuary temple of the king where food, drink, and clothing were kept for the king; his body lay in a chamber inside the pyramid. The pyramids were built in the desert. From the pyramids covered causeways led towards the royal city on the Nile. Near the valley of the Nile, on one side of the causeway stood the Sphinx, and a building on the other. In the valley a magnificent granite temple was built as an entrance to the causeway. On the left an unfinished pyramid is seen. After 3100 B.C. After Hoelscher.

3. RECONSTRUCTION OF THE PYRAMIDS OF ABUSIR. In these pyramids the kings of the Vth Dynasty were buried. The arrangement is the same as that of the pyramids of Gizeh. After L. Borchardt.

1. THE SPHINX AND PYRAMIDS OF GIZEH

2. RESTORATION OF THE PYRAMIDS OF GIZEH

3. RECONSTRUCTION OF THE PYRAMIDS OF ABUSIR

X. THE PYRAMIDS

one occupation; and this division of labour led to a series of technical inventions which made an important advance in art and industry. This advance was especially great and rapid in the arts of metal-work, weaving, and pottery. Both in military and peaceful occupations stone finally gave way to wood and metal, either copper or bronze. Ploughs, spades, harrows, spears, and arrows were now made only of wood and metal. The precious metals (gold and silver) and precious stones were freely used together with bronze by the jewellers; and the jewellery made in the time of the Pyramids and the Feudal Age of Egypt is not inferior to modern work in refinement and elegance. Woven stuffs became finer and finer, with more elaborate patterns and more variety of colour. Earthenware vessels were no longer made by hand, but on the wheel, and baked in special kilns. A method was invented for manufacturing small articles out of variegated glass. Not only were wood, potsherds, stone, and metal used for writing upon, but also paper, specially manufactured for this purpose from the pith of the papyrus, a reed which grows only in Egypt.

This great advance in technical skill made it possible for the high artistic gifts of the nation to reveal themselves in the arts of architecture, sculpture, and painting, and to carry them to a remarkable degree of excellence. The advances made by art were applied to industry, and artistic production became general.

What the palaces built in the age of the Pyramids were like we do not know, because they were made of unburnt bricks and therefore have not been preserved to our time. But many stone buildings of that period still stand on the banks of the Nile. In Egypt the architecture of tombs had a specially rich development. The belief of the Egyptians in a future life, their belief in the necessity of constructing for the dead a lasting habitation, as comfortable, beautiful, and substantial as possible, led them to discard a mere grave in the earth and to erect more and more luxurious tombs of stone for the dead to dwell in. The grave in the earth is first converted into a stone vault; then the vault emerges to the surface of the soil and becomes a pyramid—a funeral monument of colossal proportions containing within its mass of stone the dwelling-place of the dead man. For the divine king monuments of especial magnificence were constructed—

PLATE XI
EGYPTIAN LIFE IN THE TIME OF THE EARLY KINGDOM

1. PART OF THE SCULPTURAL DECORATION OF THE TOMB (*Mastaba*) OF PTAHOTEP AT SAKKARAH. The two upper rows of figures represent the desert with its typical animals, gazelles and antelopes, lions, jackals, &c. Some men are represented hunting these animals with tall, slender hounds. In the third row it is the Nile that is represented: on the left is a catch of fish, on the right two men are beginning to build a boat. Vth Dynasty. Sakkarah.

2. PART OF THE SCULPTURAL DECORATION OF THE TOMB OF TI, BARBER AND CHIEF ARCHITECT OF TWO KINGS OF THE Vth DYNASTY AT SAKKARAH. The first row of figures shows men attending to cows and young calves. The second row represents the transport of a herd of cattle across a canal or a branch of the Nile. In the water two crocodiles are watching for their chance.

3. ANOTHER PART OF THE SAME DECORATION. In the first row men are ploughing. In the second three men are hoeing, while a man, with his seed-bag on his arm, is sowing. Behind the sower a flock of rams is shown treading the seed into the soil of the field. The sower gives a handful of grain to his favourite ram.

It is noteworthy that almost exactly the same sculptural decoration is found in most of the graves of the Early Kingdom. Besides scenes of a ritual and religious character, the whole life of Egypt is represented in the richest graves: the desert with its animals, the Nile and the surrounding marshes with their fish and birds, the fields and gardens and all the various agricultural operations which went on in them, from building the dykes and canals, and ploughing, to threshing and winnowing, from planting and watering to gathering the grapes and other fruit, the pastures with scenes of cattle-breeding and slaughtering, the rich man's house with every kind of industry going on in it. All this had a magical purpose. The aim was to secure all the blessings of life—food, drink, and amusements—for the deceased. The treatment, however, is far from being ritual and schematic. The sculptors who carved the bas-reliefs were great artists, close observers of life. They show a real love for men and animals and a keen sense of humour (note e. g. the behaviour of the calves in fig. 2 and the jibbing donkeys in fig. 3).

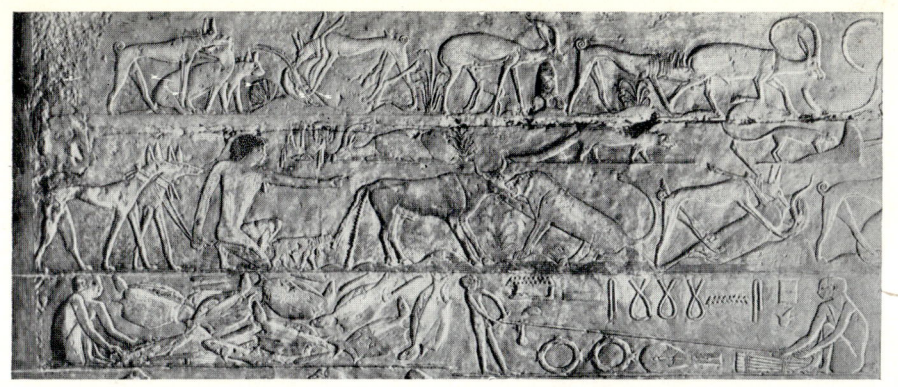

1. THE DESERT AND THE NILE. TOMB OF PTAHOTEP

2. CATTLE BREEDING. TOMB OF TI

3. PLOUGHING, HOEING, SOWING AND STAMPING THE SEED INTO THE EARTH.
TOMB OF TI

XI. EGYPT IN THE TIME OF THE EARLY KINGDOM

lordly pyramids with great stone temples in front of them. These pyramids of the Egyptian kings do not merely strike the imagination by the piling of stone upon stone : they are great works of architecture, in which artistic feeling and immense technical skill are harmoniously combined. The lines of the pyramids which cover the kings of the Fourth Dynasty—Khafre and Menkaure—are grand and severe ; the impression they produce is sublime in its simplicity, and the ideal of the architect is completely realized.

The era of the Old and Middle Kingdom—it is usual to call the age of the pyramids and the feudal epoch by these names—produced sculpture and painting not less interesting than its architecture. Owing to their view of a future life, the ordinary task of an Egyptian sculptor was to represent upon the sepulchre not only the dead man himself, but everything which the dead man might require for an untroubled life in the next world. The custom of representing the dead in a series of statues and reliefs led on to the invention of portrait-sculpture and painting. Even as early as the Old Kingdom sculptors have the skill to make striking portraits. It is not merely that they catch a likeness : in a series of statues they reach the power of conveying a type, of seizing the predominating trait in a man's character. The famous portrait-statue of King Khafre, where he is represented together with the sacred falcon, is a real masterpiece of its kind. Still more remarkable is another portrait of the same king—the famous Sphinx which rises in front of his pyramid at Gizeh. By combining a colossal head of the king with the body of a mighty lion, the artist has given to the whole statue extraordinary majesty and power. I may indicate also a series of portrait-statues, in wood and stone, of priests and officials, one of which, a wooden statuette now at Cairo, is as famous as it deserves to be : it represents a priest who lived in the age of the Old Kingdom, and the type is so expressively conveyed, that the workmen who found it at once took it for a likeness of their own chief—the sheikh of the village.

Not only were there portraits of the dead man ; but his whole life was depicted, with epic simplicity and idyllic pathos, in reliefs which covered the walls of the tomb-chamber and in miniature sculpture upon the tomb itself ; these represented all that the living man had loved and held precious. We see there the first attempts at connected narrative told

PLATE XII

EGYPTIAN LIFE IN THE TIME OF THE XIth DYNASTY

1–3. MODELS REPRODUCING THE LIFE OF THE PRINCE MEHENKWETRE OF THE XIth DYNASTY. Such models were placed in large numbers in the graves of kings, princes, and nobles of the Middle Kingdom. The purpose of the models was the same as that of the bas-reliefs in the tombs of the Old Kingdom (see pl. XI), viz. to secure for the dead everything which he had possessed during his lifetime and which he might need in his life in the nether world. The best series of such models was found recently in the tomb of Mehenkwetre. All the features of the economic life of the prince are shown in these models: his palace, his storehouses, his stables, his workshops, his fleet of river-boats, &c. The three models which are reproduced here show one of his cabin-boats, the pavilion of his villa where he inspected his cattle, and the furniture in one of the cabins of his river-boats, consisting of a chair, a couch, and two cabin-trunks. About 2200 B.C. Metropolitan Museum of Art, New York; and Cairo Museum.

1. A CABIN-BOAT

2. INSPECTION OF CATTLE

3. CABIN CHAIR, COUCH, AND TRUNKS

XII. EGYPTIAN LIFE IN THE TIME OF THE XIth DYNASTY

not in words but in images and their combinations. The whole life of a famous Egyptian passes before us in these scenes—his business as a landowner, his official occupations, his amusements. Country life is represented in its smallest details—ploughing, sowing, reaping; we witness the life of the flocks, from their birth to the shambles; the shops of the craftsmen; hunting expeditions to the marshes and deserts; pleasure-sailings on the Nile; music and dancing and wrestling-matches. Nor is military life forgotten: armies marching under kings and their generals; the siege and capture of cities; the conveyance of captives and booty by land and water; reviews of troops and soldiers on active service. For exact observation, for love of nature and animals, and even for humour, these monuments are inimitable.

In this same age Egypt made an immense advance also in the intellectual sphere; and here the decisive part was played by the discovery and rapid improvement of the art of writing. In the earliest stage each written sign (or hieroglyph, as the Greeks called it) corresponded to a definite object: it was in fact what we call an ideogram. But gradually a particular ideogram was connected not merely with a definite object but also with a definite word. The ideograms were then used to convey in writing words not corresponding to objects, and also ideas and conceptions. Thus the ideographic or pictographic stage of writing gave way to a syllabic stage, in which each sign corresponded to a syllable. Finally, the syllabic signs very early became alphabetical signs or letters, connected with one of the twenty-four consonants of the Egyptian language. Purely phonetic writing, however, was never introduced; and the Egyptians retained, to a comparatively late era, a complicated and troublesome combination of the three systems—ideographic, syllabic, and alphabetical. By means of writing, the observations made by individuals and groups of men, notably by the priests, were recorded, systematized, and supplemented by later observers. Thus a foundation was laid for many sciences—astronomy, reckoning of time and construction of a calendar, mathematics, geometry, anatomy, and medicine. In the religious sphere the uncouth incantations chanted in the Pyramid Age give place, in the Feudal Age, to hymns, composed in verse according to fixed rules and sometimes breathing a deep religious feeling. Profane literature also is produced—

PLATE XIII

EGYPTIAN JEWELLERY OF THE MIDDLE KINGDOM

1. ONE OF THE TWO PECTORALS OF THE TREASURE OF LAHUN. The treasure was found in the grave of Sat-hathor-iunut, daughter of King Senusret II of the XIIth Dynasty. The pectoral (gold openwork) shows in the centre the 'cartouche' (the name) of King Senusret II. The cartouche is supported by a kneeling man holding palm branches. On his arm is suspended a tadpole representing millions of years. The cartouche is flanked by two falcons. The front part is inlaid with lapis-lazuli and turquoise. Metropolitan Museum of Art, New York.

2, 3. THE SAME TREASURE. A necklace and a mirror.

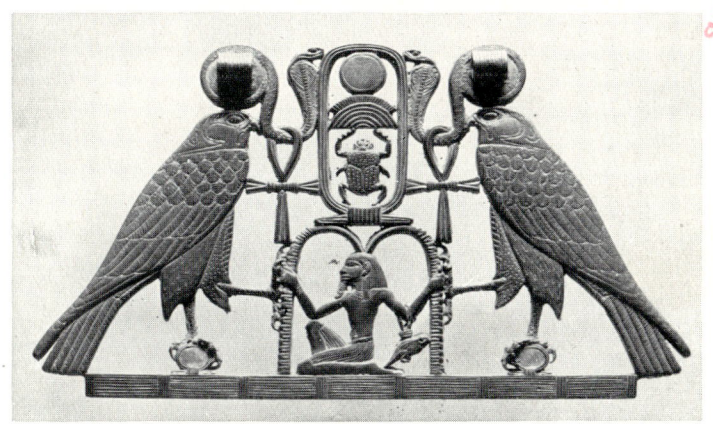

1. PECTORAL OF THE XIIth DYNASTY

2. NECKLACE

3. MIRROR

XIII. EGYPTIAN JEWELLERY OF THE MIDDLE KINGDOM

fairy tales, descriptions of travel, love-poetry. Finally, the principles of law and morality are handed down from generation to generation in written documents or codes, which embody the decisions and decrees of the kings, and especially their instructions to their successors and chief officers—how they are to rule in accordance with divine law, and how the subjects must live, if they are to please the god and the king.

In Babylonia we mark a similar advance in material comfort, artistic production, and intelligence. Here also, by

FIG. 1. *Seal impression of a clay tablet of the Kassite period found at Nippur. It shows the old Babylonian plough in use. Note the funnel for seed attached to the plough in order to combine second ploughing of a field with sowing. After A. T. Clay. University Museum, Philadelphia.*

organization and prudent direction of labour, the whole country was converted within a few centuries into cornfields and gardens. The instruments of production were continually improved: thus we have a seal representing the ingenious combination of a plough and a sowing-machine—the first sowing-machine in the world's history. The handicrafts, especially those of the metal-worker and weaver, reached a high pitch of perfection. As early as the third millennium B.C. the craftsman could make great vessels of copper or silver and cover them with carved or molten figures, representing scenes of military or religious life; large molten figures of men and animals are commonly found as adornments of the temples. Their weavers made remarkable garments in imitation of a sheep's fleece. Weapons were steadily improved and perfected. Babylonia was a military

PLATE XIV

WRITING IN EGYPT

1. STATUE OF A SCRIBE OF THE OLD KINGDOM. The statue (I reproduce almost verbally the masterly description of the late G. Maspero) represents the scribe sitting cross-legged in the attitude common among Orientals, yet all but impossible to Europeans. The face is square cut, and the strongly marked features indicate a man in the prime of life. The cheeks are bony; the ears thick and heavy; the eyes large and well open (the sockets contained eyes composed of enamel, white and black). The right hand holds the reed pen, which pauses in its place on the open papyrus scroll. Thus for five thousand years he has waited for his master to go on with the long interrupted dictation. The original of the statue was not a handsome man, but the vigour and fidelity of his portrait amply compensate for the absence of ideal beauty. About 2800 B.C. Paris, Louvre.

2. AN EGYPTIAN WOODEN INKPOT AND REED PENS. Found in Egypt. British Museum.

3. A ROLL OF PAPYRUS NOT YET USED but prepared for use by an Egyptian scribe. Found in Egypt. British Museum.

1. SCRIBE

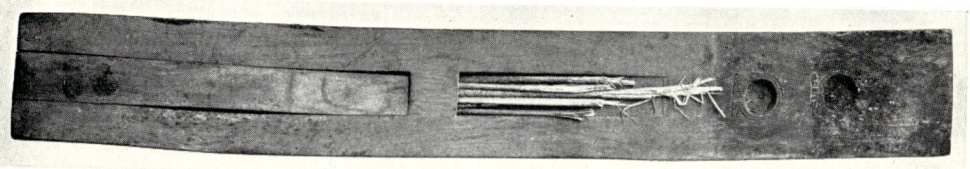

2. INKPOT AND PENS

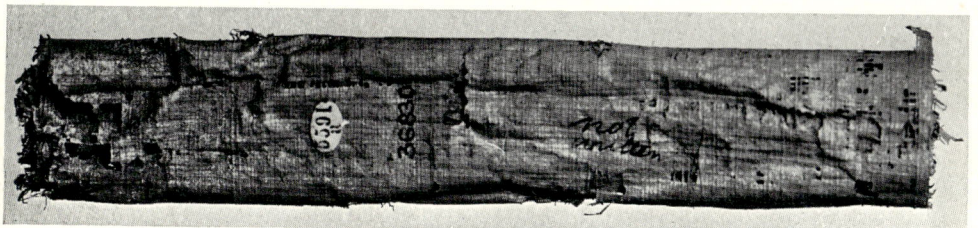

3. PAPYRUS ROLL

XIV. WRITING IN EGYPT

power, and therefore novelties were introduced into the tactics of war, such as the practice of fighting in close order, and from chariots.

In art Babylonia was not less successful than Egypt, but the development took a somewhat different direction. Because there is no stone in Babylonia, all buildings, of whatever size, were made mainly of unburnt brick with a small quantity of burnt brick added. Such buildings are, of course, easily destroyed, and of the most ancient of them only pitiful relics have survived to our times. But the conservative instinct which marks the religious and civil life of Babylonia retained, in its main features, the method of building which had once been adopted. The temples and palaces which were built by the latest kings of Babylonia were practically the same as those erected by their Sumerian predecessors. But, as these later buildings were never destroyed and gradually decayed, considerable ruins of them are still extant and enable us to judge of the earliest architecture. Among its most remarkable products were the high towers (*ziggurats*) dedicated to the sun-god and built with temples round them. They rose on mighty steps to a great height; the god's shrine was placed on the highest stage, and his worship was performed on the platform at the top. The pretty story of the Tower of Babel, preserved to us in the Bible, was undoubtedly derived from buildings of this kind. The Sumerians and Babylonians, having no stone to build with, tried to adorn the dingy brick walls of their temples and palaces with a brilliant coating of many colours; for this purpose they used rich woven carpets, or tiles coloured in imitation of the carpets. Or they covered the walls with metal reliefs and a mosaic made of various coloured substances. All these decorative methods were known in Egypt but were carried to greater perfection in Babylonia.

In their notions of a future life the Sumerians and Babylonians differed to some extent from the Egyptians. The latest discoveries at Ur show that in the early period of their life the Sumerians, like many other peoples, built for their kings large and strong subterranean graves. In these graves were buried all the gorgeous belongings of the kings, gold, silver, precious stones, &c., and men and women were immolated during the performance of the funeral rites. In later times the Babylonians did not suppose that earthly life went on beyond

PLATE XV
EGYPTIAN LETTERS

1. PART OF THE 'BOOK OF THE DEAD' WRITTEN ON PAPYRUS BY THE PAINTER NEB-SINY. Books of this kind were placed in Egyptian graves for the use of the deceased in the nether world. The object was to protect the dead by magic formulas and to guide him to and in the realm of the dead. The writing is the 'cursive hieroglyphic', a further development of the monumental hieroglyphic script seen in the inscriptions cut in stone. XVIIIth Dynasty. British Museum.

2. PAGE IX OF THE MAGICAL PAPYRUS FOUND IN EGYPT. One part of the papyrus-roll is in London, another in Leyden (Holland). It contains magical incantations and is written in the 'demotic' script, a cursive which was developed from the hieratic script, the successor of the hieroglyphic system of writing. British Museum.

1. CURSIVE HIEROGLYPHIC SCRIPT
2. DEMOTIC SCRIPT

XV. EGYPTIAN LETTERS

the grave, keeping all its joys and satisfactions. They imagined the lower world to be a place of darkness, where the departed, retaining their consciousness, were condemned to lie motionless for ages, under the stern rule of a goddess who reigned in that world. Hence they pay much less attention to the erection and adornment of tombs. Their artists devote all the power of their creative genius to the gods and to living men. They think most of religion and government, of temples and palaces, of the lives and exploits of gods and kings. Religious sculpture is of immense importance in their art. Together with human images of the gods, the Babylonian artists create a series of fanciful divine figures, in which parts of the human body are capriciously combined with parts of animals. Figures of this kind are found in Egypt also, but never with such a variety of combinations. From Sumer have proceeded all the heraldic and mythical shapes of animals which we know—the gryphon, the dragon, the sphinx, heraldic eagles and lions. And there is a remarkable novelty unknown to Egypt: these figures of men, animals, and monsters are combined by the artist in decorative and purely ornamental, almost geometrical, groups. These are the ancestors of similar groups in our decorative and heraldic art.

Equally remarkable was the success of these craftsmen in the art devoted to the glorification of the kings and the perpetuation of their exploits. Their portrait-sculpture is not so masterly or so individual as that of Egypt. We look in vain for the exact resemblance and the calm majesty which we find in the statues of Egyptian kings. Nevertheless the power and importance of the king, as such, is conveyed with sufficient clearness. But the strength of these artists does not lie here, but in the power to compose finely grouped scenes from religious and military life ; these are full of life and movement, and sometimes startling by the tragic impression they convey. One of the most remarkable monuments of this sculpture is the so-called ' Stele of the Vultures' found at Lagash ; it was dedicated to the god by Eannatum, one of the earliest rulers of Lagash. The king is represented as conquering his enemies, sweeping their corpses into huge heaps, and celebrating his victory above these heaps of dead ; at the top of the pillar, in the sky above the king and his army, vultures (or eagles) are carrying away fragments of the king's slaughtered foes. The workmanship is rude and

PLATE XVI

SUMERIAN ART

1. FRONT AND SIDE VIEW OF A FRAGMENT OF A STATUETTE OF THE TIME OF GUDEA, 'PATESI' OF LAGASH. Found at Lagash in Sumer. The lady is represented in the attitude of prayer. She wears a gold necklace and is dressed in the typical Sumerian dress with inset embroidered or woven bands. The statue is one of the greatest works of art ever discovered in Sumer. Note the religious concentration and fervour which find their expression especially in the eyes. Note also the fine proportions of the statue. After 2600 B.C. Paris, Louvre.

2. A complete wooden harp (restored) found at Ur in the grave of Queen Shub-ad. It is adorned with a gold and lapis-lazuli heifer head and shell inlays. Third millennium B.C. London, British Museum.

3. Front plaque of a large harp inlaid with shell plaques found at Ur in the king's grave. At the top is represented, in the usual way, Gilgamesh fighting two human-headed bulls. What follows in the next two rows has been variously explained. I hold it to be a scene from a folk animal-epos. It is a counterpart of the scene of the feast on the standard of pl. VII. The king is the bear. He listens to the music and beats time. The musician is an ass; the instrument a monumental harp of eight strings. At the feet of the bear-king a jackal is seated; he shakes an instrument like the Egyptian sistrum and holds on his knees a game-board (boards of this type were found at Ur). Two other animals—a wolf-cook and a lion-cup-bearer, are bringing meat and wine. In the last row is another mythological scene: the scorpion-god worshipped by a gazelle on its hind legs. Third millennium B.C. Philadelphia, University Museum.

1. STATUETTE OF THE TIME OF GUDEA

2. HARP OF QUEEN SHUB-AD

3. SHELL PLAQUE

XVI. SUMERIAN ART

primitive, but the work is full of life and tragic power. The reverse of the pillar is occupied by the powerful figure of the god who assists the king against his enemies; in one hand he holds a huge net, full of enemies of Lagash whom he has caught; he kills them one by one with his great mace. The conquest of his enemies and the capture of their fort is represented on the stele of King Naram-Sin with more grace and refinement and more skilful grouping: no Egyptian relief conveys the sense of massive movement which distinguishes the figures of the victorious king and the vanquished praying for mercy; nor shall we find anywhere in Egypt the same restrained composition, deliberate disposition of the figures, and structural harmony between figures and landscape.

In science and literature also great advances were made by Sumer and Babylon; and, as in Egypt, this development was preceded by the invention of a peculiar system of writing. In Mesopotamia also the earliest stage of writing was pictographic; but this was soon abandoned for a phonetic system. About three hundred and fifty signs were invented, corresponding to syllables. The development of writing stopped at this point and never became alphabetic, with a letter for each sound. In the absence of stone and paper, clay was used to write upon. The symbols were written with a pointed reed upon clay bricks, or cylinders, of different shapes. Hence the signs took the form of a wedge and are called 'cuneiform'; the different wedges and their combinations represented distinct syllables and words. The bricks were then baked and might remain intact for thousands of years. Every excavation in Mesopotamia reveals inscribed bricks by the thousand—the relics of ancient archives and libraries, and very miscellaneous in their contents.

The priests of Egypt accumulated a vast number of observations, which they reduced to some sort of system; but with that they were content. The same kind of work was carried on independently in Mesopotamia at the same time, with results which are probably of more importance in the history of mankind. Many of these systematic observations passed through Syria and Asia Minor into Europe, and then were transmitted by the Greeks and Romans to modern times. Thus it is certain that we derive from Babylon the division of the day and the night into twelve hours each,

PLATE XVII

SUMERIAN WRITING

1. THE FIGURE REPRESENTS A POLISHED BONE STYLUS FOUND AT KISH WHICH WAS USED BY BABYLONIAN SCRIBES. The stylus has two ends. The larger end, as shown on our figure, was employed for making wedges and heads of the cuneiform script in ordinary size. The small end makes the same elements of the script, but more minutely, and was evidently used for inserting signs into the ordinary script. The bone stylus is evidently an improved reed stylus. The discoverer of this bone stylus was able, as is shown on our figure (the hand is that of the discoverer, Prof. S. Langdon of Oxford), to make on a clay tablet every variety of cuneiform signs by slightly changing the position of the stylus in his hand. Ashmolean Museum, Oxford.

2. A PICTOGRAPHIC CLAY TABLET FOUND IN THE SUMERIAN PALACE AT KISH. It is the earliest monument of the Sumerian script where cuneiform signs are used along with pictographic signs. Its probable date is about 3500 B.C. Compare the Sumerian cuneiform texts on pl. I. Ashmolean Museum, Oxford.

3. A SUMERIAN SEAL CYLINDER FOUND AT KISH. The figures of the upper panel show hunting scenes, those of the lower probably scenes of worship. Third millennium B.C. Ashmolean Museum, Oxford.

4. A BEAUTIFUL ASSYRIAN SEAL-CYLINDER showing the holy symbol of Marduk on his sacred animal—the serpent-griffin, surmounted by the winged symbol of the god (Assur ?). Behind him sits the goddess Ishtar, or a corresponding Assyrian goddess, on a throne; before her is her star, and behind her other stars. The throne of the goddess rests on the figure of a dog. In front of the gods are two worshippers, a man and a woman. Ashmolean Museum, Oxford.

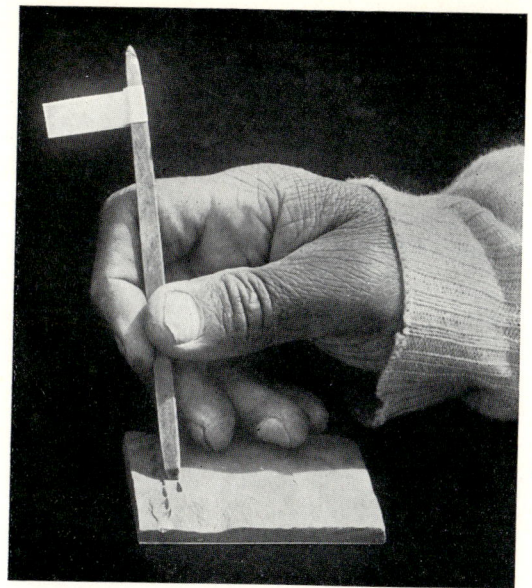

1. STYLUS

2. PICTOGRAPHIC TABLET FROM KISH

3. SUMERIAN SEAL CYLINDER FROM KISH   4. ASSYRIAN SEAL CYLINDER

XVII. SUMERIAN WRITING

the division of the year into twelve months and of the week into seven days, the naming of the days after the planets, and many of the existing systems of weights and measures. We owe also to Babylon the first exact observations of the heavenly bodies, and our introduction to the planetary and zodiacal systems with their mutual relations. The earliest of these observations probably belong to the very beginnings of Mesopotamian history. We must certainly reckon the Babylonians, together with the Egyptians, as the fathers of modern astronomy. They also created a science which has had immense influence upon mankind—the scientific prediction of the future, based on systematic observation of the internal organs of sacrificed animals, and on the movements of the heavenly bodies and their relation to the conception, birth, and future destiny of individuals (astrology). All these achievements are a step in advance, compared with Egyptian science. The Babylonians tried to connect one observation with another; they were not content merely to string them together, but sought to combine them into a more or less exact science, and to draw some scientific conclusions from them.

The same impulse appears also in their relation to the past. They are not content with a bare list of kings' names for practical ends. Their earliest records show a tendency to create a connected history of the whole nation, and not of the kings only. They use as materials: (1) the lists of kings; (2) contemporary monuments of victory; (3) consecrations of monuments to the gods by different kings; (4) temple-records of portents connected with important events, especially campaigns; (5) records of astronomical observations undertaken at the wish of the king, on the occasion of such events. Codes of portents have been preserved to our time in later lists.

In the domain of literature, the Sumerians and Babylonians are the creators of the mythological and historical epic. The poetical treatment of legends closely connected with the history of man on earth began earlier and was more richly developed in Babylonia than in Egypt. With many of these legends we are familiar, because they were borrowed by the Hebrews and perpetuated by them in the Bible; such are the Creation of the world and man, the Fall, the Flood and the Ark, the building of the Tower of Babel. Other poetic legends had great influence on later literature: such are those of Gilgamesh, the wrestler; of Etana, who first ascended to heaven in search of eternal life; of the dead and living water; how the great goddess Ishtar descended into Hell and rose again; of the death of her lover Tammuz. Greek mythology was certainly coloured by some of these legends. Further, the Sumerian hymns to their great gods are full of religious feeling and fine imagery. Of profane literature fewer monuments have been preserved; and in this respect the superiority clearly belongs to the Egyptians.

I have spoken already of the remarkable development of civil and criminal law in the ancient cities of Sumer and in Babylon. I shall note here that Sumer has furnished the earliest documents referring to international law, the earliest international compacts (as for instance between Elam and a Sumerian king), and the earliest attempts to settle disputes by arbitration instead of war; thus Mesilim, an early king of Kish, acts as arbitrator in a boundary dispute between the kings of Umma and Lagash.

VI

POLITICAL HISTORY OF THE ANCIENT EAST IN THE SECOND MILLENNIUM B.C.

A BALANCE OF POWER

THE domination of the Hyksos in Egypt and of the Kassites in Babylonia weakened both these countries while it lasted; but it also did much to develop political and civilized life in all the East. It enabled those parts of the East which, like Egypt, were closely connected with the Mediterranean, to acquire civilization by degrees: I refer to the coasts of Syria, Phoenicia, and Palestine, southern and northern Syria on the Orontes and the upper Euphrates, Asia Minor and the adjacent islands of the Aegean, and especially Cyprus and Crete, the richest and largest of these islands. The beginnings of Asiatic civilization were closely connected with districts which border on the centre of that continent; and the light of primitive culture was kindled not only in Babylonia but also, and possibly earlier, in Persia and Turkestan, and (probably) in the Caucasus. Here the central point of civilization shifts more and more from the Persian Gulf—a purely Asiatic sea—to the Black Sea, which is part of the Mediterranean, on one side, and to the Aegean on the other.

The conquests of Sargon, Naram-Sin, and their successors, Sumerian and Babylonian, were directed to the north and north-west, along the valleys of the Tigris and Euphrates, or within the 'fertile crescent' bordering on the Arabian desert —that crescent of which Babylonia forms one end and southern Syria the other. Egypt also, in quest of timber and metals, sought to acquire parts of this crescent, especially the coast of Palestine and Syria. Nubia and the Red Sea coast attracted the attention of Egypt by their wealth in gold, rare woods, and ivory; but her expeditions to Nubia and Punt (Somaliland) were not so important historically as her repeated attacks on the 'fertile crescent'.

As I have said above, the desire for conquest, common

to Babylon and Egypt, was of great importance for the life of the ancient world. By it new districts of Hither Asia were drawn, one after another, into the circle of civilization. Commercial relations, no doubt, came first, but these were extended and consolidated in consequence of military operations. The two conquering powers themselves met in Palestine and Syria and formed close commercial ties. Exchange of commodities brought in its train exchange of ideas and inventions. The two civilizations drew together and influenced each other in many ways, and created mixed cultures at the points where they came in contact.

The temporary weakness of Egypt and Babylonia under the Hyksos and the Kassites did not arrest this process but rather confirmed it. Both countries kept their wealth and their civilization. It is true that the scope of their creative activity was curtailed, but there was never a long pause. On the other hand, their superiority ceased to crush their neighbours; and these were able to develop their own power of political and social progress. It is therefore not surprising if the first half of the second millennium B.C. witnessed the formation of new kingdoms and new centres of culture in the immediate neighbourhood of Babylonia and of Egypt. We know several such centres already, and shall know more with the progress of the archaeological investigation of Hither Asia which is rapidly developing.

In close proximity to Babylonia, and taking advantage of her political weakness, a whole series of new kingdoms rise up and grow. Elam, indeed, one of the most ancient centres of civilization in Hither Asia, remains great and wealthy; Elam is the ancient enemy of Babylonia, and its culture must be almost contemporary. But it is hardly conceivable that Elam was the only kingdom within the bounds of what later became Irania. The later fortunes of Iranian Asia (of which more will be said below) show that, in the third and second millenniums B.C., this part of the world had its own government and civilization (though we know little about them), closely connected with the civilization of the Mesopotamian kingdoms. To the north of Babylonia the kingdom of Assyria begins to shape itself. Occupying the high valleys of the central Tigris and part of the fertile plain between the two rivers, it had long ago come under the civilizing influence of Sumer and Akkad, and for a long time formed one of the provinces of the Sumerian Empire which took an active part in colonizing and civilizing north-eastern Asia Minor. Its future capitals, Ashur and Nineveh, grow fast and already rival Babylon under the Kassites. In about 1720 Assyria ruled temporarily over a vast empire. Farther to the north and north-west the kingdom of Mitanni arises; its history is still a puzzle to us, but it played a considerable part in the politics of the second millennium B. C.; it seems that the ruling class was a body of Aryan, or Iranian, conquerors. Further, the foundations of civilization and government were laid on the southern and northern slopes of the Caucasus and in Transcaucasia, with its main centres near Lake Van in what is now Armenia, and northward along the course of the river Kuban. In the first millennium B. C. the kingdom of Van becomes a serious rival of all-powerful Assyria. The rulers in this part of the ancient world were the Kharri. Finally, a colony of Assyrian traders and miners settled in Cappadocia on the shores of the Black Sea, and have bequeathed to us a number of cuneiform texts which tell us of their life and history. The date of this settlement may be in the time of Sargon I or earlier; it is certainly not later than the reign of Ur-engur and Dungi. The settlers were highly civilized in Sargon's time; later they were included in the Hittite empire.

Of all these new kingdoms the Empire of the Hittites was the greatest. It grew up by degrees in central Asia Minor in the first half of the second millennium B.C., and reached the summit of its political development about 1500. Centred at Boghaz-Keui in the mountains, and leaning upon the Black Sea coast, it kept its eyes steadily fixed upon that same shore of Syria which was so attractive to Egypt, Babylonia, and Assyria. It paid less attention to the western coast of Asia Minor, although maintaining constant relations, commercial and political, with it. The history of the Hittites is beginning to be cleared up by degrees. The discovery at Boghaz-Keui of a rich store of cuneiform tablets containing the royal archives, and the study of these documents by a succession of scholars, have shown that the Hittite Kingdom gradually developed into a great feudal empire in the first half of the second millennium B.C. The first 'emperor' was the king named Labarnis (about 1800 B.C.). The dominant people of the empire spoke an Indo-European language; but earlier inhabitants of the

PLATE XVIII

LIFE IN MINOAN CRETE

1. STEATITE VASE. Found at Hagia Triada near Phaestus. An officer at the head of three soldiers is reporting to the king or the royal prince. Late Middle Minoan or Early Late Minoan. 1700–1550 B.C. Museum at Candia (Crete).

2. A GOLD RING-BEZEL. Found at Mycenae in one of the graves of the early Mycenaean kings on the Acropolis. Two groups of two warriors each are engaged in fierce battle. One of the warriors is wounded. Another has sunk on his right knee and is lifting his long sword while the hero of the scene is aiming at him with his short dagger. A fourth man tries to reach the hero with his long spear from behind his large shield. Note the pathos and the ruthless realism of the scene. The hero and his rival with the shield and spear wear scale-helmets, and are probably two kings or princes. The scene on the ring excellently illustrates many descriptions of battles in the *Iliad*. Late Minoan. 1550–1400 B.C. National Museum, Athens.

3. STEATITE VASE. Found at Hagia Triada. A religious procession of agriculturalists is represented (each man carries an agricultural implement, decorated with reeds). The men are moving in the rhythmic step of a sacred dance. They sing a hymn in honour of the Great Goddess. A priest, very like an Egyptian priest, with three attendants, is shaking an Egyptian musical instrument, the 'sistrum', sacred to Isis. The leader (a priestess) wears a peculiar dress like scale armour. Early Late Minoan (about 1600 B.C.). Museum at Candia.

1. STEATITE VASE. MINOAN KING AND OFFICER

2. A GOLD RING-BEZEL

3. STEATITE VASE FROM HAGIA TRIADA

XVIII. LIFE IN MINOAN CRETE

land, whose speech had nothing in common with the Aryan tongues, still occupied an important position; of these were the Hittites who gave their name to the empire. The process of this empire's growth is still obscure. We have seen that at one time the area later occupied by the Empire was a Sumerian province. Later it may have formed part of a great empire which arose about Aleppo; and it gradually became a great independent kingdom, at the time when Babylon was conquered by the Kassites and Egypt by the Hyksos, and when the kingdoms of the Kharri took shape. It is possible that they gained advantage over other nations by the possession of superior weapons and the free use of war-chariots. It is to be noted that the horse, and with it the war-chariot, first appears in Hither Asia and Egypt with the coming of the Aryans. The Babylonian name for the horse is 'the mountain ass'.

On the coasts of Phoenicia, Syria, and Palestine, under both Egyptian and Babylonian influence, with a strong Minoan admixture, high civilization was developed. It was concentrated round the best harbours and extended to their strips of fertile territory. Separate fortified towns grew up, each carrying on its own business of middleman, seaman, colonizer, and pirate; the most prominent of these were Gaza, Tyre, Sidon, Byblus, Aradus, and, farther north, Tarsus in Cilicia. They could easily develop their activity as middlemen, taking advantage of their neighbours' weakness and the vast resources of the 'fertile crescent'. The adjacent mountain districts, especially the Lebanon and Anti-lebanon, whose ancient cedar-groves are even now not quite destroyed, supplied them with timber and resin—the finest material in the world for ship-building. Metals they received from the southern shore of the Black Sea. Farther to the east along the Jordan in Palestine, and along the Orontes and upper Euphrates in Syria, large towns with a great historic future, such as Jerusalem in Palestine, and Aleppo, Damascus, and Kadesh in Syria, grew up by degrees. Under the influence of the caravan-trade earlier insignificant settlements became rich and powerful cities; while of smaller towns there were scores, if not hundreds. And the same holds good of Cilicia in Asia Minor. The ethnographical group to which the population of these towns belonged is unknown. We shall see later that Palestine was very early, perhaps in prehistoric times, occupied by Semites. But the original population of Syria was not

Semitic; and the same must be said of the population of the towns near the sea. They probably belonged to a non-Semitic race; for their habits were unlike those of the Semites, who only came into contact with the sea by slow degrees and comparatively late.

The Semites—including Amorites, Aramaeans, Canaanites, northern and southern Arabs—continued their nomad or semi-nomad life, except where they became blended with more civilized peoples living in cities and became accustomed to different conditions. Babylonia and Assyria had this influence upon them; so, too, to some extent, had Palestine and Phoenicia, themselves influenced by the higher civilization of Egypt.

This nomad or semi-nomad life is well described in the popular Egyptian romance which narrates the adventures of Sinuhe, a contemporary of Senusret I, who found his way to Syria and there became the influential chief of a Semitic tribe. Some facts may also be found in the Bible stories about Abraham, Jacob, Lot, and other patriarchs—stories which became part of the quasi-historical tradition concerning the early fortunes of the Jews. Of the Minaean and Sabaean kingdoms in south Arabia little is known; but they were Semitic and seem to have reached a high pitch of civilization independently.

Nor do we know certainly what race it was that inhabited Asia Minor, the Aegean islands, and the southern part of the Balkan peninsula which was one day to be Greece. Thanks to the excavations of Schliemann and his successors in Asia Minor and Greece, of Sir Arthur Evans and others in Crete, and of a succession of archaeologists in Cyprus, we are now able for the first time to judge of the political and social activity that was reached by these countries in the second millennium B.C. We can follow the gradual movement of these peoples and of Phoenicia towards the west—along the shores of Africa, Sicily, Italy, and Spain. To the trading and colonizing activity of these bold mariners the western world was indebted for its first initiation into political and civilized life. It is impossible to pronounce with confidence whether a single people, dwelling about the Aegean Sea, were the creators of this mighty advance; but, for simplicity, we shall in future speak of them as Aegeans. Nor is it certain whether this culture was born in one place or in several centres at once.

This at least is certain, that the most important centre in the earlier times was the island of Crete—that barrier between the Aegean and the part of the Mediterranean connected with Egypt and Syria, that great island, one of whose sides faces towards Egypt and Asia, whilst another looks northward to the Archipelago, Greece, and Asia Minor. Early relations with Egypt and proximity to Cyprus, whose mineral wealth was coveted in early times by Egypt and Babylonia, enabled Crete to develop an extensive culture in the late Neolithic Age. Later, when she had learned to work metal and invented a system of writing on the Egyptian model, she went rapidly ahead, organizing a civilization of her own and adapting what she could borrow from the East. One after another, great cities grew up in the bays of the island—Cnossus, Phaestus, Mallia, Tylissus, and others (the ancient Aegean names of these cities are unknown). They were not fortified, as there was apparently no danger of attack on land; their life was connected mainly with the sea, from which the rulers and their subjects drew their chief revenue. The cities lived at peace with one another, having probably quickly contrived a kind of federal government for the whole island. United Crete acquired by degrees great authority with the inhabitants of the neighbouring islands, who were, like the Cretans, traders, pirates, and colonizers; and some sort of alliance, under the leadership of Crete, may have been formed. About 1600 B.C. some great catastrophe occurred, possibly an earthquake, a foreign invasion, or internal revolution; we know at least that the palaces of Cnossus and Phaestus were destroyed (perhaps by fire) at this period; but recovery soon followed, and her most palmy days were in the sixteenth century B.C.

A similar type of civilization was simultaneously developed in Asia Minor and on the coast of Syria and Phoenicia. But, for want of investigation of the sites, the exact estimate of progress, which is now possible in the case of Crete, is beyond our reach here. Systematic excavation has only just begun in Tyre, Sidon, and Byblus; and only one site in Asia Minor is well known to us—that of Troy. Troy, like Cnossus in Crete, was the head of an alliance, between towns and tribes in the north-west of Asia Minor; but her position was more difficult, as she was liable to be attacked on land by powerful neighbours. She was therefore always a strong fortress, pro-

PLATE XIX

A CITY ON THE MAINLAND
ATTACKED BY ENEMIES WHO
COME FROM THE SEA

FRAGMENTS OF A SILVER DRINKING HORN FROM THE FOURTH SHAFT-GRAVE ON THE ACROPOLIS OF MYCENAE. The bas-relief shows a fortified city. The inhabitants come out to meet the enemies who have just landed and are moving towards the city. The upper part of one of the attacking warriors with a helmet adorned with a crest is seen in our figure on the right, below; some others are seen on some fragments not reproduced in our figure. We may recognize equally some ships which brought the besiegers to the land. The men from the city are armed with bows and slings. The women, greatly excited, are watching the battle from the walls of the city and exhorting the men to courage. The city is situated on a hill and surrounded by trees (olive-trees?). The scene is a beautiful illustration of the well-known description of the battle between Hector and Achilles in the *Iliad*. It must be noticed that such a vivid scene of battle was a novelty at that time. 1700–1550 B.C. After Sir Arthur Evans. National Museum, Athens.

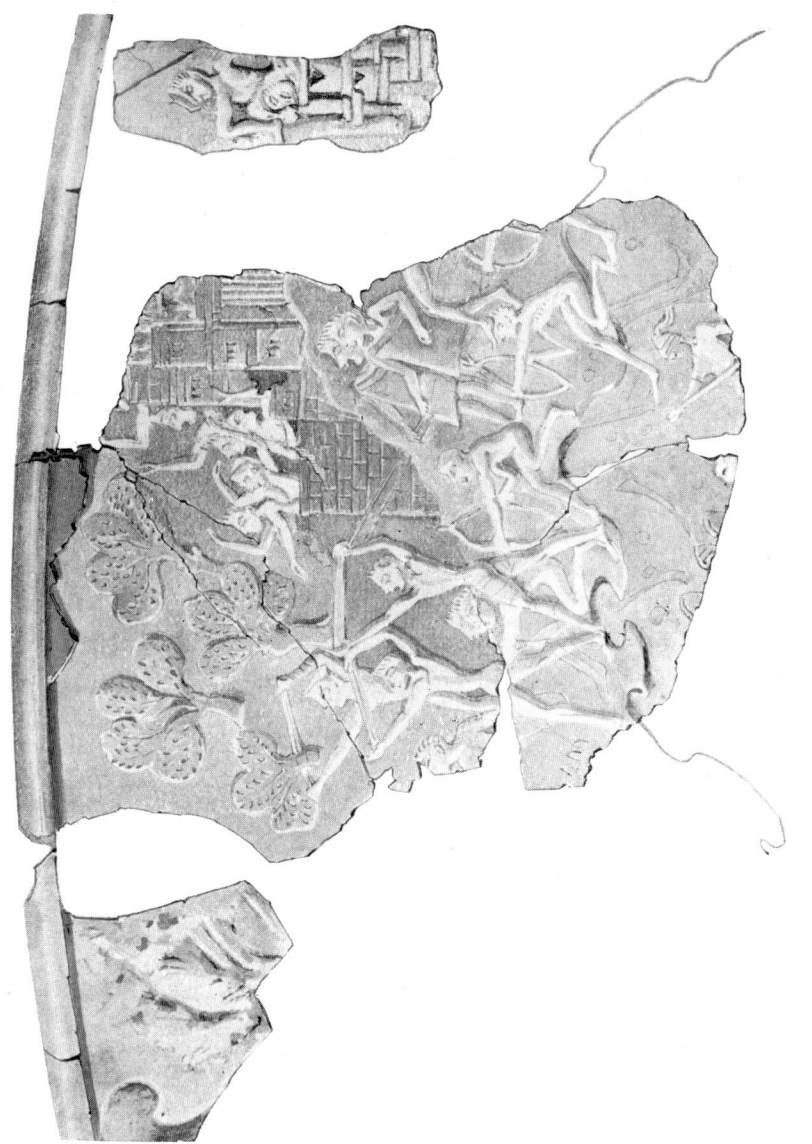

XIX. A CITY ON THE MAINLAND ATTACKED BY ENEMIES WHO COME FROM THE SEA

tected by formidable walls. I do not doubt that excavation will reveal to us in the near future similar political centres of the Aegean type, on the coast (the future Ionia) and in the centre of Asia Minor, and also on the coast of Lycia and Cilicia to the south-west.

In Greece we find just the same phenomena. In the second millennium B.C. fortified towns spring up everywhere near the sea-coast; each has stone walls, with a royal palace, temples, warehouses, storehouses, and barracks inside the walls, and dwellings for the subjects outside. All these towns grow larger and richer; and their culture gradually assumes the same Aegean type as in Crete. Our knowledge of these towns is confined chiefly to Tiryns, Mycenae, and Argos in eastern Peloponnesus, Pylus on the west coast, Orchomenus, Thebes, and Thisbe in Boeotia, and Athens in Attica; and the first two of these are the best known.

All these Aegean city-states took full advantage of the political weakness of Egypt. Whether the Hyksos had formed a large empire of which Egypt was but one part and had ruled over Crete or not is a question under debate. It is certain, however, that in the sixteenth and fifteenth centuries the Aegeans extended their political and commercial influence in Phoenicia and in Cyprus, Egypt's neighbours. From there and from Crete they certainly carried on a large trade with Egypt herself. We must suppose that their chief exports were olive oil and wine, still the pride of Greece; the inferior quality and quantity of production in the East made competition impossible.

Thus Egypt and Babylonia, the former lords of North Africa and Hither Asia, found themselves, in the first centuries of the second millennium, surrounded by a number of new kingdoms, which were steadily growing stronger and eager to extend their territory, especially at the expense of the two ancient powers. To escape being swallowed up by these rivals, Egypt and Babylonia had to be constantly on the watch.

Under the domination of the Hyksos, whose rule was hateful to the native population, any renascence whatever of the political importance of Egypt was out of the question. But at last a succession of vigorous rulers, whose power was centred at Thebes in southern Egypt, succeeded in shaking

PLATE XX

THE HITTITE EMPIRE

1. VIEW OF THE RUINS OF THE LOWER PALACE AT CARCHEMISH, one of the cities of the Hittite Empire on the Upper Euphrates (cp. pl. XXIII). The sculptured slabs which are seen on the photograph represent the army moving towards the right in a solemn procession, and the king and his family, priests and priestesses (cp. pl. XXIII) moving towards the left to meet the army. After 1000 B.C.

2. ONE SLAB WITH FIGURES OF THE SOLDIERS OF CARCHEMISH. After 1000 B.C.

3. PART OF A BAS-RELIEF which adorned one of the entrances to the palace of the chief capital of the Hittite Empire—Hatti (modern Boghaz-Keui). The bas-relief represents the Hittite War-god fully armed with a high metal helmet, metal belt, a curved short sword and an elaborate battle-axe. About 1500 B.C.

4. A SOLDIER OF ONE PART OF THE HITTITE EMPIRE, of which the capital was Samal (modern Zenjirli).

Note how different were the arms and weapons used in the various parts of the Hittite Empire. It testifies not only to gradual changes and improvements during the existence of the Empire and after its fall, but also to the fact that the Empire consisted of various peoples and races united into one federal or feudal military power.

1. RUINS OF THE LOWER PALACE AT CARCHEMISH

2. SOLDIERS OF CARCHEMISH

3. HITTITE SOLDIER OR GOD

4. SOLDIER OF ZENJIRLI

XX. THE HITTITE EMPIRE

off the foreign yoke and restoring a united national government. The struggle against the Hyksos was severe, but it ended in a complete victory for the national leaders, and the conquerors were exterminated or enslaved or expelled. When the first kings of the Eighteenth Dynasty had completed the business of liberation, it became their main object to prevent a repetition of attacks from Asia, and therefore to restore the policy of the kings of the Fourth and Fifth Dynasties, which was also that of the rulers of feudal Egypt in the Twelfth Dynasty. It was clear that Egypt would never be safe, unless she controlled Palestine, Syria, and Phoenicia, and unless her fleet was strong enough to defend her coast against maritime invasion from the harbours of Phoenicia, Crete, Cyprus, and Asia Minor. Thus the Pharaohs of the Eighteenth Dynasty were forced to adopt a policy of offence—an imperialistic policy, differing from that of their predecessors in this respect, that it aimed, not at the occasional occupation of scattered points, but at the mastery over a considerable part of Asia, and also over the great adjacent islands of Cyprus and Crete.

This policy was brilliantly carried out by the kings of the Eighteenth Dynasty (1580–1346 B.C.). The founder of this dynasty and the liberator of Egypt was Ahmose, a national hero. The first great conqueror was Thutmose I (1545–1514 B.C.). His work was interrupted by the peaceful reign of Hatshepsut, the first queen of Egypt (1501–1479 B.C.), and probably the daughter of Thutmose: she preferred the organization and development of commerce to foreign wars. But the task was resumed by Thutmose III, a nephew of Thutmose I and probably the husband of Hatshepsut. For some time he was joint ruler with Hatshepsut and remained in the background; but after her death he became one of the greatest conquerors in history and is called by many historians 'the Napoleon of Egypt'. Concerning his long reign full of glorious exploits, and concerning the empire which he created in Asia and Africa, we are well informed owing to an exact and detailed narrative of one part of his great deeds. This record, carved on the walls of the temple at Karnak, is the first chapter of military and political history in the world's literature, and is not a mere enumeration of nations conquered, towns taken, enemies slain, and booty seized, but gives a connected account of military operations. As the result of repeated campaigns

PLATE XXI

WAR AND PEACE IN EGYPT IN THE TIME OF THE XVIIIth DYNASTY

1. BAS-RELIEF FROM THE TEMPLE OF QUEEN HATSHEPSUT AT DEIR-EL-BAHARI. It represents the queen of a certain Parhu king of the land of Punt (a country situated on the southern part of the African shore of the Red Sea) with her husband and children (not represented on the part of the bas-relief published here) and accompanied by her subjects laden with gifts paying homage to the envoy of the powerful queen of Egypt. The Queen of Punt is suffering from a disease which has completely deformed her. The ships of Hatshepsut returned home laden with all the products of Punt: gold, ivory, ebony, incense, rare animals, ' serfs with their children ', &c. Many grandees of the land went with the Egyptian fleet to greet the Queen of Egypt in her own land. Cairo Museum.

2. PART OF THE BAS-RELIEFS OF THE TOMB OF HOREMHEB. To the left Horemheb as grand-vizier of Tutankhamen, in his official dress with all the gold rings given to him by the king on his neck, receives an embassy from foreign lands. An interpreter is translating to Horemheb what the ambassadors have to say and to the ambassadors the reply of the king. The group of ambassadors is full of life. Some raise their hands in supplication to the all-powerful vizier, some are prostrate ' on their bellies and backs '. Most of the ambassadors are Syrians, two are Libyans, and one is a negro. Behind the group of ambassadors are some inhabitants of Syria with their horses, probably of Aryan descent. To the left another figure of Horemheb. He is presenting to the Pharaoh and his wife some captives from the Syrian lands (the captives are not reproduced here). Behind him—the officials of the kingdom. The ambassadors, according to the fragments of the inscription, complained to Horemheb about the devastation and desolation of their lands, the hunger and misery of their people. They ask the Pharaoh to send an army to defend them from the attacks of the Chabiru and Amorites, the Semitic conquerors. Museums of Vienna, Leyden and Berlin.

1. THE QUEEN OF PUNT

2. HOREMHEB AND THE AMBASSADORS FROM THE SYRIAN LANDS

XXI. WAR AND PEACE IN EGYPT IN THE TIME OF THE XVIIIth DYNASTY

in Syria, Phoenicia, and Palestine, Egypt conquered these countries and united them to herself as tributary and subject kingdoms, each governed by members of their ruling families educated in Egypt. To assure the fidelity of these kingdoms, strong Egyptian garrisons, commanded by Egyptian generals, were stationed at important centres. Nor were the arms of Thutmose content with the conquest of Syria: there is no doubt that he consolidated Egyptian rule in Nubia also, and that he forced Cyprus and the federation of Cretan cities to be his allies if not dependants.

Thutmose III reigned for fifty-four years, more than half a century. His immediate successors—Amenhotep II (1447–1420), Thutmose IV (1420–1412), and Amenhotep III (1412–1376)—endeavoured to carry on the task of maintaining the Egyptian Empire. One of the most interesting series of official documents bequeathed to us by antiquity refers to the time of Amenhotep III and his successor Amenhotep IV, the last great king of the Eighteenth Dynasty. It is an official correspondence between these two kings and the kings of Mitanni, Assyria, and Babylon on one hand and their subjects in the Syrian lands on the other; it was found at Tell-el-Amarna in the ruined palace of Amenhotep IV. Of 350 letters 174 have been read and published, and may be supplemented by a series of letters and international compacts (about 110 in all) found at Boghaz-Keui, the capital of the Hittite kingdom, and also by a small number of letters from the archives of the ruler of Taanach in Palestine. All these documents are written in the diplomatic language of the time—the language of Sumer and Akkad. In addition to this Boghaz-Keui has supplied about 10,000 documents of various kinds in the Hittite languages. From these sources we see that the empire created by the Eighteenth Dynasty, though not world-wide, was among the strongest civilized powers of that day. Yet the Asiatic kings named above were entirely independent; and it is doubtful whether Crete long remained in a dependent position. Between these kingdoms and Egypt there are active relations, commercial and diplomatic. Together with open diplomacy secret intrigues are going on: the kings try to weaken Egypt by creating disturbance among Egyptian subjects in Asia; Egypt tries to prevent any Asiatic kingdom from growing too fast, by giving her support to the weaker kingdoms and maintaining, as far as possible, a balance of power in the East. Subsidies in money and dynastic intermarriages are the means usually employed.

But in spite of diplomacy, and in spite of repeated campaigns in Asia, Egyptian influence over that continent grew steadily weaker under the successors of Thutmose III. Egypt was not strong enough to check the growth of the Hittite kingdom, cut off as it was by the impenetrable barrier of the snow-covered mountains of Taurus. The power of Assyria also increased steadily; and both powers fomented disorder in the Asiatic provinces of Egypt. New Semitic tribes of Aramaeans and Hebrews began to spread over the Egyptian provinces. The Egyptian Empire collapsed almost entirely in the reigns of Amenhotep III and IV. The last took the name of Ikhnaton for religious reasons. The religious reform introduced by this king nearly led to civil war. He forced the people to give up their local cults for the worship of one paramount deity—Aton, the great sun-god; and the troubles caused by this innovation certainly weakened the country and diverted the king's attention from problems of foreign policy. But the chief danger lay elsewhere. Egypt's exertions had been too great for her strength: she had sent out army after army of her native population to fight in Asia and Nubia or to serve in the fleet; and at the same time the people had to bear on their shoulders all the weight of forced labour on the colossal buildings so characteristic of the Eighteenth Dynasty.

The Pharaohs never succeeded in uniting Egypt and her foreign dominions. The troubles in Asia went on, and Egyptian power could be maintained only by a succession of long and arduous campaigns. With the death of Ikhnaton in 1362 B.C., the glorious line of the Eighteenth Dynasty came to an end, and political anarchy followed for about forty years (till 1321 B.C.). To this time belongs Tutankhamen, the second feeble successor of Ikhnaton, the discovery of whose almost unviolated tomb has recently caused so much excitement.

VII

POLITICAL DEVELOPMENT AND CULTURE OF THE ANCIENT EAST IN THE SECOND MILLENNIUM B.C.

THE second millennium B.C. is very important in the history of civilization. At this time, side by side with the cultures of Egypt and Babylonia, new cultures were born and grew vigorously. Two of these we know better than the rest—those developed round the Aegean and in Asia Minor. Our knowledge, indeed, is incomplete and accidental; it is possible that systematic excavation in the East, Turkestan, Persia, and Central Asia may reveal at least one more type of culture—that which formed the cradle of Iranian civilization, just as the two former nurtured the civilization of Lydia and Phrygia and of Greece, Asiatic and European.

We know little of the primitive culture of Asia Minor. Troy is the only large city-centre that has been at all thoroughly examined. This examination, begun by Schliemann and continued by Dörpfeldt, showed that Asia Minor had its period of rich neolithic culture and also a period of copper and early bronze culture, the latter of which provided such refined products of the jewellers' art as the 'Treasure of Priam'. Hence we must suppose that the rest of Asia Minor had an early independent culture of the neolithic, copper, and bronze periods, just as the Caucasus, both northern and southern, passed through these phases. The Aegean culture (of which more is said below) affected the coast of Asia Minor and had some influence on the Trojan culture belonging to the latter half of the second millennium. Nevertheless, the Trojan civilization of that time also remains independent.

Even more individual is the civilization of the great Hittite Empire, which flourished in the latter half of the second millennium. Their form of government, in particular, is more primitive than the form created ultimately in Egypt and Babylonia. It was a group of mountain tribes, each with a fortified post like an eagle's nest, a priest-king or governor,

PLATE XXII

THUTMOSE III AND THE MIGHT OF EGYPT

1. HEAD OF A SPLENDID STATUE OF KING THUTMOSE III. Found in the temple of Amon (Karnak) at Thebes. After 1479 B.C. Cairo Museum.

2. PART OF A FRESCO FROM A THEBAN ROCK-CUT GRAVE. Syrian ambassadors are represented doing homage to the King of Egypt and bringing various gifts to him. Note the typical Syrian gold vessels which they bring as their tribute or gifts. Note also the Semitic dress and the fine rendering of the most minute features of the racial type of the ambassadors. XVIIIth Dynasty. London, British Museum.

1. THUTMOSE III

2. A SYRIAN EMBASSY TO PHARAOH

XXII. THUTMOSE III AND THE MIGHT OF EGYPT

and gods and goddesses of its own; but all acknowledged the authority of a superior king, the ruler of Boghaz-Keui, who held the key to the tableland of Asia Minor. These scattered clans, which formed in the third and second millennium B.C. a part of the Sumero-Babylonian Empire and inherited the far advanced Sumerian civilization, built up later their own civilization on local lines. The Hittite Empire had one remarkable advantage: it had free access to the rich copper mines in Asia Minor and on the south coast of the Black Sea. It is possible that they began to work the iron mines in the same districts and to use iron and steel for their weapons instead of copper. They took another great step in advance when they borrowed the Babylonian system of writing and adapted it to the local languages. Among the many cuneiform documents found at Boghaz-Keui special interest and importance attaches to the lately published code of Hittite law, which refers, approximately, to the year 1300 B.C. It shows clearly the variety of languages spoken in the empire, its feudal character, and the very important part played in it by the military class—the royal militia, who were provided with land and settled in different parts of the kingdom. The Hittite laws were undoubtedly a codification of customary law, like the Assyrian code of a slightly later date, and unlike the code of royal laws and judicial decisions of the Sumerian and Babylonian kings. The law is founded on private property. Slavery plays a prominent part. Economic life is represented as well-developed and flourishing; its main basis is cattle-breeding, but agriculture and viticulture are also freely practised; and handicrafts, especially metallurgy, are important. We note in these laws the use of Babylonian silver currency, and as regards criminal law the prevalence of a humane spirit which avoids the cruel punishments typical of the East (mutilation, flaying, &c.).

The originality of Hittite civilization, its peculiar aspect, is apparent also from the monuments of architecture, sculpture, and minor arts and crafts, discovered by excavation, especially at Carchemish and Zenjirli in North Syria and at Boghaz-Keui in Central Asia Minor. Their architecture is peculiar—an architecture of palaces and fortresses. One type of these palace-fortresses is found in northern Syria, and another in Asia Minor. The former seems to be native; the latter, which is seen at Boghaz-Keui, is the type of dwelling-house imported

PLATE XXIII

THE HITTITE KING AND THE HITTITE PRIESTS

1-3. SCULPTURED SLABS which adorn the walls of the palace and temple area of the Hittite city of Carchemish on the Upper Euphrates. Found at Carchemish and still on the spot. The figures on these slabs (hundreds of such slabs were found; they are alternately of dark basalt and of white limestone) formed long processions. One representing the Hittite army (pl. XX) covered the so-called processional wall (the outer wall of the palace- and temple-terrace); another (our plate), representing another portion of the same army with the king and his family followed by priests and priestesses meeting the soldiers, adorned the walls of the so-called Lower Palace. The king and his wife are moving slowly and solemnly, the king with the sceptre in his right hand; behind them their children are represented twice—in the upper panel moving slowly in the procession and followed by a dwarf with a standard, in the lower part playing in the royal palace; and finally the nurse, with the baby of the house in her arms, is leading a pet animal. The royal family is followed by priests and priestesses. The priestesses wear high tiaras and hold sacrificial implements; the priests or attendants of the priests carry on their shoulders sacrificial animals. After 1000 B.C.

1. KING AND FAMILY WITH PRIESTS AND PRIESTESSES

2. PRIESTS

3. PRIESTESSES

XXIII. THE HITTITE KING AND THE HITTITE PRIESTS

from Central Europe. But the main artistic features are the same in both types of building. These fortified palaces are low and massive, with strong turrets, low and impressive gates, which are finely decorated and form the most prominent feature of the building, and strong thick walls.

Their sculpture also is peculiar to themselves. Even when decorative, it is closely connected with the architecture, and displays powerful fabulous animals guarding the entrance of the buildings, or reliefs upon the walls; or it has a religious

FIG. 2. *One section of the bas-reliefs which adorn the walls of the rock-sanctuary of Yasili-Kaia near the Hittite capital Boghaz-Keui. The bas-relief shows the Great God of the Hittites, supported by two human figures and followed by two Gods who stand on the tops of the mountains, meeting his bride—the Great Anatolian Goddess Mother standing on the back of her sacred lion and followed by a God who stands on a lion and two Goddesses supported on the double-headed eagle, the sacred symbol of the Hittite Empire. About 1500 B.C.*

and political tendency, representing rows of Hittite gods and their votaries moving in austere monotonous processions, as, for instance, on the walls of Yasili-Kaia, a great shrine among the rocks that surround Boghaz-Keui. The style of these monuments has not the tragic note of Babylonian sculpture nor the refined elegance of Egypt. It is a realistic style, heavy and rude—the style of mountaineers and warriors; but it conceals rich possibilities of further development and had a great influence upon Babylonian art. Weight and solemnity are its distinguishing features. In religious sculpture the chief figure is the Great Goddess of Asia Minor—the mother of men and animals, the warrior and protectress of the king and the country; and this shows clearly the local

PLATE XXIV
THE PALACE OF CNOSSUS

1. THE STORE-ROOMS OF THE PALACE OF CNOSSUS WITH THE BIG OIL-JARS.

2. ONE OF THE STATE ROOMS OF THE PALACE as restored by Sir Arthur Evans on the spot. Note the peculiar columns growing wider above, and the capitals, prototypes of the later Doric capitals of Greece.

3. THE SO-CALLED THRONE ROOM IN THE PALACE. The central place is occupied by a monumental stone chair, and round the walls are stone benches. The walls were covered with stucco and the stucco painted. Part of this decoration has been restored from fragments by Sir Arthur Evans. It shows an eagle-griffin lying in a flower garden. There must have been a similar figure on the other side of the throne. Whether the throne was used by the king when presiding at the state council or acting as the supreme judge while the other members sat on the benches, or the throne was supposed to be occupied by the invisible Great Goddess, is uncertain. Religious and state life were closely connected in the Minoan Age. Late Minoan. 1550–1400 B.C.

1. STORE-ROOMS

2. A STATE ROOM

3. THE THRONE ROOM

XXIV. THE PALACE OF CNOSSUS

character of the whole culture. These sculptors have also represented exactly the typical features of the nation, their peculiar costume, and their way of life as soldiers, citizens, and worshippers of the gods.

With regard to future development, even more interest and importance attaches to the feats of creative genius accomplished by a series of Aegean city-states, above all in Crete and, later, in Greece. The process can be followed in Crete from neolithic times right down to the Iron Age. It is difficult to say how far this culture owed its brilliant development in the age of metals to the influence of Egypt and Babylonia. Knowledge of the metals and greater use of the sea lie at the root of Aegean civilization. We do not yet know how or whence the metals first appeared in that region; but we may be sure that they were known there almost as early as in Egypt and Babylonia. As regards seafaring, from very ancient times Aegean ships differed in appearance from both Egyptian and Phoenician craft. Perhaps the Aegeans borrowed writing, or the rudiments of writing, from the Egyptians; but they developed it independently; and possibly they owed the potter's wheel to the same quarter. The influence of Egypt asserts itself later also; but it is a mutual influence, as Egypt helps herself in turn from the treasures of Aegean genius. Though the connexion with Babylonia was looser and more fitful, the system of weights and measures may have been taken from there.

As far as we can judge from the excavations carried out of late years in the chief centres of this culture, and from the evidence preserved in the ancient Greek epics—the *Iliad* and *Odyssey* cannot, indeed, be placed earlier than the close of the second millennium B.C., but they abound in recollections of the glorious past of the Aegean kingdoms—the Aegean world consisted, as we have said already, of a number of city-states, ruled by kings and the royal troops. Both kings and soldiers led an active and eventful life. They were chiefly employed in marine trading, which was in that unruly age hardly distinguishable from piracy. The king and his retainers lived in a great palace containing hundreds of rooms; in Crete the palace was unfortified, on the mainland it was protected by strong walls. The subject population, who tilled the land and bred cattle, were scattered over the king's territory. Traders, artisans, and sailors settled close to the

PLATE XXV
MINOAN POTTERY

1. STONE VESSEL FROM ISOPATA NEAR CNOSSUS. The upper part has rows of symmetrically placed circular holes, inlaid with shell. Late Middle Minoan. About 1700. Candia Museum.

2. BEAUTIFUL POT OF THE SO-CALLED KAMARES STYLE, with white, orange, and pink floral ornaments on a black ground. Middle Minoan. 1800–1700 B.C. Candia Museum.

3. MINOAN JUG with figures painted dark on a light ground, found at Pseira. It shows dolphins swimming—one straight up, the next straight down, amid honeycombed rocks and seaweed. Early Late Minoan. About 1600 B.C. Ashmolean Museum, Oxford.

4. MINOAN AMPHORA with papyrus ornament from Isopata, Cnossus. Late Minoan. About 1500 B.C. Ashmolean Museum, Oxford.

5. MINOAN JUG with dark figures painted on a light ground: from Hagia Triada. Octopuses are shown amid stylized rocks. Late Minoan. About 1500 B.C. Ashmolean Museum, Oxford.

The figures show the condition of the potter's art in Crete at its highest development when the Cretan Empire was in its prime. Note the skilful use of polychromy and the beautiful stylization of plants and animals for decorative purposes without any rigidity but with full understanding of the principles of decorative art.

1. STONE VESSEL FROM ISOPATA

2. POT OF KAMARES STYLE

3. MINOAN JUG FROM PSEIRA

4. MINOAN AMPHORA FROM CNOSSUS

5. MINOAN JUG

XXV. MINOAN POTTERY

palace or fortified citadel of the king, inside or outside its walls. Close ties of friendship and kinship united the king and fighting men of one city with those of another in the neighbourhood, and they formed, as it were, one large family. They exchange frequent visits, feast and make merry together, and unite to take a share in the sacrifice of victims and in religious games. They make rich presents to one another and exchange compliments. But quarrels also are frequent, over spoil or beautiful women, or arising out of the mysterious and tragic crimes of a palace.

It is a striking feature of this culture that, though profoundly different from others, it was never self-centred or exclusive. It was active, enterprising, and various, as one might expect from traders, warriors, and pirates. It was probably not associated with any definite nationality. To me it presents itself as not national at all : it seems to have been created by the conditions of life on the shores of the Aegean and in the narrow valleys of the islands and the mainland. A land that was comparatively poor and cramped forced the population to sail away to the nearest islands or even to the world of the Eastern monarchies, in search of what was denied them by their own somewhat grudging soil. Hence it is highly probable that the representatives of Aegean civilization on the islands differed in race from the representatives on the mainland of Greece ; but their civilization was essentially the same with important local modifications.

In general, two varieties of it may be distinguished. The first and more ancient belongs to the south and is called Cretan; the second belongs to the north and is called Mycenean, from Mycenae in the Peloponnese, which has been investigated more thoroughly than other Aegean sites. The difference between the two is revealed most clearly by the plan followed in the construction of their houses and settlements. The Cretan house consists of a number of rooms grouped round a courtyard; the Mycenean house consists of walls erected round a hearth which forms the centre of the dwelling ; the house has a roof and a door but only one room, and its object is to make full use of the warmth diffused by the central hearth. There is an equal unlikeness in their settlements. The Cretans, being islanders and sailors, were content with the protection of their fleet and hardly fortified their cities at all ; but the dwellers on the mainland stood always in fear of their neighbours, and therefore built strong thick walls round the palace of the king and his retainers, and sometimes round the whole city. The general trend of life is equally different in Crete and in Greece. The Cretans are mostly sailors and traders. They neglect war and indulge in more pacific arts. Life in Greece is centred round war, sieges and battles.

But both types of settlements have this feature in common, that the settlement grows into a town which quickly assumes an orderly and civilized appearance. It has paved streets, houses of several storeys, drains and other sanitary contrivances, which were unknown to the East, with its huge village-like settlements grouped round a palace and temple. The Aegean way of life was more compact and thus created that kind of settlement which we call 'urban'. Such compactness was natural to men who from early times were chiefly engaged in trade and industry, and natural in a country where there were no fertile alluvial valleys for the population to spread in, and where the comparative poverty of the soil made concentration impossible except in towns not dependent entirely upon agriculture. Another peculiarity of Aegean towns is that they have no temples like those of the East, none of those huge palaces built for the gods. It appears that they worshipped mainly the powers of nature, personified in the Great Goddess, mother of gods and men. Her shrines were generally caves, or groves of consecrated trees, or small chapels forming part of palaces. Another form of worship was paid to dead heroes. The Aegeans did not build pyramids in their honour; yet their beehive tombs (which are peculiar to the mainland branch of the Aegean civilization) with a cupola roof and a long passage for entrance, hidden under mounds of earth, are not inferior to the Pyramids and the rock-cut tombs of Egypt in originality of artistic conception.

Lastly, it was a peculiarity of the Aegeans that they never sought to create anything imposing by mere size; the buildings they preferred were of moderate proportions, adorned with colour, and pleasing to the eye. Their sculptors carved no colossal shapes of gods or men; their architects did not task themselves to build a pyramid, or a row of columns in a temple—columns of such a size that a hundred men could find standing-room on the capital of each. The palaces of Cnossus, Phaestus, Mycenae, and Tiryns do indeed cover a large space: they are extensive and contain a number of small rooms and a number of courts. But the reason for this is that a number of people lived there together—the king, his court, and his retainers. The palace courts are

FIG. 3. *Plan of the Minoan city of Gournia (modern name) as excavated by an American expedition. Note the modest palace of the king, the streets, and the private houses.*

PLATE XXVI

MINOAN PAINTING

PART OF THE MURAL DECORATION OF THE PALACE OF CNOSSUS. Restored by Sir Arthur Evans. In a beautiful field or garden of crocuses or saffron a boy is gathering flowers for a religious ceremony or a feast in the palace. Note the love of the artist for nature, especially for flowers. Middle Minoan. About 1800 B.C. Museum at Candia.

XXVI. MINOAN PAINTING

extensive, because they were always filled by a crowd of men seeking air and light, and served as a public resort for the inhabitants of the palace, for divine worship or games or military reviews. In fact the palace is large because it is a whole town with a large and motley population, but it is not colossal. The only part of it that strikes one by its

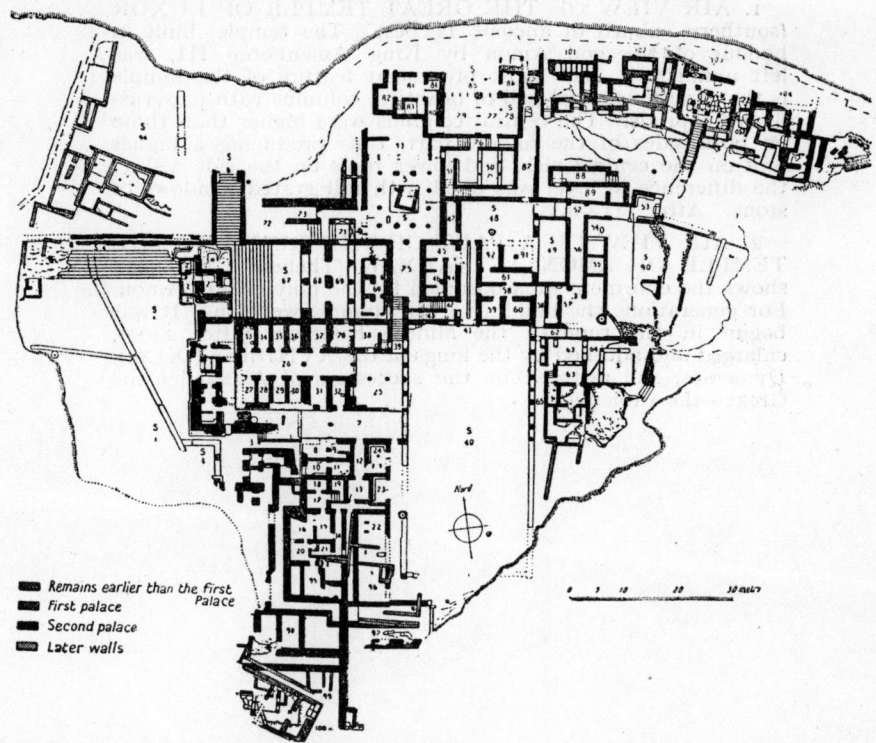

FIG. 4. *Plan of the Minoan palace at Phaestus (modern name) as excavated by an Italian expedition. The palace shows the same general features as the plan of the larger and more gorgeous palace of Cnossus. Comp. pl. XXIV.*

dimensions is the courtyard intended for religious ceremonies and shows connected with them—the earliest attempt to create a theatre.

All these peculiarities go to prove that the manner of life among the Aegeans was unlike that of the East—it was more akin to the type subsequently created by Greece, more democratic. Men lived in a swarm, with one of themselves for chief, like the queen-bee in a hive, but their life was identical

PLATE XXVII
THE TEMPLES OF LUXOR AND KARNAK

1. AIR VIEW OF THE GREAT TEMPLE OF LUXOR (southern suburb of ancient Thebes). The temple, built in honour of the god Amon by King Amenhotep III, was left unfinished. The most prominent feature of the temple is the gigantic central hall of beautiful columns with papyrus-flower capitals. The central columns were higher than those on both sides of the middle part, thus producing a higher roof on the central aisle and lower roofs on the side aisles; the difference in level was filled with tall grated windows of stone. After 1412 B.C.

2. AIR VIEW OF A PART OF THE RUINS OF THE TEMPLE OF AMON AT KARNAK (Thebes). The view shows the enormous area occupied by the holy city of Amon. For generations the building of this temple went on. It was begun in the time of the Middle Kingdom (after 2400), enlarged and adorned by the kings of the XVIIIth and XIXth Dynasties, and restored by the successors of Alexander the Great—the Ptolemies.

1. THE GREAT TEMPLE OF LUXOR

2. A PART OF THE TEMPLE OF AMON AT KARNAK

XXVII. THE TEMPLES OF LUXOR AND KARNAK

with his. In the East the king was divine and lived in magnificent isolation, an object of reverence and worship. The life of the Aegean king was more human. He had neither the will nor the power to separate himself from his comrades in war and partners in trading ventures; to them and their wives he was not, and could not be, a deity. But after death, as the best and strongest and bravest, he became a hero and his tomb became a temple.

Aegean art, so live and sparkling, is all full of humanity and individuality; it is free from the oppressive magnificence and majesty of the god-king, before whom his subjects are pitiable grains of desert sand before the sun; it bubbles like a fountain with vivacity and merriment; it thirsts for life and delights in life; it is intoxicated with sea and sun, trees and flowers, sport and war. These men reproduce life on their household utensils, on the walls of their houses, and in works of art; their fancy is not for separate figures or portraits—no portraits have been bequeathed to us by them— but for groups; and these groups are not rows of identical figures but related to one another and full of movement. The ornament is lively, impersonal, capricious, and infinitely various, finding models everywhere, both in the elegance of the geometric spiral and in natural objects, such as flowers and marine animals, and the odder these are, the better— cuttle-fish, flying fish, sea-shells.

This is why the productions of Aegean art, sometimes sketchy and impressionistic, often childish in their simplicity, impress us so strongly after the splendid monuments of the East—the refinement of Egypt and the dramatic power of Babylon. On palace walls, utensils, and ornaments these artists represent by preference scenes from the life of the spacious palace courts: young men running and jumping in honour of the god; athletes leaping over the backs of maddened oxen and clutching them by the horns; women dancing with wild ecstasy in honour of the Great Goddess; peasants returning home in procession and singing hymns to the great earth-goddess; the hero-king reviewing his soldiers. But Aegean art carries us beyond the limits of the palace, and shows us other lively pictures: bulls caught with nets in the forest; the attack on a fortress by enemies who come from the sea; the ship carrying a statue of a horse (it recalls the horse of Troy); a funeral procession and rites performed at the grave. There

PLATE XXVIII
THE TEMPLES OF DEIR-EL-BAHARI

VIEW OF TWO MORTUARY TEMPLES, built on the slope of the western cliffs of Thebes which surround the so-called valley of the kings, where most of the Theban kings of Egypt were buried in rock-hewn chambers and series of chambers. The temple to the right of our figure is the beautiful work of Queen Hatshepsut of the XVIIIth Dynasty. It consists of three terraces surrounded by porticoes. The holy-of-holies of the temple was a chamber hewn in the rock. The temple was adorned by beautiful bas-reliefs (see pl. XXI, 2), which recorded the most important events of her reign beginning with her birth, especially the expedition which she sent to the land of Punt (Somali). Many rare trees brought from this 'home of the gods' were planted in large pots on the terraces of the temple. To the left are the recently discovered ruins of the temple of Mentuhotep III of the XIth Dynasty. The temple shows the same type of building.

XXVIII. THE TEMPLES OF DEIR-EL-BAHARI

is not a trace of conventionality or tradition throughout, and there is hardly any repetition. The brightness and variety of the colours is surprising; they are laid, one on another or one beside another, in the most unexpected combinations, with a constant endeavour to get novel tints.

Nothing is more instructive than to compare this earliest European civilization with the more refined, more imposing, and more complete civilization of the East—the Egyptian civilization of the Eighteenth Dynasty, during which the nation was regenerated and a mighty empire created.

During this period the culture of Egypt reached its highest point. Much, indeed, had been done already. Technical skill had been developed to the utmost, and the Pharaohs of this dynasty could command a multitude of highly trained artists and artisans. Hardly any advance was possible in this direction: Egypt merely maintained her former level and, to some extent, developed what was old. Nor was there much novelty in the way of architecture or of ornament, though occasional hints were taken from the Aegean world, with which there were then regular and active relations. But, in general, Egypt was still not much inclined to borrow. She was content with the artistic forms worked out by herself. But we are impressed by a new and powerful creative impulse, by new and various combinations of old features to form magnificent monuments, and by perfection and beauty of execution, both in the whole and in the separate parts. At this time Egypt was able to make full use of all that the past had attained, and she created immortal monuments of brilliant beauty, strong and graceful, huge and yet shapely, harmonizing with nature, and full of enchanting detail.

The magnificent temples built by this dynasty, principally at Thebes, the capital of the kingdom, are their supreme achievement. The huge temple of Amon at Karnak (the modern name of Thebes) astonishes not only by its dimensions, which are actually unrivalled in the whole world, not only by its colossal pillars, obelisks, and statues, but also by the skill with which a number of new architectural problems are solved. I may mention perhaps the famous two-storeyed hall, simple and yet full of light; it is true that this was completed later by the kings of the next dynasty. Again, there is the hall of Thutmose III, where a series of interesting figures, in painting and relief, set forth the conqueror's services

PLATE XXIX

IKHNATON AND HIS WIFE

1. FRONT AND SIDE VIEW OF THE BUST OF QUEEN NEFERTITI, THE WIFE OF KING IKHNATON. Found in the studio of the sculptor Thutmose in the ruins of the capital of Ikhnaton at Tell-el-Amarna. Model for the workmen of the studio. Painted. The crown is blue, the band on the crown is gold inset with precious stones. The eyes were inset: they are of black and white stone covered with rock crystal. On the neck is a rich necklace. Excellent piece of realistic sculpture. After 1380 B.C. Berlin Museum.

2. SIDE VIEW OF A BUST OF KING IKHNATON. Found in the same place as No. 1. Lightly painted. The head originally wore a crown. One of the best portraits of Ikhnaton. After 1380 B.C. Berlin Museum.

1. QUEEN NEFERTITI

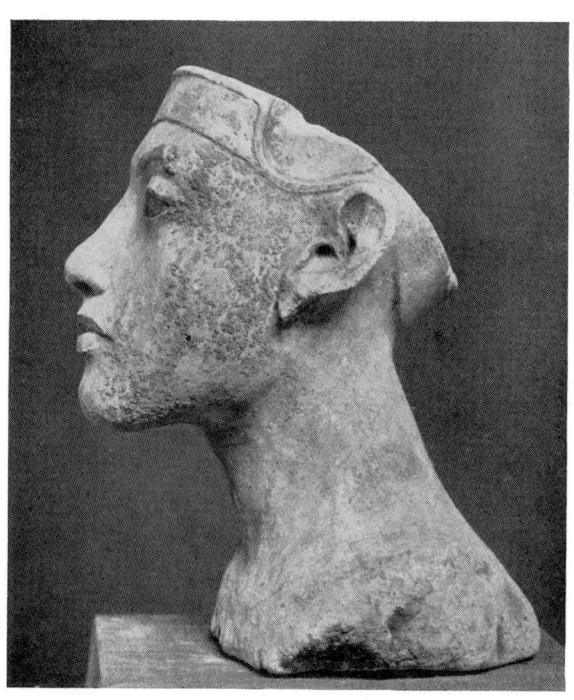

2. KING IKHNATON

XXIX. IKHNATON AND HIS WIFE

to the wealth of Egypt by the acclimatization of strange plants and animals. A different impression is produced by Luxor (the name is modern), the second Theban temple preserved to our time. There is not the same accumulation of parts as at Karnak, that city of gods. It is beautiful and shapely, powerful but not impressive in its dimensions—a dwelling-place for the great god of the Egyptian Empire, simple and clear in its plan, finished in detail. The third temple is highly interesting. It was built in the Theban City of the Dead by Hatshepsut in honour of Amon, Hathor, and the divine Anubis, and in memory of her great father, Thutmose I. A majestic avenue rises from the valley up the hill and leads to two successive broad terraces flanked by graceful colonnades. The shrine is placed on a rock at the far end of the second terrace. The walls exhibit an immense number of brilliantly coloured reliefs, depicting in full detail the queen's exploits and especially her expedition to the marvellous land of Punt in search of spices, timber, ivory, gold, and new animals and plants. The fourth great monument of this epoch was the funerary temple built by Amenhotep III in the necropolis of Thebes; but nothing remains of it except the colossal statues of Memnon (a Greek translation of the king's name); the rest was ruthlessly destroyed by Ramses II, a king of the Nineteenth Dynasty.

In their sculpture nothing is more remarkable than the portrait-statues of these Pharaohs. Not less majestic than the statues of the Pyramid Age and the Twelfth Dynasty, they are still more individualized and still more refined in technique. One of the last great monuments of Egyptian architecture and sculpture—the cave-temple of Ramses II at Abu-simbel in Nubia—reflects exactly the same spirit. Four colossal statues of the Pharaoh, surveying the Nile from the desert sands in proud majesty, guard the entrance to the spacious grotto. Here again one is struck not only by the originality of the idea but also by the skill in execution—by the power to create one complete thing out of the rock, the mighty river, and the desert, and to reflect in this combination the might and majesty of the kings, the rulers of a great empire. The refined and beautiful sculptures of King Seti I, which remain in the funerary temple built by him at Abydos, also belong to the Nineteenth Dynasty.

This solemn classical art of the Egyptian Empire is distinct

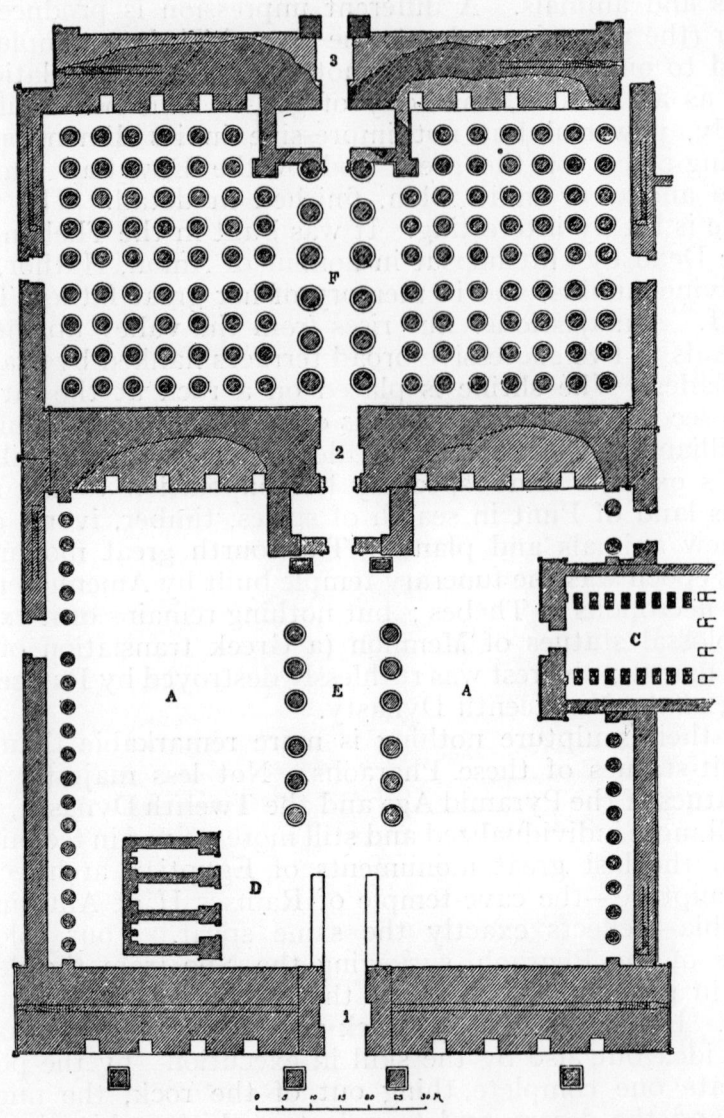

FIG. 5. *Plan of the great temple of Amon at Karnak (modern name) near the city of Thebes. Comp. pl. XXVII, 2. After Perrot and Chipiez*

FIG. 6. *Restoration of the hypostyle central hall of the temple of Karnak. Comp. the description of a similar hall in the temple of Luxor, pl. XXVII, 1. After Perrot and Chipiez*

PLATE XXX

HOREMHEB AND THE FAMILY OF IKHNATON

1. PORTRAIT STATUE OF HOREMHEB, commander-in-chief of the armies of Tutankhamen and later himself king of Egypt. Found in the temple of Ptah at Memphis. Horemheb is represented as a 'scribe' with a scroll of papyrus across his lap and his ink-well upon his knee. In his right hand he holds the pen. About 1350 B. C. Metropolitan Museum of Art, New York.

2. FRONT AND SIDE VIEW OF A BUST OF QUEEN TIY, the wife of Amenhotep III and the mother of Ikhnaton. Found in the ruins of a royal palace in the Fayum. The eyes were inset. The modelling is perfect and the portrait of a striking realism. After 1400 B. C. Berlin Museum.

3. HEAD OF ONE OF THE DAUGHTERS OF IKHNATON. Found in the ruins of the capital of Ikhnaton at Tell-el-Amarna. The eyes were inset. Wonderful portrait of a child. After 1380 B. C. Berlin Museum.

1. STATUE OF HOREMHEB

2. QUEEN TIY

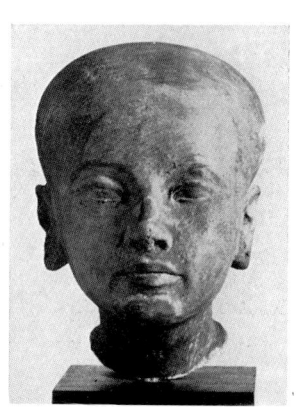
3. A DAUGHTER OF IKHNATON

2. QUEEN TIY

XXX. HOREMHEB AND THE FAMILY OF IKHNATON

from the work of those artists who were employed by Ikhnaton and were directed by him. The latter form of art was short-lived but is of remarkable interest. The novelty of it does not lie in the decoration of his palace, full as that is of life and movement and a delicate, somewhat idyllic, feeling for nature—on the floors there are flocks of geese swimming on the weed of the Nile, flocks of pigeons on the ceilings, a cat creeping up to a bird. All this had long been familiar : it only marks a stage in the development of subjects long dear to Egyptian artists. What is new is the unflinching realism with which the sculptors have represented Ikhnaton himself, his wife, his children, and his favourites ; and new, too, is the pathetic religious passion which pervades all these faces, especially that of the king himself—weak, sickly, somewhat deformed, not majestic at all, but burning with the inward fire of religious enthusiasm.

The wonderful refinement attained by the minor arts of this age is shown by the discoveries recently made in the tomb of Tutankhamen, the successor of Ikhnaton. Some of the funerary statues are refined and beautiful ; but the most interesting and beautiful things are articles of furniture—chairs and couches, chariots and miniature shrines, garments and utensils of various kinds. By means of an elaborate technique—a combination of painting (or gilding) with inlaid work—all these objects shine in the beauty of many colours. The design is masterly and almost perfect, with all the traditional peculiarity of Egyptian art, the composition lucid and well balanced. Great artists, with an age-long tradition behind them, worked to produce the marvels of Tutankhamen's tomb.

The peculiarities characteristic of Egyptian art when devoted to the service of the kings and the realm, we find repeated in the monuments which adorned the private life of their subjects, especially those who were closely associated with the king in his labours—grand-viziers, commanders-in-chief, and governors of foreign dominions. Of these we have many beautiful painted and carved rock-cut tombs, which imitate the more magnificent but similar tombs of the kings. In these graves the subjects of the kings depicted both their public achievements and their private life. Immense wealth poured into Egypt. The life of kings, priests, and officials was refined and luxurious ; every product of the then civilized

PLATE XXXI

TUTANKHAMEN FIGHTING AND HUNTING

1, 2. PAINTINGS OF A BEAUTIFUL WOODEN CASKET FOUND IN THE FAMOUS GRAVE OF TUTANKHAMEN. The casket was found full of various things, mostly parts of the king's dress. The outer face of the casket was entirely covered with gesso; upon this surface scenes and ornaments in fine miniature paintings were carried out. No photograph can reproduce all the beautiful detail; it gives only the general scheme of the composition. Our first figure reproduces the painting upon the left-hand side of the lid. It represents the king in his chariot shooting lions in the desert followed by his fan-bearers, courtiers, and bodyguards. In the field are depicted desert flora. The other side of the lid shows the king hunting various desert animals: gazelles, hartebeests, ostriches, hyenas, &c. The second figure is taken from the right-side panel of the casket. The king is shown slaughtering his enemies, probably Asiatics. He is followed by his charioteers. His enemies are routed and in full confusion. Their chariots are broken, the horses loose. The king is protected (as on fig. 1) by the two vultures of Nekhebet and by the Sun disk. The other (left) side panel shows the king slaughtering Nubians. Whether the scenes illustrate historical facts or are pure convention is difficult to decide. The art of the casket is very fine: conventional in the figures of the Pharaoh, full of life in the figures of animals and slaughtered enemies. However, it is not the realism of the art of Ikhnaton. It follows the best traditions of Egyptian pre-Ikhnatonian art. The tragic pathos of the animal figures is comparable to that of the best Assyrian bas-reliefs. It must be noted that battle scenes well known to early Sumerian art are in Egypt a creation of the warlike XVIIIth Dynasty. Later these scenes are very popular with the artists of Ramses II and III who produce beautiful creations of this type, for instance, the scenes illustrating the battle of Kadesh in six temples (Ramses II) and those of the temple of Medînet Habu (Ramses III). Compare pl. XLII. Soon after 1360 B.C. Cairo Museum.

1. A FIGHTING SCENE

2. A HUNTING SCENE

XXXI. TUTANKHAMEN FIGHTING AND HUNTING

XXXII. TUTANKHAMEN AND HIS WIFE

PLATE XXXII
TUTANKHAMEN AND HIS WIFE

BEAUTIFUL WOODEN ARMCHAIR, overlaid with sheet gold and adorned with polychrome faience, glass, and stone inlay. The legs of feline form are surmounted by lions' heads in chased gold. The arms are formed of crowned and winged serpents supporting the cartouches (name) of the king. The scene of the front panel of the back (inlaid) shows one of the rooms of the palace decorated with flower-garlanded pillars and between them a magnificent rug. In the room the king is seated on a cushioned throne. Before him the young queen, Ankhesenamen, is shown putting the last touches to the king's toilet: in one hand she holds a small jar with perfumes, the other leans on the shoulder of the king. Between them is the great disk Aton spreading his rays over the pair. Behind the queen is a table with a beautiful pectoral. The scene is treated in the style of Ikhnaton (a little less realistic) and shows the adherence of King Tutankhamen to Ikhnaton's religion in his early reign. Soon after 1360 B.C. Cairo Museum.

world was at their disposal. Though the native element still predominates, yet we see that Egypt has entered the comity of civilized countries and forms henceforth merely one member of it, though she still claimed the leadership not only in power but also in culture. A corresponding change took place in the public life of the country. Now that she was a great civilized empire, based upon a strong standing army and a skilful use of her subjects' taxable capacity, she could not preserve institutions that were suitable in the Pyramid Age or in the feudal stage of the Eleventh or Twelfth Dynasty. Like Babylon in the time of Hammurabi, Egypt under the Eighteenth Dynasty became a kingdom with a highly developed bureaucratic system. Her kings are still owners and lords of the country; but the religious aspect of their position becomes less important than their place in politics and war. Though they are still gods and sons of gods, they are, first of all, the military and political leaders of a nation which has freed itself from a foreign yoke and, in a burst of national feeling, created a great and powerful empire.

It may also be noted that the right of private property, even in land, which had begun to be recognized even under the Old Kingdom, became under the Middle Kingdom a regular institution protected by law and religion, though all property in Egypt, except that of the gods, has to pay very high taxes to the king. It is worthy of note moreover that while in the sphere of the influence of Sumerian and Babylonian civilization the structure of life is based to a large extent on private skill, initiative and property, on private commerce and industry, and on an established silver currency, Egypt shows the picture of a huge house, ruled by the king and his civil officers, of whom the first is his vizier, with thousands of scribes, humble servants of the king, who with the priests and some large landowners, generals and admirals of the king, form the thoroughly servile aristocracy of the land. The rule of this bureaucracy is based on a highly developed and refined natural economy (no recognized silver currency existed) and on a set of monopolies which yielded to the king an enormous, fabulous income. One of the chief sources of income of the kings was the rich gold mines of Nubia which in the eyes of her neighbours made Egypt a land where gold was ' like dust '.

VIII

POLITICAL HISTORY OF THE EAST AT THE END OF THE SECOND AND DURING THE FIRST MILLENNIUM B.C.

A PERIOD OF POLITICAL ANARCHY AND WORLD-WIDE KINGDOMS

ABOUT 1500 B.C. there were three Great Powers in the East and on the eastern coast of the Mediterranean: the great and strong Egyptian Empire; the Hittite Kingdom in Asia Minor; and the Aegean Kingdoms united in one great alliance under the headship of Crete. The balance of power depended upon these three and their alliances with smaller powers. But the reign of Ikhnaton dealt a heavy blow to the position of Egypt: her control of the Syrian coast was relaxed, and the Hittite Empire was quick to take advantage of this weakness and eager to usurp her place in Syria and Phoenicia; the Aegean peoples also were glad of the opportunity to ally themselves with the Libyans, her western neighbours, in order to get possession of the Delta.

But after a short period of anarchy that followed the death of Ikhnaton, Egypt was still strong enough to rally round the new dynasty, the Nineteenth, which produced a succession of able kings and commanders: Horemheb, Ramses I, Seti I, and Ramses II (1321–1234 B.C.) were able to support the tottering empire. But the effort cost Egypt dear; and the same is true of her enemies. In the Nineteenth Dynasty, as in the time after the expulsion of the Hyksos, the centre of political interest shifted from Egypt to her possessions in Asia. There the Hittite Kingdom had grown into a great political power during the reigns of Amenhotep III and Amenhotep IV, the last kings of the Eighteenth Dynasty. Encouraged by the weakness of these two Pharaohs and by their failure to grasp the political situation, Shubbiluliuma, the 'Sun-King' of the Hittite Empire, who began to reign in 1385 B.C., by a long train of intrigues stirred up a revolt against Egypt in her Asiatic possessions. Eventually Syria and Phoenicia passed into the strong hand of the Hittite king,

PLATE XXXIII

LIFE OF THE EGYPTIAN NOBLES OF THE NEW KINGDOM

1. PART OF A FRESCO FROM A THEBAN GRAVE. A party is given in the house of the owner of the grave. Married couples (upper panel) and also unmarried girls and men (lower panel) are invited. They are seated in fine chairs before two tables laden with fruit, fowls, and joints and adorned with flowers. Under the tables are jars of wine and beer. The guests are clad in their best dresses. On their heads they have elaborate wigs with a perfume box on the top of each. On the arms, necks, and ears are heavy jewels. Young boys and girls (the girls completely naked) are ministering, offering wine, flowers, and perfumes. The married couples behave solemnly, the girls are chatting and gossiping. The young man in the right corner is looking at them. End of the XVIIIth Dynasty (about 1400 B.C.). British Museum.

2. THE SAME. A hunting party in the marshes. A young man, with his wife and his little daughter, is sailing in a canoe in a thicket of reeds. In the water are various fish. The ladies are picking lotuses, the man is catching various fowl (ibises, ducks, doves) with his boomerang. His hunting cat is helping him with great energy. Late XVIIIth Dynasty (after 1400 B.C.). British Museum.

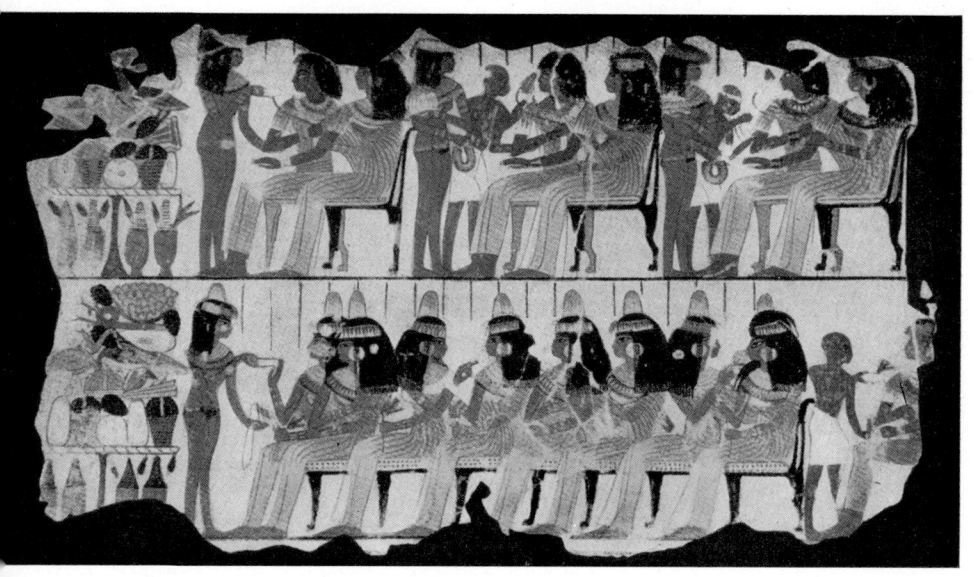

1. PART OF A FRESCO FROM A THEBAN GRAVE

2. A HUNTING PARTY

XXXIII. LIFE OF THE EGYPTIAN NOBLES OF THE NEW KINGDOM

and Egypt was entirely stripped of her Asiatic provinces. In another quarter the Hittites took advantage of troubles in the kingdom of Mitanni and reduced this rival to be their vassal.

The growth of Hittite power in Asia was a terrible menace to Egypt, who had never forgotten the long domination of the Hyksos. Therefore, under the direction of Seti I and Ramses II, she gathered all her forces for a decisive struggle against the successors of Shubbiluliuma—Murshilish II, Mutallu, and Hattushil III. The war was long and bloody. Thanks to better organization and greater wealth, Egypt succeeded in recovering a considerable part of her Asiatic possessions. The treaty between Hattushil III and Ramses II which ended the war in 1272 B.C. has been preserved in Egyptian and Hittite records, and shows that part of Syria and Phoenicia was restored. But the effort was excessive and exhausted the strength of Egypt: her creative energy dried up. It is true that Seti I and Ramses II still erect great buildings and cover the walls of their temples with the narrative of their exploits; but this is the last effort of the national genius. Together with large monuments (for the temples at Abydos and Abu-simbel, see Chapter VII), a number of hastily erected buildings, which stand no comparison with the achievements of the Eighteenth Dynasty, were put up all over the country. After the Hittite war, in which there were no conquerors but only conquered, the reigns of Merenpta and Ramses III were still a time of comparative peace and prosperity; Egypt was able to conquer and to expel the ' peoples of the sea ' which invaded it; but at the beginning of the first millennium B.C. Egypt goes rapidly downhill and plays no considerable part in history for a comparatively long time—a time of anarchy and dismemberment for what had once been a glorious kingdom.

The struggle with Egypt was no less destructive to the Hittite Kingdom. The Hittites were unable to arrest the process of dissolution in their federal empire, or to hinder the invasion of Asia Minor by foreign conquerors. A few decades after the death of Hattushil III, about 1200 B.C., the empire begins to dissolve into its component parts, under the pressure of a fresh wave of Aryan invaders—Thracian, Phrygian, and Mysian. Some districts, especially in the southern or Syrian half of the empire, such as Carchemish, Samal (Zenjirli), and Malatia, still form strong kingdoms and retain the peculiar Hittite culture; but the Hittite Empire,

PLATE XXXIV
ASSYRIAN WARFARE

1. **PART OF THE BAS-RELIEFS WHICH ADORNED THE WALLS OF THE PALACE OF ASHUR-NAZIR-PAL III, KING OF ASSYRIA (884–860 B.C.).** Found at Nimrûd (Calah). The king, protected by his lieutenant, is shooting at the besieged city. Before him is a moving tower which protects a battering ram suspended on two chains. Warriors are shooting arrows from behind the tower and from the top of it. Other Assyrian soldiers are digging down the lower wall of the city with iron crowbars. The city is fortified by strong walls. The residents of the city are shooting from the walls, women are exhorting men to courage. 884–860 B.C. British Museum.

2. **PART OF THE BAS-RELIEFS WHICH ADORNED THE PALACE OF TIGLATH-PILESER IV (747–727 B.C.).** Found at Nimrûd (Calah). A double-walled city has just been captured by the Assyrian army. Two battering-rams stand idle. From a side-gate of the city come out oxen drawing carts which carry the captives (women and children) into exile (remember the fate of the Jews in the time of Nebuchadnezzar). Flocks of sheep, goats, and oxen—the war booty—are also being driven away. Two scribes are reporting to a higher official the number of captives and cattle. After 731 B.C. British Museum.

1. BAS-RELIEF FROM THE PALACE OF ASHUR-NAZIR-PAL III

2. BAS-RELIEF FROM THE PALACE OF TIGLATH-PILESER IV

XXXIV. ASSYRIAN WARFARE

as such, disappears below the political horizon in the twelfth and eleventh centuries B.C.

This period of weakness for Egypt and the Hittites coincided with important political events, of which we know little, in the Aegean basin and Asia Minor. In the fourteenth century B.C. the hegemony of Crete suffered a crushing blow : at the highest point of its development Cnossus was destroyed, probably by an alliance of Aegean city-states in Europe. This event is probably connected with the natural development of the European kingdoms of Aegean civilization which from the very beginning were Greek, that is Achaean. It is certain that these kingdoms with their centres at Mycenae in the Argolis, at Thebes and Orchomenus in Boeotia, and at Athens in Attica, not to speak of minor states with the same civilization, were rich and powerful as early as in the seventeenth century B.C. and developed their own version of the Aegean civilization. By the fourteenth century a large Mycenean Empire had been formed. The kings of Mycenae appeared in this empire as suzerains of a host of minor feudal lords. Many wars were waged by the Mycenean kings. Greek tradition preserved the record of two of them : a war of Mycenae against Thebes and the war of the Mycenean coalition of Achaeans against Troy, celebrated by Homer in his *Iliad*. The cultural influence of the Mycenean Empire was also spread far and wide by means of an extensive commerce. It reached the route of the amber trade in the North, Sicily and Italy in the West, and Asia Minor, Cyprus and Syria in the South. The art of Phoenicia for instance shows very strong Mycenean influences.

In the thirteenth century B.C., however, this Mycenean world was in a state of confusion, caused no doubt by an important movement of peoples in the northern part of the Balkan peninsula. Our historical tradition speaks of attacks of 'sea-peoples' (among them Achaeans and Lycians) on Egypt first under Merenpta and later under Ramses III. In the later attack Philistines and Sakkari took an active part, and we hear that these peoples settled down a little later on the Palestinian shore. About the same time Pamphylia in Asia Minor was occupied by Achaeans and probably Lycia also. All these events must be connected with the dismemberment of the Mycenean Empire and the gradual emigration of the former rulers of Greece under the pressure of conquerors from the North.

Simultaneously with this unrest in the Aegean world, we

observe another important occurrence in the Balkan peninsula and Asia Minor—a powerful movement of Thracian clans. We do not know the native country of these invaders or the date of the invasion or the point from which they came. But at the end of the second millennium B. C. they appear suddenly on the north coast of the Black Sea, where they found a Cimmerian Empire with a centre on the site of the modern Kertch, and also in Asia Minor, where they collide with the enfeebled Hittites and found a number of Thracian kingdoms, of which the strongest was Phrygia. Fragments of the ruined Hittite Empire, the most prominent of which was Lydia, continue to exist side by side with these kingdoms. Some of these Thracian clans reached Transcaucasia, where they helped, perhaps, to found the powerful kingdom of Van. In consequence of all these movements the western half of the eastern world was full of disturbance at the end of the second millennium B. C.

The same process was going on within the boundaries of Syria and in all the western part of Hither Asia: great empires were broken up into small kingdoms. Palestine became for a time the strongest power. For long she had been politically dependent upon Egypt, and her culture had been strongly influenced by Egypt and Babylon. She was colonized by Amorites, and then the Amorites were subdued by Canaanites; both these peoples were Semitic. Then, at the end of the second millennium B. C., another Semitic tribe appears on the borders of Palestine—the Jews. According to the Jewish legends, they came out of Egypt and wandered long in the desert before reaching the promised land. During these wanderings in the peninsula of Sinai a law-giver, Moses, appeared among them and gave them written rules of morality in the shape of the Ten Commandments.

The weakness of Egyptian control over Palestine enabled the Jews to make their way gradually into the country and establish themselves. They had almost reached the Mediterranean, when a group of Philistine invaders, appearing from beyond the bounds of the Aegean, seized the coast and founded a powerful kingdom in Palestine. For a time the Jews were forced to submit to their excellent military organization and superior culture. By degrees, however, the Philistines, being few in number and drawing no reinforcements from without, grew weak and degenerate, while a strong impulse towards national unity arose among the Jews and brought about, at the beginning of the first millennium B. C., the creation of a strong and independent Jewish kingdom, which was headed partly by kings (for instance, Saul, David, and Solomon) and partly by the priests of the supreme god, Yahwe. But this kingdom did not last for long : its formation and early wars under Saul and David were followed by the peaceful reign and foreign glory of Solomon ; but next came a period of anarchy and internal conflict, which led to a renewal of foreign domination, first by Egypt and then by Assyria and Babylonia. The history of Judaea in its palmy days and at the time of its division into two kingdoms, its contests with its neighbours and with the great Empires of the East—all this is familiar to us, because the writings of the time, half-historical and half-religious, and also the inspired utterances of the prophets, Elijah, Elisha, Isaiah, Amos, Jeremiah, Zephaniah, Nahum, and others, are included in the sacred writings of both Jews and Christians and preserved in the book known as the Bible. In the light of contemporary records from Assyria, Babylonia, Egypt, Chaldaea, Phoenicia, Asia Minor, and the Aramaic cities, the Bible acquires a special interest, as one of our main historical sources, which tells us not only of the life of little Judaea but also of the fortunes of great empires.

The absence of strong military empires in Hither Asia accounts also for the prosperity of a number of Aramaic cities, inhabited by Semites, in Syria ; the most prominent of these were Harran, Hamath, and Damascus. The towns of Phoenicia also prospered greatly, especially Byblus, Tyre, and Sidon, which had inherited the trading connexions of the Aegean kingdoms. It is possible that these first passed permanently into the hands of the Semites at this period. In any case, the Semites developed a remarkably wide activity in trade and colonization at the end of the second millennium B. C. and beginning of the first. They strengthened trade relations between East and West, visiting the coasts of North Africa, Spain, Gaul, Italy, and Sicily. In Africa especially the Phoenicians took lasting root, and two of their African colonies, Utica and Carthage, soon became principal centres of commercial and political life.

At the beginning of the first millennium B. C. a Mesopotamian kingdom which had played no great part during the 'Balance of Power', begins to step more and more to the

PLATE XXXV

THE ASSYRIAN KING AND HIS ARMY

1. STELE OF ESARHADDON, KING OF ASSYRIA (681–668 B.C.). Found in one of the capitals of the Hittite Empire at Zenjirli (ancient Samal). Behind the head of the king there are figures of Assyrian gods standing on fantastic animals, and the symbol of the great god Ashur. Before the king kneel two captured kings: Taharka, the Nubian king of Egypt, and Ba'alu, king of Tyre (Phoenicia), begging for mercy. The king holds a rope by which the two kings are ringed through the nose. In fact Esarhaddon never captured Taharka and is merely boasting. After 671 B.C. Berlin Museum.

2, 3. PARTS OF THE BAS-RELIEFS WHICH ADORNED THE PALACE OF NINEVEH (Kuyundshik). One shows a mounted heavily-armed soldier shooting an arrow; the other, a war-chariot drawn by horses and containing a driver and three soldiers. Note the wonderful mastery in representing the horses: they are full of life, much more so than the men. Time of Ashur-bani-pal (668–624 B.C.). Paris, Louvre.

1. STELE OF ESARHADDON

2. MOUNTED SOLDIER

3. WAR CHARIOT

XXXV. THE ASSYRIAN KING AND HIS ARMY

front of the stage. I refer to Assyria. Strongly influenced by Babylonia, Assyria gradually grew to be an independent kingdom. The people were Semites and not numerous ; they were ruled by a king and lived near the central Tigris ; they were strong in the warlike spirit of their herdsmen and husbandmen, and had long been accustomed to look down with envious eyes from their mountains upon the rich plain of Babylonia, the valleys of Asia Minor, and the Syrian and Phoenician cities. As early as in the fourteenth century they appear as completely independent and dangerous rivals of the Hittites and of Babylon. The fall of the Hittite Empire gave them a long coveted opportunity to try their strength once again in the sphere of foreign conquest. Led by Tiglath-pileser I (1110–1100 B.C.), they were successful for a time and subdued part of eastern Asia Minor, as far as the Black Sea. This success was not lasting. But in the ninth century B.C. Assyria resumed her policy of conquest under more favourable conditions, led by her kings Ashur-nazirpal III (884–860) and Shalmaneser II (860–825). Her third attempt, in the second half of the eighth century and in the seventh century B.C., was crowned with still greater success. A series of Assyrian kings, beginning with Tiglath-pileser IV (747–745), carried on fierce and continuous warfare and conquered Babylonia, Elam, the Syro-Phoenician coast, and Palestine; even Egypt succumbed to them for a time. The names of Sargon (722–705), Sennacherib (705–681), Esarhaddon (681–668), and Ashur-bani-pal (668–624) left a deep and permanent impression on the minds of their contemporaries. The fame of their cruel wars and not less cruel sway over the conquered nations made its way even to Greece, where about this time begins a fresh and brilliant advance in civilization and political life.

The history of the Assyrian conquests, the organization of Assyria for peace and war, and her religion and culture, are thoroughly well known. To us her kings are not mere names connected with certain historical incidents, but real men. Archaeological exploration of Hither Asia began when the ruins of Kalhu and Nineveh, Assyrian capitals, were ransacked and robbed in the middle of last century. Since then interest in Assyria has never slackened : successive expeditions have by degrees explored the ruins of all the four capital cities—Ashur, Kalhu, Dur Sharrukin, and Nineveh, which were, one after another, the residences of the great kings. Excavation has been rich in results, and has not only revealed to us the architecture, sculpture, painting, and artistic industry of the Assyrians, but has also laid bare the entire life of the people, by discovering thousands of written documents belonging to that time. These are the relics of the public archives and royal libraries; among the latter the library of Ashur-bani-pal is especially full and interesting. Most of these documents are the cylinders common in Mesopotamia, with cuneiform inscriptions in the Assyrian, Akkadian, and Sumerian languages. We have also monumental records, chiefly of an historical nature: inscriptions on reliefs, recording the history of this or that reign and of kings who adorned the palaces; also detailed annals of each reign, carved on flagstones which paved the palace temples. Great historical importance attaches to the questions addressed by the kings to the god and the god's answers, which were revealed to the priests after examining the liver of a victim, and which generally bear reference to public events. Then there is the official and sometimes confidential correspondence of the kings, and a small number of documents dealing with private law. One of the latest discoveries is the code of law which was recently published.

In these historical documents and monuments, all the public life of the country passes before us in complete detail, especially the campaigns and conquests of each king. There the kings enumerate the names of the nations and cities against whom they fought, the number and sad fate of the captives, the booty seized, the contributions levied on the conquered, and the tribute they had to pay thereafter to Assyria. The extension of the Assyrian kingdom began by the incorporation of neighbouring tribes who lived in the 'Assyrian triangle', formed by the Tigris and its tributaries. At the same time constant warfare was waged with Babylonia, formerly the suzerain of Assyria. When the Kassite rule over Babylonia fell (about 1180 B. C.), political anarchy followed, and repeated changes of dynasty. Aramaic tribes appeared, one after another, from the north and west; the Chaldeans attacked from the south, and Elam from the east with the tribes from the tableland of Irania. Under these conditions every active king of Assyria found it easy to make himself practically master of Babylonia; and this was easier because the merchants, who were the ruling class in Babylonia, preferred the domination of Assyria, which professed to carry on Babylonian culture, to the rule of nomad Semites or half-savage mountaineers. Nevertheless, Babylon was never permanently conquered by Assyria. Her national spirit woke again, whenever Assyria was weak, and strove for independence. And even the Assyrians themselves, aware that their civilization came down from the glorious past of Babylonia, were not inclined to make a final settlement with their rival and reduce her to a province.

After strengthening themselves in the 'Assyrian triangle', the kings of Assyria began to advance towards the west, where movement was easier and the prospect of booty more tempting than on the north and east. The situation in the western part of Hither Asia was remarkably favourable. Egypt was unable to maintain her sway over Syria, Phoenicia, and Palestine; and the united kingdom of the Hittites had ceased to exist. Thus the richest districts on the Mediterranean coast were left to themselves and naturally broke up into a large number of small kingdoms. Each of the coast towns was independent, and many inland towns, especially Damascus, asserted and developed their freedom. All these towns lived mainly by trade and industry, and even their constant wars against each other could not prevent them from growing rich. It is true that attempts to unite may be observed among them. On one side, the Jews, and on the other, Damascus, the great centre of Aramaic trade, endeavoured to take the lead in the cause of unification. But both attempts failed: they were dashed to pieces against the exclusiveness and passion for independence which were as strong in each city and tribe of that day as we shall find them later in Greece. Under these conditions it was an irresistible temptation for Assyria to send her armies to pillage one rich city after another, and to penetrate farther and farther west. By degrees incursions became regular campaigns, and contributions gave place to tribute. The establishment of Assyria in north Syria led to decisive engagements against Damascus and Judaea and the complete subjugation of both nations after a long and bloody struggle. The seizure of Palestine made a collision with Egypt inevitable; the weakness of Egypt enabled the Assyrian kings to invade her borders with success; and Esarhaddon was even able for a time, just before the Assyrian monarchy came to an end, to reduce her to the status of a province.

PLATE XXXVI
THE PERSIAN KINGS

1. PART OF THE SCULPTURAL DECORATION OF THE GREAT HALL WITH A HUNDRED COLUMNS IN THE PALACE OF KING DARIUS (522–485 B.C.) at Persepolis. The king is shown fighting a horned lion, a personification of the brute forces of nature. End of the 6th or beginning of the 5th cent. B.C.

2. HEAD OF KING DARIUS FROM THE ROCK BAS-RELIEFS OF BEHISTUN (see next plate). Note the diadem, the skilful trimming of the beard and of the hair. The head is not a real portrait: it represents not the personal features of Darius but an idealized head of the Great King of Kings of the Persian Empire. End of the 6th cent. B.C.

3. ONE OF THE BODYGUARD OF KING DARIUS. A long row of such figures adorned the walls of the staircase which led to the terrace on which his palace of Susa was built. Enamelled bricks. End of the 6th or beginning of the 5th cent. B.C. Paris, Louvre.

4. KING DARIUS FIGHTING HIS ENEMIES AND TRAMPLING OVER THEIR SLAIN BODIES. Between the king and his enemies is the holy symbol of Ahuramazda (the winged Sun-disk and the medallion with the bust of the god). Cast of a cylinder-signet. End of the 6th or beginning of the 5th cent. B.C. British Museum.

1. DARIUS AND A LION

3. THE BODY-GUARD OF KING DARIUS

2. HEAD OF KING DARIUS

4. DARIUS FIGHTING HIS ENEMIES

XXXVI. THE PERSIAN KINGS

In view of these conditions, it is easy to understand the success of the Assyrians in extending their empire westwards. They paid small attention to Asia Minor, where new kingdoms, partly Indo-European (Phrygia, for instance, and Lydia), were being shaped out of the ruins of the Hittite Empire. Their relations or wars with Asia Minor were merely casual and never ended in the permanent conquest of large territories. Far more serious for Assyria was the question of her northern and eastern boundaries. I have said earlier that a strong centralized kingdom, with a capital on the shores of Lake Van, grew up in Transcaucasia near the lakes of Van and Urmia at the end of the second millennium B.C. It was formed out of local tribes, the ancestors of the future Armenians and Georgians, together with at least two bodies of foreign invaders, of which the former were Iranians from the east, and the latter Thracians from the north. This kingdom was called by the Assyrians Urartu, from the name of Mount Ararat, and the inhabitants were called Haldians. We are comparatively well informed concerning its fortunes. Our information does not come solely from Assyrian documents. Excavation in Transcaucasia during the last half-century has brought to our knowledge not only a number of Haldian cities—their capital, near the city now called Van, was Turushpa or Tushpash—but also a great quantity of cuneiform inscriptions in the Haldian language, recording the conquests and buildings of their kings. From these and contemporary Assyrian records we can gather how great and substantial was the activity of these kings, how much they did for the organization and economic life of the country, especially in the sciences of hydraulics and metallurgy, and what a pitch of civilization they attained in the eighth and seventh centuries B.C. The names of the Assyrian kings themselves are hardly greater in Eastern history than those of the Haldian monarchs—Sardur I, Ishpuina, Argishti I, Sardur II, and also their feebler successors, Rusa I, Argishti II, Rusa III, and Sardur III. In spite of a succession of campaigns and many victories, Assyria was unable to master these rivals and defeat their constant struggle for expansion. The independent existence of the Haldian power came to an end only with the existence of the Assyrian Empire. Nor was Assyria more able to cope with her neighbours on the east, the Mannai and Medes, mountaineers of Iranian stock, who

PLATE XXXVII

KING DARIUS AND THE REBELS

1-3. ROCK BAS-RELIEF AT BEHISTUN NEAR THE 'GATE OF ASIA', on the great road which leads from Babylon to Ecbatana. The bas-relief is placed high up on the rock and is in a very good state of preservation. In a long inscription in three languages (Babylonian, Elamitic, and Old Persian, all in cuneiform script) which proved the key for deciphering cuneiform writing, King Darius relates in substantial detail how he quelled the rebellion of the usurper Gaumata and his supporters. The inscription is a beautiful piece of solemn prose and ought to be read in full by all students of ancient history. The bas-relief tells the same story in pictures. The king, followed by two assistants who carry his bow and his spear, makes the gesture of adoration towards the holy symbol of Ahuramazda. He is shown trampling upon the figure of Gaumata, who lies prostrate under his feet. A row of rebellious satraps all strung on one rope are led towards the king as a sacrifice to Ahuramazda. It is an interesting series of figures, each of which represents the ethnographical peculiarities and dresses of the various tribes and peoples comprised in the Persian Empire (figs. 2 and 3). End of the 6th cent. B.C.

1. THE KING BEFORE THE SYMBOL OF AHURAMAZDA

2. PRISONERS

3. PRISONERS

XXXVII. KING DARIUS AND THE REBELS

were neighbours also of the Haldian kingdom and were later to inherit the Assyrian power. Long, too, and stubborn was the struggle of Assyria against Elam, the ancient rival of Babylon, which constantly strove to snatch Babylonia from Assyria. The conquest of Elam in the reign of Ashur-bani-pal, with the destruction of Susa, their capital city, was the last great achievement of Assyria; but it proved ruinous to the conqueror. The removal of her rival made her not stronger but weaker: it had required an immense effort on the part of Assyria, and besides it untied the hands of those Iranian tribes who had always been blocked by Elam in their westward movement towards the rich and civilized cities of Mesopotamia.

Such were the conditions under which the Assyrian Empire was gradually created. Apart from the general political conditions, which have been mentioned already, Assyria owed her success to her internal organization and to the foreign policy of her kings. These kings were the first in the Eastern world who were able to create a purely military empire, founded upon an army enrolled from the native herdsmen and husbandmen and from the population of conquered kingdoms, excellently organized, and carefully trained. At the same time a number of technical improvements were introduced, which at once gave them an immense advantage in the struggle against their neighbours. The most important of these innovations were as follows. Instead of a militia levied for a single expedition, they created by degrees strong and well-trained bodies of infantry, armed with bows, pikes, and swords, protected by iron breast-plates, and accustomed to fight in close order. Together with the slow and heavy war-chariots, which till then had represented both cavalry and artillery in eastern armies, they created speedy detachments of mounted men heavily armed, who broke the ranks of the enemy by the weight of their charge and proved incomparable in pursuit. The improvement in siege operations was even more important. To an army of the second millennium B.C. a fortified town was an almost insuperable obstacle: if it was not taken by assault, a long and wearisome siege was the only resource. The Assyrians were the first to apply the scientific knowledge of the time to military problems. A number of different engines, especially rams, and the development of subterranean mining, made the fortresses of

PLATE XXXVIII
SCULPTURES OF THE PERSIAN PERIOD

1. BAS-RELIEFS WHICH ADORN THE GREAT STAIR OF THE PALACE OF KING XERXES (485–465 B. C.) AT PERSEPOLIS. The first bas-relief represents the Syrians led by a Persian high official to offer their tribute to the king. The second shows the Bactrians doing the same. Beginning of the 5th cent. B. C.

2. BAS-RELIEF SHOWING TWO PERSIAN LADIES (probably wives of high officials of the Persian king) RIDING ON HORSEBACK AND PRECEDED BY A SERVANT. Found in Asia Minor near Daskylion. 5th cent. B. C. Constantinople, Osmanic Museum.

1. TRIBUTE BEARERS

2. PERSIAN LADIES

XXXVIII. SCULPTURES OF THE PERSIAN PERIOD

the East helpless against their assaults. The remarkable speed and activity of their armies, unrivalled in the military history of the East, should also be mentioned.

Further, the Assyrians brought to perfection a systematic terrorization of their adversaries. Measures, which by other powers, especially by Egypt, were resorted to only in exceptional cases—the massacre of the whole population in conquered towns and villages, and horrible tortures inflicted on the leading victims—became a rule in the policy of Assyrian conquerors. The accounts of their campaigns enumerate with wearisome monotony the punishments inflicted after each victory; to flay men alive, to impale them by hundreds, to cut off legs, arms, noses, and ears, and then to keep their mutilated rivals shut up in cages—such was the invariable custom of all their generals. Small wonder that the very name of the Assyrians inspired panic terror, and that the mere approach of their armies often forced strong kingdoms and cities to surrender and beg for mercy. We shall see later that their skilful organization of their conquests was another factor in the success of the Assyrians.

Their rule was brought to an end by the constantly increasing pressure of the Iranians and Thracians on their eastern and northern frontiers. As early as the eighth century B. C., in the reign of Sargon, Thracians from Cimmeria in the north made their way right to the boundaries of Assyria; and, later, hordes of wandering Iranians—Scythians migrating from the east—appeared within the empire. This movement must be connected with events which were taking place on the northern coast of the Black Sea. The Cimmerians, as we have seen already, had founded there a powerful kingdom; but they were forced to yield the mastery to the nomad Scythians who had for many centuries been firmly established on the steppes of south Russia. The Haldians and Assyrians, being unable to resist the pressure first of the Cimmerians and then of the Scythians, let the invaders pass through their territory. Asia Minor was soon inundated by the Cimmerians, Syria and Palestine by the Scythians. The former carried their devastating incursion as far as the shores of the Aegean and destroyed a number of the Greek settlements; the latter penetrated to the very borders of Egypt. The ancient Greek poets of Asia Minor and the Jewish prophet Jeremiah speak in eloquent terms of the terror inspired by this invasion. But

PLATE XXXIX
LATE EGYPTIAN SCULPTURE

1. BRONZE STATUETTE INLAID WITH SILVER AND GOLD OF QUEEN KAROMAMA OF THE XXIInd DYNASTY (947–740 B.C.). She was an Egyptian princess who married a Nubian (Sheshonk); he became king of Egypt and the founder of the so-called Bubastite Dynasty. Note how graceful the statuette is and how jealously the Egyptians preserved the glorious traditions and great technical and artistic achievements of the past. 947–925 B.C. Paris, Louvre.

2. STATUE OF QUEEN AMENIRTIS, wife of King Piankhi of the XXVth Dynasty of Egypt (728–715 B.C.). King Piankhi ruled at Thebes and was a descendant of the Theban king-priests of the XXIst Dynasty. The statue shows the same delicacy and technical skill which characterize the statuette of Karomama. 728–715 B.C. Paris, Louvre.

1. QUEEN KAROMAMA 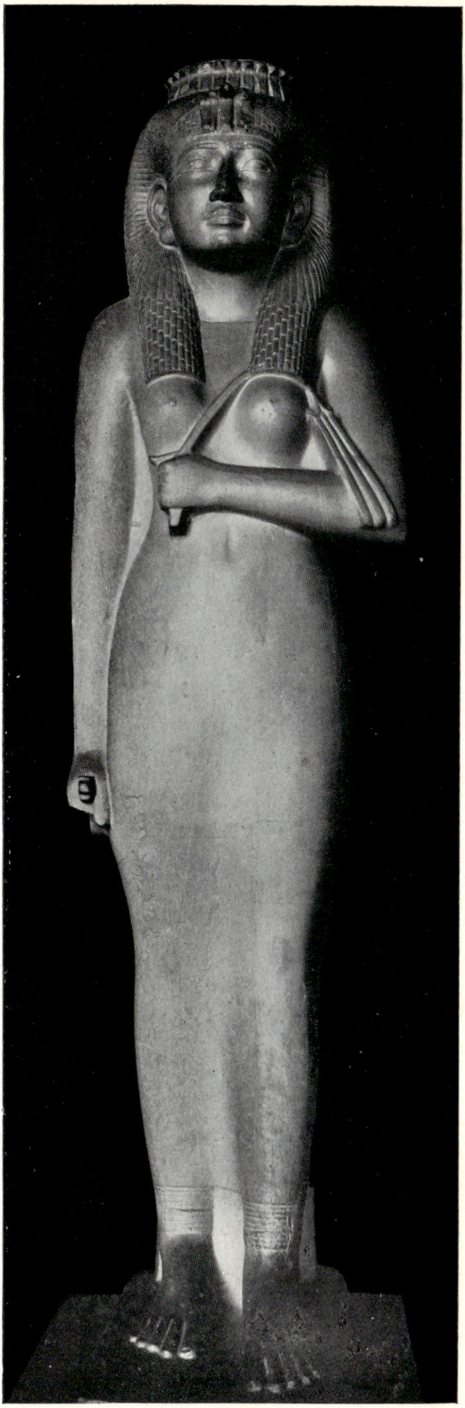   2. QUEEN AMENIRTIS

XXXIX. LATE EGYPTIAN SCULPTURE

no powerful kingdom was founded by either people. Having no reinforcements from without, they either exterminated one another, or were destroyed in detachments by the powers of southern Asia, or melted away among the local inhabitants. What was left of them settled in Cappadocia and Armenia.

But these two waves were followed by a third. The Iranian tribes of Medes and Mannai, who had adopted much of the civilization of their ancient neighbours, the Babylonians and Assyrians, grew stronger by degrees, and their pressure upon Assyria steadily increased. On the death of Ashur-bani-pal they united under the command of the Median King Cyaxares and crossed the Assyrian frontier. They formed an alliance with Babylonia, where, after many years of complete subservience to Assyria under Esarhaddon and Ashur-bani-pal, a new and strong dynasty had taken rise in the southern part of the country; and in 612 B.C. they took Ashur and Nineveh. The destruction of Nineveh, the extermination of the army, and the extinction of the reigning family, put an end to the Assyrian Empire. The subject peoples hailed with joy their deliverance from a reign of terror: the Jewish prophets, Zephaniah, Nahum, and Ezekiel, show clearly enough how the news of Assyria's downfall was received. But even before the destruction of Nineveh the empire was beginning to break up. Egypt first revolted, under the leadership of Psammetichus I, founder of a new dynasty, the Twenty-sixth, which lasted for more than a century, down to the conquest of Egypt by the Persians under Cambyses, and was supported by a mercenary army consisting mainly of Greeks and Anatolians. Herodotus, an Anatolian himself and the first Greek historian, gives a detailed account of this force. These Pharaohs—Psammetichus I, Necho, Psammetichus II, Apries, and Amasis—resided at Sais and secured to Egypt one more period of advancing civilization and political development.

The foreign policy of Egypt, though successful in the south, met with strong opposition in the east—in Syria and Palestine. This check was caused by the renewed strength of Babylon. Following Egypt's example Babylon revolted from Assyria. In alliance with the Medes, Nabopallasar, founder of the new Babylonian kingdom, succeeded in organizing opposition to the Assyrians and then in retaining his power by virtue of the alliance. The reign of his son,

PLATE XL

THE ART OF NEO-BABYLONIA

1, 2. FIGURES OF A BULL (symbol of the god Adad) AND OF A SNAKE-DRAGON (symbol of the god Marduk with the body and head of a snake, forelegs of a lion, hindlegs of an eagle) which adorned the Ishtar gate of the temple of Marduk at Babylon. Made of coloured glazed tiles. Similar figures (lions and dragons) adorned the processional street which led to the temple of Marduk. The use of glazed coloured tiles (the colours used were—blue, yellow, red, and white) is typical of Babylonian architecture. It penetrated also very early into Egypt. From the Babylonians it was taken over by the Assyrians and by the Persians (see pl. XLIII). It still survives in the East. The Ishtar gate and the processional street were built by King Nebuchadnezzar II (604–562), the greatest ruler of the last Babylonian Dynasty and the founder of the Neo-Babylonian Empire. Berlin Museum.

1. A BULL

2. A SNAKE-DRAGON

XL. THE ART OF NEO-BABYLONIA

Nebuchadnezzar, was especially distinguished : he succeeded in wresting from Egypt all the western part of Hither Asia, and inflicted a series of terrible blows upon the Jews, who were partisans of Egypt.

But neither Egypt nor the new Babylonian kingdom kept their independence for long. They were unable to resist the growing power of the Iranians, the destroyers of Assyria, who were not only firmly established in the eastern and northern districts of that country, but had also mastered the Haldian kingdom. The new Iranian kingdom now received a powerful impulse towards a career of conquest by the transference of power from a Median dynasty to a Persian. These Persian kings belonged to the most southern branch of the Iranian stock. In 550 B. C. the Median kingdom was conquered by Cyrus, the fifth king of the Persian tribe, which had probably been long connected with Elam and had inherited from that source its civilization and capacity for political development. The Medes accepted Persian rule without much opposition : there was kinship between the two peoples, and they spoke nearly the same language.

From the beginning of his reign Cyrus proved that he inherited the imperial aims of Assyria. The position in the East was now very much what it had been when the Assyrian kings began their career of conquest. The appearance of a balance of power was deceptive. Babylonia, though a great kingdom, was weak internally, and the population was degenerate. Egypt, as we have seen, relied upon mercenary troops for support. The kingdom of Lydia was somewhat stronger but no match for Persia, which united under her own civilized rule the inexhaustible forces of the Iranian people. Hence it is not surprising that Cyrus found it easy to seize Lydia, his strongest rival, in 546 B. C., and to add to Persia the Greek cities on the Asiatic coast which had paid tribute to Lydia. Next came the turn of Babylon in 538 B. C. Nabonid, the last king of Babylon, taken up with his antiquarian and religious fancies, had alienated his priests and nobles, and was unable to make any worthy resistance to the invader.

The submission of Babylonia was naturally followed by the establishment of Persian rule over all Hither Asia ; and the whole of Asia Minor fell into the same hands when Lydia was destroyed. It was impossible for Egypt to hold out against the masters of these dominions: she was conquered by Cambyses, the son of Cyrus, in the reign of Psammetichus III, the successor of Amasis. Thus a new world-empire was created in the East by Cyrus and Cambyses. This Persian Empire was not Semitic, but Indo-European. It was consolidated by Darius, son of Hystaspes, the able successor of Cambyses. Darius not only maintained all the conquests of his predecessors and checked the centrifugal forces of his vast empire, but also devised a suitable framework of government, of which more will be said later (see Chapter IX). It is probable also that Persia owed to him her new religion— the religion of the notable prophet and reformer, Zoroaster (see Chapter X).

IX

CULTURE AND ART IN THE EAST DURING THE FIRST MILLENNIUM B.C.

THE stormy life of the East, with its constant bloody wars and constant transference of power from one people to another, did not hinder its advance in civilization and art. The ancient centres of culture, especially Thebes in Egypt and Babylon in Mesopotamia, continued to spread their influence over the world. Even in her most troubled times Egypt still built temples and adorned them with painting and sculpture; her workshops still poured out over all the world a multitude of articles for domestic use and many works of art. The level attained by her in the Eighteenth and (to some extent) in the Nineteenth Dynasties was not reached in the first millennium B.C. Yet the period between the Assyrian and Persian ascendancies—what is called the Saitic period—witnessed a revival in architecture, painting, and sculpture, and especially in the applied arts. More than ever before, the products of her workshops and factories—made of faience, glass, ivory, precious metals, papyrus, and flax—were in demand in all the world's markets, and were conveyed thither by Greek and Phoenician middlemen. At this period the Greeks had a trading-station of their own in Egypt itself—the city of Naucratis.

The cultural and economic life of Babylonia also was still vigorous, in spite of constant political upheavals, changes of dynasty, and long periods of foreign domination. As will be shown later, Babylon was the chief centre of Assyrian culture, and an object of emulation to all the Assyrian monarchs; she filled, in fact, the position which Greece filled later in her relations to Rome, and which France has filled in our own time in relation to other civilized countries. Babylon preserved also her controlling power over the trade of Mesopotamia. The great merchants, united in powerful trading companies, were the most influential class among her inhabitants. The palmy days of Babylon were the end of the seventh century B.C. and the first half of the sixth—the interval between the Assyrian and Persian invasions. The excavations carried out by German archaeologists in the last years before the European War, revealed the extent and richness of the buildings erected by the kings of the latest dynasty. Magnificent ruins of their vast temples and frowning fortified palaces are still standing. The tiles which adorned the

Fig. 7. *Restoration of the Ishtar gate of the temple of Marduk at Babylon. Comp. pl. XL. After Koldewey.*

monumental gates of the goddess Ishtar—gates that led to Nebuchadnezzar's palace—are astonishing for brightness and richness of colouring, and for the capricious fancy of the artist. It is true that there was little novelty either here or in contemporary Egypt: the temples, palaces, and ziggurat-towers are constructed on the old plan; the old methods and subjects reappear in the decorative sculpture; but the old has been artistically used, and skill in execution has been brought to the highest pitch.

Other centres, as well as Egypt and Babylonia, continued to develop the creative genius of the East. Something was said of these in Chapter VII; and when we come to Greece, more will be said there of the course taken by the great Aegean civilization. The Hittite culture was inherited by a number of independent Anatolian kingdoms, of which Phrygia and Lydia are the best known to us, though our knowledge even of them is very imperfect. The façades of Phrygian tombs, carved on rock and richly adorned with sculpture which was probably covered with painting, undoubtedly develop subjects of Hittite art, and combine with them geometrical patterns brought from Europe to Asia Minor by peoples of Thracian stock. But the influence of Babylon is powerful too, and accounts for the many figures of fabulous

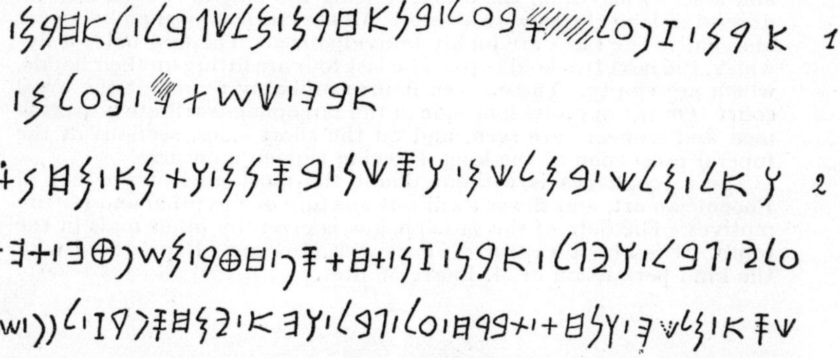

FIG. 8. *The Phoenician inscription on the sarcophagus of Ahiram king of Byblus. Found at Byblus. The inscription says that Itoba'al, the son of Ahiram, made the sarcophagus for his father as his eternal dwelling. At the end are imprecations against those who violate the sepulchre and the sarcophagus. 13th cent. B.C. After Dussaud. Museum of Beyrouth.*

animals and for the heraldic combinations of them. It is important to notice also, that Phrygia possessed its own system of writing, whose history has not yet been cleared up: it may be connected with the Aramaic system (for which, see below) or with the later development of the Aegean system.

Lydia was a connecting link between the East and Greece, and of late years we have begun to learn more about Lydian civilization. The American excavations at Sardis, which are still unfinished, bear eloquent testimony to the connexion of Lydia both with Assyria and with the Greek cities on the coast of Asia Minor. But the only artistic objects discovered so far have been small articles of jewellery and pottery. The system of writing is peculiar but related to the Greek system. Lydia made one great advance in the first invention of coined

PLATE XLI
ART OF CYPRUS, ASIA MINOR, AND PHOENICIA

1, 2. SARCOPHAGUS OF KING AHIRAM OF BYBLUS (Phoenicia). (Cf. fig. 8—inscription on the sarcophagus.) The sarcophagus was found at Byblus in the tomb of King Ahiram. It consists of a cover and the body of the sarcophagus, both made of the local stone. On the cover are represented two lions (the heads of the lions form the projecting handles of the cover), and to the right and left two figures of the king reclining on the cover (life-size). The body of the sarcophagus is supported by four large lions with their backs to each other. Round the top runs a frieze of lotus flowers. On one of the long sides of the sarcophagus (which is reproduced in our fig. 1, detail in fig. 2) King Ahiram is represented, seated to the right on a monumental chair supported by two figures of winged sphinxes with human heads and lion bodies. The king is dressed in a long heavy cloak with sleeves, and holds in his right hand a cup, and in his left a ' lotus ' flower. His feet rest on a pile of cushions. He has a beard and long hair. In front of him stands a table with offerings on it : an ox head on one plate and a set of loaves on the other. Facing the king are seven men all dressed in long cloaks with sleeves. All are clean shaven and all wear long hair. The faces are highly individualized. The first holds a fly-whisk, the next two hold cups. The last four are lifting up their hands, which are empty. These seven figures probably represent the royal court. On the opposite long side of the sarcophagus tribute bearers—men and women—are seen, and on the short sides, sections of the funeral procession of the king, showing women mourners.

The sarcophagus is without doubt the most ancient product of Phoenician art, and shows a curious mixture of Egyptian and Hittite motives. The date of the sarcophagus is given by other finds in the tomb. It is about 1200 B.C. Beyrouth Museum. Reproduced with the kind permission of M. Pierre Montet.

3. ENTRANCE TO A GRAVE-CHAMBER HEWN IN A ROCK IN PAPHLAGONIA. The columns are low and heavy. On the walls near the entrance are carved various animals, partly naturalistic, partly fantastic. In the upper part of the pediment is an eagle with outspread wings. The date is uncertain. The sculptures seem to be later (5-4th cent. B.C.) than the construction of the grave (8th cent. B.C.).

4. A CYPRIAN SARCOPHAGUS. Found at Amathus (Cyprus). Shows a procession of chariots followed by armed foot-soldiers. The style and ornaments show a curious mixture of Phoenician (i.e. Babylonian and Egyptian) and Greek elements. 6th cent. B.C. New York, Metropolitan Museum of Art.

1. SARCOPHAGUS OF KING AHIRAM OF BYBLUS

2. DETAIL OF SARCOPHAGUS OF KING AHIRAM OF BYBLUS

3. ENTRANCE TO GRAVE-CHAMBER

4. A CYPRIAN SARCOPHAGUS

XLI. ART OF CYPRUS, ASIA MINOR, AND PHOENICIA

money. In spite of the activity of commerce in the East, and in spite of the fact that the metals had long been the basis of exchange in both Egypt and Babylonia, the natural idea of devising, for the purposes of exchange, a metallic unit with its weight and purity guaranteed by the government, had never been thoroughly carried out. It is true that in some documents belonging to the age of Sennacherib, the Assyrian king speaks of coins cast by him and weighing a shekel or half a shekel; but the fact that none of these coins have been revealed by the thorough exploration of the Assyrian capitals, shows that this royal coinage was neither abundant enough nor regular enough to drive out the prevailing custom of using metal as one only of the units of exchange and accepting it in payment by weight. But in the seventh century B. C. the Lydian kings began to coin money out of pale gold. They were soon followed by the Greek cities of Asia Minor; and coinage quickly became the indispensable instrument of all the commerce of the time.

The culture of the Haldian kingdom of Van is also connected with the Hittite civilization. Before 1914 Russian scholars began systematic excavations which showed that the capital city Turushpa, the modern Van, was full of rich palaces and temples. The kingdom was rich in metals, and the art of working them was highly developed. The metal statues of gods and men remind one of Assyria, while the animal figures and the ornament are much akin to those of the Hittites. The Haldians used the Babylonian cuneiform, having no native system of writing. Their kings paid great attention to providing water for the towns and irrigation for the fields, and were very successful in this department.

As was said above, the culture of Palestine and Phoenicia was created by the influence of Babylonia and Egypt. Palestine flourished especially in the time of David and Solomon and their successors. The Bible tells us marvels concerning the splendour and magnificence of Solomon's temple at Jerusalem. But those descriptions, and also the discoveries made at Jerusalem and other cities of Judaea, prove that the Jews never created an art of their own. Solomon's temple was a combination of Egyptian and Babylonian elements. More originality was shown by the Phoenician cities—aristocratic republics of commerce, ruled by princes who belonged to the great merchant families. It is certain that the Phoenicians acted mainly as middlemen. Their ships sailed to Greece, Italy, Sicily, Spain, Africa, and Britain for metals, slaves, and raw material of different kinds that was not too bulky; they offered in exchange articles manufactured in Egyptian and Babylonian workshops, spices, and precious stones. But they also made wares themselves for export. Their purple fabrics were famous all over the world; and graves in Italy and Cyprus have revealed a number of silver and bronze vases made by them. It is true that the figures on these vases are mere copies of Egyptian and Babylonian patterns.

In the civilization of Hither Asia in the first millennium B.C. an important part is played by the Aramaeans, a Semitic stock, who made their way, without fighting, into all parts of the country and settled down in compact bodies, especially in Syria. It is still a puzzle how they were able to drive out of general use the Babylonian language and cuneiform writing, which had been to some extent international in the second millennium, and to have their own speech and character accepted instead. But it is certain that in the first millennium most documents in Hither Asia, and many even in Egypt, were written in this character, and that a knowledge of this language was indispensable, at all events for persons engaged in commerce. Unlike the complicated cuneiform and Egyptian systems, this character was simple and easily learned; and this may account for its success.

It is, however, certain that the leading part in the civilization of this period was played by the great ruling monarchies, first by Assyria, and then by Persia. These states also display the greatest quantity of creative energy. Unfortunately, we know very little about Persia in the time of her world-empire. For there have been no systematic excavations in the country except the French exploration of the two capitals, Persepolis and Susa. Assyria, where excavation has been carried on continuously for more than a century, is much better known. First of all I shall note one new and characteristic feature in the civilization of both countries—the strong feeling in the higher classes of their dependence upon the past, their keen interest in that past, their eagerness to imitate it and to preserve and restore its monuments, and the special attention they pay to their ancient religious literature. The same historic interest appears also in relation to contemporary

XLII. ASSYRIAN ART

PART OF THE BAS-RELIEFS WHICH ADORNED THE PALACE OF ASHUR-BANI-PAL AT NINEVEH

The king is represented in his chariot hunting lions. Many lions and lionesses are killed or wounded. The various stages of their agony are wonderfully represented with a masterly observation of details and with tremendous pathos. One lion though wounded by many arrows fiercely attacks the chariot of the king, biting wildly at one of the wheels. The king strikes him with his spear. The scene is full of movement and shows Assyrian art at its height. 669–626 B. C. British Museum.

events. These were recorded in their chronological order with unrivalled exactness and wealth of detail. The annals of the Assyrian kings record carefully and precisely all incidents, especially of military operations; and a series of reliefs upon the palace walls illustrate the records and form a kind of military history in pictures.

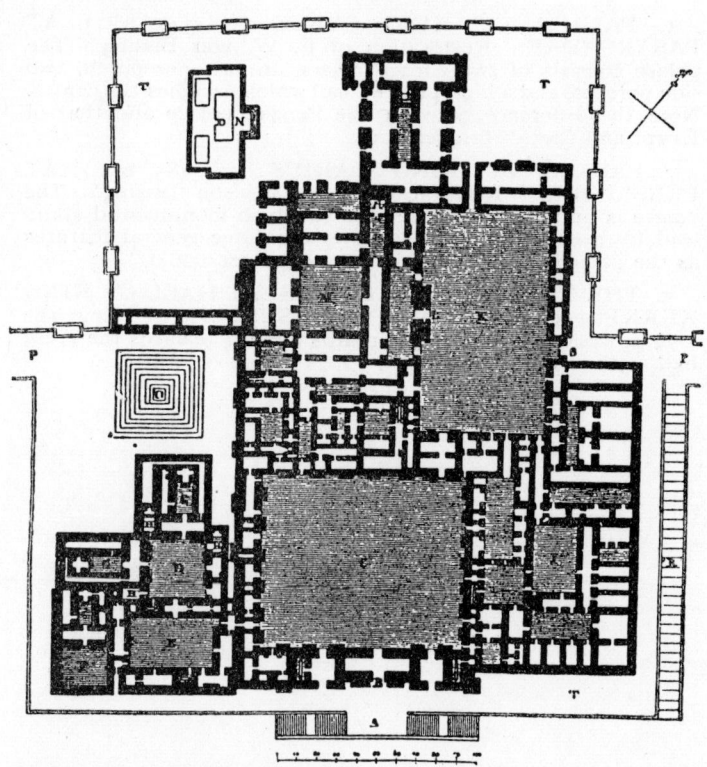

FIG. 9. *Plan of the palace of King Sargon at Khorsabad. Note the 'Ziggurat', or great tower-temple of the God Ashur and the series of courts surrounded by various rooms, of which some are store-rooms. Note also the massive entrance gate and the solid walls which make the palace look like a fortress.*

The wealth that poured into Assyria, and the eagerness of her kings to surpass their predecessors and contemporaries in pomp and magnificence, combined to stimulate building operations. Ashur, Kalhu, and Nineveh, the capital cities, and especially the last two, were not inferior in splendour to Thebes and Babylon. Dur Sharrukin, the fortified castle of Sargon in the north of the country, was majestic and rich. In

PLATE XLIII

THE PALACES OF THE PERSIAN KINGS

1. PALACE OF KING CYRUS (558–529 B.C.) AT PASARGADAE. Restoration of F. W. von Bissing. The palace consists of two corner-towers, an entrance porch, two side porches, and a high pillared hall which occupies the centre. Note the difference between the Persian palace and that of Egypt and Crete. 6th cent. B.C.

2. PALACE OF KING DARIUS (522–485 B.C.) AT PERSEPOLIS. Restoration of F. W. von Bissing. The palace is built on a high terrace to which monumental stairs lead from the ground, and shows the same general features as the palace of Cyrus. End of the 6th cent. B.C.

3. THE STAIRCASE OF THE GREAT HALL OF KING XERXES (485–465 B.C.) AT PERSEPOLIS, showing the long procession of the king's guards moving towards the great hall. 5th cent. B.C.

1. PALACE OF KING CYRUS AT PASARGADAE

2. PALACE OF KING DARIUS AT PERSEPOLIS

3. STAIRCASE OF THE HALL OF KING XERXES AT PERSEPOLIS

XLIII. THE PALACES OF THE PERSIAN KINGS

the architecture of these capitals and palaces (the latter especially) we are struck by the half-military and half-religious note that reflects so clearly the essential character of the Assyrian Empire. The king's palace is his fortified camp and, at the same time, the fortified dwelling-place of the great god Ashur. It is surrounded by strong walls crowned with high towers; outside there are ponderous gates, guarded by colossal statues of oxen and lions with human heads—the genii who watch over the king. The chief place within the walls is occupied by the ziggurat, a huge tower-temple sacred to Ashur that rises high into the sky. Round this are ranged living-rooms and reception-rooms for the king and his courtiers, for his retainers and probably also for the priests of the god. Nearer the walls there are magazines of arms and provisions in subterranean halls and galleries. All these buildings were constructed mainly of brick. But these bricks were covered with tiles, brilliant in colour and fantastic in design, with metal ornament, and with long panels of reliefs, probably coloured also. The pavilions used by the king on campaign, so often represented in the palace sculptures, have the same note of military magnificence, with their luxury of eastern carpets and the carved capitals of the pillars supporting the ceiling.

In this architecture and ornament there is nothing new, nothing original. The walls and gates with their guardian genii were inventions of the Hittites; the tower-temples owe their origin to Babylonia, and the pavilions are taken from the nomad Bedouin of the desert and Iranians of the steppes. From the last source Assyria got also the rich trappings of her war-horses and war-chariots. In general, we notice everywhere a continuation of Babylonian tradition—in the historic reliefs depicting the royal campaigns, in the tiles with their mixture of colours, in the conventional splendour of the king's robes, in the passion for creating fantastic and fabulous monsters, neither men nor animals nor birds nor reptiles nor fish, intended to impersonate good and evil spirits.

But the influence of Babylonian tradition is seen most powerfully in the very spirit of Assyrian art. Let us recall that even in Sumerian sculpture the favourite subjects were dramatic and realistic pictures of military life, with a great deal of painful and distressing detail. This tendency reaches its height in Assyria. Historical sculpture there is realistic,

PLATE XLIV
PERSIAN ORNAMENTAL ART

PARTS OF A FRIEZE OF COLOURED (not enamelled) BRICKS ON THE PALACE OF SUSA. One part shows two winged genii with human heads crowned by high tiaras, curled wings and lions' bodies. Above is the symbol of Ahuramazda. The other shows the typical Persian horned and winged lion-griffin. Beautiful specimens of the majestic ornamental art of the Persian Empire. 6th–5th cent. B.C. Paris, Louvre.

1. WINGED 'GENII'

2. HORNED AND WINGED LION-GRIFFIN

XLIV. PERSIAN ORNAMENTAL ART

and quite unlike the simplified and conventionalized pictures of battle and conquest which we find in Egyptian art. Assyrian art is full of life; the life is harsh and cruel and tries one's nerves; but it is neither fictitious nor conventional—it is genuine, and therefore the more appalling. The artist is attracted especially by scenes of death, destruction, torture, and suffering. No one has ever surpassed the Assyrians in conveying the death-agony of animals killed in the chase. The figures of dying men are stiffer; but in them also, and in the men who are being flayed alive, or whose eyes are being burnt out, the genuine awfulness of suffering is palpable. In these immense pictures every detail is true to life: the landscape, of mountain or forest, through which the army makes its way by rugged paths, or of marshes, with endless overgrowth of reeds; the rivers, with rafts covered with soldiers and resting on inflated goat-skins; the forts, proudly lifting their battlements on the mountain-tops; the Assyrian camp with the king's pavilion, camels, mules, and horses; the invincible charge of the heavy cavalry side by side with Bedouins on camels; the kings out hunting, with their thoroughbred horses and dogs, and the terror of the flying and falling animals—antelopes, roe deer, gazelles, wild asses—or the furious resistance of the lions. Nor is the romantic and idyllic note entirely unrepresented. Side by side with pictures of massacre and torture, these artists are capable of drawing a touching scene of family life; they can evoke a feeling of pity and sympathy for the miserable captives, forcibly transferred to unknown and dreaded countries, or driven like cattle to the pen for prisoners. There is a marked element of humour also in both tragic and pathetic subjects. The technical power is astonishing: even the Greeks never succeeded in catching so completely and conveying so realistically the essential features, external and internal, of animal life. Only the Roman Empire, in the historical sculptures erected by victorious princes, produced something to rival these artistic chronicles of Assyria.

But Assyrian art is not entirely traditional. Their craftsmen could refashion what was old, make it their own, and import into it a new and original element; and here lies the power and greatness of creative art, to whatever country it belongs. The art of Assyria grows and develops under our eyes. Beginning with rude imitation of Babylon, it proceeds to its first attempts at creation in the time of Ashur-nazir-pal; under Sargon and Sennacherib it grows strong and develops; and under Ashur-bani-pal, on the eve of Assyria's downfall, the sculptures of the palace at Nineveh mark the height of its attainment, where skill in composition vies with refinement of execution.

But if Assyria is of permanent importance in her contribution to art, and if her system of government reveals, as we shall see later, a new epoch in political history, yet in intellectual creation—literature, science, and law—the Assyrians accomplished nothing. They republish, with some trifling additions, the ancient monuments of Babylonian literature, but they have none of their own; and in science their only achievements are some improvements in the practice of war. About their law we are ill informed: the number of their legal documents is contemptible, especially in comparison with Babylonia. It is true that part of an ancient Assyrian code, dated about 1500 B.C., has lately been discovered; but the date itself makes it impossible to believe that these laws remained in force when the empire reached its highest point. The ancient code reflects a primitive state of life, social and economic; it has no connexion with the laws of Babylonia, but reminds one of the Jewish law and, to some extent, of the Hittite code. Fragments of the code of Hammurabi have been found at Nineveh, and seem to show that Babylonian law was adopted eventually by Assyria.

The art practised in the great world-empire of Persia bears a strong general resemblance to the art of New Babylon and Assyria. It also is a borrowed and miscellaneous art; it also depends largely upon ancient Babylonian tradition, but lacks that vein of creation which gives life to the later Assyrian work. Another strong influence, however, is present—that of the Greeks in Asia Minor, who created, as we shall see later, their great original art in the seventh and sixth centuries B.C., especially the latter. Lastly, Persian art is remarkable, especially in the department of applied art, for certain features which were undoubtedly due to the Iranians themselves, such as the endeavour to use, for the purpose of ornament, the figures, in whole or in part, of animals. This peculiar style was most highly developed in the Scythian-Iranian kingdom established on the northern coast of the Black Sea.

Culture and Art

The most original part of Persian art is their palace architecture. The palaces of Persepolis and Susa differ from those of Assyria and Babylonia. The column, so richly developed in the Egyptian temples and not unknown to the Hittite builders, plays a very small part in Mesopotamian architecture; but in these Persian palaces it reigns without a rival. They are not fortresses nor, as in Assyria, combina-

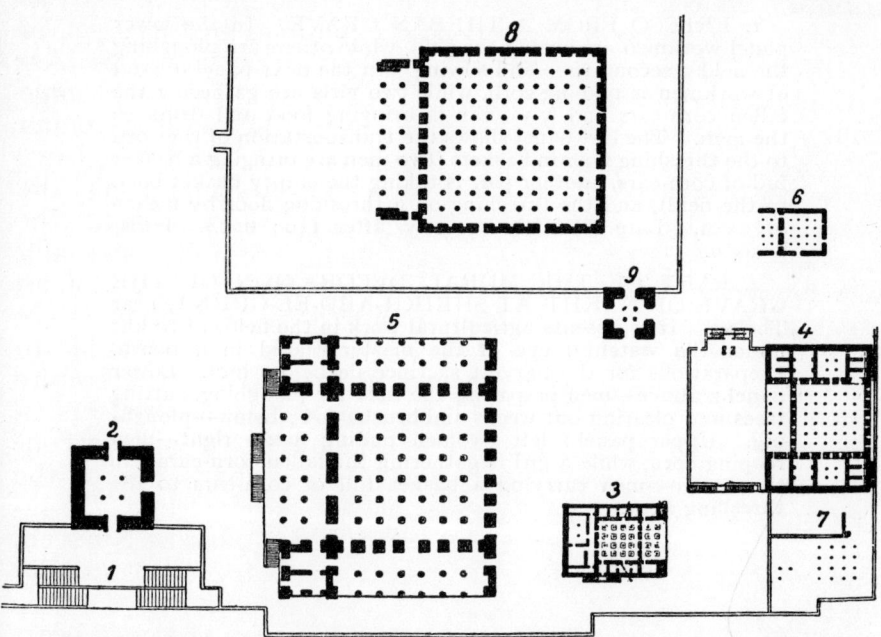

FIG. 10. *Plan of the palaces of the Persian kings at Persepolis.* 1. *The open stairs leading to the terrace on which the palaces were built.* 2. *The entrance gate of Xerxes.* 3. *The palace of Darius.* 4. *The palace of Xerxes.* 5. *The great reception hall of Xerxes.* 6. *A pavilion.* 7. *The building of Artaxerxes III.* 8, 9. *The hall of the hundred columns and the entrance gate to it. Comp. pl. XLIII. After F. Sarre.*

tions of a fortress and a temple. The palace is a vast ornamental pavilion, with a roof supported by a forest of columns; it is built on a high and broad terrace of stone, and a magnificent staircase leads up to it. The *apadana* (as it was called) is the reception-hall of the great king, where his throne rises in the background, and where he gives audience to his subjects and to foreign ambassadors, surrounded by his 'court' and his warriors. The columns are very peculiar: they do not resemble either Egyptian columns with their capitals shaped like the lotus or papyrus, or the columns of Greece; the

PLATE XLV

AGRICULTURAL LIFE IN EGYPT OF THE NEW KINGDOM

1. FRESCO FROM A THEBAN GRAVE. In the lower panel workmen are hoeing the field, while others are ploughing the field a second time and sowing. In the next panel a band of workmen is reaping corn, while two girls are gathering the fallen corn-ears and a woman is bringing food and drink to the men. The last panel shows the transportation of the corn to the threshing floor in baskets (two men are bringing a basket full of corn-ears, another pair is taking the empty basket back to the field), and the threshing on a threshing floor by means of oxen. Late XVIIIth Dynasty (after 1400 B.C.). Paris, Louvre.

2. PART OF THE MURAL DECORATION OF THE GRAVE OF NAKHT AT SHEIKH-ABD-EL-GURNA, near Thebes. It represents agricultural work in the fields of Nakht under the watchful eye of the master seated in a booth. Preparations for the harvest sacrifice lie before him. Lower panel: above—men preparing the field for ploughing, cutting trees and clearing out weeds and brushwood; below—ploughing. Upper panel: left—women pulling flax; right—men reaping corn, while a girl is gathering the fallen corn-ears; in the centre—men carrying a basket full of corn-ears to the threshing floor.

1. FRESCO FROM A THEBAN GRAVE

2. MURAL DECORATION FROM THE GRAVE OF NAKHT

XLV. AGRICULTURAL LIFE IN EGYPT OF THE NEW KINGDOM

1, 2. MURAL DECORATION FROM THE GRAVE OF NAKHT

XLVI. AGRICULTURAL LIFE IN EGYPT OF THE NEW KINGDOM

PLATE XLVI

AGRICULTURAL LIFE IN EGYPT OF THE NEW KINGDOM

1. THE SAME GRAVE. Agricultural work. Upper panel: men winnowing. Lower panel: men measuring corn under the supervision of Nakht.

2. THE SAME GRAVE. The upper panel shows vintage and treading of grapes; the lower, catching of wild fowl in a pond and preparing it for the kitchen (the birds were kept in the large jars seen above). About 1415 B. C.

capitals represent the fronts of animals combined together, especially of oxen turned in opposite directions. This is undoubtedly due to the Iranian custom, already mentioned, of using animals in sculpture.

The reliefs which adorn the palaces and the exterior of the rock-hewn tombs are of interest also. Similar in type to those found in Asia Minor, they resemble most closely the

FIG. 11. *Restoration of the buildings on the palace terrace of Persepolis. Comp. pl. XLIII. After Perrot and Chipiez.*

carvings on the Hittite palaces and shrines. They represent stately processions of victorious soldiers and conquered nations approaching the king; or rows of warriors flanking a staircase which leads to the palace at Persepolis. Scores of figures representing conquered peoples are carved on the triumphal monument of Darius at Behistun; and in the inscription below Darius tells of his conquests. This is an excellent example of the majestic and stately court-style of the Persian monarchy, so far removed from the disquieting realism of Assyrian sculpture.

X

POLITICAL, SOCIAL, AND ECONOMIC ORGANIZATION OF THE WORLD-EMPIRES OF THE EAST

IN reviewing the political and cultural development of the Eastern monarchies during the first three millenniums of their existence, I have indicated more than once the fundamental differences, political, social, and economic, which divide them so sharply from western, and especially from Greek, institutions. In the East a definite type of social and political community, almost everywhere identical and differing only in detail, formed itself by degrees. These beginnings of a polity, in the East as in other parts of the world, are closely connected with a particular tribal organization. This gradually grows into a city, and the city at the same time becomes a state. But in the East, as opposed to Greece, the city with its small territory is unable to maintain its political independence, or to create institutions based upon self-government of a more or less democratic type. From causes already mentioned power in these separate city-states became concentrated in the hands of an individual—the king; and the chief object of these different kings was to unite a number of cities under their own sceptre, so as to create a large centralized monarchy. This unity was generally secured within the limits of a single nation, that is, a group of clans speaking the same language and worshipping the same gods.

Within this union the foundations of a political, social, and economic framework are laid, and, once laid, prove to be more permanent and substantial than the nation which devised them. Owing to conquests and attacks from without, resulting in the seizure of the country for a long period by people of different origin and different creed, the ruling class of the population changes, but the fundamental framework remains the same. Thus, in Babylonia, the transference of power, from Sumerians to Semites, from Semites to Kassites, from Kassites back to Semites and Elamites, next to Semitic Assyrians, and finally to Indo-European Medes and Persians, makes little change in the framework of the state constructed originally by the Sumerians. Nor is this altered by the accretion of foreign dominions inhabited by a different stock. And we observe the same phenomenon in Egypt also.

The ties which bind a kingdom and community into one whole are, first, religion and, secondly, the king's power, which is closely connected with religion. The king's power from the first takes an absolute form: it is unlimited, divine, and responsible to heaven alone; it demands blind obedience from the subjects and relies upon the army, the officials, and the priesthood. The first of these is the most obedient instrument in the king's hands. Originally, the army consists of a militia which includes the whole population. In cases where a kingdom was formed by conquest, the adult men of the predominant people form the nucleus of the army. In Egypt, except during the episodes of foreign domination, and in Assyria, liability to military service was universal. And when the kingdom grew into an empire, incorporating a number of conquered nations, though the army was supplemented by contingents of the foreigners, its nucleus remained the same. Further, a special standing force is created for the personal protection of the king—his bodyguard, which generally consists of the strongest and most active members of the ruling nation. At a later date the kings of the great Eastern empires prefer to enrol mercenaries in this force. In most Eastern monarchies there was no standing army except the bodyguard, and soldiers were only enlisted when the necessity arose. In the great empires, however, where the royal power rested mainly on military force—for instance, in Egypt under the Eighteenth Dynasty, in Assyria and Persia— the need of a standing army was so great that part of the militia was converted into a permanent force, and detachments of mercenaries were formed to supplement the militia. The army played no great part in the politics of these Eastern monarchies, and very seldom overthrew the king: such an event is almost confined to the world-empires of Assyria and Persia at the latest periods of their development, when mercenary soldiers had begun to form an important part of the standing army.

The officials and the priesthood were less trustworthy as supporters of the king's power. As we have seen already, the history of the Eastern monarchies presents a series of changes between centralization and decentralization, according as centripetal or centrifugal forces prevailed. Thus in Egypt, during the first five dynasties, the former tendencies were stronger, and a united Egyptian kingdom was created for the first time; but next comes decentralization and the Feudal Period of Dynasties Six to Thirteen; this gives place, first, to the foreign domination of the Hyksos, and then to a new period of centralization under the Eighteenth and Nineteenth Dynasties. Later we note a new growth of the centrifugal forces and a perpetual struggle between the two principles which lasts till the date of the Persian conquest. The process in Babylonia is the same. First comes concentration in the Sumerian and Sumerio-Akkadian period; this is followed by the centralized government of Hammurabi; in the Kassite epoch, the organization of the state is purely feudal and extremely primitive; next comes the period of confusion and of Assyrian domination, and, finally, the restoration of centralized government in the time of the New Babylonian monarchy. In Assyria we know little about the period of concentration; but the time when the empire was strong and flourishing was a time when power was completely centralized. Of Persia more will be said later.

Whenever the centralized kingdom prospers, the officials and the priests are obedient instruments in the king's hands; they are his personal agents and entirely dependent upon him. But when the central power is weak, the officials and priests, who act for the king in civil and religious business, try to secure greater independence of action, relying on their wealth and personal influence with the population, and finally succeed in forcing the central authority to concede rights and privileges, which break down the unity of the kingdom, by making certain officials and priests independent rulers in the districts committed to their charge. But, as I have said already in Chapter IV, even in feudal Eastern kingdoms the government of parts of the realm is founded on the principle of absolute obedience to their superior on the part of officials; so that each feudal ruler, within his own domains, is just as absolute a monarch as the king of a united kingdom, and requires complete subservience from his own officials and priests and from his subjects in general.

The general population played no political part at all. We hear nothing of popular risings or revolutions with the

PLATE XLVII

INDUSTRY IN EGYPT OF THE NEW KINGDOM

1, 2. PART OF THE DECORATION OF THE TOMB OF APUKI AND NEBAMUN, sculptors and painters at the court of Amenhotep III, at Sheikh-abd-el-Gurna near Thebes. The owner of the tomb (his figure is not reproduced in full on our plate) is supervising the work in two workshops: that of carpenters (upper panel) and that of jewellers and engravers (lower panel). The finished articles from the two shops are brought to the owner for inspection (inlaid cloisonné work, used for trinkets, bracelets, and clasps for necklaces; fluted gold and silver vases; a painter's pen-case; caskets fitted up to receive jewellery); and a man is weighing in a balance gold to be given to the workmen. The carpenters are busy making a catafalque for a dead man; the sides of the catafalque were covered with symbolic figures—Osiris and Isis signs. Some are carving and painting these amulets, others are fitting them on the catafalque, one is making the planks for the amulets. Of the jewellers one is fitting a box for a pectoral of Amenhotep III (the pectoral is seen hanging on the wall above him, compare our pl. XIII, a pectoral of the XIIth Dynasty). His companion is grinding down the surfaces of two pieces of inlay against one another. Above him is a dish full of precious stones and a saucer with polishing material. Next the 'draughtsman Pasinisu', as the inscription says, is engraving an inscription on a libation vase. A specimen of decorated vases is shown above him. The next man is fitting an 'uraeus' (royal snake) to the head of a royal sphinx (gold). Two men are polishing and engraving libation vases of alabaster, and one is heating a piece of metal in the fire by means of a blowpipe.
1385–1370 B.C.

1, 2. DECORATIONS FROM THE TOMB OF APUKI AND NEBAMUN

XLVII. INDUSTRY IN EGYPT OF THE NEW KINGDOM

aim of securing a right to share in the government. The people did not even conceive the possibility of any political and social system, except that which had been formed by the passage of centuries. To them the power of the god and the king was not a subject for discussion but an article of belief. To the government, that is to the god and the king, belonged full and unlimited right to dispose of the person, labour, and property of the subject. It might require of him military service, just as it thought good. For tilling the land of the king and the god, for making canals and dikes, for constructing roads, for transporting men and goods required by the government, the subject was bound to give his time and labour without a murmur, and also the labour of the animals belonging to him. Finally, the subject was also bound to surrender to the government part of the produce of his labour: the court must be maintained, the worship of the gods must be performed, new temples or palaces or royal tombs must be built, military expenses must be defrayed. If the work was too heavy or food not forthcoming for the men summoned to forced labour, the only means of protest was a strike. But there was no germ whatever of political protest in these strikes.

Within the limits of this relation between government and people we observe certain differences, mainly formal and theoretical, in the different countries. In Egypt, but for some temporary and exceptional arrangements, the king considered himself the sole owner of the soil, recognizing in the subject no right except that of using it for a time; but in Babylonia the government recognized and upheld the right of private property in land. In spite, however, of this theoretical difference, the practice, as regards the possession of land, became identical in all the Eastern monarchies. We find it in Egypt under the empire, in Assyria, in the New Babylonian kingdom, and in Persia. Where small holders of land survived for a time, as in Assyria, Persia, and Asia Minor, they died out by degrees. The king, the temples, and the higher classes were lords of the soil. It was tilled by serfs bound to the soil which they tilled and the place where they lived, and forced, not only to surrender part of the produce to the government and landowner, but also to labour at such public works as irrigation, roads, bridges temples, and palaces; they had also to provide for transport. In industry we observe the same conditions. The workshops were owned by the king, the temples, and a group of wealthy merchants; the artisans were either serfs or slaves. Industry was closely connected with the large estates and came under the same management. Trade, large and small, was more independent of the king, the temples, and the large landowners; but the trader, unless he was agent of one of these powers, had to pay various taxes.

Agriculture was the basis of economic life. Industry and trade were concentrated round the temples and the palace. The ruling aristocracy, the royal bodyguard, the merchants and craftsmen lived in close proximity to the king and the god, and converted the settlement round the temple and palace into a city defended by walls. These city-states, ruled by the god and the king, were the earliest germs of political life over all the East, and especially in Hither Asia. Within the city, indeed, a certain unity grew up between men of the same profession and social standing, such as the royal bodyguard, the officials, the priests, the artisans, the merchants. These might form a sort of corporation, chiefly on a religious basis.

As separate cities developed into kingdoms, certain traditions and forms of self-government grew up simultaneously in the cities. The kings, representatives of the central principle, observe a cautious attitude toward such traditions. Even in great centralized empires like Egypt, and still more in Assyria and Persia, the kings were forced to reckon with these traditions and the set form which time had given to the life of these cities. The result is that in the great monarchies the cities are granted a certain measure of self-government, sometimes, as in Assyria, assured by charters, and referring especially to taxes and imports levied on the population. But this self-government does not go beyond certain definite limits. The mastery of the city remains with the king; as he chooses, he can extend or maintain existing rights; he can grant self-government to new cities or take it away from those which have enjoyed it. In the eye of the government, a city is the centre of a given territory and the residence of the ruling power; any rights that have grown up in the course of history are not binding on the king. And this is the fundamental difference which divides the Eastern empires from the Hellenistic monarchies and the Roman Empire.

Within the East there was no tradition of self-government upheld by the city population. The king of Assyria or Persia was the heir, not of the sovereign power of the people inhabiting a certain city, but of his predecessors, who were god-kings like himself.

In the East government was identified with the king. He was the fountain and centre of power. The legislative, judicial, and executive powers were concentrated in his hands. He might bind himself by the laws he had himself made by the inspiration of the god; but he was free to change these laws and to interpret them as he liked. Part of his power he might transfer to others; but their power owned the king as its source, and his officials acted exclusively in his name.

Such were the main features of the organization, political, social, and economic, which we find in the Eastern kingdoms, both small and great. In great empires, indeed, life was more complicated, and the mere fact of their existence raised a number of new problems, unknown to monarchies of narrower dimensions. For great powers like Egypt, Assyria, Babylonia, and Persia, one fundamental question was the treatment of conquered kingdoms, which had possessed, before they were conquered, a political system and government of their own. By the Old Babylonian kingdom, by Egypt down to the Eighteenth Dynasty, and by Assyria in her early stage, this question was simply settled. The conquered country retained its system and its rulers; it was bound merely to pay tribute to the victorious king, to help him in his military enterprises, and not to keep up friendly relations with his enemies. But it was impossible on this principle to build up a permanent and substantial kingdom including many nations; for the vassals naturally strove to recover their independence, and this led to constant and prolonged warfare. A change, though not a change of principle, was made by the Pharaohs of the Eighteenth Dynasty. Though they retained the system of vassalage in their foreign possessions, they stationed detachments of their own soldiers at the most important strategic points to act as garrisons. Thus the commanders of these garrisons became, to some extent, governors-general of large districts, through whom communications passed between the vassals and the suzerain, and who could dispose of the tribute and the detachments of auxiliary forces furnished by the vassals.

PLATE XLVIII

THE EARLIEST TEMPLES OF EGYPT

1. RESTORED VIEW OF THE CLERESTORY HALL IN THE VALLEY TEMPLE OF KHAFRE AT GIZEH (cp. pl. X). The stone piers of this hall are made of solid blocks of polished granite. The statues which originally adorned the hall were found in a well in an adjacent hall (the head of one of them is reproduced on pl. V). After 3100 B.C. Restoration of Hoelscher.

2. RESTORATION OF THE SUN TEMPLE OF THE KING NE-OUSER-RA OF THE Vth DYNASTY. The sanctuary was situated near Abusir (cp. pl. X, the pyramid of the rulers of the Vth Dynasty). The city stood in the valley near the Nile. A beautiful entrance gate in the middle of the city gave access to a causeway which led to the terrace of the temple. Through another gate the worshipper entered the temple court which was surrounded by a wall. The main building in the court was the Obelisk, the holy symbol of the Sun-god Ra. Before the Obelisk stood an altar for sacrifice, and to the left a chapel for divine service. To the left of the temple in the desert a stone image of the Sun-ship was placed. In this ship the Sun was supposed to make his daily journey. Restoration of L. Borchardt.

1. CLERESTORY HALL IN THE TEMPLE OF KHAFRE AT GIZEH

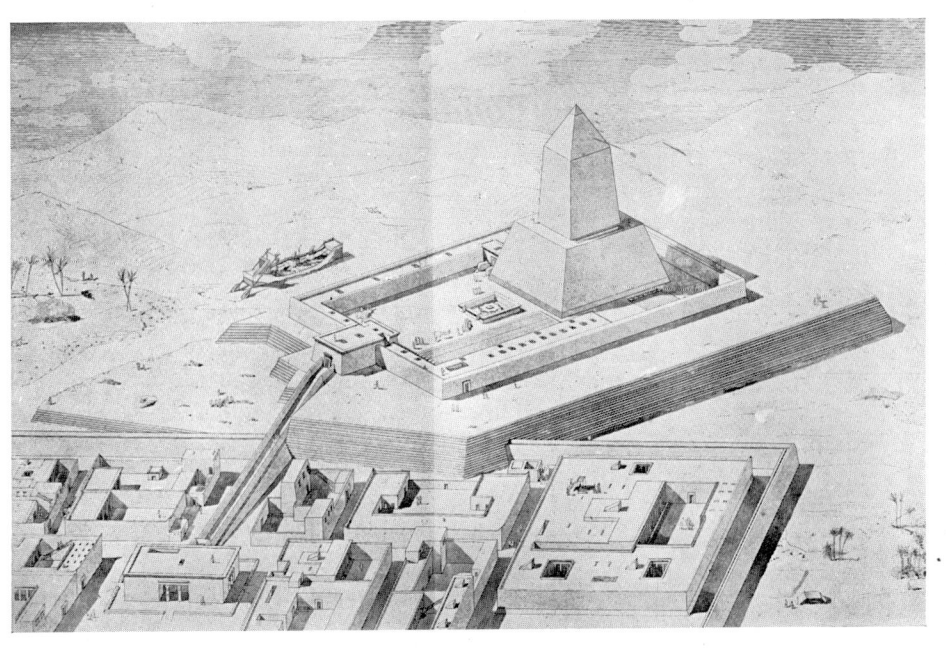

2. RESTORATION OF THE SUN TEMPLE OF KING NE-OUSER-RA

XLVIII. THE EARLIEST TEMPLES OF EGYPT

A further step towards the organization of a real empire was taken by Assyria in the reign of Ashur-nazir-pal. The Assyrians now began to incorporate territories within their own kingdom, substituting for the local authorities governors appointed by the Assyrian king, and establishing everywhere, as an imperial institution, the worship of the god Ashur and his vicegerent on earth, the King of Assyria. When the subject peoples, nevertheless, revolted and struggled obstinately for independence, the Assyrians resorted to extreme measures : they removed whole nations by force, taking scores of thousands away from their own country to foreign lands, and filling their places with colonists from other parts of the empire. The kingdom of New Babylon followed the same policy ; the transference of the Jews from Palestine to Babylonia is a familiar instance. But this policy, as much as the plan of massacring all opponents, earned nothing but hatred for Assyria.

The next step in the direction of uniting a heterogeneous empire was taken by the Persian kings. In this monarchy the distinction between the ruling country and the conquered peoples was gradually effaced. The vassal kingdoms passed by degrees into the position of provinces, ruled by the king's officials and generals. Eventually, just as happened later during the Roman Empire, the word ' province' or ' satrapy' ceased to signify the external authority of the ruling kingdom, and became merely a synonym for an administrative division of the territory ; and Persia itself, with the other Iranian parts of the monarchy, became one such division, though possibly privileged in some respects. Thus we see for the first time the idea of a kingdom not connected with a definite nation—the idea of a heterogeneous empire, subdivided not into nations but into administrative districts. This reform was never completed by Persia, and the empire continued to be a union of kingdoms and cities once independent ; but this was a novelty—that the parts of the empire were not ruled by native kings but by Persian governors (or satraps), whom, indeed, the local population were regularly accustomed to consider as their kings. The important point is this, that the Persians were the first to take decisive steps towards the creation of a real empire, centralized though heterogeneous, and united. From a number of measures taken by the kings we can see that they looked upon their empire as an indivisible

PLATE XLIX

THE ROCK TEMPLES OF ABU-SIMBEL

1. FRONT VIEW OF THE GREAT TEMPLE. The front is carved in the living rock. Before the front is a fore-court hewn out of the rock, to which a flight of steps ascends from the river. The entrance door of the temple, which is entirely excavated in the rock, is flanked by two pairs of colossal (65 ft. high) seated statues of Rameses II (1292–1225 B.C.), of excellent workmanship. The second colossus on the south has been deprived of its head and shoulders, which lie on the ground before it. To the right and left of each colossus and between their legs are small figures of members of the royal family. Upon the two southern colossi a number of Greek, Carian, and Phoenician inscriptions were carved by soldiers of King Psammetichus II (593–588 B.C.). The first are among the most ancient of all extant Greek inscriptions. Over the front is a cornice with a row of cynocephali worshipping the rising sun. In a niche above the entrance door the name of the king is represented by large figures, one of them the falcon-headed Sun-god worshipped by two figures of the king. The rock temple itself is very large and beautiful and consists of two hypostyle Halls, the Sanctuary, and eleven chambers.

2. PART OF THE FRONT OF THE SECOND ROCK TEMPLE OF ABU-SIMBEL, founded by Rameses II and dedicated to the Goddess Hathor and to the wife of the king. The front is adorned with six colossal standing figures: two of the king and one of the queen on each side of the narrow door. Near the colossi are smaller figures of the royal children. The temple excavated in the rock consists of a hypostyle Hall, a Sanctuary, and a chamber.

1. FRONT VIEW OF THE GREAT TEMPLE

2. PART OF THE FRONT OF THE SECOND ROCK TEMPLE

XLIX. THE ROCK TEMPLES OF ABU-SIMBEL

whole: the introduction of a uniform coinage and the construction of great military roads, piercing the kingdom from end to end, are among the most convincing of these measures.

While introducing central government and insisting on the unity of the empire as a political organism, the Persians, in dealing with the private affairs of their subjects, did not follow the example of Assyria but showed themselves tolerant and humane. They did not force either their religion or their language upon the whole kingdom. In their dealings with dependencies of the empire, they did not even use the Persian language and cuneiform writing which they had borrowed from the Elamites, but the more widely diffused language and character of the Aramaeans. Nor did they insist upon the use even of these; but the inhabitants of the different satrapies used the local languages and systems of writing. For Lydia this is proved by Lydian inscriptions of that date; and the same privilege was enjoyed by Phrygia, Lycia, Cilicia, Phoenicia, Palestine, and Egypt. This tolerance, this unwillingness to force their language and culture upon foreigners and make their empire Iranian, made it possible for the Anatolian Greeks, who were Persian subjects, to develop their own culture with such brilliance, in spite of the political overlordship of Persia. The same cause explains the notable advance in Jewish literature at this time—the Persians restored to their native land the Jews who had been exiled by the Babylonians—and the great prosperity enjoyed by the Phoenician and Aramaean cities and by a number of civilized centres in Asia Minor.

The separate parts of the empire retained their local peculiarities also in their social and economic life. The Persian administration and the Persian army were mere superstructures. Private life went on unchanged. It is true that in Egypt and Babylon ancient dynasties came to an end and were replaced by Persian kings; but the essence of kingly power remained the same. To an inhabitant of Babylon the Persian monarch was ordained and anointed by the god, Marduk, just as his predecessors had been; he merely began a new dynasty of Babylonian sovereigns. The usurpers welcomed this attitude and showed the greatest respect for the religious and political traditions of Babylon. So in Egypt Cambyses and his successors were perfectly willing to appear as the sons of the god, Ra-Amon, to bear on local monuments

PLATE L
EGYPTIAN RELIGION

1. PART OF A BAS-RELIEF FROM THE MORTUARY TEMPLE OF RAMESES I (XIXth Dynasty) at Abydos, begun by himself and finished by Seti I his son. The temple was dedicated to Osiris, the god of the Nether World. The king (in one case Seti, in another Rameses) is represented as making offerings to the holy symbol of Osiris, in the presence of Horus the son of Osiris, and Isis his wife. The sculptures are among the best specimens of the delicate and refined art of the XIXth Dynasty. About 1315 B.C. New York, Metropolitan Museum of Art.

2. STATUETTE OF RA-AMON, the supreme God of Egypt, the Sun-god. British Museum.

3. STATUETTE OF ISIS, the wife of Osiris, with her infant son Horus in her lap. Before her is the sacred royal serpent 'uraeus'. British Museum.

4. STATUETTE OF OSIRIS, the god of the Nether World, dressed like a mummy. British Museum.

1. SETI IN ADORATION BEFORE OSIRIS

2. RA-AMON　　　3. ISIS, WIFE OF OSIRIS　　　4. OSIRIS

L. EGYPTIAN RELIGION

purely Egyptian titles, and to be represented in the dress and with the attributes of the Pharaohs. One understands how the general course of life in both countries remained unaltered under the new régime. In these cases, indeed, the rapid adoption of the foreign monarch was a simple matter, because the power of the Persian king was, essentially, much the same as the regal power in Babylon and Egypt. But the Persian government showed the same pliability in other parts of the empire, where the former constitution had been opposed in principle to the ideas of Eastern monarchy. Thus the Phoenician cities, where the government was a commercial oligarchy, continued to live as before under the Persians; Palestine preserved, and even strengthened, its theocratic constitution, half-political and half-religious; and a number of small Anatolian kingdoms, fragments of the Hittite Empire, where the chief priests of the principal temple bore rule, were equally unmolested. Even the Greek cities in Asia Minor, whose constitution (to be discussed later) differed so sharply from that of any Eastern monarchy, were not forced to fight in defence of that constitution. Content with political superiority, the Persians suffered each of these city-states to govern itself as it thought good. They did, indeed, in the struggles of Greek parties, support their own favourites, especially the tyrants who crop up all over Greece in the sixth century B.C.; these tyrants, however, were not Persian nominees but leaders of a party in their native cities.

Under such a system of government it is not surprising that Persian rule was not burdensome to the majority of the ruled. Many parts of the empire, such as Babylonia, Phoenicia, and some districts of Asia Minor, were entirely satisfied with the position thus created; others, though attempting from time to time to recover their freedom, endured the Persian yoke on the whole with reasonable submission. The attitude of the subject peoples was much influenced by the fact that Persian overlordship opened wide possibilities of economic development to all the Eastern world. Internal peace, light taxation, unhindered communication between all parts of the empire, the royal patronage of international trade, the introduction of a common coinage for the whole empire, and the new roads which intersected it from end to end—all this made the exchange of commodities extremely easy; facility of exchange stimulated production throughout the realm, in agriculture, cattle-breeding, and manufactures;

and this economic development was suffered to enjoy complete freedom. The Phoenician cities, in close connexion with their powerful colony of Carthage, captured one Western market after another; the Greek cities in Asia Minor were not prevented from communicating with their compatriots in the Aegean islands and the Balkan peninsula. To simplify this intercourse, the Persians did not insist even upon their monopoly of coinage: they allowed all Anatolian Greek cities to coin their own silver and some, Cyzicus for instance, to coin gold.

In this tolerance and absence of rigidity on the part of the Persian government there were elements of strength and also of weakness. These qualities brought wealth to the empire, both material and intellectual; to the latter the chief contributors were the Greeks and Phoenicians, who turned up everywhere either as traders or travellers or mercenary soldiers and sailors. On the other hand, they fostered disruption among the most active peoples of the empire, and the economic advance of these peoples supplied means for organizing the struggle for freedom. It is, however, to be noted that, but for a shock from without, the disruptive process might have gone on for centuries without impairing the political unity of Persia. Again, the army was weakened by the imperial policy followed by the Persian kings. The nucleus of native Persian soldiers steadily dwindled; most of the troops were either drafted into the ranks from the provinces, or were mercenaries, especially Greeks. Finally, the prolonged existence of the empire had a corrupting effect upon the ruling dynasty. The kings came to be entirely cut off from their subjects, and, while keeping up relations with the motley population of the empire, lost touch with their own nation; they surrounded themselves with a narrow ring of courtiers and officials, or even shut themselves up in the yet narrower circle of their own overgrown families—polygamy, at least for the sovereign, was a feature of all Eastern monarchies. Nevertheless, the form of Eastern despotism which we find in Persia is of great historical importance. Its main principles in the government of a heterogeneous empire did not die with it, but were inherited by Alexander the Great, the avowed successor of the last Persian king; from Alexander they descended to the Hellenistic kings who succeeded him, and from them to the Roman emperors, who finally bequeathed them to modern Europe.

XI

RELIGIOUS DEVELOPMENT IN THE EASTERN WORLD

THE primitive religious beliefs of the East differ in no respect, as regards their main features, from the beliefs of mankind elsewhere, so far as these are known to us. The origin of religion is a difficult subject to discuss within the limits of a short history of antiquity. It is a debated question, and the number of answers given to it by different investigators—historians, sociologists, and philosophers—is almost infinite. Some facts, however, may be considered as established. The development of religious feeling in man is closely connected with his cultural development. The belief in a deity, in a divine principle that exists together with man and above him, was born when reflection upon his own life first dawned upon primitive man; and this belief has accompanied him from that time throughout his long advance in civilization.

As primitive stages in religious development we may reckon, first, the deification of natural forces, friendly or hostile, and also of certain animals which especially strike the imagination; and, secondly, the belief that there exists in man himself, and in other animate and even inanimate things, something distinct from matter, and which does not perish together with matter; and this involves the belief in a future life. The number of divine elements in man's life was unlimited. Everything in nature might become, and did become, an object of reverence, that is, of worship; and the forms of this reverence naturally took a mysterious and magical shape. Man sought to live at peace with the divine powers and under their protection, and to secure, by whatever means, this peace and protection for himself. Thus it is easy to understand how each group of men living together produced from their midst one or more chosen persons who knew more than the average man about divinity. These men

PLATE LI

SUMERIAN, BABYLONIAN, AND ASSYRIAN RELIGION

1. RESTORATION OF THE ENTRANCE TO THE TEMPLE OF TELL-EL-OBEID, near the Sumerian city of Ur. The staircase leads to a porch of two columns which is built before the gate leading into the temple court. The temple was built on a high artificial terrace, the walls of which are adorned with friezes reproduced and described in pl. VIII. About 3000 B.C. Restoration of C. L. Woolley, Joint Expedition of British Museum and Pennsylvania University Museum.

2. A STONE STELE BEARING THE TEXT OF A CHARTER OF PRIVILEGES WHICH KING NEBUCHADNEZZAR I OF THE IVth BABYLONIAN DYNASTY GRANTED TO RITTI-MARDUK, commander of his war chariots. The stone is protected against violation by the figures, symbols, and standards of Babylonian gods carved on the stele in the fashion first introduced by the Kassite kings for their boundary stones. About 1140 B.C. British Museum.

3. FRAGMENT OF AN ASSYRIAN BAS-RELIEF SHOWING SOME ASSYRIAN DEMONS: a set of lion-headed, eagle-legged monsters fighting each other with daggers, and another demon with a human torso and head and a lion's body. British Museum.

1. RESTORATION OF ENTRANCE TO THE TEMPLE OF TELL-EL-OBEID

2. STELE WITH FIGURE OF BABYLONIAN GODS, ETC.

3. BAS-RELIEF WITH FIGURES OF ASSYRIAN DEMONS

LI. SUMERIAN, BABYLONIAN, AND ASSYRIAN RELIGION

were able by rites and incantations to 'control the spirits'—an expression common in primitive magic; by communication with the deity they could discover how to appease him; and, in general, they were possessors of some mysterious power and some special knowledge. Thus we may account for the origin of wizards, sorcerers, and priests.

It is perfectly easy to understand why man wished to keep his god constantly near him, to be in unbroken communication with him, and to know what or who should be addressed in prayer. In the belief of primitive man, all nature and all more or less mysterious objects and appearances around him were divine and permeated with divine power; and therefore he worshipped trees and springs and animals and meteoric stones and human beings (male and female), and various objects of peculiar shape and mysterious origin, and images of gods made by man. Places where such objects were found, and places where the deity, often invisible, was supposed to be constantly present, became sanctuaries. In these sacred spots and groves and mountain-tops men gathered together to put up their prayers to the god.

Most natural of all was it for man to conceive of god 'after his own image',—to represent god in human shape. Birth and death were the riddles which struck the mind of man most forcibly, with which his religious reflections were connected, and towards which the effort of his imagination was directed. Because the mystery of birth is closely connected with woman, men began to imagine the deity in female form, perhaps even before the male form was used for this purpose. The likeness between the productive power of woman and that of nature, especially of the soil, was so obvious that the worship of woman and earth together was established early and lasted long. It is probable, too, that the soil was first tilled by women, and this would help to account for the institution. Then the fertilizing power of the sun, and of the sky with its showers of rain, was equally obvious and also found its analogy in the part played by the male in human generation. Hence the fertilizing powers of nature were worshipped in the shape of a man; and the gods were married to goddesses and had families, like men. The life of nature and of man was observed; catastrophes which humanity had survived were recalled; the struggle of man with nature and his sufferings were noted; and all this took

PLATE LII

MINOAN RELIGION

1. BEZEL OF A GOLD RING. Found at Mycenae. The Great Goddess is represented seated on a rocky ground beneath her sacred tree. Above her in the heaven, symbolized by the sun and the moon, are divine emblems: the double-axe and a small figure protected by the double shield—the shield goddess. On the left row of lion-heads. Near her are seated two little handmaids; one is offering her a spray, the other plucks fruit for her from the tree. Two women votaries present flowers: to one of them the goddess presents three poppy-heads, the other holds some lilies. The scene represents no doubt the epiphany of the divine world to her worshippers. Late Minoan. About 1500 B.C. Athens, National Museum.

2. BEZEL OF A GOLD RING. Found at Mycenae. A shrine of the Great Goddess is represented standing perhaps on the top of a mountain. The doors of the forecourt, which is surrounded by a wall and consists of three terraces, stand wide open. A paved road leads to the cult-room of which the front is represented. Behind the front grow two trees. Two other trees grow outside the walls of the forecourt. Before the shrine two priestesses are worshipping the invisible Goddess by performing a sacred dance. Similar shrines are known at Paphos in Cyprus and at Byblos in Phoenicia. Late Minoan. About 1500 B.C. Athens, National Museum.

3. FAIENCE STATUETTE, PAINTED. Found in the Palace of Cnossus among other sacred objects in a temple-depot. The figure represents either the Snake-goddess herself or her priestess. Her arms, her waist, her tiara are surrounded by snakes. Snake-goddesses are familiar figures in Oriental religions. Middle Minoan. About 1700 B.C. Museum of Candia, Crete.

4. PAINTED SARCOPHAGUS. Found at Hagia Triada. Cult of the gods and of the dead. The right half of the fresco is occupied by the mummified figure of the dead man standing before his grave-monument. Three male-priests bring him gifts: the first, a ship for his last voyage, the others, animals. The left half represents a sacrifice (of blood and wine) by two ladies at the double-axe shrine of the Great Goddess. On the axes are two doves, the birds of the Great Mother. Between the axes is a large *crater* for the liquid offerings. Behind the offering ladies a priestess is playing the lyre and singing the praise of the Goddess. After 1400 B.C. Museum of Candia, Crete.

1. BEZEL OF A GOLD RING

2. BEZEL OF A GOLD RING

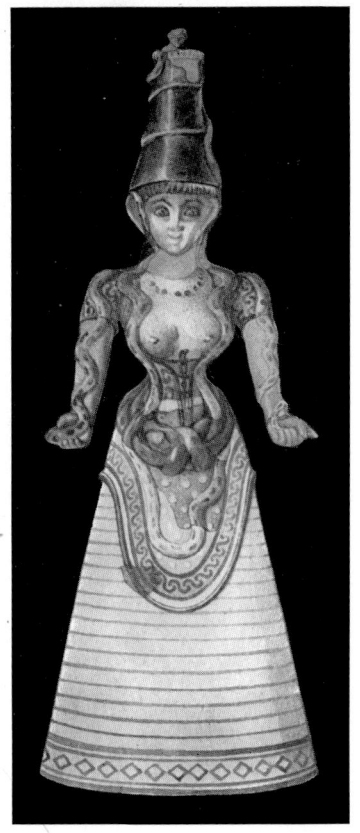

3. PAINTED FAIENCE STATUETTE

4. PAINTED SARCOPHAGUS FROM HAGIA TRIADA

LII. MINOAN RELIGION

a mythical form and became a connected narrative, dealing with the life of the gods and the history of their relations to man. The form of these myths was determined by the social organization of this or that group, by the predominance of women or men within the family and clan—'matriarchy' is the name commonly given to the former condition and 'patriarchy' to the latter—and the chief part in the most ancient myths was played by a female or male deity, round whom the other gods and goddesses, infinite in number, were ranked. Thus from polytheism and anarchy in the world of gods a transition was gradually made, not so much to monotheism as to monarchy in heaven, similar to the monarchy which had been developed in the family and in the state. A supreme deity, ruling over all the rest, was now imagined. In some parts of the world, such as Asia Minor, the Great Mother held this position. Sometimes a great male deity, generally the Sun, warrior and fertilizer, made his appearance as her divine consort and even as her superior.

The belief in a future life was simultaneously developed, especially in Egypt, where the survivors did their utmost to secure a comfortable and peaceful existence for the immortal part, the *Ka*, as they called it, of the human being. Thus they came to embalm the body, to erect for the dead a lasting habitation, and to fill it with all that he might require in a future life. Sometimes the objects themselves were deposited there, but it was the rule to substitute representations of them in painting or sculpture.

The political development of the East and the creation of solidly organized kingdoms hastened the transition from the anarchy of polytheism to the supreme rule of one god. Even in the separate Sumerian city-states and in the *nomes* of Egypt we find gods singled out as guardians of the kingdom and its rulers; and the same thing is observable in Asia Minor, Syria, and Phoenicia. When larger kingdoms were formed, the god of the ruling race became pre-eminent; such was the position of Marduk in Babylonia, of Ashur in Assyria, of Teshub in the Hittite kingdom, and of Ra-Amon in Egypt. Round these were grouped all the other gods, their assistants and coadjutors, often members of their family—parents, children, brothers, and sisters. The gods of conquered kingdoms were readily admitted into this family. This establishment of one supreme god, while easily reconcilable with polytheism, is opposed to monotheism, which recognizes no god but one.

The chief god of a kingdom becomes also the guardian of its constitution, its peculiar social and political system. Public order, founded on law and certain traditional rules of general behaviour, is closely connected with religion and comes under its protection. The god becomes a law-giver, a creator of the rules of social morality which are formed by degrees. Religion and morality draw closer and closer till they become indistinguishable. Thus the laws of Hammurabi were delivered to him by the god, and therefore submission to these laws becomes part of every believer's religious duties. To live in accordance with the rules of morality becomes, in Egypt, a pledge and a condition of peace and happiness after death, 'in the fields of Ialu', the mythical abode of the blest. But this bliss is reserved for those who prove worthy of it after judgement before the great tribunal of the dead, presided over by Osiris.

This process, by which public worship became centred on a single god or closely connected group of gods, is comparatively well known to us in the case of Egypt. The priests, who devised the earliest religious teaching and the earliest theologies, are conspicuous in the process. In pre-dynastic Egypt there is religious chaos; but then, by degrees, as we saw above, the gods of the ruling cities emerge; and the priests of Heliopolis succeed in bringing to the front the local Sun-god Ra, with whom are associated eight other gods; the whole group was called the Nine Gods or Ennead. But now the centre of the kingdom shifts to Thebes, and Ra, while remaining the chief of the Holy Ennead, becomes identified with Amon, the local deity of Thebes. A series of myths is connected with these Nine Gods; genealogies are assigned to them; a connected story, dealing with the origin of the world and the relation between gods and men, makes its appearance—a story which in some parts recalls Babylonian teaching on the same subjects. Then Osiris, god of the 'western world' (i. e. the world of the dead), claims a place by the side of the sacred nine. The legend of Osiris and Isis and their son Horus takes a poetic form: it describes the struggle of Osiris against Set, the chief of the powers of darkness, his death, and the mourning of Isis; then she searches for his body and finds it, but it is torn to pieces by

Set and the pieces are scattered all over Egypt; Isis mourns again and begins fresh wanderings in search of her husband's body; Horus fights with Set and conquers him. We have here the eternal myth, discussed later on, which tells of day and night, winter and spring, life and death. To the like effect is the tale of the god Ra—how every twenty-four hours he travels through the realm of the dead and is born again out of his own substance.

The endeavour to concentrate worship upon one principal deity, who should be the god of a united Egyptian empire, reaches its highest point in the religious reform of Ikhnaton, of which I have already spoken. In opposition to the theology of the Theban priests, he put forth his worship of the sun's disk—Aton, the creator and ruler of the world. In all the sculptured monuments dedicated by Ikhnaton to Aton, the god is not once represented in the figure of a man or an animal. He is always the sun's disk, sending forth rays, each of which ends in a human hand. Even if Ikhnaton's reform had a political purpose—even if it was directed against the powerful guild of priests and intended to create a deity acceptable to all the subjects of the empire alike—yet it is certain that the reformer had also a purely religious end in view: he wished to create a worship more abstract and spiritual, clearer and simpler, addressed to one supreme god; other gods might exist together with him, but only to personify special parts of his divine essence.

We notice the same general development in the kingdoms of Mesopotamia—Sumer, Akkad, Babylonia, and Assyria. Here, too, the chaos of primitive fancies concerning the divine gives way to gods and goddesses with a definite sphere of activity, who are mainly personifications of natural forces, e. g. the Sky, the Sun, Water, the Moon. Here too among those deities who watch over the different kingdoms a great goddess is conspicuous—Ishtar or Mother Earth, parent and warrior, goddess of the creative and productive powers in nature and man. Here too the priests of each city endeavour to reduce the host of gods to a definite hierarchy, promoting the most powerful of them, arranging them in trinities and groups of trinities, and assigning to each his special place in the government of the world and its inhabitants.

As in Egypt, so in Mesopotamia the gods, while still representing natural forces, become at the same time pro-

PLATE LIII

HITTITE RELIGION

1. STATUE OF THE GOD HADAD. Found in the Lower Palace of Carchemish (see description of pl. XXIII). The god, ponderous and majestic, is represented sitting. The base of the statue is formed by two lions which an eagle-griffin with human body is mastering.

2. ONE OF THE SLABS FOUND AT CARCHEMISH. It adorned the wall of a staircase leading to the royal palace (see description of pl. XXIII). The bas-relief represents the Great God of the Hittites and his priest. The god (Teshub) is the god of the sky and the thunder; his symbol is the axe; he is winged. The priest offers him his own symbols. Both stand on the back of a lion.

1. STATUE OF THE GOD HADAD

2. THE GREAT GOD OF THE HITTITES AND HIS PRIEST

LIII. HITTITE RELIGION

tectors and organizers of civilization, founded not merely on military power but also on conceptions of right, order, and morality. In many Babylonian hymns and prayers the worshipper appeals to the god, not only as the personification of power and might, but also as the fountain of justice, mercy, and forgiveness, who punishes the guilty and rewards the upright. The moral element becomes steadily more prominent in the religion of Babylonia and Assyria.

As a united kingdom grew up round Babylon, Marduk, the great god of that city, became king of gods and men throughout Babylonia ; and the priestly theology strove to connect with him and to subordinate to him all the other deities who had once been powerful in the Sumerian and Akkadian cities. Marduk's father is Ea, god of the watery element and of human civilization ; his son is Nabu, worshipped in Borsippa close to Babylon, the god of knowledge and science, of writers and craftsmen. Two powerful trinities existed before : Anu (the Sky), Enlil (the Earth), and Ea (Water) mentioned already ; Sin (the Moon), Shamash (the Sun), and Adad (the Storm). Both of these became subject to Marduk : he is the king and ruler of gods, the one god to whom earthly kings, his coadjutors, address their fervent prayers. This idea of a single supreme deity is still more clearly expressed in Assyria, where the great god Ashur, symbolized by a winged and featureless solar disk, is not connected with any one city or with any one natural phenomenon. He is the one god of the great Assyrian kingdom, ruling over all whom the Assyrian arms have subdued ; and, as the kings believe themselves the masters of mankind, therefore Ashur is the god of the whole world.

Unlike Egypt, absorbed in contemplation of a future state, Babylon and Assyria think mainly of earth and earthly life. This accounts for the extraordinarily rich development of prophetic lore in both these countries. All the methods of divination, which have been so immensely important in human life even down to our own time, draw their origin from Babylon. Divination by the entrails, especially the liver, of a slaughtered animal—a system which passed from Asia to the Etruscans in Italy, and from them to Rome ; prediction of the future either for individuals or kingdoms, determined by the combination of the heavenly bodies ; the interpretation of all portents or apparent portents, of all rare and capricious phenomena in life and nature, such as the birth of monsters, or a rain of blood or stones; and finally the interpretation of dreams—each of these methods derives from Babylonia, and each of them was there worked out with system and logic and set forth in manuals of scientific form. In demonology also, or the lore of evil spirits who bring disease and misfortune, we mark the same connexion of science with religion and superstition. Incantations against

FIG. 12. *Restoration of the 'Ziggurat', or tower-temple of Marduk (the 'Tower of Babel' in the Bible) in the Esagilla sanctuary at Babylon. After Koldewey.*

these spirits are found in thousands among the cuneiform texts on Babylonian cylinders; and often rudiments of medical knowledge are mixed up with them. In order to drive out from the patient's body the evil spirit that caused the disease, incantation was often supplemented by prescriptions; for the magic power which could free a man from an evil spirit was attributed to drugs. Divination, incantation, and magic are characteristic of all primitive religions. They existed in Egypt also; but nowhere except in Babylonia were they worked out so systematically or reduced to such an apparently scientific shape.

Another remarkable feature of Babylon, which is found, indeed, in all Semitic nations and above all in the Jews, is the rich imaginative power of their religion, which found expression in numerous productions of religious and semi-religious literature. The hymns and prayers addressed to the gods of Babylon and Assyria are full of religious inspiration and unfeigned religious feeling. The Babylonians in their epic poetry sought to explain the mighty secrets of nature,

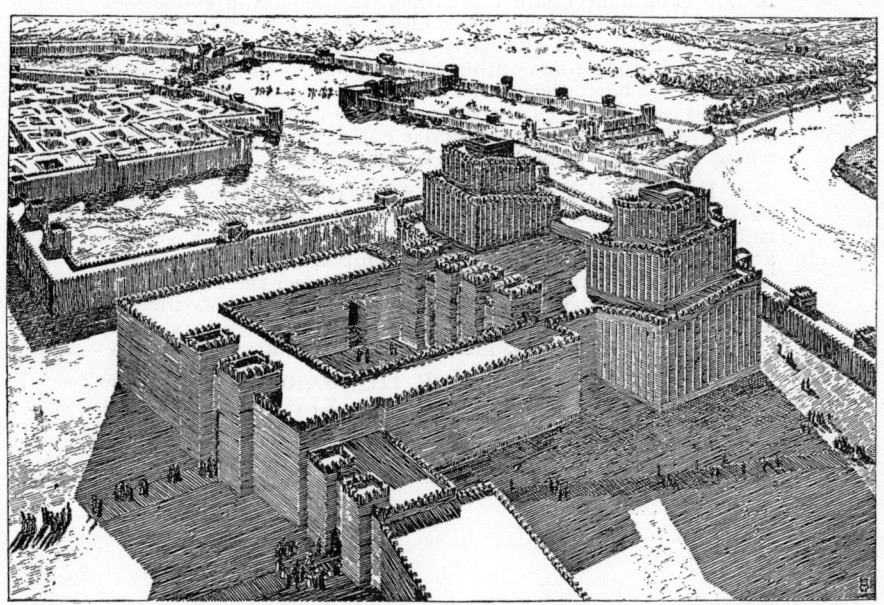

FIG. 13. *Restoration of the temple of the Assyrian god Anu-Adad at Ashur, one of the capitals of the Assyrian Empire. The temple was built by King Shalmaneser II (860–825 B.C.). After Andrae.*

connected with the life of gods and men. A poem on the creation of the world, closely akin to the Book of Genesis, tells how Marduk, the god of light, order, and civilization, strove mightily against the monster Tiamat and his army of weird and terrible beings—personifications of the primitive chaos. The creation of the world is referred to also in the poem about the Flood, which destroyed the world and its inhabitants, except one man who was saved in his ark by divine inspiration. A mysterious poem, rich in imagery, gives tidings of the mysterious under-world, into which the goddess Ishtar descended; it is akin to all those poems which sym-

PLATE LIV
PHOENICIAN RELIGION

1, 3. TWO ARCHAIC STATUETTES OF PHOENICIAN GODS, one male, the other female, found at Tortose (Phoenicia). The male figure was armed, the female (a goddess or a priestess) lifts her hands in adoration. The style and the dress are similar to the early Hittite sculptures. Note the typical belt and helmet of the god (cp. pl. XX) and the necklace with the archaic prehistoric pendant, worn by the goddess or priestess. The eyes of the figures were inset. Note the rude but powerful art and the religious enthusiasm of the Semites which these figures breathe. Paris, Louvre.

2. BAS-RELIEF WITH THE FIGURE OF ONE OF THE SEMITIC BAALS. Found at Amrith in Phoenicia. In the right hand he holds a whip, in the left, a lion. Above him are the Solar disk and the wings symbolizing the Solar god. The god is standing on a lion, and the lion on the tops of two mountains. In the dress, the style and the symbols there is a mixture of Assyrian, Egyptian, and Hittite elements, while the religious ideas are Semitic. Beyrouth, Collection Peretié.

4. ONE OF THE SIDES OF THE SARCOPHAGUS OF AMATHUS (see the description of pl. XLI). The bas-relief shows four naked goddesses of fertility. On the top of the lid are two sphinxes. 6th cent. B. C. New York, Metropolitan Museum of Art.

1. PHOENICIAN GOD   2. ONE OF THE SEMITIC BAALS   3. PHOENICIAN GODDESS

4. SIDE OF SARCOPHAGUS OF AMATHUS

LIV. PHOENICIAN RELIGION

bolize the death of nature in winter and her resurrection in the spring. Poems about the heroes Gilgamesh and Etana tell how man endeavoured to penetrate the mysteries of life and death and to gain immortality; they tell also of man's eternal struggle against the malignant forces of nature.

In the instances of Egypt and Babylonia we have seen how, in the most civilized Eastern countries, religion passes out of its primitive chaos to order and system; and how its moral and spiritual aspect becomes, especially in the more

FIG. 14. *Upper part of the stele of King Esarhaddon of Assyria (comp. pl. XXXV, 1). Near the head of the king the great Assyrian gods and goddesses are represented standing on their sacred animals. Near them are the stars, the moon, the winged symbol of the Sun, and Venus, the star of Ishtar. Near the head of the king are sacred sceptres of various Assyrian gods.*

enlightened classes, more and more predominant over the primitive terror and superstition born of terror.

These moral and spiritual aspects of a creed reach their highest point in the religion of the Jews. Yahweh, or Jehovah, the god of the Jewish people, was essentially just such a god as Marduk or Ashur. Their worship, like that of other Semitic peoples, was addressed to the deity of the Sun and the Sky. We do not know when and how this worship was supplemented by new and sublime religious conceptions, preached by the Hebrew prophets in the first millennium B. C. This entire reconstruction of their religious conceptions is connected by Jewish tradition with the personality of Moses, a great religious law-giver, and with the exodus of the Jews from Egypt. (It is possible that they found their way there at first as one among that group of Semitic clans, to which

PLATE LV

PERSIAN RELIGION

1. DETAIL FROM A BAS-RELIEF OF ONE OF THE PILLARS OF THE PALACE OF XERXES AT PERSEPOLIS. It shows a part of the baldaquin which protected the figures of King Darius and of King Xerxes. The figure reproduces the beautiful embroidered rug of the baldaquin with the winged symbols of Ahuramazda, rows of lions and rows of rosettes. Above is a large winged symbol of Ahuramazda. After F. Sarre.

2. TWO PERSIAN ALTARS OF FIRE-WORSHIPPERS which still stand in a rocky spot at the top of a mountain at Husein Kuh, near Persepolis. After F. Sarre.

3. ONE OF THE ACHAEMENID ROCK-GRAVES BEHIND THE PALACE TERRACE AT PERSEPOLIS. The entrance to the grave is surmounted by a monumental throne which is supported by two rows of the subjects of the king. On the throne, raised on a platform, the king, armed with his bow, adores the sacred symbol of Ahuramazda before a burning altar. To the right of the symbol we see the combined disk of the Sun and the crescent of the Moon. After F. Sarre.

1. BAS-RELIEF FROM PALACE OF XERXES AT PERSEPOLIS
2. PERSIAN ALTARS OF FIRE-WORSHIPPERS

3. ROCK-GRAVE BEHIND THE PALACE TERRACE AT PERSEPOLIS

LV. PERSIAN RELIGION

the name of Hyksos is given by tradition.) The tradition tells us that to Moses upon Mount Sinai were revealed the Tables of the Law, or the Ten Commandments. We can hardly doubt that the new religious ideas proclaimed by the prophets were the work of one or several religious reformers. For great religious reforms are always connected with definite personalities, in whose head and heart the confused aspirations of their contemporaries take shape and are expressed with precision : at nearly the same time a similar reform of religion was started in the Iranian world by Zoroaster. The new discovery attributed to Moses put forward two ideas especially: first, God is one, and there is no room for other gods beside him ; and, secondly, this one god is outside the world of matter, a purely spiritual power that made and governs the world. At the same time God appears as the creator and maintainer of morality, who dictates to man rules of conduct and requires prompt obedience.

Closely connected with these fundamental points was hostility to everything irreconcilable with them—polytheism, nature-worship, bowing down to idols, departure from the laws of morality. All these essential points were emphasized and more powerfully expressed by those whom the Jews called 'prophets'—a succession of men imbued with these beliefs and devoting their lives to the task of proclaiming them to others.

At first this new doctrine remained within the boundaries of the Jewish nation and kingdom : Jehovah was the god of the Jews, and of the Jews alone. The triumph of the doctrine depended upon the triumph of the nation as such— upon its political and material prosperity at the beginning of the first millennium B. C. But their destiny was not such that this connexion could be fully maintained. The sufferings and humiliations experienced by the Jews during their struggle for freedom against Assyria and the kingdom of New Babylon were explained by the prophets as resulting from their departure from the Covenant of Moses, their concessions to materialism and polytheism, and their disobedience to the moral dictates of the Law. In the exile and dispersion due to the domination of Babylon, the Jewish religion rises for a time to the region of universality : it seeks to detach itself from a single nation and to become the religion of mankind. As preached by some of the prophets, the one god of the

Jews is converted into the one God whom all nations are bound to recognize and, sooner or later, will recognize. But the final inference from these premisses was never drawn. The restoration of the Jews from captivity was followed by a national reaction, which took a specially marked form against the successors of Alexander the Great and once more limited the Jewish religion to one place and one people. From this limitation it was never able to free itself. It was never spread abroad by religious propaganda, but moved with the dispersion of the Jews that followed the domination of Greeks and Romans over Palestine. It shut itself up within the shell of national exclusiveness and never found strength to issue forth again.

The cosmopolitan tendency is seen elsewhere. During the Persian empire many other religions, at first merely local and national, became spiritualized and moralized, broke loose from their local origins, and went forth beyond the limits of a single kingdom and a single nation. Within the Persian monarchy, not only was the state religion spiritualized by the reforms of Zoroaster, but other worships lived and grew, offshoots of the ancient Eastern beliefs which deified the powers of nature. Thus the cult of the Sun, common to all Semitic peoples, the Anatolian cult of the Great Mother, the Egyptian cult of Osiris and Isis—all these became more refined, worked out more precisely their main ideas, concentrated on one of these, and endeavoured to make as many converts as possible, without regard to their race or political connexions. In all these religions the mystical element becomes prominent. Their chief dogma becomes by degrees the union of man with God, his approach to God by means of repeated mysterious and symbolic rites, his cleansing from earthly taint by baptism, his consecration and participation in the mystery contained in the great central myth concerning the god or goddess. All these myths, whatever their form, are connected with the mystery of death and resurrection; and they are all definitely naturalistic, inasmuch as they symbolize the death of nature in winter and her resurrection in spring. In them all we see the figure of a dying god, suffering pain and parted by death from his divine consort, but united to her again after his resurrection. In the Persian religion of the Sun-God Mithra there is more than this: the god is not only a sufferer but a hero, an athlete, a martyr, who fights for mankind and makes subject to them the powers of darkness in nature.

But all these doctrines were surpassed, both in depth of religious feeling and in moral elevation, by the religion of Zoroaster. Like the Hebrew prophets, Zoroaster reached the conception of a single spiritual God, Ormuzd or Aura-Mazda, in whom the principle of good is personified, while the evil principle is embodied in Ariman or Angra-Mainu. The two principles strive eternally in life and nature, and in the struggle men take part. Man is responsible for his actions, good or bad; he is master of his fate; his will determines his line of conduct. If he struggles against evil, confesses God, and cares for the purity of his body and soul, then, after four periods, of three thousand years each, in the world's history, when the time shall arrive for final victory of good over evil and of Ormuzd over Ariman—the general resurrection of the dead and the Last Judgement will assure him his place among the saved and the righteous. It is remarkable that these two tenets of a future life and of two contending principles in human nature, although the former was unknown to the ancient Jewish religion, were adopted by it at a later time and then taken over in their entirety by Christianity.

GREECE

XII

GREECE AND THE AEGEAN KINGDOMS

WE have seen that in the third and second millenniums B. C., when the East attained the highest point of her creative genius in civilization, Crete was one of the most brilliant centres of this culture, and that a number of smaller kingdoms round the Aegean gradually grouped themselves about Crete and copied her civilization. We have seen also that about 1400 B. C. the maritime empire of Crete was dissolved and the leading part in the culture and politics of that region was transferred to the Aegean kingdoms which had grown up on the coasts of Greece. We cannot trace the development of these kingdoms in that age of storm and confusion. But recent discoveries, derived from documents which formed part of the library of the Hittite kings, encourage us to hope that in the near future the history of early Greek settlements in Asia Minor will become better known to us. This at least is clear, that the peaceful rule of Crete had passed away. The Aegean world was full of unrest and disturbed by war after war. I have spoken already of the allied expedition against Troy carried on by European kingdoms of Aegean type; of the campaigns in which the 'sea peoples' fought against Egypt; of two detachments of Aegeans, the Philistines and Etruscans, which cut themselves loose from their surroundings and settled down, the first in Palestine and the second in Italy. I have spoken also of the form which Aegean civilization assumed in its Greek centres of development. The still extant ruins of the fortified palaces of Mycenae and Tiryns with their massive gates and walls, their mural and floor decorations, their sculptures and metalwork, and the beautiful vaulted graves of the kings scattered all over Greece, which have yielded a profusion of admirable examples of the various arts and crafts, many of them, especially in the later times after the fall of Crete, no doubt made in Greece and not imported from abroad, testify to the splendour and originality of the Greek version of the Aegean civilization. But at the end of the second millen-

PLATE LVI

MYCENEAN GREECE

1. GENERAL VIEW OF THE RUINS OF THE FORTIFIED PALACE OF TIRYNS in the north-eastern part of the Peloponnese in Greece. Tiryns was first excavated by Schliemann. A typical example of the Mycenean fortresses which were scattered all over the southern and central part of Greece, and which reached the highest point of their development after 1400 B.C.

2. THE VAULTED CORRIDOR (which probably served as a store-house) INSIDE THE FORTIFICATION WALLS OF TIRYNS. Huge blocks of stone were used for building the walls. The later Greeks ascribed this type of building to the mythical Cyclopes. It is probable that the wall existed on the hill of Tiryns before the palace of the Minoan type (see fig. 16) was built on the top of the hill.

3. RECONSTRUCTION OF ONE OF THE FRESCO-FRIEZES DISCOVERED IN THE PALACE OF MYCENAE. It shows a warrior, three grooms and four horses. The frieze belongs to a comparatively early period of the Minoan civilization of the mainland (soon after 1400 B.C.). After A. J. B. Wace. National Museum, Athens.

1. TIRYNS

2. VAULTED CORRIDOR AT TIRYNS

3. WARRIOR, GROOMS, AND HORSES

LVI. MYCENEAN GREECE

nium B.C. Aegean culture in Greece grows coarser, and more primitive forms of life and art prevail. It appears that the creative forces of Mycenean Greece were exhausted.

This decline is contemporary with the great movement of peoples spoken of above. On the Balkan peninsula this confused period led to the distribution of peoples in Greece as we know it in historical times. What exactly happened in Greece at the end of the second millennium B.C. and the beginning of the first we do not know. There are many questions to which science so far can give no positive answer. The key to their solution lies in exploration by archaeologists in Greece and Asia Minor. At present we must be content with surmises. It seems that the Thracian and Illyrian movement in the north of the Balkan peninsula drove the stocks belonging to Northern Greece southward towards the centres of Aegean-Greek civilization. The division of that quarter into a number of independent kingdoms perpetually at war with one another made it impossible for any of them to resist the invaders, who were not inferior to the Aegeans in military equipment and used the same bronze weapons of highly developed forms. Some of these stocks, indeed, may have used iron weapons also, which were still unknown to the Aegean world. The appearance in Greece of these Greek conquerors drove out many inhabitants, especially the ruling classes, of the Aegean-Greek kingdoms from their old abodes towards the east and south.

There conditions were in their favour. In Asia Minor the Hittite empire had been destroyed, partly by the struggle with Egypt, partly by the invasion of Thracians who had spread there also. Hence the exiles, Aegeans and Graeco-Aegeans, seized the opportunity to establish themselves on the rich coast of Asia Minor, driving out the old inhabitants, who had their own comparatively high culture, akin to that of the Aegeans. These in their turn sought new abodes in Syria, Phoenicia, Palestine, Egypt, Sicily, Italy, by routes which had long before been opened up by Aegean trade. It is therefore quite probable that the Philistines were a part of the Greco-Aegean population expelled from Crete, or inhabitants of the south coast of Asia Minor who were forced to migrate. The Etruscans also, who appeared in Italy not earlier than the end of the second millennium B.C. or the beginning of the first, probably came from Asia Minor.

In Greece these new Greek stocks, moving forward to

the coast and finding their way from there as far as Asia Minor, inherited from their predecessors their cities, the boundaries of their kingdoms, and a part of their technical skill. How many waves of population succeeded one another on these coasts we do not know; but there was certainly more than one. By degrees, however, when the Dorians had appeared in southern Greece and large numbers of them had settled in the Peloponnese, the troubled sea began to calm

FIG. 15. *Reconstruction of the north-western angle of the courtyard of the palace of Mycenae. The architecture and the decoration (ornamental friezes) were very like those of the later parts of the palace of Cnossus in Crete. After A. J. B. Wace and W. Lamb.*

down, more permanent national kingdoms began to take shape, and once more the beginnings were developed of a peculiar culture—liker that of the East, and therefore of higher quality, in Asia Minor, and more primitive in Greece itself.

The political organization of Greece was dictated by the geographical and economic conditions. Nature had divided her into small economic units, and she was incapable of creating large political systems. So it had been during the prevalence of the Aegean culture, and so it still remained. Each valley was self-centred, and its inhabitants jealously guarded their pasture and arable land. The best parts of the country, especially its rich valleys, are open to the sea and shut in by land—separated from the central high valleys and plateaux by formidable barriers. They are more in touch with those neighbours from whom the sea divides them than with those whom the land brings near them. It is easier for them to exchange goods and ideas by sea than by land. Hence civilization develops quickly on the coast but slowly in the centre of the country.

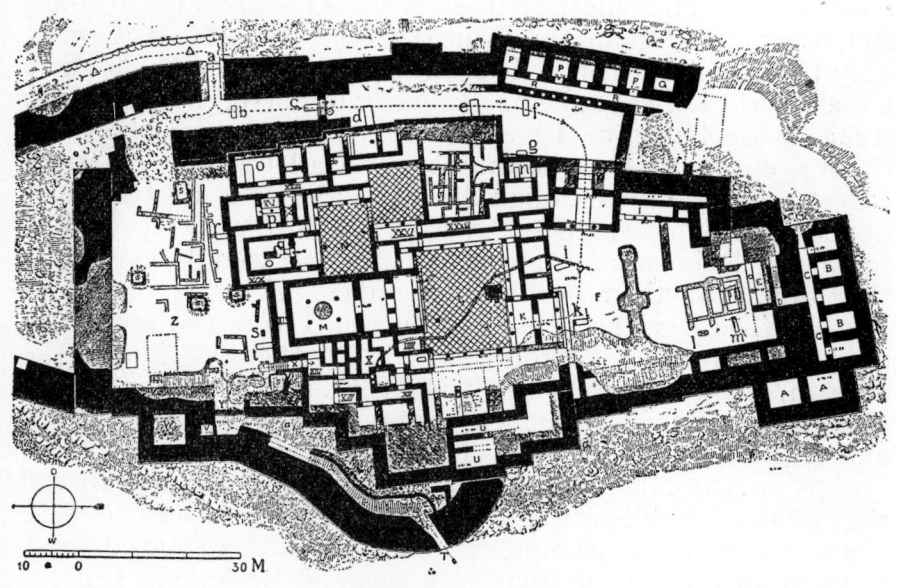

FIG. 16. *Plan of the fortified palace of Tiryns. The palace is surrounded by powerful ' cyclopean ' walls (see pl. LV, 2). The centre of the palace consists of a large northern house (megaron) with a spacious forecourt and a tower gate which led to the court. This central building is surrounded, in the Minoan fashion, by an irregular complex of halls, chambers, and passages.*

The type of life, however, is the same in all parts. Stocks, and portions of stocks, form petty political units which keep jealous guard of their independence. To protect themselves and their property against attack, they build fortified refuges on the hill-tops, and these by degrees are converted into cities, which offer a market for their produce, a centre of religious life, and a residence for their kings, leaders in war, and priests. The city becomes the focus of a larger or smaller territory, inhabited by farmers and shepherds who live either in detached houses and cottages scattered over the country, or together in villages (demes). Such city-states steadily increase in number. Among them there always existed groups united by the tie of a common language, or, more strictly speaking, a common dialect of the one Greek language. The distribution of these dialects in Greece, the islands, and Asia Minor, throws light on the process by which the resettlement of Greece by Greek stocks took place. Three dialects are sharply distinguished, and probably correspond to three successive waves of conquerors. The oldest of these is the Arcadian and Aeolian-Achaean; the Ionian comes next; and the Dorian is probably the third and last. The three groups divided the whole Greek world between them. Thessaly in northern Greece was Achaean-Aeolic from time immemorial; and also central Greece, except Attica, became so, and all the north-west of Peloponnese. The Arcadian dialect belonged to central Peloponnese and the island of Cyprus. Ionic dialects prevailed in Attica, Euboea, and most of the Aegean islands, especially the largest of them—Imbros, Lemnos, Chios, Samos, and Naxos. The Dorians were firmly established in the south and east of Peloponnese, Aetolia, and the southern islands of the Aegean, Crete and Rhodes being the largest and richest of these; they left a permanent impression also upon Boeotia and Thessaly. There was a similar distribution of these groups in Asia Minor. The northern coast of the Aegean and that of the Black Sea were Aeolic; the central coast, closely connected with the islands, was Ionian; and a small district to the south, connected with Rhodes and Crete, was Dorian. Thus the Ionians cut in like a wedge between the other two groups, and their chief centre was not in Greece but in the islands and Asia Minor.

Some of the districts which were independent and wealthy kingdoms in the Aegean and Mycenean ages still remained the centres where civilization and political life were most vigorous. Such were Sparta in the south of Peloponnese, Argos in the north-east, perhaps Olympia in the north-west; Corinth and Megara on the Isthmus; while in central Greece there were Delphi in Phocis, Thebes in Boeotia, and Athens in Attica; in northern Greece there was Larissa in Thessaly. The same rule applies, even more generally, to Asia Minor. The most ancient and important cities were all older than the Greeks: Miletus, Ephesus, Smyrna were centres of economic, political, and religious life long before the appearance of Greeks in the country. And the same thing is observable in Crete and in Rhodes.

The system, economic, social, and political, of these ancient Greek communities is described in the Homeric poems—the *Iliad* and the *Odyssey*, which probably were put together and assumed the form in which the Greeks knew them and in which they have come down to us, not earlier than the ninth or eighth century B. C. These poems describe the past, not the present : they refer to the time when the redistribution of Greek stocks was everywhere going on, and when not a few features of the Aegean past were noticeable in the life of the aristocracy. It is likely that separate legends concerning the heroes of the *Iliad* and *Odyssey* who took part in the conquest of Troy—legends which served as material for Homer—appeared in Aeolian Thessaly as early as the Graeco-Aegean period. They were worked over later in Aeolian Asia Minor and assumed their final form in one of the Ionian cities there. But in spite of the complicated origin of the poems, it is possible for us to pick out what is characteristic of the life of these Greek stocks in the earliest period of their existence.

We observe in them all nearly identical institutions, economic, social, and political—institutions connected in one way or another with the Aegean stage which the different parts of Greece passed through. The ruling element in all Greek cities of the Homeric Age is the aristocracy, embodied in certain families which play the leading part in the life of each clan. Each of these families traces its descent to a single founder—a god or hero ; and to one of them belongs the king who directs the clan in war and peace. Each family is subdivided into groups—*phratries* or brotherhoods—mainly of a military and religious nature. Next to these families comes the general population, divided from one another by occupation, place of residence, and social position. Some members of this plebeian class or *demos* own land, others, as tenants or serfs, till the land of their masters, others hire out their labour to employers, and others live in the city as artisans. There are also slaves, as is natural in a society where war is constant and clans are for ever shifting from place to place.

How this social system grew up we do not know. Greek tradition regards these ruling families as descended from heroes who came to Greece, some from the north and some from the east, and were closely connected with the most ancient myths about the gods and heroes. A considerable part of these myths was inherited by the Greeks from the Aegeans and Graeco-Aegeans who preceded them. This suggests that the aristocracy of Homeric Greece was composite—consisting partly of the military chiefs who led their clans to conquer Greece, and partly of the ruling families in the conquered kingdoms. So the lower classes also belonged partly to the conquering stock, and partly to the original population of the conquered country.

The system of land-ownership in ancient Greece corresponded with this division in the origin of the population. In some districts the conquerors probably found a large number of cultivators who had long been in serfdom to a group of the directing and ruling families; and this system they maintained. The origin of the system is unknown; but to the inhabitants of some districts, e. g. the Thessalians, Cretans, and Spartans, it seemed immemorial and was long kept up among them. Elsewhere, as in Attica and Boeotia, there were probably no serfs at the time of the conquest; and there the land was divided between the conquerors and the conquered, though no doubt the former, and especially the leading families, claimed the lion's share. The conditions on which the conquerors owned the land are not quite clear. In the Homeric poems we find joint ownership by a whole family existing side by side with individual ownership. Perhaps the former system is older, and the division of the clan into families was universal among the conquerors and only by degrees became a privilege of the aristocracy, to the exclusion of the population generally. In that case private ownership was probably a development of the earlier system. Persons expelled from the family for delinquencies and crimes, younger sons in a large family, or free men working for wages, could retire to the edge of the cultivated territory, and there clear away forest and drain marshes, till they made farms which belonged to them personally and to their families.

The farming of the Homeric Greeks consists mainly of agriculture and stock-raising; but horticulture, especially the growing of vines and olive-trees, is also developed by degrees. The last industry, however, is only in its early stages; Greece is still a land of cornfields and flocks. Cattle, swine, sheep, and goats are the common animals; to own horses is a privilege of rich and noble families. The stock owned by such families is sometimes very numerous, and a man's wealth is measured by his head of cattle. Little buying is done, and that unwillingly; most necessaries are produced at home. Domestic manufacture supplies not only food but also clothes, furniture, agricultural implements, and foot-gear. The whole family works: the men plough, sow, plant trees, reap, mow, look after the cattle, milk the cows and goats, make butter and cheese, go out hunting; the women spin, weave, embroider, wash linen and clothes, cook the food. Hard work is no humiliation and is not considered burdensome or oppressive. Odysseus boasts that he had no superior in reaping and mowing, that he could build a ship and his own bed and adorn it with cunning patterns. His old father Laertes enjoys working in the garden. Penelope, a queen, weaves every day in the palace with her maidens. Nausicaa, a king's daughter, washes the linen and clothes of her brothers. Work is done in the house by all the members of the household. The slaves and houseless hired servants form a part of the household as a social and productive unit. Though the hardest and most repulsive labour falls to their lot, yet they are neither machines nor animals. Like the other members of the family they come under the patronage and protection of the household gods, and humane treatment is secured to them by religion and custom.

Only the more difficult work is done by professional craftsmen who are paid for their labour. To build a ship or a good house or strong walls for a town is not a job that any one can do; and therefore the specialist is called in. The merchants play a conspicuous part. The mysterious knowledge of prophets, priests, and physicians is highly prized; so is the loud voice of the herald and the skill of the singer and musician.

Commerce, so brilliantly developed in the Aegean age, was not brought to a standstill even by political anarchy and the constant shifting of population. The Greeks were helpless without metals and could not get on without them; and they prized the fine productions of Eastern industry and art, so strikingly superior to the primitive objects that issued from their own workshops. The old routes to the sources of this wealth were never forgotten: the Greeks inherited this knowledge from the Aegeans. From the same source they learned

PLATE LVII
EARLY GREEK POTTERY

1. A LATE MYCENEAN VASE showing two sphinxes facing a geometrized tree in an heraldic position. About 1300 B.C. British Museum.

2. A COLOSSAL ATHENIAN VASE which was originally used as a grave monument. The skilful technique is similar to that of the Minoan times. The ornamentation consists of a series of geometric motives in various combinations. The figure-scenes are treated in the same geometric spirit and are very primitive. They represent a funeral with the deceased laid out on a bier, surrounded by his wife and children and by mourning women tearing their hair. The lower frieze shows warriors on foot and in chariots, some carrying large shields. Found near the Dipylon gate of Athens. 8th cent. B.C. Metropolitan Museum of Art, New York.

3. AN ATTIC VASE showing strong Oriental influence in its ornaments and in the figure of Centaur (half-man, half-horse), goat, plants and bird on the neck. Late 8th cent. B.C. Berlin Museum.

4. A RHODIAN JUG adorned with Oriental plant ornaments, geometric patterns and a row of naturalistic animals (wild goats). 7th cent. B.C. Private collection, England.

5. A CORINTHIAN POT showing the same Oriental type of ornamentation: floral ornaments and rows of animals (sphinxes and panthers). About 600 B.C. Metropolitan Museum of Art, New York.

The plate shows the general evolution of pottery in early Greece.

1. A LATE MYCENEAN VASE

2. COLOSSAL ATHENIAN VASE, VIIIth CENT. B.C.

3. ATTIC VASE, LATE VIIIth CENT. B.C.

4. A RHODIAN JUG

5. A CORINTHIAN POT

LVII. EARLY GREEK POTTERY

the art of navigation, the tradition of which had never died out in that sea. But their way of life was primitive, and what they could offer by way of exchange was not specially attractive. Their wealth was confined to slaves and a certain amount of raw produce. Hence their expeditions in search of what they needed were more like piratical inroads than commercial ventures. Plunder, not purchase, was the purpose that carried them to Asia Minor, Egypt, the coasts of the Black Sea and of Italy. But these descents were dangerous and not always profitable, while their need of metals was urgent. Thus trade was not entirely squeezed out by piracy, and the Phoenician merchants were welcome guests in Greece. Articles of Eastern production, whether stolen or received in the way of trade, were imitated locally; thus local industries were improved, and a profitable trade in such goods, either imported or produced locally, sprang up between the inhabitants of the coast and their neighbours who had no access to the sea.

The political system of Greece probably remained much the same as it had been in the Aegean age. The separate kingdoms were still ruled by a king, who relied upon the armed force of the clan and especially upon the richest and strongest of his companions in arms. The royal power was exercised by the man who was stronger, more ready-witted and intelligent, richer and better armed, than the rest. Wealth, knowledge, and the power to rule he inherited from his ancestors, as they had from the god; for all royal families, and noble families in general, traced their descent from heaven. But, for all his divine origin, the king was no eastern despot: not a god himself nor the master of his subjects, he was the head and leader of his clan and the chief of his heaven-descended family.

Round him are ranged other similar heads of old and distinguished families, who are his regular advisers and his brothers-in-arms. This small group has considerable wealth, and owes that wealth to their enterprise, activity, and excellent bodily training for warfare on land or sea. All the members of such families are well armed: each has a breastplate, a helmet and greaves, a good sword and spear, and a bow that carries to a distance. They drive into battle in chariots. They are perfectly skilled in all the niceties of single combat, by which battles are often decided. Hence the aristocracy are indispensable to the clan and kingdom, and their high position is secure. But the members of this group are all equals; they are all descended from Zeus just as the kings are; they are necessary to the king, as he is to them, and therefore are not merely his obedient servants.

So the plebeian members of the clan are not the slaves of the king and aristocracy. They acknowledge the superiority of their leaders; but their leader and king is not their owner, and they are not his slaves. An unsuccessful or degenerate king cannot reckon upon the support of the clan; and it is easy for some one else, richer and stronger, more intelligent and successful, to take his place. The life of a king is by no means a bed of roses, but full of danger. He reigns while he fights, and he fights with his own hands. If he is rich, it is because he knows where and how to direct the arms of the clan, and how to organize its economic and military life. He is surrounded by envy and hostility. Greek tragedy tells us of more than one sinister episode from the lives of these primitive kings. Horrible crimes and bloody revenges, murders and revolutions, were common in the kingdoms of the Homeric Age.

XIII

ANATOLIAN GREECE. ECONOMIC REVOLUTION IN GREECE IN CENTURIES VIII—VI B.C.

IT is one of the most notable features of the migratory epoch in Greece, that the redistribution of population at the end of the second millennium B.C. and beginning of the first drove out a number of clans, and parts of clans, first to the islands and then to Asia Minor. There is no doubt that the emigrants were exceptionally active, enterprising, and ambitious. Some of them, belonging to the old population of Greece, had been unable to defend their kingdoms against the new-comers, and preferred to emigrate rather than come to terms and submit to new masters. Others belonged to the invading clans and looked on Greece as merely a temporary halting-place in the course of their instinctive march to the south and east, whose wealth was well known to them. Both alike brought with them from Greece the habits of civilized existence which had grown up there, either from the continuous influence of Aegean culture, or from the independent development of that culture by the Graeco-Aegean population of southern and central Hellas.

The emigrants established themselves in Asia Minor by force of arms and seized the choicest parts of the coast, especially the fertile valleys at the mouths of the chief rivers —the Granicus, the Scamander, the Caicus, the Hermus, the Maeander—and lying near to the most convenient harbours. They found here conditions of life not very different from what they had left behind. The Anatolian coast had long been civilized: it kept up regular communications with the East and was familiar with the routes of maritime trade in the Straits, the Sea of Marmora, and the Black Sea. Hence when the Greeks had established themselves in Asia Minor, they could not help inheriting Anatolian traditions. The Late Aegean culture which they brought with them was bound to blend with the form which culture had already taken on the spot; Graeco-Aegean religion took over many Anatolian religious ideas ; and, finally, a mixture of blood between the immigrants and the local aristocracy was inevitable.

The system, social, economic, and political, which prevailed in these Anatolian kingdoms before the Greek invasion, is somewhat obscure. But from survivals of that system and from the picture of Troy drawn by Homer we must suppose the existence of fortified cities as the centres of political life. The king's palace was in the city, and his retainers lived there. The form of later institutions makes it probable that the chief sanctuary was habitually placed close to the city— a sanctuary consecrated to one of the many Anatolian Mother-Goddesses, who continued to be, in later times, the chief objects of religious worship in that country. The worship of the goddess was performed by a numerous class of priests, whose head was perhaps king of the city and adjacent territory. It is possible, however, that even at that early time there was a special chief priest, distinct from the king : we know that in some cults of the Great Mother the chief priest was bound to be a eunuch. Below this aristocracy of priests and warriors came the general population, who tilled the soil for their superiors. Peasants who lived on temple lands were counted as slaves of the god ; and so were the numerous workmen employed in shops belonging to the temple. The inhabitants of land not owned by the temple were, in all probability, serfs belonging to the king, his favourites, and his warriors. We must suppose that these relations were formed during the existence of the great Hittite Empire. It is probable that the fortified towns were built then, and that the aristocracy of the conquering Hittites settled down in them. But the temples and temple lands were older than the Hittites. Before the Hittites came, the king and the chief priest were probably identical.

When groups of emigrants from Greece conquered one of these kingdoms after another, their first business, no doubt, was to establish their power, define their relations to the local inhabitants, adapt themselves to new conditions, and defend their possessions against fresh swarms of invaders from the west. They were few in number and the place was strange. Hence the difficulty of their position dictated a policy of agreement in their dealings both with the local population and with subsequent colonists. It is certain that the Greeks spared the rich and powerful temples on the Anatolian coast.

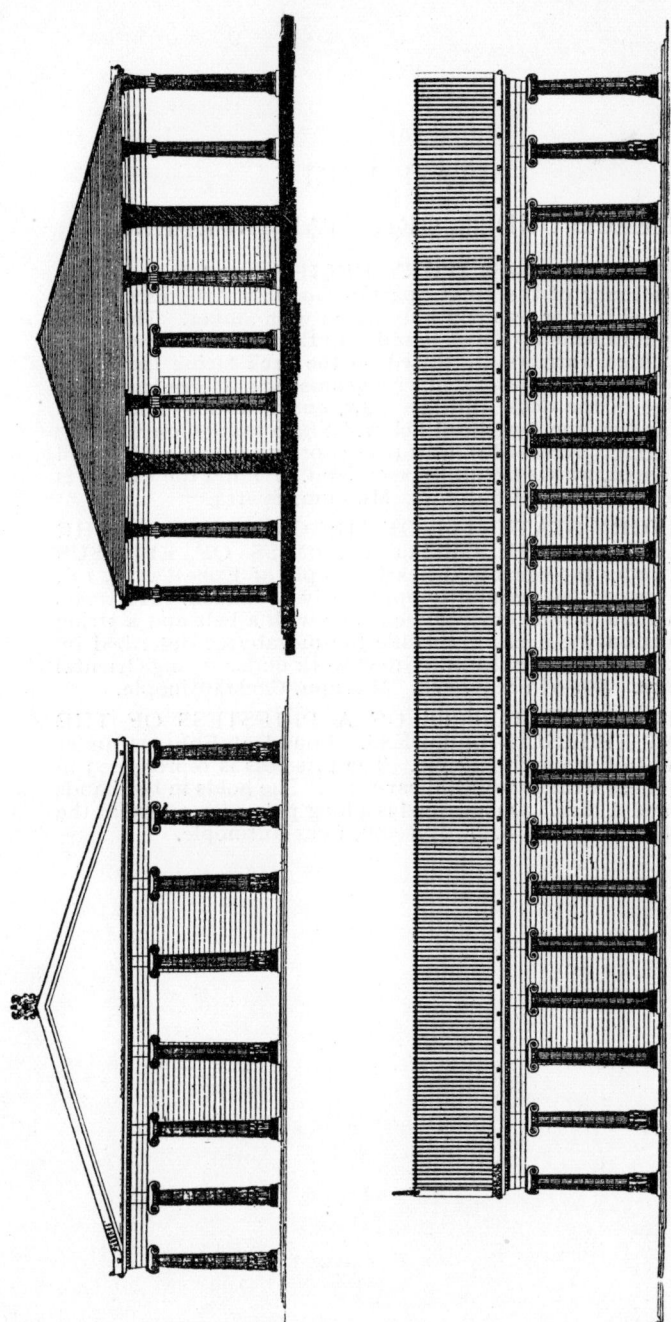

FIG. 17. *Restoration of the sixth-century temple of Artemis at Ephesus. After Hogarth.*

PLATE LVIII

GREECE UNDER ORIENTAL INFLUENCE

1. SEMICIRCULAR IVORY RELIEF found in Sparta in the sanctuary of the great Spartan Goddess Artemis Orthia. The raised border was probably inlaid with amber. The relief represents a warship about to sail. In the water are three large fish. Three warriors are seated on the deck facing the stern. Five round shields decorated with geometric patterns hang over the edge of the deck. Of the crew, one is fishing, another is crouching on the long beak below. Three sailors are working the rigging. A bearded man (the captain) is saying farewell to a woman, who is meant to be on land. Behind the woman is a large bird. About 600 B.C. Museum, Sparta.

2. IVORY STATUETTE OF THE OVERSEER OF THE TEMPLE OF THE GREAT GODDESS OF EPHESUS found under the ruins of the early temple of Ephesus (fig. 17). The overseer (*megabyzos*) is apparently a eunuch. He wears a high tiara, a long embroidered robe with a belt and a string of beads on the neck. Just like the megabyzos described by Xenophon in the *Anabasis*. Greek work under strong Oriental influence. 8th–7th cent. B.C. Museum, Constantinople.

3. IVORY STATUETTE OF A PRIESTESS OF THE GREAT EPHESIAN GODDESS. Found at Ephesus under the ruins of the early temple. The priestess is represented in a long dress with heavy gold ear-rings. She holds in her hands a jug and a dish. On her head is a long pole with a bird at the top. 8th–7th cent. B.C. Museum, Constantinople.

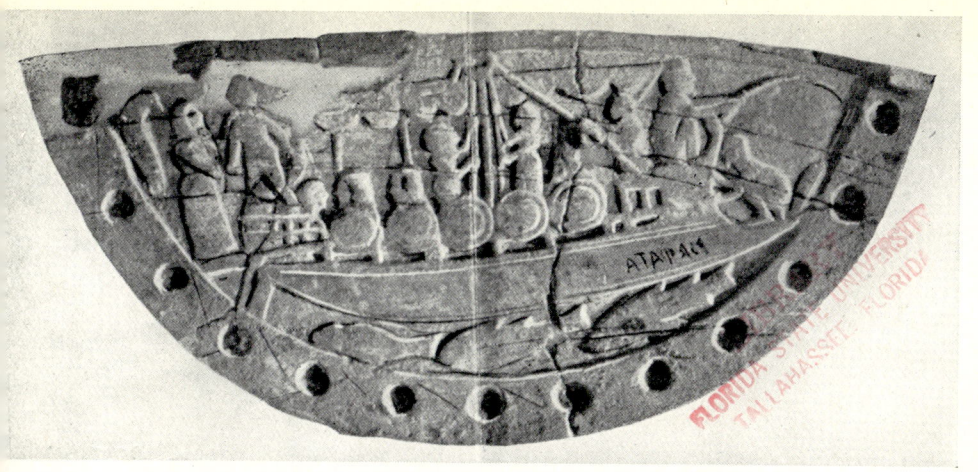

1. IVORY RELIEF FROM SPARTA.   SPARTAN SHIP

2. IVORY STATUETTE FROM
EPHESUS.   HIGH PRIEST

3. IVORY STATUETTE FROM
EPHESUS.   PRIESTESS

LVIII.   GREECE UNDER ORIENTAL INFLUENCE

The cult of the Great Goddess had been familiar to them even in Greece. Hence their first object was to secure for themselves the protection of the local goddess; and they secured it by maintaining her temple and the immunities of the temple. This is why we find later a large and wealthy temple of some local deity with a Greek name standing near most Greek cities in Asia Minor. If the deity was male, he was called Zeus or Apollo by the Greeks, and every goddess became Artemis. Some of the Greek names, indeed, had been taken over by the Greeks in their own country from the Aegeans or from the pre-Greek population of Hellas. This policy of agreement can be traced at Ephesus, for instance, with its famous temple of Artemis, or at Miletus, where a shrine of Apollo existed from the earliest times. In all probability the Greeks and the ruling aristocracy of the conquered cities combined to form a single dominating class, with the local population of tillers and herdsmen to work for them. It is probable that the Greeks seldom came into armed collision with fresh groups of settlers. Generally they admitted such freely to their kingdom, and sometimes guided them to districts in the neighbourhood that were ripe for the spoiler.

This conciliatory policy was the necessary result of the political situation, already described in Chapter VIII, in the eastern world at the beginning of the first millennium B.C. The first Greek settlers found the Hittite empire still strong and became its vassals. After its disruption its place was filled by the Phrygian kingdom, whose power and wealth were very well known to the Greeks—a fact sufficiently proved by the stories current among them of Midas, the great King of Phrygia who 'bathed in gold'. When Phrygia was broken by an invasion of Cimmerians, Lydia by degrees took its place. Lydia had withstood the pressure of these devastating marauders, who spread as far as the Greek cities in Asia Minor and destroyed some of them in the seventh century B.C. The kingdoms of Phrygia and Lydia had both kept up constant relations with Greece. Carrying on an extensive trade with the East, they resented the interposition of the Greeks between themselves and the sea, and therefore strove to add these Greek cities to their own dominions. The settlers had to exert themselves to the utmost to defend their independence. Under these conditions, every addition to the population of the Greek cities increased their power of resistance; and the better their relations with the native inhabitants, the less likely they were to be betrayed by them. In spite of all, they were unable to maintain their freedom against the last kings of Lydia, or against Persia, when she took the place of Lydia in Asia Minor. They were all obliged to submit to Cyrus and his successors. Their internal life went on unchanged; for, as we have seen, the Persians did not interfere with the institutions of the cities.

These institutions were partly brought from European Greece by the settlers and partly taken over from their predecessors in Asia Minor. The form of government in most of the communities was not monarchical. It is probable that the conquest of the Anatolian coast was effected under the rule of kings; but our historical tradition, at least, refers almost exclusively to a contest between different forms of popular government—aristocracy, or government by a few rich and noble families, and democracy, or government by the whole people. The aristocracy probably consisted of those descended from the original conquerors, who had shared among themselves the conquered land and the serfs connected with it. The lower classes would probably include later settlers, who lived chiefly by industry and trade; some of these would be rich and influential citizens, while others would be plain artisans, small traders, and labourers.

The economic life of the settlers was based mainly on agriculture and stock-raising. Further, the culture of the vine and olive was successfully carried on both in the Aegean islands and on the Anatolian mainland. The production of wine became a Greek speciality, notably in the islands, some of which, such as Lesbos, Chios, and Samos, are really inseparable from the mainland. The soil of these islands, less suitable for agriculture, is excellent for vines, which supply splendid wine, sweet, fragrant, and strong—exactly the qualities prized by the inhabitants of Hither Asia, where viticulture was unsuccessful and the produce of the grapes indifferent. A kindred industry was the production of olive oil, which gradually became, throughout Greece and in parts of the East, essential for diet, health, and illumination. Olive oil drives out butter; olive oil drives out lighted brands and torches, just as paraffin drove out tallow candles and has now given place to electricity. Thanks to her wine and oil, Greece, and especially Anatolian Greece, was able for the first time to produce wares which earned respect for her in the world's markets. The revolution in cultivation, caused by the development of these two industries, had a notable influence upon the life of the whole Greek world. In Greece one district after another took up these novelties. The islands and European Greece were soon able to compete successfully with Asia Minor, especially in the production of oil, and captured the markets in the east, south, and north.

Nevertheless, Asia Minor did not lose her predominance in the economic life of the Aegean coast. In districts occupied by Greece since the time of the Hittite dominion industry as well as agriculture was firmly established. The technical skill of Aegeans and Egyptians, of Mesopotamia and Phoenicia, found a refuge in the Anatolian temples, which were not merely religious centres, but also important centres of art and the scene of animated fairs. The conditions were specially favourable for the textile industry, and for work in wood and leather. The central plateau of Anatolia fed enormous flocks of sheep, which had long been famous for the exceptionally fine quality of their wool. The country was rich in minerals, and in the materials for vegetable dyes that could match the Tyrian purple extracted from marine shells. In metallurgy Anatolia was not inferior to the Transcaucasian kingdom of Van: gold she produced herself; and silver, copper, and iron were shipped to her along the coast from the land of the Chalybes on the southern shore of the Black Sea. This route had been familiar to the Carians even before the Greeks set foot in Asia. The natural wealth of the country had long been known, and to it was due the prosperity of the Hittite empire.

The Lydians, as the heirs of the Hittites, raised the industry and trade of the country to an unprecedented height. Nor were the Greeks on the coast left behind in the race. They soon acquired from the native inhabitants technical skill in the manufacture of textiles, and bettered the instruction. They learned to work in wood and leather, and to make fine jewellery of Anatolian gold after Lydian patterns. They brought with them into the country the ancient speciality of the Aegeans—the manufacture of excellent vessels of clay for oil and wine, and of lamps for illumination. They took full advantage of the high quality of Greek clay, especially clay from the islands; and their natural taste made these objects

PLATE LIX
ORIENTAL AND GREEK COINS

(*a*) ELECTRUM (PALE GOLD) STATER OF ASIA MINOR. On the reverse two oblongs incuse. Early 7th cent. B. C.

(*b*) GOLD STATER OF CROESUS, KING OF LYDIA. Foreparts of lion and bull confronted. R. Two incuse squares. 560–545 B. C.

(*c*) SILVER DIDRACHM OF SYBARIS IN ITALY. Bull to the l., head turned to the r. R. The same incuse. 6th cent. B. C.

(*d*) ELECTRUM STATER OF CYZICUS ON THE SEA OF MARMORA. Head of a man r. R. Incuse square of mill-sail pattern. 5th cent. B. C.

(*e*) SILVER STATER OF MILETUS. Lion's forepart r. R. Square incuse. 6th cent. B. C.

(*f*) SILVER STATER OF OLBIA ON THE BLACK SEA. Head of the goddess of fertility Demeter. R. Sea-eagle holding in its claws a tuna or a sturgeon. Name of the city inscribed. 3rd cent. B. C.

(*g*) SILVER DIDRACHM OF AEGINA. Sea-tortoise. R. Incuse square divided into eight triangles. 6th cent. B. C.

(*h*) GOLD DARIC OF PERSIA. The Great King running r. with bow and spear. R. Incuse square. 5th cent. B. C.

(*i*) GOLD STATER OF LAMPSACUS ON THE SEA OF MARMORA. Bearded head l. in laureate conic cap (the god Cabeiros ?). R. Forepart of a winged horse. Early 4th cent. B. C.

(*j*) TETRADRACHM OF ATHENS. Head of Athena r. R. The owl and the olive fruit. Abbreviated name of the city. 5th cent. B. C.

(*k*) SILVER STATER OF CORINTH. Helmeted head of Athena r. Behind the little figure of Victory (Nike). R. Pegasus (winged horse) running r. 4th cent. B. C.

(*l*) GOLD STATER OF PANTICAPAEUM ON THE BLACK SEA IN THE CRIMEA. Head of a god of fertility r. R. The Persian lion-headed griffin with spear in the mouth (military strength) and a corn-ear under its feet. First two letters of the name of the city. 4th cent. B. C.

(*m*) GOLD STATER OF PHILIP THE GREAT OF MACEDONIA (358–336 B. C.). Youthful male head r. R. Biga to r. and the name of the king. About 345 B. C.

(*n*) TETRADRACHM OF ALEXANDER THE GREAT (336–323 B. C.). Head of youthful Herakles with the features of Alexander r. R. Seated statue of Zeus the father of Herakles l. and the name of the king. About 325 B. C.

For the Greek coins of Sicily and Italy see vol. II, pl. XII.

All the coins are in the British Museum. Note the first attempts at coinage made in Asia Minor and the early and speedy spread of it in Asia Minor, Greece proper, and in the colonies. The Lydian, Oriental and the depending Greek coinage is mostly in gold and pale gold, the Greek almost exclusively in silver. Note also the great variety of types, mostly the heraldic emblem of the various cities or the figures of their chief gods. On the coins of monarchical states appears the figure or the head of the king. As various as the types are the standards used by the cities: Babylonian, Phoenician, Aeginetic, Euboean, Attic, &c. The chief monetary unit of the Asiatic coinage was the stater divided into thirds and sixths, the monetary unit of Greece was the drachma multiplied by two, four, &c. (didrachm—2 dr. ; tetradrachm—4 dr. &c.) and subdivided into obols (1/6 of the drachma) and into chalci (1/8 of the obol). Since the standards, the value of gold and silver and the prices of the products varied, no equivalents in modern coins can be given for these units.

LIX. ORIENTAL AND GREEK COINS

1. Clay statuette found at Tanagra in Boeotia. The statuette represents a Boeotian peasant ploughing his field. The workmanship, though primitive (note the almost geometric oxen), is unusually good. The group is full of life. Note the primitive plough, of which all the parts as we know them from literary sources (e.g. Hesiod) are perfectly recognizable. 6th cent. B.C. Paris, Louvre (Bull. de corresp. hell. xvii (1893)).

2. Clay statuette found at Tanagra in Boeotia. A street cook seated on a square stone, before him his transportable stove. He is cooking meat or pastry. Probably early 6th cent. B.C. Berlin, Lapiquarium.

3 and 4. Two clay statuettes found at Thebes in Boeotia. One represents a man playing the lyre with five strings. In his right hand he holds the 'plectrum', with his left he moves the strings. The second represents a man writing on a diptych, i.e. a double wooden tablet covered with wax. In his right hand the 'style'. Greek letters (three lines) are seen on the tablet. The letters give no sense. Is the musician a Homerist, and the writer a poet or a modest scribe. Early 6th cent. B.C. Paris, Louvre.

LIX A. GREEK LIFE IN THE VIth AND Vth CENTURY B.C.

masterpieces of decorative art, as unique in their kind as the Aegean vases. Their woven fabrics, leather and wood manufactures, gems, weapons, and metal articles for household use and furniture, were bartered for wine and oil from the islands and from Greece; and these, together with wine and oil of their own production, were exported to east and west. Thus the foreign trade of the Anatolian Greeks became very extensive, including Lydia, Greece, and the Greek communities now springing up in the west, in Italy and Sicily, and in the east, along the Straits, the Sea of Marmora, and the Black Sea. For the purposes of this trade, Lydia and the Anatolian cities now began, for the first time, to make use of coined money—gold, electrum (pale gold), and silver.

Trade and commerce became even more active when Persia took the place of Lydia in Asia Minor. I have shown already how the existence of the world-empire of Persia, together with the construction of roads and the introduction of a single monetary system for the whole kingdom, assisted the growth of trade in the Persian monarchy generally. When the Greeks became part of this empire, they made full use of all these advantages. Their merchants steadily squeezed the Phoenicians out of the Aegean world and drove them to the western part of the Mediterranean. From that time all the attention of the Phoenicians was given to the western district of the north African coast, where their colonies of Utica and Carthage prospered greatly; to the south coast of Spain, with its rich mines of silver, copper, and tin, including Tartessus, a wealthy centre of trade and industry; to the north-west coast of Italy, where the Etruscans were always faithful allies and regular partners in business, and where there was a considerable supply of metals—copper and iron; and to the south coast of the British Isles, from which they exported tin.

This commercial prosperity of the Greeks in Asia Minor affected their social and political life as well. In consequence of it their cities take the lead in the life of the country. Their growth is irresistible, and adventurers in search of gain crowd into them. A new aristocracy—the great merchants, the owners of vineyards and olive groves and of large factories —grows up beside the old landowning aristocracy and acquires a considerable part of the land. They own whole fleets of merchant vessels. Slave labour begins more and more to displace free labour in mercantile business. Slaves work in the vineyards and factories, and serve as rowers on the ships.

The growth of trade makes it necessary to seek new markets for produce; and the growth of urban population makes it impossible for each small community to find food for itself from its own territory. Therefore the new markets must provide not merely raw products for industry and more slaves, but foodstuffs as well. Corn, above all, is needed. Flocks and herds are too small to provide meat for every one; beasts are no longer bred for the butcher but for their milk and wool and their use in agriculture. Fish becomes a substitute for meat. The leading speculators therefore look

FIG. 18. *Paintings of a black-figured cup showing the hoeing and ploughing of the field, transportation of big jars (oil or wine), and other scenes of rustic life. Like others of this period the pictures are full of life and humour. 6th cent. B.C. Paris, Louvre. After Perrot and Chipiez.*

out for districts where fish can be caught in great numbers for salting. These conditions stimulate colonization in all places suitable either for the extensive production of cereals or for a fishing industry. The places which prove most suitable are—the shores and seaside valleys of Italy and Sicily; the coasts of the Balkan peninsula, the Straits, the Sea of Marmora, and the Black Sea; there was an inexhaustible supply of tunny-fish in that region, and of freshwater fish at the mouths of the Danube, the Dniester, the Bug, the Dnieper, and the Don. These coasts, known to the Greeks at an earlier date, were now populated by crowds of new Greek colonists—tillers of the soil and fishermen, not working for themselves alone, but also for an extensive and steadily growing market.

The economic revolution, beginning in the eastern part of the Greek world, soon made itself felt in the west also, and especially along the line of the coast. Here the disruption of the family had long been going on, and small separate holdings had been formed on the territory of each community. In some places this process resulted in a division of the land between the families of the predominating stock, who finally reduced the conquered native population to a state of serfdom. This was apparently the origin of the system in Sparta, Thessaly, and Crete. But in most of the other communities— we know more about Attica and Boeotia than about other countries—the disruption of the family resulted in the creation

FIG. 19. *An excellent black-figured cup signed by the painter Theozotos. It shows a herd of goats with the shepherds and the dogs. 6th cent. B.C. Paris, Louvre. After Morin-Jean.*

of two classes, a number of smallholders and a group of large landowners, members of the royal house and other great families. The life of the poor farmer, driven by the pressure of great neighbours to the hills and marshes, is excellently drawn for us in the poetry of Hesiod, a Boeotian peasant. He depicts a hard life on a little patch of land, with no brightness in the present, constant care for the morrow, and no hope for the future.

At this time the economic revolution already mentioned began. The demand for wine and oil forced the large owners to give up the production of cereals and take to vineyards and olive-trees. This industry is suitable for slave-labour, because it requires a number of hands directed by a single owner. The result was a great increase in the number of slaves. In the cities, as, for instance, in Athens and Corinth, trade and industry began to grow. Each city tried to produce for the market something individual and unknown to other cities; they improved their methods of production and the quality of their goods. Money now made its appearance. At first it was very dear, and it was possible to buy a quantity of goods for a small sum.

This economic advance did nothing to improve the position of the smallholder. Holdings became smaller and smaller. That vines and olive-trees were lucrative was proved by the

FIG. 20. *One of the votive plaques of which scores were found in a sanctuary of Poseidon, near Corinth, the great centre of commerce and industry of Greece in the 6th cent. Our plaque represents miners working in a pit. 6th cent. B.C. Berlin Museum. From 'Antike Denkmäler'.*

example of the large landowners; but capital was needed for this new enterprise, and capital was all in the hands of the merchants and manufacturers in the city. Money was dear, and high interest had to be paid for loans. It was necessary to borrow money for other purposes—to keep the farm going in bad seasons, to divide an inheritance and form new holdings, to clear away forest and drain marshes. All this tended to the wide development of the money-lender's business and the growth of debt among the smallholders. They were exposed to a terrible risk: if they could not pay, first the land and then the debtor himself and his family became the property of the creditor.

In the meantime, this expansion of industry, trade, and navigation opened up wide possibilities for ambition both within the city and beyond the borders of the country. Cities became crowded and new colonies were formed. All the Greek coasts took an active part in colonizing the west, north, and east. Miletus, Cyme, and Clazomenae throw off swarm after swarm; and colonists in considerable numbers go forth from Euboea and other islands and from the Peloponnese. Certain cities of European Greece come to the front in the world's markets. Thus the city of Chalcis in Euboea begins to work its copper mines intensively and to flood the market with the metal; Aegina takes advantage of its position between Asia Minor and Greece to become a great exchange for the barter of goods; and both cities begin to coin silver in abundance. Corinth, situated on the isthmus between the Peloponnese and Greece, becomes the centre of exchange with Italy: it pays better to break cargo at the isthmus than to sail round the stormy coasts of the Peloponnese. Corinth stirs up the Ionian islands and colonizes considerable parts of the Italian and Sicilian coast. Much the same part is played by Megara, a centre for the production of fine fabrics, and by Sicyon in Achaia, the best harbour in the north of the Peloponnese.

FIG. 21. *One of the votive plaques from Corinth (see fig. 20). The picture shows an oven for making pottery, one of the specialities of Corinthian industrial life. 6th cent. B.C. Berlin Museum. From 'Antike Denkmäler'.*

To the economic development of this age we must ascribe the Greek colonization of all sites on the Mediterranean coast that offered a prospect of reasonable prosperity for the settler. Italy and Sicily were soon covered with colonies, till the southern coast of Italy and the eastern half of Sicily were densely populated with Greeks. Tarentum, Sybaris, Croton, Epizephyrian Locri, Rhegium, Elea, Cumae, and Naples, in Italy; Agrigentum, Gela, Syracuse, Tauromenium, and Messana, in Sicily—all these cities gained wealth and power. Central Italy was in the hands of the Etruscans, who were themselves enterprising merchants and skilled agriculturists,

PLATE LX

GREEK VASES. 7TH–6TH CENT. B.C.

1. PROTO-CORINTHIAN JUG (made at Corinth or Sicyon) divided into four friezes. Two of them are shown in our figure. One represents two armies of hoplites clashing in battle. The shields of one army which are seen from the front side show the various armorial devices of the warriors. A fluteplayer between two rows of soldiers plays a military tune (remember the war-songs of Tyrtaeus). The other frieze consists of dogs running after animals. 7th cent. B.C. Villa Giulia, Rome. After *Antike Denkmäler*.

2. ARCHAIC POLYCHROME ' HYDRIA ' (WATER POT) from Caere in Etruria. The vases of this type were probably made somewhere in Ionia. The picture on the hydria represents the Greek legend of how Herakles came to Egypt, was captured by the Egyptian King Busiris, was brought to an altar and here broke loose and knocked down Busiris and his Egyptians. Some negroes are running to the scene of action to help their king. The scene is full of life and humour. 6th cent. B.C. Oesterreichisches Museum, Vienna. After Furtwängler-Reichhold.

1. PROTO-CORINTHIAN JUG.   GREEK WARRIORS

2. ARCHAIC HYDRIA FROM CAERE.   HERACLES AND BUSIRIS

LX. GREEK VASES.   VIIth to VIth CENT. B.C.

and therefore barred their coast against the Greeks. The
Phoenicians had seized western Sicily, and there the influence
of Carthage predominated. When the Greeks had occupied
the east coast, they were forced to begin a long and obstinate
struggle against the Carthaginians, who were supported by
the Etruscans. The east coast of Italy was peopled by Illyrian
settlers coming from what is now Dalmatia, on the east of the
Adriatic. These Illyrians were bold navigators and pirates
who defended the Adriatic against Greek penetration. In
Gaul things were different: that country had not yet been
occupied by the Indo-European stock of Celts from the north,
and its native inhabitants—Ligurians and Iberians, the first
conquerors of southern Gaul—welcomed the Greeks gladly.
Massilia became the centre of Greek colonization on the south
coast, and was supported against Phoenicians and Etruscans
first by the local population and then by the Celts. The
Greeks managed also to establish themselves here and there
on the south coast of Spain.

In the east the same process went on as widely. Here
the Greeks began by occupying all the eastern shore in the
north of the Balkan peninsula, with both banks of the Straits
and the Sea of Marmora. The peninsula of Chalcidice, with
its rich mines, was covered with Greek cities. A number of
large settlements grew up on the banks of the Straits and
the Sea of Marmora. Conspicuous among these were Cyzicus
on the south of the Sea of Marmora, and Byzantium and
Chalcedon on the European and Asiatic sides of the Bosphorus. Here began a perfect network of Greek stations for
trade and the fishing industry—Heraclea, Amisus, Sinope,
and Trapezus, south of the Black Sea; next, on the west,
north, and east coasts all the best fishing-stations at the
mouths of the Balkan and Russian rivers; a number of
harbours in the Crimea, along the Caucasian and Crimean
coasts of the Cimmerian Bosphorus, and on the Caucasian
coast. The chief settlements on the western shore of the
Black Sea were Apollonia, Mesembria, Tomi, and Ister. Tyras
stood at the mouth of the Dniester, Olbia at the mouth of
the Bug and Dnieper, Cercinites, Chersonesus, and Theodosia,
on the Crimean coast; Panticapaeum and Phanagoria on the
shore of the Cimmerian Bosphorus; Tanais at the mouth of
the Don; Dioscurias and Phasis on the Caucasian shore.
Behind these coast-towns, the Balkan peninsula and Asia

Minor were inhabited by Thracian tribes of Indo-European origin, who tilled the soil and raised cattle. In the steppes of south Russia, about 800–700 B.C., a powerful kingdom of nomad Scythians had destroyed the Cimmerian kingdom and taken its place; and the same relations existed between them and the Greek colonies on the Black Sea as between Persia and the Greek cities in Asia Minor. I have said already that the Scythians were another branch of the same Iranian stock to which the Persians belonged.

The wider the extension of Greek colonization on the shores of the Mediterranean and the Black Sea, the more fierce became commercial activity in Greece itself and Asia Minor. One new market after another was opened for trade and industry. The wealth of Greece increased by leaps and bounds. But this growing wealth brought with it changes in political and social life. Classes grew up, and with them class hatred and class contests. The aristocracy of birth found their superiority contested by the aristocracy of the purse; and both were threatened by the numbers of the labouring population. The lavish expenditure of the minority, the luxury with which they surrounded themselves, their exploitation of the masses, and the increasing number of slaves, were not passively endured: they begot active jealousy and hatred, which broke out in the shape of a cruel, and often inhuman, struggle between classes. Thus at Miletus the people were at first victorious and murdered the wives and children of the aristocrats; then the aristocrats prevailed and burned their opponents alive, lighting up the open spaces of the city with live torches. Read the verses of Theognis, and you will understand the intense hatred and mutual contempt which the opponents in this unending struggle felt for one another.

XIV

SPARTA: HER SOCIAL, ECONOMIC, AND POLITICAL SYSTEM

FROM the eighth to the sixth century B.C. the political and social development of Greece kept pace with her economic growth. As the chief feature in this development we must reckon the gradual formation and establishment of that peculiar Greek institution, the city-state. This process was not everywhere simultaneous or identical. Some parts of Greece retained for centuries the clan system of government and all the peculiarities of the Homeric Age; among these were Arcadia in the Peloponnese, the Aetolians in the north-west of central Greece, their neighbours, the Acarnanians, and the inhabitants of Epirus. Others developed urban institutions, proceeding from stage to stage in the course of this development. The essential peculiarity of the latter system is this—that political life is concentrated in one place. This place is the city: it is the religious, political, and economic centre of the district united round it and reckoned as territory belonging to the city. All the inhabitants of this territory are citizens and jointly organize the life, political, economic, social, and religious, of the whole community. Foreigners, serfs, and slaves are the only persons excluded from the ranks of the citizens. In these city-states political power passes by stages from the hands of the clan king to the body of citizens, first to a group of leading families closely associated with the king in his duties, next to all landowners, and finally to the citizens generally; the first of these stages is called 'aristocracy', and the last 'democracy'.

The whole body of citizens draws up rules for the behaviour of each citizen individually and of the associated body. These compulsory rules receive the name of laws. They represent the conscience of the community, and express the will of the citizens in each city. As in the East, law is the means by which notions of right and justice are conveyed to the populace; but there is a difference. In the East, law is a divine revelation vouchsafed to the king himself, unalterable and binding on every man because it is the god's command. But in Greece, though the law enjoys divine protection, it is not a divine revelation nor an unalterable rule of behaviour laid down once for all. In Greece laws are made by men. If a law offends the conscience of the majority, it can and must be changed; but while it is in force, all are obliged to obey it, because there is something divine in it and in the very idea of law. To break its injunctions entails punishment not only from men, the guardians of law, but also from gods. This rule of law in the city—of law created by the whole body of citizens—is one of the most characteristic features in the public life of Greece.

In any given territory the city has no rivals of a similar character. There may be other places where the population is concentrated; but these have no independent political life, and their inhabitants are citizens only of the central community. In private life the old clan divisions are kept up: each citizen is member of a brotherhood (*phratria*), family, and tribe (*phyle*); the last is a large subdivision of a clan. There is also a geographical division into districts (demes), each of which has some town or village as a centre. Within the limits of one clan there are often several city-states forming an alliance; one example is Boeotia. Such alliances are often due to certain cults common to a number of city-states, and then the alliances are called 'amphictyonies'.

Such is the general outline, identical in all city-states. But within the limits of this outline each city-state develops in its own way, so that endless varieties of the same system present themselves. We know most about the constitution of two city-states, which gradually step to the front of political life, and in whose history, as in a mirror, the whole history of Greece is reflected. I refer to Sparta in the Peloponnese, and Athens in central Greece. Next after these are ranked other states: Argos and Olympia in the east and west of Peloponnese; Messene beside Sparta; Sicyon on the northern shore of Peloponnese, not far from the Isthmus; Corinth on the Isthmus; Boeotia, including a number of cities, of which Thebes was the strongest and richest; Phocis, also including many cities which formed a religious alliance round the great shrine of Delphi; and Megara, close to Corinth and the nearest neighbour of Athens. A number of large cities, of which something was said in the preceding chapter, grew up in the islands nearest Greece, especially Euboea and Aegina. The chief cities of Euboea were Chalcis and Eretria.

Among these city-states a peculiar position is occupied by Sparta. In general, her constitution is not markedly different from the type just described. She is a community of citizens, such as we find elsewhere throughout Greece. But in this constitution there are a number of peculiar features, some of which, in a slightly different form, recur in Crete with its scores of cities and in the fertile plains of Thessaly; and these peculiar features gave Sparta her individuality and forced even Greek historians and thinkers to regard her system as exceptional.

Sparta forms the natural centre of Laconia, the fertile valley of the Eurotas. Of her early history we know little. In the Graeco-Aegean age Laconia was among the most powerful kingdoms of the Peloponnese. At the time of the Trojan war it was ruled by 'fair-haired' Menelaus and 'fair' Helen his wife, who, according to Homer, was the cause of the war. Homer represents Menelaus as one of the richest and most enlightened of Graeco-Aegean kings; and this is natural, because the Eurotas valley grows excellent crops, and the Laconian Gulf, into which the Eurotas flows, has several convenient harbours which offer the shortest passage from Crete to Greece.

According to tradition, Laconia was conquered by Dorians at the end of the Dorian invasion and became the chief stronghold of the Dorian stock in the Peloponnese. In the eighth century B.C., and again in the seventh, Sparta, having become the capital of Dorian Lacedaemon, carried on stubborn warfare against her neighbour Messene, to acquire the fertile lands owned by this richest district of the whole peninsula. About the second of these wars we get information in the verses of Tyrtaeus, a poet born at Athens, who played a prominent part in the victory obtained by Sparta over a federation of Peloponnesian states, which had helped Messene to assert her freedom. Excavations carried out by Englishmen at Sparta have shown that she was at this time a rich country and in the van of Greek civilization. Her culture is of that semi-oriental type, together with a considerable number of Aegean survivals, which is noticeable in all the progressive districts of Greece in that age.

Whether the peculiar features of the Spartan system had taken shape as early as this time we do not know. By Spartan tradition they were assigned to a single reformer, the divine Lycurgus. But we must certainly regard Lycurgus as a mythical personality. There is evidence that he was worshipped at Sparta as the sun-god. Still it is very probable that tradition is right, in considering the later system, as it is known to us from the sixth century to the fourth, as the result of one reform or of several carried out successively. We may suppose that these reforms were started amid the dangers and difficulties of the Messenian wars, when the inhabitants were forced to put forth all their strength in order to save the kingdom.

The chief peculiarity of the system is this. A group of families, numbering not more than 25,000 persons, living in Sparta and called Spartiates, dominated over a population which was nearly twenty times as numerous. Of this subordinate population one part were called Helots. The Helots lived on separate farms in the domain of the city and in some parts of conquered Messenia; their position was that of state slaves, and the families of Spartiates made use of their labour. Another part were called *perioeci* or provincials. They lived in Laconia and Messenia, in the cities and the domains belonging to the cities; they enjoyed personal freedom and a certain measure of self-government; but in military and political affairs they were entirely subordinate to the dominating group. We do not know how this system came into existence. It is very likely that there were serfs in Laconia during the rule of the Graeco-Aegeans, and that the Dorians took over the institution. Some of the Messenians were reduced to slavery after the Spartan conquest already mentioned. It is probable, also, that the status of the Perioeci was due to the conquest, at some date, of independent cities, which were then united to Sparta as allies but inferiors.

The reform, already mentioned, of the Spartan constitution did not create these two inferior classes. Its object was rather to change the organization of the ruling class, and to define precisely the relations between it and the two others. It was, from first to last, emphatically a military reform, aiming at a military organization for the ruling class, who were probably identical with the group of Dorian conquerors. Within this group the reforms were democratic and socialist;

it is the first attempt in history to introduce a thoroughgoing system of state socialism. The system retained some relics of the time when Sparta also was ruled by a group of aristocratic families. Thus the kings—two kings, one from each of the noble families of Europontidae and Agiadae—were still

FIG. 22. *Laconian black-figured cup. Two young soldiers are carrying on their shoulders a slain warrior. 6th cent. B.C. Berlin Museum.*

at the head of the government. There was also a body called *gerusia* or Council of Elders, consisting of thirty members including the two kings; these were drawn from a definite group of noble families and formed the chief instrument of government. But both these institutions were survivals. The real power belonged to the *apella* or popular assembly, consisting of all adult Spartiates who possessed full rights of citizenship and served as cavalry and infantry in the army.

They elected the Council; they also elected the Ephors (overseers), who were the real rulers of the country and guardians of the constitution. It is true that the Assembly voted only on business submitted to them by the Ephors and previously discussed by the Council—individual citizens had no power to initiate legislation; but nevertheless no important decision and no law was valid unless it was confirmed by the popular assembly.

The peculiarity of Sparta was not the constitution: it was the creation of an absolutely unique social organization, intended to increase the military strength of the country. All social and economic relations were based on absolute subordination of the individual to the state, and on the conversion of all the dominating class into a standing army, ready at any moment to take the field. Every adult Spartiate was, first of all, a soldier. Though he had a house and family of his own, he did not live there; and his days were not spent in providing for them or in productive labour, but entirely devoted to constant military training. Every adult Spartiate enlisted in one of the military divisions of the citizen army, and spent all his time in special clubs (*phiditia* or *syssitia*), where he was compelled to take part in the common meals. As all his time was taken up by his club life and training, the state relieved him of material cares by supporting him and his family. This was effected by giving to each man a considerable allotment of land together with one or more families of Helots. The Helots were bound to provide their owner and his family with a fixed annual quantity of foodstuffs, and to act as his servants in peace and on campaign. Part of the Helots' tribute went to pay the Spartiate's subscription to his club, and part to maintain his family. The allotment was the Spartiate's own property, and he might bequeath but could not sell it. If he could not force the Helots to produce from the land enough to pay his club-subscription, then the State took the land from him and transferred it to some one else. There was always competition for it, because the allotment generally passed to the eldest son, and the younger sons, who had been brought up like all other Spartiates, were constantly on the look-out for the chance of a vacant allotment. That part of the territory which was not divided into allotments was the private property of the Spartiates and might be bequeathed to sons or daughters.

From early childhood the Spartiate was trained to live for the State. A boy born in such a family, if he was pronounced healthy by a special board of elders, came at once under public supervision. Deformed or sickly infants, boys and girls, were exposed by the government, when they either died or were picked up by some charitable Helot. To the age of seven the children were cared for by their mothers and special government nurses. At seven the boys were removed from their families and entered a military group commanded by a young Spartiate; here they learned marching, gymnastics, music, and reading. They ate plain food cooked by themselves, and their bedding was of reeds gathered by themselves on the banks of the Eurotas. Gymnastic and military competitions were constantly held for their benefit. In order to develop independence, ingenuity, and dexterity, they were encouraged to steal and especially to steal food. But the unsuccessful thief was mercilessly beaten, not for stealing but for being found out.* The girls went through much the same course of physical exercise as the boys, in order that the future mothers of Spartiates might be healthy. After marriage they led a comparatively idle life in the houses of their husbands.

Morally and socially the position of the Helots was deplorable. They were in absolute slavery to the Spartiates. They were kept under constant supervision; and from time to time the most vigorous among them were murdered. The most wary and intelligent of the young Spartiates were constantly moving about in their midst as secret agents of the government, turning up where they were least expected and dispatching undesirable Helots without trial. The economic position of the Helots was not so bad: their tribute of produce to their masters was strictly defined and not burdensome; and they had full liberty to improve their land and accumulate savings. But the Perioeci were much better off. The Spartiates were forbidden to engage in trade and industry, and not encouraged to sell their landed property, even when it was not divided into allotments; and therefore the Perioeci monopolized all the business of the country. They worked the rich iron-mines of Laconia; they manufactured weapons for the army, implements for agriculture, and articles for domestic use. Trade also was in their hands exclusively. The Spartiates, however, disapproved of foreign trade, and tried to make home products satisfy their needs. They feared that foreign goods would bring with them new demands and new ideas. For the same reason they retained iron coinage as the only recognized medium of exchange, though of course it was not current outside Sparta. The Spartiates kept a watchful eye on foreign visitors and resorted freely to the deportation of undesirable persons from other countries. This spirit tended to isolate Sparta from the rest of the world: she became self-centred—almost exclusively an inland power with a strong army but without ships either for war or commerce.

Such was the organization, political, social, and economic, which made Sparta a powerful factor in the life of Hellas. She alone possessed a standing army, large enough, considering the conditions of that age, strictly disciplined, and excellently trained. The other city-states, living under different conditions, had at their disposal a mere militia of citizens who were mustered only at the beginning of military operations. This military superiority made a strong impression upon contemporary observers, and they were therefore inclined to idealize the Spartan system. And it did enable Sparta to develop an extensive activity for conquest in the seventh and sixth centuries B.C. After the subjection of Messenia this policy was first directed against the neighbouring states of Elis, Arcadia, and Argolis. Arcadia, after long warfare, concluded an alliance with Sparta, recognizing her headship in their joint political and military proceedings. The attempts of Argos to make herself the leading power in central Peloponnese brought her into collision with Sparta, and also armed Elis against her, together with Corinth and Sicyon, the cities on and near the Isthmus. In the sixth century Sparta was able to disarm Argos and deprive her of Cynuria, a district bordering on Lacedaemon, and to make Elis, Sicyon, and Corinth members of a Lacedaemonian military league directed by herself. This was the first considerable league of the kind in the history of the Greek nation; and it made Sparta the controlling power in Greek politics, especially in times of difficulty and danger.

XV

ATHENS AND ATTICA FROM 800 TO 600 B.C.

SIDE by side with Sparta there grew up by degrees in Greece between 800 and 600 B.C. another considerable political power, which was destined to take the lead for several centuries in the politics and civilization of all Greeks. This was the city-state of Athens, the economic and political centre of Attica. We have seen how Sparta deliberately chose to confine her activity to operations by land and recognized no industry but agriculture. Athens, on the contrary, at all times made full use of her favourable geographical position and the resources of her territory.

The peninsula of Attica runs out eastward to the sea. Her harbours are connected with the East by a chain of large and small islands, which stretch to the coasts of Ionia and Caria in Asia Minor. She is divided from central Greece and, in particular, from Boeotia by mountains which are fairly high but easily crossed. The island of Aegina in the Saronic Gulf forms a bridge between the Dorian world of the Peloponnese and the Ionian world of Attica and the islands. The Isthmus of Corinth cuts off Attica from the west, so that she has no direct and natural access to the Gulf of Corinth. The natural wealth of the country, though not great, was sufficient to support a considerable population. The valleys of the Cephissus and Ilissus, if tilled with care, produced fair harvests ; the valley of Eleusis was more fertile. The soil was everywhere excellent for growing olive-trees. The mountains grew fairly good timber, which made ship-building possible. With regard to metals, there were mines of silver and lead, but no iron and no copper. Good clay provided fine material for the potter. The quarries of the adjacent mountains, especially Pentelicus, afforded excellent sorts of stone, marble, and lime, so that building on a large scale could be carried on.

It was more important to Attica that here the conditions were favourable for uniting a considerable territory round one political centre. She forms a single geographical unit, whose most convenient exit to the sea is formed by the two harbours of Athens, Phalerum and the Piraeus. Thus it was possible in Attica, as in Sparta, to form a single kingdom with a rather large territory. A divided Attica would have remained what she was in the Graeco-Aegean age—one among many centres of civilization and political progress; united, she became the single powerful political centre of the richly gifted Ionian stock, possessing sufficient population and sufficient natural wealth to make her the mistress of all Ionians, just as Sparta endeavoured to become the mistress of all Dorians. We must remember that the rest of Ionia was broken up into small political units in the islands, and that its development and expansion in Asia Minor were cramped first by Lydia and then by Persia. Political rivalry with Attica was impossible for any of the other city-states in central Greece; Boeotia was divided into a number of cities and had no satisfactory outlet to the sea; Corinth was a purely commercial power, her territory was always negligible, and she had also powerful rivals at her very doors—Megara on the Isthmus, and Sicyon on the north coast of the Peloponnese.

In Attica the process of unification was unlike the corresponding process in Sparta. One reason for this may be that there was no class of serfs as a basis of economic life in Attica of the Mycenean age, and that the new order was established, not as a result of conquest, but by evolution and agreement. At all events, instead of foreign invasion and the reforms, military and social, of Lycurgus, we find a transaction of uncertain date, connected with the name of a mythical king, Theseus, and called by the Greeks *synoecismos* or *sympoliteia*. It is quite possible, in Attica as in Sparta, that the mythical name conceals the real name of some great statesman belonging to the eighth century B.C. But the transaction itself was this—that the separate communities of Attica, each of which had possessed its own individuality and its own centre for politics and finance, now agreed to form a single kingdom, with Athens for the single centre of political, economic, and religious life. It is not known whether this measure was preceded by a gradual rise of Athens which proved her superiority in war and peace to the other communities of Attica. But it is highly probable that this concentration, which was resorted to later in several parts of the Greek world, was due to several causes—the gradual destruction of the kingly power and the formation of a strong aristocracy in each of the separate communities, and the certainty that these aristocrats must join forces if they were to cope with domestic and foreign dangers. At any rate, tradition is

FIG. 23. *The palace of Thetis, the mother of Achilles, as represented on the so-called François vase (Attic black-figured). The palace shows the typical forms of a 'megaron' (comp. fig. 1 and pl. LXI). 6th cent. B.C. Archaeological Museum, Florence. After Furtwängler-Reichhold.*

unanimous that the change in Attica was gradual and peaceful, and free from the revolutionary convulsions familiar to the Ionian world of that age.

We know little about the constitution of Attica after this concentration was carried through. But it is probable that the class of large landowners, who at that time were also traders and pirates, took the lead in political and economic life. The rulers of the community, chosen from among the members of the ruling aristocracy, were three in number: first, the king who was also the chief priest; secondly, the polemarch who commanded the armed forces of the kingdom; and, thirdly, the archon, the representative of civil authority. With these were associated six junior archons, called *thesmothetae*, as judges and guardians of the law. The nine chosen rulers of the state, or magistrates, to use the Roman term, did not form a single corporate body. The king, who had once been the head of the administration, gradually began, from about 650 B.C., to lose all political importance, retaining only his religious functions. Power was concentrated almost entirely in the hands of the polemarch and archon. At the same time the tenure of all these archons or magistrates, which had been permanent, became limited. Eventually it became the custom at Athens for all the representatives of authority to hold office for one year.

The magistrates were elected, laws were passed, and perhaps decisions on war and peace were taken, by the *ecclesia* or popular assembly, which consisted of all citizens with full rights, that is, all those who formed part of the citizen army and fought in defence of the country. Together with the magistrates there acted a council of elders, the chief body of the state for political, religious, and judicial business; it was called the Areopagus after the hill on which its meetings were generally held, and was filled by representatives of the noblest families and, probably, by ex-magistrates.

Together with these gradual changes in the system of government there grew up a new political and social division of the population. The ancient division into four tribes, phratries, and families was retained; but a further redistribution was made into three social and economic groups. The first of these contained the large landowners, the second the traders and artisans who lived in the city, and the third the smallholders. At the same time the political rights and military duties of each citizen began to be reckoned not by his birth but by his property and income. The aristocracy became a timocracy. The necessity of creating a larger and stronger army was probably the cause of this innovation. The land-owning aristocracy, who had originally borne the whole burden of defending the country, was inclined to shift a part of this burden to the shoulders of other well-to-do citizens, and to concede to them in return a part of their own political rights. This new division for military and civil purposes was founded on the comparative wealth of various classes in the state—wealth connected with the possession of land. The highest class consisted of persons called *pentakosiomedimnoi*, those landowners who drew from their lands an annual income of not less than 500 *medimni* (700 bushels) of corn; the second class contained those whose income from

FIG. 24. *Black-figured water-pot (hydria). The picture shows Athenian women filling their water-pots at a public fountain and chatting. 6th cent. B.C. Paris Louvre. After Perrot and Chipiez.*

land was not less than 300 *medimni*. These two classes served in the army as cavalry: when summoned, they had to appear on horseback and wearing the full equipment of the hoplite or heavy-armed foot-soldier; and as their horses were not used in battle but merely for mobility and to pursue a beaten enemy, they were, properly, mounted infantry. The third class consisted of those whose income was not less than 200 *medimni*; they were called *zeugitae*, and served in heavy armour but had no horses. Political rights were confined to these classes. Below them came the *thetes*, who lived by the labour of their hands and possessed no definite and regular income; some of them served as rowers in the fleet and perhaps carried the baggage of the army.

The financial revolution described in Chapter XIII affected Attica as well. There also, owners of vineyards and olive-groves made their appearance, the class of traders and artisans grew larger, and the population of the city increased steadily. In this new capitalistic society the position of the smallholder became more and more irksome. Money is needed for improvements, for additions to stock, and for the transition from corn to vines and olives; and when his sons set up for themselves, money is needed to stock their holdings. At the same time money is scarce and dear, while the law regarding debt is extremely harsh, and its application rests with the upper classes, the very people who own capital and lend money. Thus the smallholder is ruined and deprived not only of his property but of his freedom also by the law of debtor and creditor. Many escape this fate by becoming tenants of land which once belonged to them but is now owned by representatives of the wealthy classes. The conditions of such leases are very harsh: the tenant is entitled to no more than a sixth of the produce. The discontent of the lower classes grows steadily and takes an acute form. They seek and find men to lead them and organize them for the struggle against the dominant classes. Their war-cries are a fresh division of the land and the abolition of debt. In order to carry out this programme, an armed rising takes place, directed by the leader, who attempts, with the support of the masses, to concentrate in his own hands military and civil power. Disturbance of this kind was especially rife throughout most of the Greek world in the seventh and sixth centuries B.C. In many places the acuteness of class-warfare called forth 'tyrants' or 'judges' (called *aesymnetae* by the Greeks), whose business it was to smooth down extremes in either direction, to create a new and more democratic system, to devise and establish in writing the basis of a constitution and of civil and criminal law. They met with stout opposition from the aristocracy, especially the old aristocracy of birth and landed possessions; but they often found supporters, not only among the lower classes who possessed no political rights, but also among the middle class and the new aristocracy of commerce and industry. It is not without cause that this period in Greek history has been called the age of revolution and tyranny.

The history of Attica, during the course of these developments in the Hellenic world, is marked by one distinctive feature. For there the transition from one stage of civil government to another was accomplished more quickly and more peacefully, with none of those atrocious convulsions which make the life of many contemporary communities resemble an almost uninterrupted conflagration. In the course of a single century Attica made a clean sweep of her ancient institutions connected with the clans and families, and, for the first time, created a democratic state on the basis of a carefully considered legal system—a system no less logical, but more flexible, than the military system of Sparta. It is a remarkable fact that the constitutional changes of this period are everywhere associated with men of genius and brilliant personality—the first professional politicians, whose mythical prototype in Attica is the royal reformer, Theseus.

The dawn of political development in Attica reveals another semi-mythical figure in the lawgiver Draco, to whom legend attributed the oldest written code of law. These laws are of interest, because they testify to the severity of the early criminal legislation which prevailed in an aristocratic Greek community; but it is hardly possible to believe, on the authority of late witnesses, that Draco was really the author of the first written constitution of Athens. Still we may well believe that party conflicts between the classes grew more and more acute in Attica, and that repeated attempts were made to set up a tyranny. There were many models to copy from: either at this time or earlier tyrants were ruling in Asia Minor, Italy, and the islands, and also nearer home—in Megara, the rival which contested with Athens the possession of the prosperous island of Salamis, and in the commercial cities of Corinth on the Isthmus and Sicyon on the north coast of Peloponnesus.

The great social and political reformer, Solon, is the first really historical name in Athenian history. Men of action, of this type, are common in Greece in the late seventh and early sixth centuries B.C. They are prominent and able representatives of noble families, men who have assimilated the results of Ionian culture, thinkers and rationalists, who believe in the omnipotence of government and statesmen to change social and economic relations, and who realize the effect of eloquence and literary propaganda. They are convinced that the causes of the never-ending class-conflict are clear to them, and consciously endeavour to reform out of existence that which they reckon as the root of the evil. With this object in view, many of them were forced to resort to armed force, and to make themselves tyrants, while others attempted to gain the same end by the peaceful method of legislation. Solon belonged to the latter class. Concerning his achievements even ancient writers knew little more than we do. Some writings by him, half-literary and half-political, have been preserved—short poems, which depict vividly the condition of Attica and speak of their author's reforms. Tradition associated with his name some essential features of democracy at Athens. A number of laws written and placarded on wooden tablets were attributed to him with perfect justice; but a number of anecdotes, of doubtful historical authenticity, were piled by degrees upon the foundation of this fact. This composite tradition explains the different views taken even by ancient historians concerning the nature and extent of his reforms.

Nevertheless there is no difference of opinion on the main and essential points. Solon was elected archon in 594 B.C. The course of historical development had made the archon at this period the virtual master of political affairs. As archon Solon at once brought forward a series of reforms, upon which the future progress of Athens was built up. His main achievement was to mitigate the severity of the law which then decided the relation between debtor and creditor in Attica. Allotments of land which had been mortgaged to the rich were restored to the owners, and the debts cancelled. Freedom was restored to those who had lost it for non-payment of debt. It was made illegal to advance money on the security of land or of the landowner's person. Serfdom and slavery due to debt were abolished for all time coming. The amount of land that any individual might own was definitely fixed. The export of corn from Attica was forbidden; olive oil alone might be exported. The purpose of this last measure is obvious: it was to make speculative cultivation of arable land unprofitable and to simplify the transference of such land to smallholders. It is true that these reforms pleased neither of the contending parties: the poor hoped that all the land would be divided afresh and all debts cancelled, while the aristocracy lost heavily and had to seek new outlets for the investment of their capital. But, all the same, Solon had done a great work. The class of small landholders had been strengthened, and measures taken to maintain their strength. On the other hand, the capitalists' wealth was turned into a more profitable channel: the growth of olive-trees for the export of oil was stimulated, and trade and industry in general were encouraged. About this time Athens began to strike her own coinage and brought chaos into order by introducing a uniform system of weights and measures throughout Attica.

On the basis of these social and financial reforms Solon built his constitution. The chief innovation here was the admission of the lowest class, or *thetes*, to the citizen body, and so to a place in the popular assembly and in the army. A new and important institution was the *Heliaea*, a law-court, in which any citizen could be a judge, membership being determined by ballot in which every class of citizens, from the *pentakosiomedimni* to the *thetes*, could take part. Thus three most important functions of government—the election of magistrates, legislation, and the supreme control of conduct—were handed over to the whole body of citizens, irrespective of the class to which each belonged. On the other hand, the privileges of the highest classes were maintained: the magistrates, whose number and duties were unchanged, were still elected from the two highest classes exclusively. The Areopagus, or council of elders, retained its importance, but a new institution was added to it. This was the council of four hundred, with one hundred members chosen from each of the four tribes; it prepared the business which was afterwards discussed and disposed of by the popular assembly.

Though the reforms of Solon did not end the strife of classes, they paved the way to a victory for the popular party. The years that immediately followed his archonship were full of this strife. But it should be noted that Athens nevertheless was strong enough to begin a spirited foreign policy. She engaged in a struggle with Megara for the possession of Salamis; and there is no doubt that she also wished to claim a share in the commerce between the different parts of Greece. This foreign war, in which all the citizens, including the *thetes*, took part for the first time, had two important consequences. It was the first time that Attica interfered in the affairs of other Greek states, and imitated Sparta in trying to rule her neighbours and extend her territory at their expense. A collision with Sparta, who had been consolidating her leadership in the Peloponnese, was now inevitable; and the question was raised—who was to be the controlling power on the Isthmus, the bridge between central Greece and the Peloponnese? and who should take the lead in trade with the west? Secondly, this first considerable campaign revealed the importance of including every citizen in the army and of entrusting entire command to one capable general. Successful in the struggle against Megara, the Athenians owed the conquest of Salamis and Nisaea, the port of Megara, to the skilful leadership of Pisistratus, one of their own body. When Pisistratus ceased to lead them, all their former achievements came to nothing, and the dispute about the Isthmus was decided against the interests of Athens.

Pisistratus was undoubtedly a prominent figure in Athenian history, not less important, and perhaps even more important, than Solon himself. Solon was a lawgiver and reconciler; Pisistratus was a military commander, the leader of a definite party, and a tyrant. After his success against Megara he came forward as the champion of the smallholders, and in 561–560 B.C. by their aid seized power at Athens. The aristocracy then united with the class of merchants and traders and forced him to go into exile for a time. But after some years' banishment he returned to Athens, supported by the tyrant of Naxos and some Thessalian troops. He was cordially received by a considerable body of the citizens, who were weary of party strife and sore at their discomfiture in the struggle with Megara. This time he remained at Athens as the supreme ruler of the state until his death in 528 B.C., when he bequeathed his power to his sons, Hippias and Hipparchus. They ruled for eighteen years.

The rule of Pisistratus may be considered as a turning-point, in many respects, in Athenian history. His tyranny did not destroy a single one of the democratic foundations which Solon had laid. His power was a mere superstructure on the top of Solon's constitution. The power of the aristocratic families was weakened, partly because most of them were banished and their land distributed among poor citizens, partly because the aristocratic bodies, the magistracy and the

Areopagus, lost influence entirely and began to die away, thus clearing the ground for new democratic institutions in the future. When the tyranny fell and it was necessary to reconstruct public life, that life was not founded on a discredited and enfeebled aristocracy, but on a democracy strong and conscious of its strength. And the old organization by families and clans had now given place to a new system

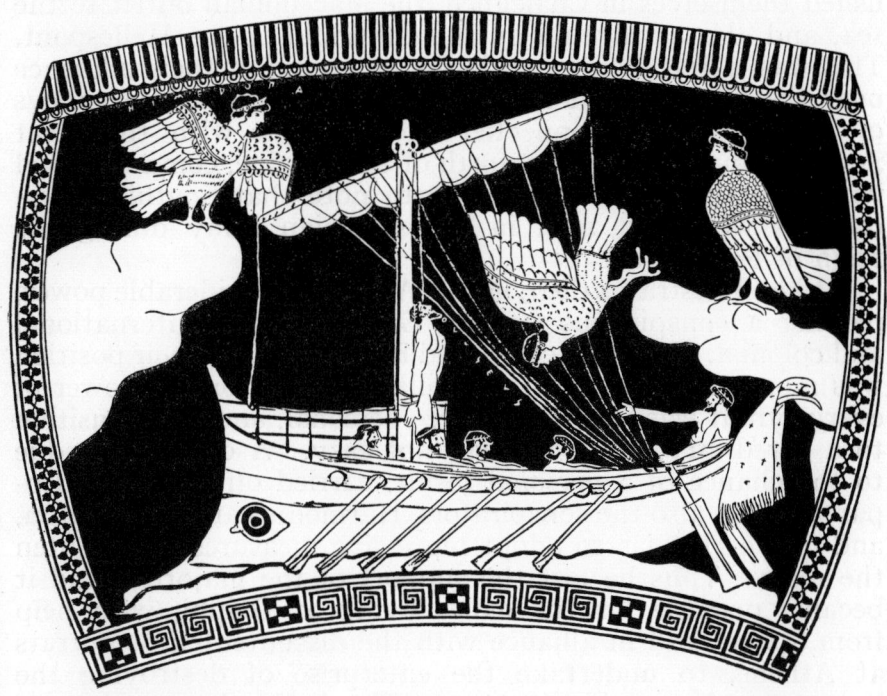

FIG. 25. *Red-figured vase. The picture shows Odysseus on his ship tied to the mast and the Sirens on the rocks singing him their alluring song. The ship gives a good idea of early Greek merchant ships. Early 5th cent. B.C. British Museum.*

introduced by Pisistratus, by which the people were divided into *naucrariae*, districts for the purpose of military service and taxation.

The foreign policy also of Pisistratus had an important effect upon the future development of Athens. A powerful fleet and considerable improvements in the army assured to Athens a voice that must be heard in Greek politics. From this time onwards the strongest Greek powers of the day—Boeotia, Thessaly, and, above all, Sparta—had to reckon with

Athens. Pisistratus, however, did not carry on a policy of conquest in southern and central Greece, satisfied with the safety from attack assured to him by his strong army and fleet. The sole object of his foreign policy was to make Athens powerful on the north-east coast of the Balkan peninsula, and on the shores of Macedonia, the Hellespont, and the Bosphorus. Thanks to him, the Athenians established themselves in Chalcidice, the Macedonian outlet to the sea, and also at Sigeum on the threshold of the Hellespont. This was a first step towards the extension of their influence over the Thracian Chersonnese, by which the fertile valleys of Thrace, closely connected at that time with the great Scythian kingdom on the north of the Euxine, communicated with the sea. It is interesting to note that Scythian mercenaries were first seen in the Athenian army during the reign of Pisistratus.

When Pisistratus died, he left Athens a considerable power, playing a conspicuous part in Greek politics, international and colonial. His sons continued his work; but their position was more difficult, as in all similar cases. For the power of every tyrant was in a high degree personal, and the transition to a hereditary monarchy was not easy. A conspiracy, due to the chance of a personal insult, carried off not only Hipparchus but also the conspirators, Harmodius and Aristogiton, and drove Hippias to adopt repressive measures and tighten the reins. Thus he lost the support of the majority, and it became possible for the exiles living at Delphi, with help from Sparta and in alliance with the discontented democrats at Athens, to undertake the enterprise of destroying the tyranny and restoring freedom. Thanks to the exertions of the Alcmaeonid family, the attempt succeeded: Hippias withdrew from Athens; and it became a question what shape this freedom, gained by an alliance between aristocrats and democrats, should assume.

Just as before the reforms of Solon, again a series of civil commotions preceded a radical reform carried out by Cleisthenes, one of the Alcmaeonidae. Cleisthenes supported an advance towards democracy. The aristocrats opposed his policy tooth and nail and called in assistance from Sparta; but this interference merely added to his strength and popularity. After a short occupation the Spartans were expelled from the capital, and Cleisthenes could begin his reforms and carry them through without interference from without or opposition from within.

The work of Cleisthenes differs from that of Solon and Pisistratus in this respect: he did not attempt to tinker at the existing system, but carried out a complete scheme which he had thought out in detail. His governing idea was to create a well-proportioned and completely co-ordinate state, based on the political equality of all the citizens, and on the participation of all in the working of the government machine. Existing institutions were neither destroyed nor abolished, but their life left them and entered into the new political bodies created by Cleisthenes.

The radical innovation due to the statesmanship of Cleisthenes was that he systematically introduced into the constitution the representative principle. At the same time the political centre of gravity was shifted to the representative bodies, and especially to the *Boule* or Council of Five Hundred, which became the main lever of the government machine. For this purpose Cleisthenes began by changing the whole system by which the citizens were classified, and created electoral districts of entirely new composition. The former division into tribes and phratries, though it continued to exist, lost all political importance. In place of these, the demes, or parishes grouped round the villages and small towns of Attica, became the chief electoral unit and the centre for the population in each place. All persons domiciled within the deme were registered as belonging to it, and the franchise was conferred upon every person so registered. The capital itself was divided into demes. It was no longer obligatory to belong to a family or phratry or one of the old tribes. The demes were divided, according to their locality, into three groups: the city of Athens, the coast, and the plain of Attica with the hills. In each of these groups one of the main divisions of the population naturally outnumbered the rest: the commercial and trading element predominated in the city; sailors, dockyard hands, and fishermen on the coast; and landholders, large and small, in the interior of the country. Each of the above-mentioned groups was divided into ten *trittyes* with several demes in each; and three *trittyes*, one from each group, formed a tribe, so that ten new tribes were created out of the thirty *trittyes*. In this way each of the three social classes was represented in each tribe.

These tribes became the foundation of all political and military activity. Each of them elected a military unit, chosen from its own members and commanded by an officer called *strategus*. The popular assembly voted by tribes; and the tribes elected the magistrates and the members of the judicial assembly and Council of Five Hundred. Within the tribe each deme had a local activity of its own, with an elective administration, a demarch, a local council, and a budget. The authorities attended to the local business, the local cults, and the local order. They were obliged to supply to the state lists of electors and tax-payers. The tribes also had representative bodies, with functions similarly limited. But the competence of the demes was strictly limited to local business of secondary importance. All important matters, even of local interest, were discussed and decided at Athens by the central assemblies. Attica was so small that no considerable municipal activity could find room beside the activity of Athens.

The demes and tribes were thus organized on purpose to secure an exact representation of the citizens in the Council of Five Hundred, the governing body of the whole country. This first endeavour to govern by means of a House of Representatives is highly instructive. Each deme, in proportion to the number of citizens on its roll, chose candidates for the council, and from these candidates the members of council were elected by lot, fifty in all being taken from each tribe. The existing House reviewed the moral qualifications of new members and rejected the unworthy. The council was not merely a deliberative body associated with the executive power, which was still retained by the board of the nine archons: it was a governing body, dealing with finance, war, and foreign policy. The magistrates, except in the case of some religious and judicial functions, were merely the executants of its decrees. Closely associated with the council were the *colacretae* and *strategi*, two boards now added to the magistracy; the former had to do with finance; each of the latter commanded ten companies of militia. The Council of Five Hundred was naturally too numerous a body to deal with ordinary business. Therefore such business was undertaken normally by a quorum, called a prytany, of fifty members, who held office for a tenth of the year under a chairman who sat for one day. Part of the prytany remained on duty day and night, eating and sleeping in the *Tholos*, a round building provided for the purpose.

Legislative powers did not belong to the council: laws

FIG. 26. *Reconstruction of the famous throne of Amyclae (near Sparta) described by Pausanias: the foundations have been excavated recently. The early sanctuary consisted of the grave of a hero (Hyacinthos), and on it an archaic statue of Apollo. Later a famous Ionian artist, Bathycles (6th cent. B.C.), built round the early sanctuary a majestic throne richly adorned with sculptures. After Fiechter.*

were discussed and passed at meetings of the *ecclesia*, the popular assembly. Judicial authority remained with the *heliaea*, the court of popular representatives, elected by the demes on the same principle and by the same method as the council. The magistrates—the nine archons, *colacretae* and *strategi*—were elected as before from the first two classes only, i. e. from the well-to-do citizens. This limitation of democratic ideas was dictated by necessity; for the state did not pay the citizens for the discharge of their public duties, nor even reimburse them for their incidental expenses. The army also definitely assumed the character of a national militia. Each tribe provided a regiment of infantry and a squadron of cavalry commanded by elective officers, called *taxiarchi* and *hipparchi*. The polemarch remained as a survival. Each of the ten *strategi* commanded the army in turn. The question of the navy, left untouched by Cleisthenes, was solved at a later date.

The reforms of Cleisthenes completed the creation of a strong and solidly organized Athenian state. While aiming at the same object as Sparta, Athens had attained it by different means. Her government was not based, as at Sparta, on the predominance of a single class over a subordinate population: she relied on attracting the whole body of citizens to the business of government; and she excluded none except the slaves and the foreigners resident at Athens, called *metoeci*. When the new system was created, these two groups formed a comparatively insignificant minority of the population, and it was not till much later that the question of their position became acute. This Athenian principle of government deserves to be called democracy, because the real master and ruler of the country was the people.

The constitution of Cleisthenes began working in 502 B. C. It did not, indeed, end the strife of parties or the uneven distribution of wealth. Both these evils remained, and there were conflicts, sharp and sometimes prolonged. But their acuteness was mitigated and almost abolished by the attitude of mind due to these reforms. Every citizen learned to regard the government not as an external and alien thing, but as something identical with the body of citizens, and each justly looked upon himself as a working part of the government machine. No Greek took such pride as the Athenian in his city and country; and nowhere in Greece was the consciousness of citizenship or the feeling of true patriotism so strongly developed.

XVI

CIVILIZATION OF GREECE IN THE SEVENTH AND SIXTH CENTURIES B.C.

THE seventh and sixth centuries B.C. were a great creative epoch in the history of human civilization. Those laws of thought, political organization, and art, which mark out European civilization generally and distinguish it in many important respects from the civilizations of the East, began to take shape at this time. The chief peculiarities of Greek culture, both then and later, were its individual, personal character and its boldness—the unbounded hardihood, one might say, with which it stopped at nothing, and its entire independence of religion, though the latter maintained a separate existence beside it.

But together with this bent towards individualism, we observe another trait which is easily reconcilable with it. Throughout Greek history we find among all Greeks an increasing consciousness that they belong to one nation and form one body; and this unity was indicated, not only by a common religion and a common language, but also by a common civilization, more or less identical among them all. This national feeling was powerfully promoted by colonization and the trade which kept pace with colonization. The tie that bound a colony to the Greek world was never broken: the colony always felt herself the true daughter of her mother city and resembled her almost exactly in all respects. On the other hand, the deep gulf that separated the Greek view of life from that of their new neighbours was realized with exceptional clearness by the colonists.

Let us begin by dwelling for a little on the second of these traits, the feeling of nationality. In the dawn of Greek history it showed itself in religion. The primitive religious beliefs of the Greeks were the same as those of other peoples, the same as in the East—animism, or the belief that there exists in living beings an immortal part which is not identical with matter, the belief in a future life being derived from this; fetishism, or the belief in a mysterious power residing in

PLATE LXI

EARLY GREEK ARCHITECTURE

1. RESTORATION OF THE FRONT OF AN ARCHAIC TEMPLE EXCAVATED RECENTLY AT PRINIAS ON THE ISLAND OF CRETE. The temple consists of a porch (*pronaos*) of three pillars, one standing free, the two other forming the ends of the walls, with a frieze and a flat roof above and with 'acroteria' (top figures) on the roof, and a 'cella' (*naos*) entered by a door adorned with sculptures. Light was admitted into the cella through the door; the flat roof had a central opening over a large altar. The cella was divided into two naves by two columns. The temple of Prinias with a few others represent the earliest stage of Greek architecture. The restoration is of course problematic, but it seems evident that the type of the temple is derived from that of the Mycenean 'megaron' (see fig. 23), i. e. the Greek Nordic house. The characteristic parts of later Greek architecture (the Doric or Ionic columns, the porch of two, four or six columns, the pediment) are missing in these early temples. While the temple is very archaic and the ornaments and the figures of animals have a strong Oriental aspect, the sculptures of the frieze and of the door-posts are Greek and not very primitive. The archaic temple and sculptures of Crete show that the legend about the most ancient Greek architect and sculptor, Daedalus of Crete, is not a mere invention. 7th cent. B.C. After L. Pernier.

2. THE SCULPTURED DOOR-POSTS AND FRIEZE OF THE TEMPLE OF PRINIAS.

3. RECONSTRUCTION OF THE TEMPLE OF APOLLO AT DELPHI. This temple of the 6th cent. B.C. shows all the typical features of the Greek Doric temples, the porch supported by six Doric columns, the architrave, the frieze of triglyphs, the pediment with the sculptures, the roof and the top figures over the pediment (*acroteria*). After Replat.

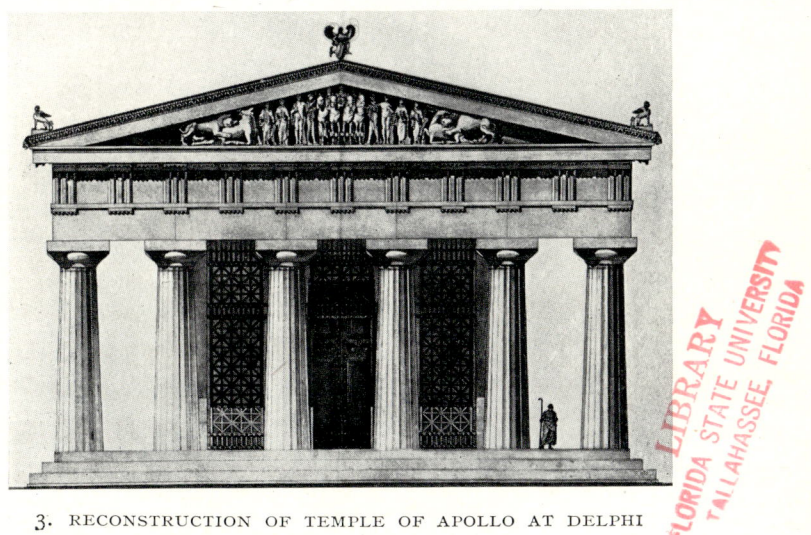

1. RESTORATION OF ARCHAIC TEMPLE AT PRINIAS

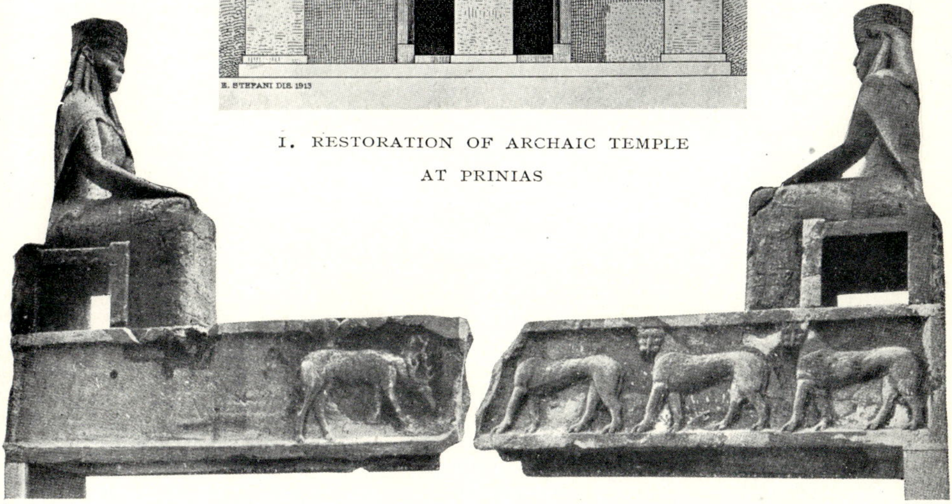

2. DOOR-POSTS AND FRIEZE OF THE TEMPLE AT PRINIAS

3. RECONSTRUCTION OF TEMPLE OF APOLLO AT DELPHI

LXI. EARLY GREEK ARCHITECTURE

certain inanimate objects, such as trees and stones; totemism, or the belief in the divinity of certain animals; and polytheism, which believes in an infinite number of gods and in the divinity of such natural phenomena as the sun and moon, thunder and lightning, rivers, springs, and forests. There was

FIG. 27. *Red-figured cup. The beautiful picture shows the god Apollo killing the Titan Tityos, who attacked Apollo's mother Leto. The mother of Tityos, Ge (the Earth), tries vainly to protect her son. The picture gives an excellent idea of Apollo as the god of right and civilization fighting against anarchy and barbarism represented by the elemental forces of nature. Attic work of about 460 B.C. Munich Museum. After Furtwängler-Reichhold.*

no national religion and could not be, because there was no nation. Each stock, each *gens*, each brotherhood (*phratria*), and each family had its own gods and its own rites.

It was the appearance of the so-called Homeric poems, during their first spontaneous expansion over the Aegean islands and Asia Minor, which first made the Greeks conscious that they were a nation. Through these poems and through their mighty culmination in the *Iliad* and *Odyssey*—a culmination which touched religion also and endeavoured to single out the common element in the religious ideas of all Hellas—the Greeks gained a clear conception of their national unity and realized the racial peculiarities of their life and religion. These poems set the figures of the chief gods before the eyes of the Greeks, gave to each of them a distinct form, forced men to believe in their nearness to humanity, and equipped them with attributes which every Greek recognized in himself.

Homer united the gods in one comprehensive family; the great monarch Zeus the Thunderer was the head of this family and governed it just as the Graeco-Aegean kings governed their households. At the same time Homer exalted the gods and Zeus in particular to a height beyond human attainment, placing them on the summit of Mount Olympus and illuminating them with the light of ineffable beauty. Homer became the Bible of the Greeks—the source from which they drew their conceptions of divinity, and which fixed for ever the divine images so familiar even to us. Supreme Zeus, ruler of gods and men; queenly Hera, his divine consort; Poseidon, lord of the sea; Ares, the terrible warrior; Hermes, the messenger of the gods; Aphrodite, born of the sea foam, ever young and lovely in her divine beauty; Hephaestus, the halting smith; the radiant Apollo—all these were clothed once for all in permanent forms of ineffable poetic loveliness.

Yet among these gods there was one in particular who became especially near and dear to every Greek, and with whom they connected their new conceptions of divinity and its part in human life. This was Apollo. Originally the god of light in particular, but also the god of agriculture and stock-raising, he assumed by degrees new attributes. Like Heracles, a champion of humanity against the dark forces of nature, he comes forth as a defender and saviour. He overcame with his arrows the formidable Python, the serpent which personified the dark and dangerous forces of the underworld; and men, in gratitude for this exploit, built him his bright temple at Delphi, where all nature proclaimed the power of light to conquer darkness. Together with Heracles he was a builder of cities and their protector, and the patron of Greek civilization, especially of music. His first paean or song of victory he sang over the body of the slain Python. His oracles guided men along the path of truth and justice and advised them in their public and private affairs.

Still more important is the fact that, with the figure of Apollo, morality makes its first appearance as a part of religion. The god himself undergoes a humiliating penance for the slaughter of the Python, and feeds the flocks of Admetus. From his shrine at Delphi he holds forth a helping hand to others who have stained themselves with blood ; by repentance and purification they are reconciled with their own consciences and with society ; the god absolves them from their sins ; for the matricide only there is no absolution. The religion of Apollo had a very great influence on Greece. The temple of Zeus at Olympia was not the only shrine where all Greeks worshipped : Apollo had two such temples—one at Delphi, the centre of an alliance, one of the most ancient in Greece, between several communities, and the other in Delos, where the religious life of all the Ionians was concentrated. In Asia Minor the place of Delphi was taken by the temple of Apollo at Didyma near Miletus, a shrine familiar to all Greeks. Pindar, one of the greatest Greek poets, claims to be a prophet who reveals the religion of Apollo and glorifies the god of light.

The worship of Demeter in her temple at Eleusis also became universal among Greeks. Demeter, the Great Mother, had been worshipped earlier by others ; but the Greeks raised this cult to a high point of poetic symbolism and moralized it. Whereas Apollo was a god of all Greece, revered in every city and, as the 'god of our fathers', in every family, Demeter was more exclusive. She admitted to her mysteries only a chosen band of believers, only those who were pure in a ritual and moral sense. Yet there was no distinction of sex or station : even slaves were included ; but no foreigner was admitted. To the initiated she promised complete regeneration, or rather, a new birth during this life and bliss hereafter. At the solemn ceremony of initiation, her worshipper, cleansed from earthly taint, drew near to the deity and was united with her.

A third cult, which spread by degrees over all the Greek world, was that of Dionysus. It reached Greece in the seventh century, coming probably from Thrace, and was quickly diffused through Greece, Asia Minor, and Italy. By Thracians and Greeks Dionysus was conceived as a suffering god : he personified the vegetation which dies in winter and is renewed in spring. In his youth he was torn to pieces by the Titans, the dark forces of earth, but is born again from himself, as young and beautiful as before. His worshippers, women

PLATE LXII

GREEK ARCHITECTURE IN ITALY AND SICILY

1. TWO OF THE FAMOUS TEMPLES OF THE GREEK CITY POSEIDONIA (modern Pesto, Latin Paestum) IN SOUTH ITALY. Poseidonia was one of the flourishing Greek cities of Italy in the 6th and 5th cent. B.C. Later the city was in complete decay and the place infested by malaria. This explains the splendid state of preservation of the ruins as shown on our figure, which shows two of the temples: in the foreground, the so-called temple of Poseidon with six Doric columns on the fronts and twelve on the sides, a regular Doric temple; farther off, the oldest and the largest, the so-called 'Basilica' with nine columns on the fronts and eighteen on the sides, an excellent example of an early Doric temple. The 'Basilica' belongs to the early part of the 6th century B.C., the temple of Poseidon to the 5th.

2. THE MOST ANCIENT TEMPLE ON THE ACROPOLIS OF THE BRILLIANT CITY OF SELINUS IN SICILY. Of the five temples on the Acropolis one was not yet finished when the city was destroyed by the Carthaginians at the end of the 5th cent. After this catastrophe the city never recovered, and in 250 B.C. it was finally destroyed during the first Punic war. The sculptures of some of the temples present good examples of Greek archaic art. 6th century B.C. Reconstruction, problematic in details. After Hulot-Fougères.

3. FANCY RECONSTRUCTION OF THE CITY OF SELINUS. After Hulot-Fougères.

1. THE TEMPLE OF POSEIDON AND THE 'BASILICA', POSEIDONIA (PAESTUM)

2. THE MOST ANCIENT TEMPLE OF THE ACROPOLIS, SELINUS

3. RESTORATION OF THE CITY OF SELINUS

LXII. GREEK ARCHITECTURE IN ITALY AND SICILY

especially, held nightly revels in his honour by torch-light on the mountain-tops. Dancing in ecstasy to the sound of cymbals and drums, they tore in pieces a sacrificed animal, whose blood they drank with wine, and so participated in the being and eternal life of their god. A group of religious reformers, who traced their descent to the Thracian minstrel, Orpheus, and called themselves 'Orphics', purified this worship of its rude primitive features and spiritualized it. The sacred writings of the Orphics taught that the soul, imprisoned in the body as a punishment for sin, is capable of purification. This purity is attained by a life of strict morality, even of asceticism, by participation in the great secret of Dionysus, the suffering god, and by initiation into his mysteries. To the initiated an endless life of happiness after death was promised. This doctrine gradually became united with the kindred mysteries of Eleusis. Dionysus-Iacchus was united to Demeter and her daughter, Kore; and this trinity became the object of the Eleusinian rites. The Orphic cult of Dionysus was propagated outside Greece by a succession of missionaries who founded everywhere communities of believers, of which the most important and long-lived belonged to the Greek cities in south Italy. Among them were many thinkers of a religious turn, notably Pythagoras, one of the founders of scientific mathematics and astronomy, and the head of an Orphic community which at one time governed the wealthy city of Croton.

These shrines, most of which were also oracular seats, were resorted to by all Greeks and served as a symbol of national unity. I have mentioned already the temple of Zeus at Olympia and those of Apollo at Delphi, Delos, and Didyma. Other oracular shrines were those of Poseidon near Corinth and of Zeus at Dodona in Epirus. The temples of the healing god, Asclepius, were national also. The sick and suffering flocked thither from all Greece, and schools of medicine were formed there by physicians, the pupils of the divine healer.

In connexion with some of these holy places competitions in honour of the god were instituted in athletic games, music, and poetry, and were open to all Greeks. From time immemorial the gods had been worshipped, not in Greece alone, with dance and song and competitions of various kinds. In these contests the youth of Greece sang hymns of praise in the god's honour; or reproduced scenes from his life in rhythmic choral dances, accompanied by music and singing;

PLATE LXIII
EARLY GREEK SCULPTURE. STATUES

1. THE MARBLE STATUE OF CLEOBIS OR BITON, carved by the sculptor Polymedes of Argos; found at Delphi. Cleobis and Biton were the two young men who drew the car with their mother, priestess of Hera at Argos, to the temple. In reward for their piety the goddess let them fall asleep after the sacrifice, never to awaken. The statue is one of the earliest products of Greek sculpture. The influence of Egypt is strong, but the statue is individual and shows a close study of the human body by the Greek pupils of Egyptian sculptors. About 600 B.C. Museum, Delphi.

2. A BEAUTIFUL AND ALMOST COMPLETE MARBLE STATUE OF A PRIESTESS OR GODDESS found recently in Attica The statue shows all the peculiarities of Greek archaic art when the Greeks were gradually becoming emancipated from the rigidity of early art and beginning to take delight both in the details of the feminine dress and in the rendering of the movement of the human body and in giving expression to the faces. Early 6th cent. B.C. Museum, Berlin.

3. MARBLE STATUE OF A SEATED GODDESS of West-Ionian workmanship. It is a beautiful work of mature archaic sculpture, elaborate in details and splendid in its general conception. Early 5th cent. B.C. (time of the Persian wars). Museum, Berlin.

4. MARBLE STATUE OF APOLLO from the west pediment of the temple of Zeus at Olympia (see fig. 28). The sculptures of this pediment represent the fight between men (Lapiths) directed and helped by heroes (Pirithous and Theseus) and the Centaurs, representing the elemental forces of nature. Apollo stands in the centre and dominates the pediment sculptures by his beautiful majestic figure. He is helping the Lapiths and represents the forces of civilization and order. About 460 B.C. Museum, Olympia.

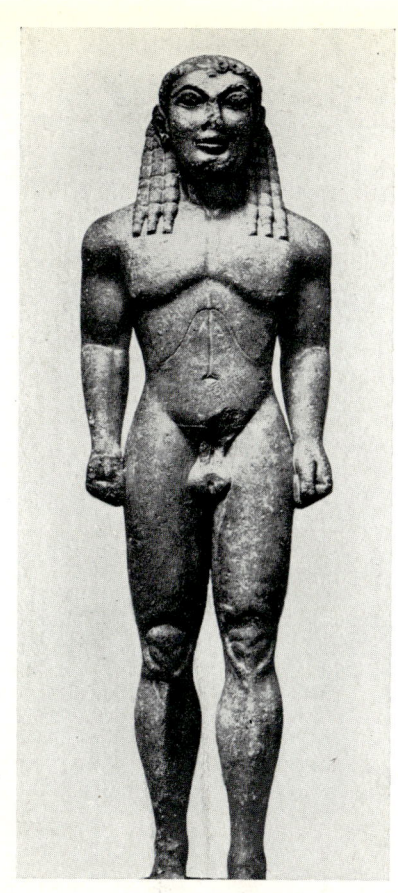
1. CLEOBIS OR BITON

2. GODDESS OR PRIESTESS

3. SEATED GODDESS

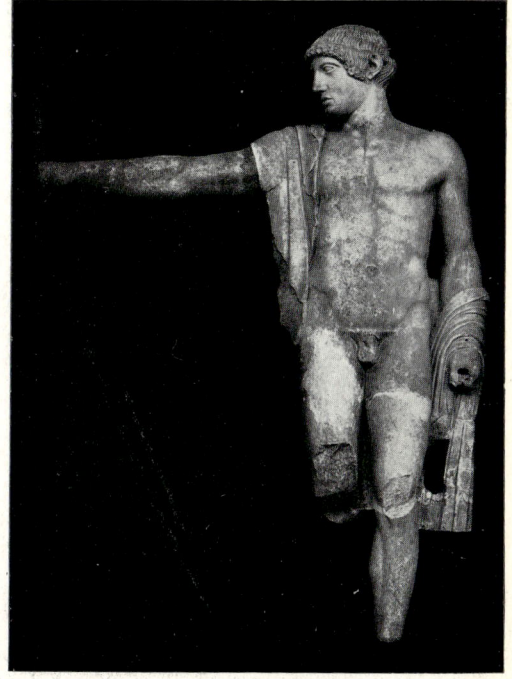
4. APOLLO

LXIII. EARLY GREEK SCULPTURE

or vied with one another in running, jumping, wrestling, and the throwing of the discus and the javelin; or appeared as drivers of chariots drawn by the swiftest horses.

In these games and in the very nature of the Panhellenic shrines the two characteristics of the Greek genius and of Greek life are conspicuous. The god was glorified by all Greeks: during the games thousands of Greeks from Greece proper and the colonies gathered at Olympia or Corinth met, conversed, discussed questions of interest to a section or to them all, and united in combined rites and offerings. But, on the other hand, almost every community in Greece or the colonies prided itself on its 'treasury', a beautiful chapel-like building within the temple precinct, where its great deeds were told in painting and sculpture; each community brought thither its best artists and best athletes, and coveted the honour of raising a statue of their victorious townsman on the open space in front of the temple. Not only did each city in this way assert its individuality, but the competitors did the same with equal emphasis. These youths were eager to excel, to thrust themselves forward, to display to all Greece their personal superiority. They strove with persistent toil to attain perfection of mind and body, and to wrest the prize from rivals like themselves, who had submitted to the same training for the same object. Their highest reward was gained when all Greece, in the person of the chosen judges, acknowledged them as national and public heroes, crowned them with a wreath of twigs from the sacred tree, and permitted their statues to be placed beside those of the gods.

The Greek, however strongly he felt himself a part of the Greek nation, was, first and foremost, a citizen of his own community and would sink his individuality for it, and for it alone. The interests of that community touched him nearly and often blinded him to the interests of Greece as a whole. Throughout Greek history the forces of disruption were stronger and more active than those of centralization; rivalry and separation, which found vent in wars between the states, were stronger than the tendency to agreement and coalition— a tendency which showed itself in treaties, alliances, and national arbitration, and laid the foundations of European international law. To the Athenian the temple of his native goddess, Athena, on the Acropolis, the symbol of a united community and kingdom, was dearer than the temple of Poseidon in Calauria, the centre of a religious alliance between several communities akin to Athens, and dearer than the shrine of Apollo at Delos, the religious centre of all who used the Ionic dialect. Nevertheless, Attica, united round Athens, Boeotia, rallying round Thebes, Argolis, concentrating round Argos, and Sparta, ruling a number of Dorian communities and clans—each of these powers sought to become the centre of a still more extensive union; but each of them regarded such a union as a point scored in the competition between

FIG. 28. *Restoration of part of the 'Altis' (the sacred area) of Olympia. In the centre, the temple of Zeus; to the right the great altar of ashes on which the sacrifices were performed. The temple was surrounded by minor buildings and by many votive statues (to the left the famous Nike of Paionios) and monuments. After Bohn.*

states, and treated the members of the union not as allies with equal rights but as inferiors.

The individual character of the national genius is seen with special clearness in the region of thought and of art, where local patriotism, far from hindering the development of personality, in many cases even encouraged it. The communities were just as proud of their great thinkers and artists as of their champions who won prizes at Olympia, and strove as eagerly for pre-eminence in culture as in politics. Discovery and invention, which in the East had been impersonal things, lose that character in Greece and are closely connected for all time with the personality of the discoverer.

Civilization of Archaic Greece

It is significant that all the earliest discoveries of the prehistoric past were attributed by the lively imagination of Greece to a definite inventor, who was, in many cases, not even a Greek. Thus the Greeks could tell at once that Prometheus had taught mankind the use of fire, and that Daedalus was the father of sculpture; they knew who invented the potter's wheel, and who was the first to forge weapons of copper and iron. Much more did they make mention of those

Fig. 29. *Restoration of part of the 'Altis' of Olympia. The centre is occupied by the temple of the Great Mother (Metroon), to the left the terrace of the treasuries; in front of the temple and the treasuries are altars and votive monuments. After Bohn.*

who created their own civilization—that civilization which distinguished them from all 'barbarians' who spoke no Greek. Greece was proud of them, and with good reason: they laid the foundation of all our modern civilization, which is as individual as that of Greece.

In matters of science, technical skill, and art the Greeks were, in many respects, pupils of the East, and they never forgot this. It was in Asia Minor, where they were in constant connexion with the East, that they started on the path of progress themselves. But, while drawing freely from the stores of Eastern civilization, they refashioned all they received, and stamped a fresh character upon it. Their genius recognized no tradition, no unalterable rules. They approached each fresh problem as a matter for investigation. If the problem was solved, the next investigator treated the solution as merely a starting-point for further inquiry. Nature, the world, and man became at once for them matter for this kind of reflection and investigation. They were not content to register what they saw and accept its mythological explanation. They felt the rule of law in nature and tried to make it clear. Their first question was not ' How ? ' but ' Why ? ' When foreign travel made them acquainted with new countries and strange seas, they perpetuated their knowledge by drawing maps, and also at once began asking: ' What is the whole world ? what is its shape, and what its relation to other worlds, the sun, moon, and stars ? ' And having raised such questions, they suggested answers—answers which were at first childishly simple, no doubt, but scientific and not mythological. Thus they became the creators of scientific geography, cosmology, and astronomy. Before the end of the sixth century Pythagoras in Italy knew that the earth and the stars were of spherical shape.

In their study of the world, the Ionian inquirers and thinkers—or philosophers, as they called themselves—endeavoured to separate the chief and fundamental element in the creation. That a single substance underlies all matter was held first by Thales ; and the question was discussed further by Anaximander and Anaximenes. All these three were Milesians. Thales found the primary substance of matter in water ; Anaximenes found it in air ; Anaximander, the creator of scientific prose and the first to publish his theory in a book, insisted on the infinity of the world, or rather worlds, and their perpetual interchanges. He also was the first to make a map of the world known to him. Still more profound were the views of Xenophanes, who migrated to Elea in south Italy and there founded the Eleatic school of philosophy. The unity of the world was his chief dogma. He believed one god to be the directing force of the world. ' He is all eye, mind, ear ; he directs all things without effort by the power of his reason.' Polytheism and the legends told of the gods he treated as mere inventions of human imagination. God was perceived by reason, and reason led men to the knowledge of things. God is also moral force, and men should pray to God, in order to attain the ideal of justice. This is not the place to dwell on the beginnings of European science ; but it is proper to repeat, that in Greece for the first time humanity treated nature and man as a problem that could be solved by reason.

In literature the same spirit of individuality is supreme. The Homeric poems may have owed their birth to a school of poets; but to the Greek they were the work of a blind

Fig. 30. *Red-figured pot for wine and water (krater) found at Acragas in Sicily. One side of this krater is adorned with the figures of Sappho and Alcaeus, the two greatest lyric poets of archaic Greece. There was a legend based on some poems of the two singers that Alcaeus fell in love with Sappho and was rejected by her. This scene is represented on the krater. Attic work of about 480 B.C. Munich Museum. After Furtwängler-Reichhold.*

old minstrel, whose native country was unknown but whose personality was near and dear to every Greek. Homer is followed by a long succession of great writers in poetry and prose. A strong and brilliant personality belongs to each of them, and their work has such a definitely personal note that each of them has told us, in greater or less detail, his own biography in his writings. They all of them put their soul into their poetry. The first famous woman, the poetess Sappho, paints a most vivid picture of her own life, with the clubs or schools of Lesbian girls for a background—her passion for various members of the sisterhood, her jealousy of their future husbands, and the feelings with which she escorted them to a new life in households of their own.

The poets who were contemporary with Sappho reflect in their poetry all the life of Greece—a life full of movement, variety, and adventure. They are the true children of their time. They trade and travel and fight; they take an active part in revolutions; they flee from the battle-field or lead their comrades-in-arms to victory with their songs; they feast and love and are jealous; they lash the character and conduct of their fellow-citizens. Alcaeus of Lesbos is a trader, a warrior, an active politician. Archilochus of Paros is a needy adventurer, a stern warrior, an injured and resentful lover. Tyrtaeus, not himself a Spartan, sings his marching songs to the ordered ranks of Spartan hoplites. Anacreon of Teos, a poet in the courts of tyrants, sings of love and wine. Then there is Solon, the great Athenian reformer; Theognis of Megara, an injured and venomous aristocrat; Terpander of Lesbos, Simonides of Ceos, Stesichorus of Sicily—inspired writers of choric songs in honour of the gods. Last and greatest of the lyric poets is Pindar of Boeotia, that swan with strong snowy pinions, as he was called by later Greek and Roman bards, the inspired prophet of Apollo, who crowned with glory the conquerors at the Panhellenic contests. The poetry of them all has a personal note and conveys the individuality of the writer; the style, metre, and thought of each are his own. Most of the early philosophers already mentioned put forth their theories in poetic form.

But, together with poetry, prose also comes into existence. Of Anaximander I have already spoken. Travellers into far countries brought home with them many new impressions, and made acquaintance with foreign lands—their climate and flora and fauna, their religion, manners, customs, and history. Full of these new impressions, they told them to their countrymen at markets and on public squares, in temples and blacksmiths' shops; and from these narratives sprang the first tales of history, geography, and ethnography; they were called 'tales' (*logoi*) by the Greeks, and their authors 'tale-makers' (*logopoioi*). The earliest tales were in verse; such is the story of Aristeas, how he travelled to the land of marvels, through the Black Sea regions and the land of the Scythians to Central Asia. Here legend and fact are bound up together ; but, with Hecataeus of Miletus, prose takes the place of verse, and the narrative becomes a half-scientific treatise, in which mythology and history are fantastically blended with geography and ethnography. He is followed by Herodotus, the father of history and the first Greek historian ; but still the distinction between science and literature is incomplete.

Political life was another source of prose literature. Disputes and discussions in the streets and at council-boards, attempts to write down and express exactly legal and constitutional principles in codes of law, decrees of law-courts and public assemblies—all these were written out in prose form and perpetuated on wood or stone or bronze. Hence proceeds the prose literature of law and politics, the speeches made before courts and assemblies, and the more austere and rigorous literature of official proceedings.

The singing and dancing of a chorus had long been used to express religious feeling. These differed at different festivals and in different cults ; and in the worship of Dionysus they took a peculiar form which underwent a remarkable development in Attica. At the vintage festival it was customary for the chorus to dress up as birds or frogs or other animals, to come forward under the direction of the leader who presented them to the public, to sing songs of different kinds, and then to go off in a merry, noisy procession led by flute-players. This procession was called *comos*, and the performance itself comedy. At the spring festival of Dionysus, instituted by Pisistratus, the singers were disguised as goats and satyrs (imaginary half-animal creatures, spirits of the fields and forests, and the constant companions of Dionysus). These took turns with the 'answerer' (the Greek name for actor), who replied to the chorus in metre. From the goat-masks (*tragos* is the Greek for goat) the acting was called tragedy. The new form of ritual had a great success and became an established part of these festivals. From this humble beginning, Aeschylus, of whom more is said below, created Greek tragedy, one of the noblest triumphs of the Attic genius.

But religion was not content with expressing itself in the form of poetry, music, and dancing : the Greeks wished to see and touch their gods and give them dwellings worthy of their majesty. Zeus, Apollo and Demeter, Aphrodite, Dionysus and Poseidon, first came really home to their hearts when

PLATE LXIV

EARLY GREEK SCULPTURE. RELIEFS.

1. ATTIC GRAVE STELE OF MARBLE. The front of the stele bears the figures of the deceased, a young man, and of a young girl, probably his sister. The boy is naked and holds the funerary fruit, the pomegranate, in his left hand, and an athlete's oil flask on his wrist. The girl holds a flower. The stele was painted as well as carved. The heads are the finest part of this beautiful work of art. They are still conventional, but show a feeling for beauty of line and a strong decorative sense. 6th cent. B.C. Metropolitan Museum of Art, New York.

2. MARBLE GRAVE STELE FOUND AT CHRYSAFA, NEAR SPARTA. The figures of the deceased are represented seated on an arm-chair. Behind the throne is the snake, symbol of the nether world. The deceased are represented as hero and heroine enjoying a drink of wine. A youth and a woman bring them offerings: a cock, a pomegranate, and a flower. The relief, though not of very early date (late 6th cent.), is very conventional and recalls wood-carving. Berlin Museum.

3-4. TWO SIDES OF A BASE WHICH WAS FOUND WITH TWO OTHERS IN THE WALL OF ATHENS, which was built either in 337-322 B.C. or in 307, and for which the material of the wall built by Themistocles was used. The reliefs of this base are most beautiful examples of Athenian sculpture in the period of Pisistratus. One of the reliefs (No. 3) shows two wrestlers in the centre. The wrestler on the right is seizing the left arm of his opponent and is about ' to swing round to the front and by getting underneath him to throw him by leverage '. The wrestler on the left is trying ' to stop this swinging movement by placing his right hand on his opponent's left shoulder '. The athlete on the left of the group seems to be a jumper; the figure on the right is a javelin-thrower. The slab thus represents three of the five games of the pentathlon, the runner and the discus-thrower being omitted. The second relief (No. 4) is a complete novelty in sculpture. It shows a cat and dog set on to fight by two young men. The dog—a Laconian—is ' in the attitude of excited play ', the cat ' is frightened and enraged '. The third face of the base (not reproduced) shows a ball game. On the second base there is a relief showing a game very similar to modern hockey. About 520-510 B.C. National Museum, Athens.

1. ATTIC GRAVE-STELE

2. MARBLE GRAVE-STELE FROM NEAR SPARTA

3. WRESTLING

4. A CAT AND DOG FIGHT

LXIV. EARLY GREEK SCULPTURE

painters and sculptors, after long experiment, began to find fitting artistic forms for the divine inhabitants of Olympus. In sculpture we are able to follow their experiments, because a fairly large number of the statues which served to adorn the shrines and temples have been preserved, some of them the actual divine images which were worshipped by the faithful, while others were votive offerings—statues and statuettes dedicated to the god by his worshippers. Not a few of these have been found in different parts of the Greek world and are preserved in our museums. The painting with which the temples were adorned has perished; but the types of divinity created by the painters are repeated in the decoration of Greek vases, a subject we shall deal with later.

It is probable that painting preceded sculpture in representing not merely separate forms of the gods but scenes taken from mythology and perhaps also groups of worshippers. Sculpture followed the example, when it became the custom to adorn certain parts of a temple—pediment, frieze, and metopes—with reliefs and sculptures in the round or in bas-relief. Though their chief attention was given to religious subjects, the artists did not confine themselves to figures of the gods.

Greek art, and especially Ionian art, made immense progress in the course of the sixth century B.C. The delicate and beautiful floral ornament, which became one of the main features of Greek art, was perfected at this time. In the representation of men and animals advance was slower, especially in sculpture, which had to meet many purely technical difficulties; but by degrees these difficulties were surmounted. Beginning with a wooden post or board hewn into human shape, or with a stiff and lifeless idol of stone, the artist advances further and further in the truthful representation of the human body, conveys more and more accurately the anatomical structure and muscular surface, and reproduces the individual features with ever-increasing skill. The appearance of motion is added: one foot is advanced, the arms are raised, attempts are made to convey rapid movement and even flight, especially in the sculpture of imaginary winged figures. Treading in the footsteps of the painter, the sculptor learns to carve groups and to subordinate them to their architectural purpose.

Typical figures of the gods are evolved by degrees—Zeus in his majesty, Apollo, the graceful stripling, the ripe charms of Aphrodite, Athena, the stately maiden and formidable

PLATE LXV

GREEK POTTERY OF THE 6TH CENT. B.C.

1. PICTURE ON THE INSIDE OF A SPARTAN KYLIX (CUP). Black figures on a white background. King Arcesilas of Cyrene in Africa (Cyrene was a Spartan colony) is shown watching the lading and weighing of goods, possibly ' silphion ' (a plant peculiar to Cyrene and extensively used in Greek diet). Note the realism with which the scene is painted, the intense movement in the picture, and a good sense of humour. The masterly rendering of the animals (the pet animals of the king, the monkey, and the birds) is quite remarkable. The scene illustrates well the growing commerce of Greece in the 6th century, and the part which the Greek colonies played in this commerce. 6th cent. B.C. Cabinet des Médailles, Paris.

2. ATTIC BLACK-FIGURED AMPHORA. On the shoulder a combat of warriors, on the body a marriage procession. It is possible that the man in the chariot is Heracles being driven by Athena to his permanent home, Olympus. Hebe is his divine bride. Apollo is playing the marriage hymn on his lyre. Style of the painter Execias. About 540 B.C. Metropolitan Museum of Art, New York.

3. AN ATHENIAN KYLIX (CUP). Black figures on red ground. From the workshop of the potter Nicosthenes. It is a beautiful scene full of life and elegance, showing two ships racing. About 530 B.C. Paris, Louvre.

4. AN ATTIC BLACK-FIGURED AMPHORA. Eos, the goddess of the dawn, mourning in a garden over the body of her son Memnon, who was killed by Achilles in the Trojan war. His arms are piled under one of the trees. Note the extensive use of landscape elements. About 550–540 B.C. Vatican, Rome.

1. SPARTAN KYLIX.
KING ARCESILAS OF CYRENE

2. ATTIC AMPHORA. WEDDING

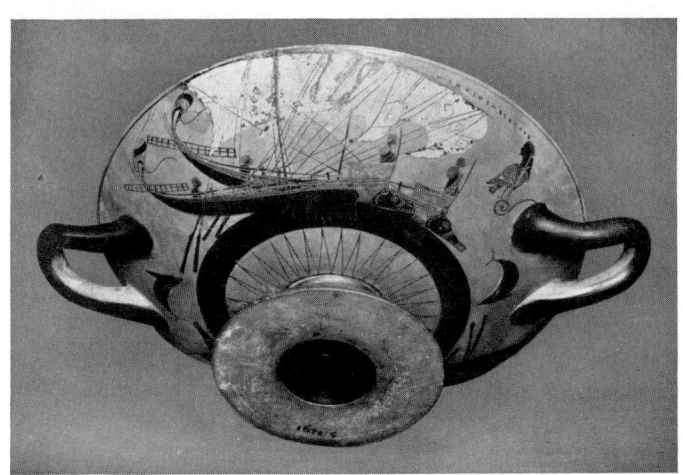

3. ATHENIAN KYLIX. ATHENIAN SHIPS

4. ATTIC AMPHORA. EOS AND MEMNON

LXV. GREEK POTTERY OF THE VITH CENT. B.C.

fighter. Art makes the attempt to embody ideas in colour and stone, and to create typical figures of humanity; and this power of creating types remains one of the leading features of Greek art. At the end of the sixth century, however, we notice in Ionian art the formation of some conventional tradition, some mannerism, some tendency to exaggerate details at the expense of the whole. Statues found on the Acropolis and dating from before the Persian wars prove this clearly. These defects of ancient Ionian art are shared to some extent by the sculpture of Greece proper.

The temples, the abodes of the gods, were worthy of their inhabitants. The modest house with its four walls, front room, and two posts at the entrance, is converted by degrees into a majestic hall flanked by pillars, which, together with the walls, support the roof. These pillars, with their bases and capitals, become the main feature of the temple and define the order to which it belongs. The pillars themselves, the stone entablatures which crown them, the raised foundation, the walls and roof of the building, combine to form one artistic whole, where there is nothing arbitrary, but every detail is calculated and planned, where painting and sculpture are in strict keeping with the main lines of the structure, and where, nevertheless, nothing is stereotyped. There are no two temples in Greece which are exactly alike. The column, the main feature of the temple, is not confined to a single form. The massive Doric column has a flat cushion for a capital; the Ionic column, invented in Asia Minor, is more graceful and more elaborate, with its sculptured base, shapely fluted shaft, and the double volute of its capital; and then, still more graceful and more elaborate, comes the Corinthian column, whose capital reproduces the highly decorative foliage of the prickly acanthus. Noble columnar temples rise in all the great centres of Greek life. The temples of Artemis at Ephesus, of Zeus at Olympia, of Apollo at Delphi, of Hera at Samos—how clearly they convey the peculiarities of the Greek genius in all parts of Greece! In Italy and Sicily there still stand majestic productions of that genius, wonderful in the boldness of their plan and the harmony of their outlines.

But Greek art does not confine itself to the temples: from the earliest times it permeates the whole of life. There is no clearer proof of this than the common pottery used for domestic purposes. Like the Aegean ware, and perhaps under its influence, it dislikes monochrome. And in no department is the variety and creative power of Greek genius equally conspicuous. Two simultaneous influences can be distinguished. The first is of Eastern origin. It prefers motley groups of animals, partly real and partly due to Eastern fancy; in the latter case the bright colours do not reproduce nature but confer on her a richness that does not belong to her. Though the type of this pottery is the same everywhere, there is much local variety: if an Eastern vase from Rhodes be compared with another from Corinth, the comparison will show at once how much each presents that is local and peculiar. The other style is not Oriental but European. Poor in its choice of colour, and stiff in its simplified geometrical ornament, it develops quickly: ornament gives place to the human figure, though the figure is at first angular and stiff, and next the figures are combined to form groups. From this modest beginning the Attic vase is developed by degrees —the vase with black figures on a red background, in which the human figures are the main thing and the animals and floral ornament the accessories. These Attic vases, whose makers sign their names with pride on their work, reproduce before long each new artistic tendency and idea. While decorating these articles of everyday use, the artist feels freer than when working for temples and shrines. In painting vases he reflects all the full and various life of Greece—first of all, its religion, but not that alone. Love and feasting, the merriment of a holiday, weddings and funerals, men at the market or in the workshops, women in the seclusion of their apartments, children at their games, youths and girls in the palaestra and gymnasium—all these are revealed to us by the observant eye and ready hand of the Athenian vase-painter. And their mastery of design and drawing rivals even the majestic lines of the Greek temples themselves.

Such was Greece in the seventh and sixth centuries B.C. Without effort, in an impetuous outburst of genius, she overcame all the obstacles in her path. She knew what the East had accomplished, valued it, and made use of it; but she struck out for herself and created her own peculiar culture— a culture far more natural and intelligible to us than the civilizations worked out earlier by the East.

XVII

THE PERSIAN WARS

THERE is no doubt that in Hellas of the sixth century B.C. the leading part in economic and civilized life belonged, not to Greece proper, but to the Greek colonies in Asia Minor and, in some degree, to those in Italy and Sicily. The Greek cities of Aegina, Chalcis, Eretria, Corinth, Sicyon, Sparta, and Athens were far poorer and less civilized than Miletus, Ephesus, Samos, and Lesbos in the east, or than Sybaris, Croton, Gela, Acragas, and Syracuse in the west. The colonies had richer and more fertile territories, more extensive markets, and easier communication with the East. On the other hand, the position of these outposts of Hellenism was, from the political point of view, very precarious. In Asia Minor and also in Italy the cities were exposed to attack from their neighbours by land. The Sicilian Greeks were constantly menaced by the great maritime power of Carthage, backed by a powerful federation of Etruscan cities, to say nothing of their nearest neighbours—the tribes who inhabited the interior of the country. But even so they were safer than the Greeks in Asia Minor. For Etruria, though rich and civilized, was cut off from the colonies by the mountains of central Italy; their other neighbours were still in a primitive stage of development; and Carthage was only beginning to realize her strength and the necessity of a fight to a finish with the Greeks.

In Asia Minor the situation was different. The coast was occupied by Greeks. But even here a considerable part of the population which continued to live on the soil seized by the Greeks was neither Greek nor uncivilized. Before the Greeks came and conquered them, these tribes had enjoyed their own civilization and political institutions; and they kept this fact steadily in mind. They felt themselves closer to their Asiatic kinsmen than to their new masters. The record of central Asia Minor was distinguished, and traditions of the Hittite Empire survived in the new kingdoms of

Phrygia, Lydia, and Lycia. Of these kingdoms Lydia lay nearest to the Greeks. During the seventh and sixth centuries B.C. she had survived the invading Cimmerians and Scythians, had rapidly grown strong and rich, and had become a powerful empire with distinct political and economic aims. As mediator between the East and the new world of Greece, and belonging to both of them by her position, nationality, and culture, Lydia was always pressing towards the sea. But the coasts were occupied by Phoenicians and Greeks. To oust the former was impossible: first Assyria, and then Persia, stood in the way. It was far easier and more natural for Lydia to expand towards the west, in the region of the Greeks.

The Greeks in Asia, just like the Greeks at home and in the West, all shared the same blood, religion, and culture, but were divided into a number of independent states, each with its own policy and traditions, which ran counter to the policy and traditions of its neighbours. Hatred and jealousy of these neighbours moved them more than hostility towards powerful but distant Eastern empires, about which they knew and cared little. Moreover, social and political strife was constantly going on inside each state, and led the contending parties to seek for support, irrespective of the source from which it came. And, finally, the strategic position of these cities was excessively weak. The territory of each was, in most cases, a river-valley, divided by a mountain ridge from the territory of its next neighbour along the coast. Thus communication was difficult by land; by sea it was not difficult but, owing to the much indented line of the coast, took much time. Meanwhile, the territory was freely exposed to the attack of an army from the interior of the country.

Of all these facts the Lydian Empire took full advantage and soon became preponderant in the political life of these cities. While giving much to the Greeks in the way of a civilization and commerce, Lydia took from Greece all that Greece could give, and the difference between the Lydians and Anatolian Greeks became fainter and fainter. By degrees Lydia was admitted to the band of Greek states as one of themselves, just as Macedonia was admitted at a later date. Lydian ambassadors, bearing rich gifts to Delphi and other Greek shrines, were as welcome guests as the ambassadors of Greek powers. It is not surprising that the Anatolian cities were speedily absorbed by Lydia in the seventh, and still more in the sixth century, and that such resistance as there was did not take the form of a combined national effort against an Eastern foe. The resistance was unmethodical and entirely ineffective. All the Lydian kings—Ardys, Sadyattes, Alyattes, and Croesus—worked deliberately at the task of subduing the Greek cities, and their activity prevented the Greeks from observing the growing power of the Medes and Persians. Hence the catastrophe of 548 B. C., when Cyrus defeated the armies of Croesus and took Sardis, was a complete surprise to the Greeks, who were now confronted by the Persians, a quite unknown enemy. Their sympathies were all on the side of Lydia, and Sparta even prepared to send part of her army to help Croesus.

Persia had little difficulty in conquering the Anatolian Greeks. Greece was far away and comparatively weak, while they themselves were crippled by disunion and the mild but corrosive policy of Lydia. All the coast soon became a part of the great Persian monarchy. But the new masters made little change in the internal life of the cities. Each of them retained its autonomy, kept up regular communications with the rest of the Greek world, and continued to be important as a centre of trade and industry. They were only bound in future to pay part of their revenue to their conquerors, and to provide soldiers and ships for the unending wars waged by Persia against Babylon and Egypt. To all this the Anatolian Greeks were accustomed. They resented only the frequent interference of Persia in their party squabbles, and the support which they gave to tyrants. Tyranny became in time the prevailing form of government in the cities.

The absorption of these Anatolian Greeks was an important political factor in the history of the Persian Empire. These new subjects brought with them ideas and habits entirely unlike the ideas and habits which characterized all the rest of the kingdom. On the other hand, it was a political absurdity to rule Asia Minor and not to rule the coast also. But the ruler of the coast was bound to come in contact with the islands and with the complicated politics of all the Balkan peninsula and the Black Sea coast—a coast which was densely populated by colonists, mostly Anatolian Greeks. Thus, by the conquest of Asia Minor, Persia was drawn into European politics and forced to define, in one way or another, her policy in relation to Europe. The simplest solution of the problem, at least from the point of view traditional with Eastern conquerors, was this—that Persia should conquer and absorb Greece, thus including not merely a part but the whole nation in her Empire.

Conditions seemed to favour the execution of this project. Public affairs in Greece proper differed little from public affairs in Anatolian Greece. Both countries were divided into small states constantly at war with one another; in both there was the same jealousy between cities, the same internal division of each city into social and political parties, and the same readiness to make use of any allies in order to gain the immediate realization of political and party objects. Such political conditions made it seem an easy matter to conquer Greece. What Persia could throw into the scales in this contest seemed enormous and decisive—a great army, well organized and well disciplined; an excellent fleet, manned by Phoenicians and Anatolian Greeks, the most skilful sailors of the age; and the inexhaustible material resources of a wealthy kingdom. Distant campaigns must, no doubt, be undertaken; but did not the Persian armies march to the recesses of Central Asia and the boundaries of India? and had they not recently conquered mighty Egypt herself?

In extending their power the Persian monarchs never acted at random. They were excellent strategists: each campaign was rigorously thought out and carefully prepared. To them it was clear that the absorption of the Greeks in Europe was impracticable, unless the Persian frontier was advanced so as to meet the frontiers of the Greek states by land and sea. This meant that, before annexing Greece to their dominions, they must conquer the Greek islands and, above all, the north of the Balkan peninsula, the seat of the Thracian tribes, who were well known to the Persians in Asia Minor. There was this complication, however, that there Persia was confronted by the aspirations of another Iranian power—the Scythian Empire, which had by this time established itself firmly on the north of the Black Sea, and had also come into contact with the Greeks. This Scythian pressure towards the west and south Persia was bound to check before she turned elsewhere. At the time she did not contemplate the conquest of the Scythian kingdom in south Russia. That might be a problem in the remote future; but the pressing business was to drive the Scythians back from the

Danube and prevent them from extending their sway to the Balkan peninsula. Darius undertook the task in a great campaign against Scythia about 512 B. C. He probably went no farther than the steppes between the Danube and the Dniester, and it seems that he succeeded on the whole; for the conversion of Thrace into a Persian province went on quickly and steadily after this date, with no hindrance from without.

Darius was prevented from carrying out his plans further by the revolt of the Ionian Greeks. The causes of this revolt we can only surmise; but it was certainly not connected with any Panhellenic movement intended to check the further advance of Darius; it did not even extend to the whole of Asia Minor. The southern and northern Anatolian Greeks took part in it, and a timid attempt to help them was made by Athens and by Eretria in Euboea, but no other power in Greece proper joined in. In fact it was hardly more than a revolt of Miletus and a few other Ionian cities. We must suppose that it was due to local causes and was undertaken because the Greeks overrated their own power and underrated that of Persia. Though they were well aware of Persia's weak points, it is obvious that they were blind to her real strength. The struggle was stubborn and prolonged (from 499 to 494 B. C.) but ended in the destruction of Ionia. Miletus was burnt to the ground and took long to recover from the heavy blows inflicted upon her.

This revolt played an important part in the history of relations between Persia and Greece: it confirmed the belief of Persia that it was imperative to proceed at once with the conquest of the Balkan peninsula. It is therefore not surprising that the first business of Darius, after crushing the revolt, was to send a force to the shores of the Hellespont and to northern Greece, in order to strengthen the authority of Persia, which had been weakened in these districts by the revolt. This was the immediate object of the campaign of 492 B. C.; but the large number of land and sea forces employed shows that, if all went well, a continuation of the campaign was contemplated, and an advance of the fleet and army into central Greece. But a large part of the fleet was wrecked off Mount Athos, and without the support of all their ships it was difficult to supply a large army through a long and troublesome campaign. Thus the Persians were

PLATE LXVI
THE ORIENT AND GREECE

GREEK POTTERY OF THE 5TH AND 4TH CENT. B. C.

1. RED-FIGURED WINE-VESSEL (*KRATER*) FOUND AT CANUSIUM IN ITALY. The leading idea is the triumph of Europe over Asia. The most important part (our figure) represents the preparations of Darius for his eventful expedition into Greece. Darius is consulting his council, one of the Persian nobles is speaking. Below, the treasurer collects the war-tax from the tax-payers. In the upper row to the left the divine protectors of Greece (Athena, Hera, Zeus, Nike, Apollo, Artemis), to the right the personification of Asia led into war by the goddess 'Apate'—Deceit, Illusion. It is the first act of the great historical drama treated by the great Aeschylus in his 'Persians' and by Herodotus in his 'Histories'. Italiote Greek work of the 4th cent. B.C. Naples Museum. After Furtwängler-Reichhold.

2. RED-FIGURED 'AMPHORA' (vessel with two handles). The picture shows the Lydian King Croesus on the pyre after his army was defeated by the Persian King Cyrus. The story was famous in Greece and was used by Herodotus to show how unstable fortune is and how quietly a 'wise' man takes the inevitable. Attic work of about 500 B.C. Paris, Louvre. After Furtwängler-Reichhold.

3. RED-FIGURED CUP. Achilles is represented slaying the Amazon Queen Penthesilea, with whom, according to the epic poets, he was in love. To the right, one of the Greeks; to the left, one of the Amazons in Oriental costume. Attic work of about 460 B.C. Munich Museum. After Furtwängler-Reichhold.

1. RED-FIGURED KRATER. KING DARIUS

2. RED-FIGURED AMPHORA. DEATH
OF CROESUS

3. RED-FIGURED CUP. GREEKS
AND AMAZONS

LXVI. THE ORIENT AND GREECE. GREEK POTTERY OF
THE VTH AND IVTH CENT. B.C.

forced to confine themselves to their main purpose, which was to strengthen Persian authority by the annexation of Thrace and Macedonia.

The campaign of 492 B. C. was only a first attempt. It was followed in 490 by a second, whose object, publicly announced by the Persian king, was to punish Athens and Eretria for their part in the Ionian revolt. This object was formally communicated to the Greek states by ambassadors who demanded of them 'earth and water' as a symbol of submission; what they really required was their neutrality in the coming contest. The proximity of the Persian dominions induced many of the Greek states not to reject these demands. But the real object of Persia was, undoubtedly, different. Making use of her naval superiority, she hoped by her second campaign to accomplish the task which Mardonius had begun, and not only to create a common frontier with Greece by land but also to connect Persia with Greece by a sea route, starting from the cities of Ionia and proceeding through the islands to the natural goal in Europe, that is, Attica and its harbours and the harbours of Euboea. Attica once seized, Persia had no other rival to fear at sea and might count on the conquest of Greece as certain. Considering the internal discord of Greece, it was easy to pit one state against another, and before long to knock out Sparta, the hope of Greece by land, with one decisive blow.

To seize Attica seemed a very simple matter. There was no quarter from which Athens could look for help. Close beside her was Aegina, a dangerous foe and rival; Sparta was far away, slow to act, and hardly conscious of her danger; Boeotia was openly hostile. There was no strong fleet at Athens; and the army of Attica had not much experience and no glorious traditions behind it. The new-born democracy found itself vigorously opposed by the aristocracy, which still retained some strength. Hippias, the last tyrant, was still living and hoped to return in the train of the Persian army. For these reasons Darius believed that Athens could be disposed of by a force landed from his ships; and this force, though considerable, should consist entirely of infantry, because the transport of a large cavalry force would require too many ships, and heavy ships, which were more exposed to the danger of shipwreck.

His calculations proved partly true and partly false.

Athens did, indeed, stand alone. But Aegina's intention of assisting the Persians was thwarted by Sparta. At Athens the friends of Persia were ready to act; but they would take no risks: the democratic army of Athens must be beaten first. Sparta did not refuse to support Athens, but her support was long in coming. The danger that threatened Athens and all Greece was enormous; and Athens recognized this, but Greece did not. When the Persian troops were landed on the plain of Marathon, Athens had either to surrender or to accept a decisive battle without any great hope of victory. The chances on her side were not many, but there were some. The chief of these was, that the invaders were infantry, and that the excellent cavalry, which was the chief military arm of Persia, was taking no part. This being so, the small compact army of Athenian and Plataean citizens—an army of infantry equipped with heavy weapons and covered with iron mail—inspired by their deadly peril, and fighting on their native soil and under familiar conditions, proved more than a match for their enemy. The Persians were much more numerous; they were picked troops and well provided; but they were light-armed and fought under strange conditions and had just completed a long voyage. It was a great piece of fortune for the Athenians that they were led by Miltiades, a skilful commander, who was familiar with the Persian army, having served with it during the Scythian campaign as the tyrant of some Greek settlements and local tribes in Thrace. His remarkable talents for war and his knowledge of the enemy played a great and almost decisive part in the brilliant and famous victory of Marathon.

The two armies which fought at Marathon were neither of them large, but the battle is of capital importance in the world's history. In the chain of Persian policy one link, and an essential link, was broken. Yet the battle might have remained merely a splendid exploit in the history of Athens, had it not been followed by a succession of crises in Persia which gave Greece a respite and a breathing-space for the next ten years. Darius, though he made serious preparations for it, was never able to fit out another expedition against Greece. After the failure at Marathon great caution was necessary. But he was old; the bureaucratic machinery of Persia worked slowly; in 486 B.C. Egypt revolted, and in 485 Darius died. Xerxes, his successor, needed time to take his bearings and strengthen his position at home. This delay was highly advantageous to Greece : it increased her resources and raised her spirit. The fame of Athens stood high in Greece. When her treasury was filled by thorough exploitation of the silver mines of Laureium, and when Themistocles came to the front and, with equal boldness and wisdom, insisted on the necessity that Athens should build a great fleet in order to resist future invasions, there was not a power in Greece that would have wished to hinder this addition to her military strength. Sparta and Aegina felt that opposition on their part was impossible. Still more important, the attitude of Greece towards the Persian peril changed during these ten years : all Greeks now realized that they might be enslaved by Persia, and realized also that the conflict was inevitable. Not that all Greece was preparing for the conflict throughout the ten years. Individual states did something in this way ; but the important thing was this—that a public opinion, a feeling of common nationality, was formed to meet the struggle. But again, this does not imply that some of the states were not ready to yield and even to fight for Persia ; but this had come to be looked upon as treason to the nation, and not as a legitimate course of policy.

Thus the next campaign, begun by Xerxes in 480 B. C., was carried on under different conditions. The preparations made by him were extraordinarily careful, and the plan of campaign excellent. The supply department was ably organized. The plan of 492 B. C. was adopted again : the army was to march along the coast, escorted by a vast fleet ; the business of the fleet was to secure the provisioning of the forces and to guard it from being attacked in the rear. Great anxiety prevailed in Greece. Originally it was intended to bar the invader from Greek soil, by meeting him where the vale of Tempe gives admission to Thessaly. But Themistocles, who commanded the Greek army dispatched to Thessaly, soon made it clear that this plan could not be executed, because it was easy to go round the pass. It was therefore necessary to abandon Thessaly to the invader. A second plan, pressed by the Athenians and all central Greece, involved co-operation of the fleet and army at Thermopylae, the key to central Greece: the army was to defend Thermopylae, and the fleet was to resist any attack by sea upon the rear of the army. But Sparta put forward a rival plan of her own : she insisted that the Isthmus should be defended and all central Greece abandoned without a blow. The plan of defending Thermopylae was practicable, if the army on the spot was large and the fleet did its duty. But, though the fleet did not fail, Sparta and some of the allies sent forces which were insufficient for the defence, and the Persians were able to march round the comparatively small body of defenders. The Greek fleet thereupon sailed away to the coast of Attica. Some of the defenders of Thermopylae retreated; others, including Leonidas, the Spartan commander, were slain in unequal fight. The Persians had entered Greece.

Attica was their first victim. Boeotia, like most of central Greece, submitted to the invaders and rendered them zealous service. There were fresh disputes about the plan of campaign. To defend Athens was impossible, and the population of the city and of Attica was removed to Salamis and Aegina. Attica was soon overrun, and Athens was sacked and burnt. That it was now the turn of the fleet to act was beyond question; but where was the battle to be fought: off Attica or off the Peloponnese? The Spartans insisted that the Isthmus should be fortified and the Peloponnesian coast protected from invasion—a hopeless plan, considering the superiority of the Persian fleet. The Athenians, and especially Themistocles, demanded that the Greek ships should be concentrated between Salamis and the coast of Attica, where there was a chance of success because the gulf was too narrow for the Persian fleet to deploy in. Corinth and Sparta protested and even threatened to withdraw their ships to the coast of the Peloponnese; and Themistocles had great difficulty in securing that the battle should be fought at Salamis. Xerxes also wished this: he hoped to crush the united Greeks and to catch all their fleet in a trap by closing both ends of the gulf.

Battle was given and accepted; and the Greeks were completely victorious. It became necessary for the Persians to change their whole plan of campaign. Their fleet was not, indeed, utterly destroyed at Salamis; but it was so much crippled that the superiority at sea passed over definitely to the other side. And while the Greeks were masters of the sea, it was impossible to maintain a large invading army. They had fears also for their communications with their own country. Therefore Xerxes, with a considerable part of his army, started on the difficult march homewards. Part of the army was left in Thessaly with the object of renewing the strife in the following year, 479 B.C.

The situation of Greece, even after the victory of Salamis, was still precarious. To have beside her, perhaps for ever, a Persian province in northern Greece, with a strong army, was a terrible menace. But to this result the policy of Sparta tended. She continued to insist that central Greece must be abandoned and the Isthmus fortified. Meanwhile, the Persians re-fitted their fleet and sent it to defend the coast of Asia Minor; and they reinforced the army of Mardonius, a skilful general, who passed the winter in Thessaly. The spring brought them back to Greece. The plan of Mardonius was to cause a definite rupture between Sparta and Athens and then to conclude a separate peace with the latter. Once he had the Athenian fleet on his side, he could disregard the fortification of the Isthmus, and the conquest of the Peloponnese was assured. The Athenians were in a difficult position. They had to face a second invasion and a second devastation of their country; for Sparta obstinately refused to send her own forces and those of her allies to central Greece. Nevertheless, the Athenians found strength in themselves to return a decided refusal to the proposals brought by Alexander, King of Macedonia, the envoy of Mardonius. Attica was again occupied, her population was again removed to Salamis, and the destruction of Athens was this time completed.

When Sparta realized that the patience of Athens was nearly exhausted, and that, if Sparta continued to insist on defending the Peloponnese, a separate peace between Mardonius and Athens and the utter collapse of the Spartan plan of campaign were inevitable, then, and not till then, she decided to give up this plan and dispatch her army to Boeotia. A strong Spartan army took the field at once, and was joined by the militia of other Greek states; the whole number amounted to 100,000 infantry, heavy-armed and light-armed. Mardonius at once evacuated Attica. The two armies met not far from Plataea. At first the Persians had the upper hand. Mardonius had excellent cavalry as well as a strong force of infantry. Hence Pausanias, the Spartan king, who commanded the allied Greek army, was hampered in his movements and obliged to keep to the hilly ground between

Boeotia and Attica. The difficulty of the Greek position increased with the duration of the campaign. The Persians had the fertile lands of Boeotia and Thessaly for a base, whereas the Greeks had to draw all their supplies from as far off as the Peloponnese. Again, the Persians were united under one command; but the Greek generals were apt to quarrel even on the field of battle. The Greeks were saved by an error on the part of Mardonius. When Pausanias shifted the front of his army towards the hills, for protection against the Persian cavalry, Mardonius took this manœuvre for a retreat, and gave battle under circumstances which made his cavalry useless. As at Marathon the Persian infantry were beaten by the hoplites; but this time the hoplites were Spartans.

At the same time, in order that the Persian fleet might be kept aloof from the struggle in Greece, the Greek ships sailed eastwards to the island of Samos, where a Persian army and fleet were stationed at Mycale. The Greeks disembarked and offered battle. Betrayed by the Ionian Greeks, who predominated in that division of the Persian army, the Persians were cut to pieces.

As the result of Plataea and Mycale, the Persians were forced to abstain from any further interference in Greek affairs and to abandon the conquest of Greece.

While these events were taking place in Greece an equally stern struggle was going on in the West between the Sicilian Greeks and Carthage. I have spoken already of this important Phoenician colony on the north coast of Africa, of her commercial relations and growing prosperity. By degrees Carthage reduced to subjection the other Phoenician colonies on that coast and also a number of tribes in the interior. In the sixth and fifth centuries B.C. she was a strong imperial power, governed by a small group of her noblest and richest citizens, and possessing a powerful army and fleet, manned partly by citizens and partly by mercenaries. Her trade was directed chiefly to the north and north-west. I have said already that she had to face the competition of Greek cities in Sicily, Italy, and Gaul, and that this led to constant bloody collisions. At the beginning of the fifth century, simultaneously with the third Persian invasion of Greece, and possibly in collusion with Persia, she equipped a powerful fleet and collected a large army, and hurled them upon Sicily, hoping to seize the whole island and expel the Greeks at one blow. Fortunately for the Greeks, Sicily was in such a position that she was prepared to meet the foe. Gelon, tyrant of the city of Gela, an able and ambitious statesman, had created a powerful empire in Sicily; and Syracuse, the richest and strongest city in the island, had come under his sway shortly before the Carthaginian invasion. Making use of the resources thus obtained and of the general apprehension, he collected a great army and met the invaders near Himera. The skill of the general and the favourable conditions—the Carthaginian cavalry had been wrecked while crossing from Africa—gave victory to the Greeks. It was long before Carthage was in a position to renew her attack.

Greece had defended her freedom. Persia and Carthage, it is true, were still great powers, but Persia advanced no farther: she had to think of defence instead. Greece had escaped the fate of Asia Minor: she never became, even for a time, the province of an Eastern monarchy.

XVIII

THE ATHENIAN EMPIRE

AFTER Plataea and Mycale the struggle with the Persians in Greece proper was at an end. Persia recognized that, as things were, she was unable to conquer Greece and cut it up into Persian satrapies. But this does not mean that war between the two nations was ended: it still dragged on, inevitably; and the only question was, what form the struggle would take, and which side would play the active or the passive part. It was possible for Persia to abandon all hope of immediate conquest, and yet to maintain her common frontier with Greece and her possessions in the Balkan peninsula, Asia Minor, and the islands.

The period of fifty years which divides the battle of Plataea from the beginning of the Peloponnesian war is a period about which little is known. Herodotus ends his history with the taking of Sestos in 478 B.C.; Thucydides made it his business to describe and explain the great struggle between Sparta and Athens for primacy in Greece; and the later historians—Ephorus, Theopompus, and others—who recorded not episodes merely but the whole of Greek history, have come down to us, if they have come down at all, in mere fragments. Those fifty years were not marked out by any central incident of arresting interest, and therefore found no historian fit to rank with Herodotus or Thucydides.

It was impossible that Persia should give up the struggle. But she had suffered such shrewd blows in Greece that the ponderous framework of the Persian Empire, with its immense territory and motley armies, obviously needed some respite in order to concentrate these armies and prepare for a fresh attack. But this respite Greece refused to give. She never stopped fighting, even temporarily; instead of defending herself, she became aggressive. She made it her object to push the Persians back to Asia and deprive them of immediate contact with the Aegean. This military object was at the same time a national object: what mattered most was to restore their independence to the Greek cities on the Aegean coast. We are ill informed of the way in which this policy was carried out. I have said above that we have but meagre records of the period following the Persian wars; and such information as we have refers mainly to the internal affairs of Greece and not to the struggle against Persia. These internal affairs became more complicated as Athens rose in political importance. There was increasing friction between her and her neighbours; and behind those neighbours was Sparta, ever turning a suspicious eye on the increasing wealth and importance of Athens.

The main incidents, however, of this struggle are known. It was directed originally by Sparta. Before the war Sparta had been the chief political and military power in Greece; to her, with Athens coming next, had belonged the first place in the actual conduct of the war; her army had won the battle of Plataea. But Sparta was ill suited to take the lead in a contest which was waged chiefly by sea and on the outskirts of the Greek world. Such a war demanded a more flexible and active machine than the constitution of Sparta. Her military strength was limited and could not be squandered here and there in large numbers. Her domestic affairs, her relations to the Helots and Perioeci, made it necessary to retain at home a large military force, the majority, indeed, of those Spartiates who formed the nucleus of the army. This concentration of Spartan force in Greece, instead of Asia Minor and Thrace, was required also by the complicated political situation of the Peloponnese, where Sparta's leadership depended upon military superiority alone. Finally, as we have seen, Sparta was an agricultural and inland kingdom: her wealth was limited, and no war could be carried on with success at sea and on the outskirts of the Greek world without large expenditure.

All this taken together inevitably drove Sparta to resign the leading part in the further struggle against Persia. But a leader there must be, and the only possible leader was Athens. Her fleet was the best in Greece; her army was considerable, including as it did all the citizens of the state, i.e. the immense majority of the population inhabiting Athens, the Peiraeus, and all Attica; and the fleet could easily convey detachments of the force to wherever they were

PLATE LXVII
ATHENS OF THE PERSIAN WARS

GREEK POTTERY OF THE 5TH CENT. B. C.

1. ATTIC CUP (red figures on black ground) from the workshop of Euphronios, the great Athenian potter and painter of the late 6th and early 5th century. Found at Caere in Italy. The picture, which is splendidly illustrated by the beautiful victory-song (*paean*) of Bacchylides, recently found, represents the Athenian national hero Theseus. He had been challenged by the Cretan King Minos to prove that he was really the son of Poseidon. Fearless, he jumped from his ship into the sea, and supported by a sea-monster Triton met the sea-queen Amphitrite in her palace. His protectress and the patron of his city, Athena, assisted him; and he received from the queen both recognition and rich gifts. The picture is one of the most beautiful of archaic vase paintings. It is important from the historical point of view as well. It shows that, from the time of Pisistratus, Athens regarded herself as the mistress of the sea. About 500 B. C. Paris, Louvre.

2. ATTIC CUP (red-figured) showing an aged citizen helping a young man to put on the arms of a hoplite. The expression of deep sorrow is masterly. Such were the fathers of those who fought for their country at Marathon, Salamis and Plataea. About 480 B.C. Vatican, Rome.

3. ATTIC CUP (red-figured) in the style of Duris. Oedipus is seated on a rock meditating over the riddle of human life which the Sphinx, a beautiful winged woman with a lion's body, has asked him. A beautiful symbol of the time of the great Greek thinkers, especially the Sophists, who tried over and over again to find a logical solution of the riddle of life. About 480 B. C. Vatican, Rome.

4. ATTIC CUP (red-figured) in the style of the painter Duris. The picture shows Jason, the first Greek sailor, who went on the ship Argo to Colchis in the Caucasus to bring back the golden fleece. He met here the dragon which guarded the fleece, entered its huge body or was swallowed by it, was rescued, and finally killed the monster. The picture shows Jason coming out of the dragon's mouth under the protection of Athena. The fleece hangs near by on a tree. The picture demonstrates how early Athens became interested in the Greek colonies on the Black Sea and wished to be recognized as their protectress. About 480 B. C. Vatican, Rome.

5. A GRECO-PERSIAN GEM showing the Persian king fighting a Greek hoplite. Arndt collection. 4th cent. B C. After W. Weber.

1. RED-FIGURED ATTIC CUP. THESEUS AND AMPHITRITE

2. RED-FIGURED ATTIC CUP. ATHENIAN WARRIOR AND HIS FATHER

5. GRECO-PERSIAN GEM. PERSIAN KING AND GREEK WARRIOR

3. RED-FIGURED ATTIC CUP. OEDIPUS AND THE SPHINX

4. RED-FIGURED ATTIC CUP. JASON AND THE DRAGON

LXVII. ATHENS OF THE PERSIAN WARS. GREEK POTTERY OF THE Vth CENT. B.C.

needed. Besides, after the democratic reforms of Cleisthenes, her domestic affairs were in order ; and indeed the citizens, busy with military enterprises, had no time to think of anything else. And lastly, the spirit of patriotism had risen high in Athens, in consequence of Marathon, Salamis, and Plataea ; and the fame of the Athenians, as excellent soldiers and sailors and sagacious politicians, was very great. It is no wonder that Athens coveted the direction of the struggle against Persia, and obtained it.

Though Greece proper, i. e. the cities dotted about the Balkan peninsula, was not much concerned in this contest, to the islands and the cities in Asia Minor it was a matter of life and death. These parts of Greece took therefore an active part in it, combining, under the presidency of Athens, in a marine confederacy with a centre at Delos—a confederacy which gave birth to the Athenian Empire. The principles of this alliance were—that each of the allies should take part in the war and be represented at the council of the league in proportion to his military strength ; and each might contribute money instead of men and ships. Under these conditions it was natural that the presidency should belong to Athens. Possessing larger forces and greater wealth than the other allies, she commanded a majority of votes in the council ; she alone had men enough and energy enough to convert the money of the allies, in case they were unwilling or unable to take an active part in the war, into ships and soldiers. On the Athenians, as directors, the chief responsibility fell ; and their importance on the council was naturally in proportion to their responsibility.

By the action of this confederation the Aegean was gradually cleared of the Persians. The Hellespont and the Sea of Marmora joined the alliance, or, in other words, became Athenian waters ; the most important points were garrisoned by colonies of Athenian citizens ; and by degrees the Persians were squeezed out of the southern Aegean also. The chief actors in this systematic warfare against Persia were new. Aristides, a general at the battle of Plataea and founder of the Confederacy of Delos, had left the scene. So had Themistocles, the hero of Salamis and the creator of the Athenian fleet. His last achievement was to fortify Athens and the harbour of Piraeus with walls. With her land and sea bases thus fortified Athens could carry on freely her activity at sea, and could be indifferent to the possibility of attacks by land against her capital and harbour. Later, like most statesmen of the Athenian democracy, Themistocles was prosecuted and exiled. His remaining days he spent in Persia.

The chief figure at Athens now was Cimon. He led the aristocratic party and supported the 'balance of power' in Greece, that is, a policy of peace and agreement with Sparta and the other Greek states. Thus he was peculiarly well fitted to direct the foreign policy of Athens, as things then were. Like his father, Miltiades, and like Themistocles, he had great ability. His chief exploit was his victory over the Persians at the river Eurymedon in 468 B.C., which decided the mastery of the southern waters. After this defeat the Persians had no marine base except the coasts of Palestine, Syria, Phoenicia, and Egypt.

This battle completed a series of operations against Persia, which were closely connected with the invasion of Greece. The Greeks realized clearly that the danger of a fresh invasion was not to be feared in the immediate future. But this did not imply that the struggle was over. Persia was still a strong marine power with outlets to the Mediterranean, and sooner or later she might return to a policy of attack with increased experience and increased knowledge. But no Greeks except the Athenians realized this danger. The rest felt themselves free from immediate menace, and thought it unnecessary to preserve, with an eye to the future, the naval organization which they had created for the contest with Persia. Thus a process of decomposition began in the confederation. The allies resented the supremacy of Athens and aimed at complete political independence.

There were now two alternatives before Athens—either to renounce the mastery of the Aegean and revert to the state of things before the Persian wars, or to convert the confederation into an Athenian Empire; in other words, to rule the allies instead of presiding over them, a result which could only be secured by force. She was induced to take the second of these courses, partly by her conviction that the struggle with Persia was not yet over, and partly by other considerations. Athens had become a great city: a large part of the Aegean trade was concentrated there; and she had become an important centre of industry. The population had greatly increased: to the citizens were added a multitude of aliens (*metoeci*) who did not possess the franchise but settled in the city in order to carry on trade and industry; the number of slaves also had risen greatly. The loss of mastery over the sea would certainly have arrested this development; and also it might have forced on Athens a return to the conditions that existed before the Persian wars; and such a return would inevitably have brought with it serious internal con-

FIG. 31. *Red-figured cup. The picture shows a beautiful pack donkey, a familiar figure in all the bazaars of the East. Attic work of about 480 B.C. Boston Museum. After Hartwig.*

vulsions. Hence she chose the second course and proceeded to convert the confederation into an empire, in which the citizens of Athens ruled over the citizens of other states, and the contributions of the allies became tribute instead.

This decision affected the whole policy of Athens, both at home and abroad. The leaders of the democratic party—first Ephialtes and then Pericles—became assertors of the imperialistic ideas and aspirations cherished by the citizens. The activity of Ephialtes was short-lived: soon after his first public appearance he was mysteriously murdered. But Pericles guided Athenian policy for many years, and always found support in the popular assembly. He was a strict and consistent champion of the view that Athens should be at once a democracy and a great imperial power; he was an excellent orator, and a wary and sagacious statesman. It is with good reason that the time between the banishment of Cimon in 461 B. C. and the beginning of the Peloponnesian war is generally called the Age of Pericles.

The decision was taken, and Athens became the centre of a great empire, a democracy herself, but with a number of states dependent on her and ruled by her in all matters except those of purely local interest, and thereby deprived of their political independence. This decision altered the policy of Athens towards her nearest neighbours and towards Sparta, and also affected her relation to the Persian monarchy; and in both cases the new policy was due to economic causes and mainly to commercial considerations. The victory over Persia had severed Greece from the East. The East was no longer one of the chief markets for Greek exports, chiefly wine and olive oil, and for the raw material, bought by Greek merchants in the West and on the Black Sea and exchanged for the products of Eastern manufacture.

Between the seventh and fifth centuries B. C. Greece created her own flourishing manufactures, developed and improved her production of wine and oil, and found for her wares a number of markets, where they were appreciated more and more and found increasing sales. The chief markets were Italy, Gaul, and Spain in the west, Macedonia, Thrace, and the Black Sea coast in the north and north-east. The Phoenicians were her only rivals. Driven out of the Aegean, they were still masters of the lucrative trade with Egypt (though the Greeks tried to compete with them there as early as the seventh century B. C.), and tried hard to oust the Greeks from all the western trade. It is therefore no wonder that the imperial fleet of Athens aimed its first blows at the Phoenicians, attacking them in Cyprus and Egypt, the main centres of their trade in the eastern Mediterranean. Success in the struggle for these markets would have enabled Greece to attack Phoenicia itself. But both these Athenian expeditions ended in failure. When endeavouring to support the Egyptian revolt against Persia (456–454 B. C.), they lost a considerable detachment of soldiers and a powerful squadron of ships ; in Cyprus, having recalled Cimon from banishment to lead their army, they won a battle (450 B.C.) but reaped no considerable advantage from it. Cimon died of disease during the campaign. They were forced to make peace with Persia and leave the question of Phoenicia to be settled by future generations.

Athens was unsuccessful against Persia, because she was at the same time drawn into strife with her nearest neighbours and with Sparta. Her empire was by no means consolidated at this time, and she was forced, as we shall see later, to fight against her own allies or subjects. In this case the war with Aegina, Corinth, and Boeotia was due to the same economic and commercial motives which had embroiled her with Persia. Aegina was an old enemy and a rival. Corinth with her western colonies excluded Athens from the Italian coast and the great grain-markets of Italy and Sicily. But for Athens, with the growth of her manufactures and the conversion of her fields into vineyards and olive groves, the import of raw material and foodstuffs was a question of life and death. Italy and Sicily could supply both her needs more fully than any country except Egypt. The northern markets, still only in process of development, could not produce enough to satisfy the needs of the great Athenian Empire, increased as it was by the accession of the Ionian cities, which were now cut off from the East and could no longer draw their food-supplies from that quarter.

Repeating the policy which they had employed against Phoenicia, the Athenians did not attack Corinth directly, but tried to weaken her by seizing Aegina and forcing her into the alliance, by depriving Megara, the neighbour of Corinth and Athens, of all commercial importance, and by establishing her own ascendancy in Boeotia. This attempt to extend her influence in Greece proper naturally involved collision with Sparta, to whom (and to all Peloponnesians) the neutrality of the Isthmus was of vital importance, because they depended largely on the import of corn and raw material from Italy and Sicily. The struggle dragged on from 459 to 447 B.C., and Athens in the end was unsuccessful. Aegina, indeed, became part of the Athenian Empire ; but she was unable either to cut off Megara from the sea or to strengthen her own position in Boeotia. Again she was obliged to end the war by an unprofitable peace which was concluded, first in 452 B. C., for five years, and then, in 446, extended to thirty. Sparta consented to make peace, though the question of Athenian ascendancy in central Greece was by no means settled. But she could not help herself: she was weakened by a long struggle against the Helots, from 464 to 459 B. C., and by repeated complications with Elis and Arcadia, members of the Spartan military league, and with Argos, her stubborn enemy.

Unsuccessful in her grand imperialistic schemes, Athens was now obliged to deal with the affairs of her confederacy, in other words, of her new dominions, and to consolidate her position in those parts of the world where her supremacy was as yet undisputed—in Thrace and on the Black Sea coast. The wish to impress the dependent cities and extend the bounds of the empire explains the cruise undertaken by Pericles in 445 B. C. In command of a great fleet he visited the coast of the Black Sea and the Crimea, where a number of military colonies were planted, probably by Pericles himself, and many Greek cities were annexed to the empire. While Athens was fighting Persia and her Greek neighbours, the process was going on which converted the maritime confederation into the Athenian Empire. In 454 B. C. the treasury of the league was transferred from Delos to Athens; most of the allies, except Samos, Lesbos, and Chios, became dependent and paid tribute; and they were all obliged at this time to refer most of their suits at law to the decision of the Athenian courts. All this was exceedingly displeasing to the 'allies', as the subjects of the Athenian Empire were still officially called; and they resented the constant interference of Athens in the internal affairs of cities which still considered themselves independent. Thus Athens had constantly to deal with 'revolts' among the allies. Some of these, e. g. the revolt of free Samos, which refused to remain a member of the league, and the revolt of Byzantium, were very formidable and were quelled with great severity.

The internal life of Athens was influenced by her ambitious foreign policy. The consistent development of that policy was guided mainly by the lower classes—by the citizens engaged in navigation, trade, and manufacture. They were the masters, and all public institutions were re-fashioned, to suit them, in the spirit of extreme democracy. The political centre of gravity was now transferred from the Council of Five Hundred to the popular assembly, in which the law required that all important business should be decided, such as questions of foreign policy, of war, and of food-supplies. Once in each prytany (a period of thirty-six days) the public assembly reviewed the proceedings of the magistrates, with power to suspend and bring them to trial, in case of any irregularity. Under these conditions the magistrates confined themselves to executing the decisions of the assembly; and the council merely discussed beforehand the business which the assembly had subsequently to decide. Every member of the assembly had the right to speak and even to initiate legislation. But the latter right was hedged about with certain safeguards. A new law was passed, not by the whole assembly but by a special committee; and if it failed to pass, its mover might be fined or even put to death. (This became the rule soon after the death of Pericles; up till then bills of legislation were worked out by a special committee, discussed by the council, and finally passed by the assembly.)

The board of ten generals (*strategi*) acquired great importance at the same time and formed a kind of cabinet. This was a survival from the troubled times of the Persian wars. All foreign and domestic policy was concentrated in their hands. If their policy was successful, they might be re-elected an indefinite number of times; in case of failure, they were tried and sentenced to exile or death. Their high position was quite natural in a state where the centre of gravity lay in foreign and military affairs, and in the ruling of an empire. There was also an army of executive officials, all appointed annually by lot, and serving partly in Athens and partly abroad. Their chief business was the finance of the empire.

There was a third body which played an important part in public life. This was the Heliaea or judicial assembly in which citizens were paid for their duties. This body monopolized by degrees all the forensic business of Athens. It consisted of 6,000 members, 600 taken by lot from each tribe. They were divided into committees of 500, but the number was sometimes greater than this, sometimes less. The jurors swore to give their verdict in accordance with the laws, and, in cases where the law could be interpreted in more than one way, according to their conscience. The number of suits, especially when swollen by business of the empire, was very large and took long to decide. The magistrates merely prepared the case and took no part in the decision. Advocates and defenders were not admitted to the court : each party had to appear in person. The verdict was determined by a simple majority.

Such was the final form of democracy. Neither in foreign nor in domestic affairs did it lead to any specially brilliant consequences. To it, in considerable measure, Athens owed her failure in the struggle with Sparta, and her fall.

XIX

THE PELOPONNESIAN WAR

THE continued existence of the Athenian Empire started a problem in Greek politics. Which was the stronger, the centralizing forces personified in that empire, or the opposite tendency towards independence in each separate community? It is remarkable that the Athenian democracy, while taking the path of imperialism, at the same time supported the democratic cause in all the states dependent on Athens. She reckoned that the democrats, most of whom belonged to the industrial and trading class, would support the commercial imperialism of Athens, even if injury were done to the political independence of the separate communities. However selfish the policy of Athens might be, yet she made the seas safe for traders and admitted her allies to some share in the advantages of her commercial ascendancy.

'Self-determination' and 'a balance of power'—these had once been the watchwords of most Greek cities. Now they were proclaimed chiefly by the adherents of aristocracy—the wealthy landowners and smallholders. Sparta sympathized to a certain extent with this programme: she was prepared to concede to her allies a larger measure of self-government, even in political affairs, than Athens was willing to grant. She supported, therefore, in all ways the aristocratic and oligarchic factions which existed in every Greek community and even at Athens. She left no stone unturned, that the conservative policy, which was bitterly opposed to Athenian imperialism and sympathized with the constitution of Sparta, if not with her military league, might become the policy of as many Greek states as possible.

But the difference between the Spartan attitude and the Athenian attitude towards these fundamental questions of Greek politics does not explain why these two powers were infallibly bound to meet in armed conflict—a contest which was destined to continue till the strength of the combatants

PLATE LXVIII

WAR IN THE ART OF THE 5TH CENT. B.C.

1. RED-FIGURED CUP painted by Brygos. The pictures represent the capture of Troy by the Greeks with all its horrors. On one side we see Priam taking refuge at the altar of Apollo, and Neoptolemos, the son of Achilles, using the boy Astyanax to brain him with. On the other side a wild fight is going on. The heroic woman who defends her boy is Andromache. Attic work of about 480 B.C. Paris, Louvre. After Furtwängler-Reichhold.

2. RED-FIGURED WINE-CUP (*kantharos*) painted by Duris. The picture shows the fight between Greeks, led by Heracles, and Amazons. The idea is to represent the victorious fight of Greece against the East. Attic work of about 490–480 B.C. Brussels Museum.

1. RED-FIGURED CUP. CAPTURE OF TROY

2. RED-FIGURED WINE-CUP. HERACLES AND THE AMAZONS

LXVIII. WAR IN THE ART OF THE Vth CENT. B.C.

was utterly exhausted, and to end in the complete triumph of the separatist tendency. The turn of events in the first half of the fifth century B. C. was such, that the coexistence of a maritime Athenian Empire and a Spartan league of inland states enjoying some measure of political independence was perfectly possible; and this might seem the most reasonable solution of the difficulty for an indefinite time to come.

The explanation of the conflict is therefore to be found not merely in the fundamentally different view of politics taken by two almost equally matched powers in Greece, but also in a succession of accompanying incidents, which ripened and hastened on the clash of arms. The growing trade and industry of Athens and the states in alliance with her, including the islands and Anatolian cities, made the question of the Western markets, which had not been settled by the wars of 500–450 B. C., still more acute. Corinth and Megara would not and could not put up with the increasing competition of Athens in Italy and Sicily. The success of Athens in her trade with the West is proved by this one fact—that from 500 B. C. her pottery drove out, all over Italy, the product of all other Greek centres of the manufacture. If imports from Athens grew thus, the exports from Italy and Sicily—corn, cattle, and metals—would soon pour exclusively into the Piraeus; and then Athens would have an ascendancy, not merely commercial but political also, in all the north and west of the Peloponnese. For those districts could not support their own population and depended absolutely upon food exported from the West; but this trade would be monopolized by Athens. Sparta also, though not interested in export trade to the West, was menaced by this danger and therefore inclined to listen to the complaints of Megara, Corinth, and Sicyon.

It was a turning-point in the long rivalry, political and economic, between Athens and the Peloponnese, when Athens made up her mind that certain questions concerning Megara and Corcyra were ripe for settlement. Pericles was induced by continual friction with Megara to take the decisive step of declaring a blockade of the city. And at the same time Athens was compelled to take a definite line in the Western question. In 433 B.C. Corcyra, a rich colony of Corinth and the natural bridge between Greece and the West, finding that her commercial interests were constantly at variance with those of her mother city, expressed her readiness to enter into alliance with Athens. To do this was to cut off from Corinth her last chance of stemming the rush of Athenian trade to the West, and to put the control over the western trade-route, which was commanded by the harbours of Corcyra, in the hands of Athens. For the presence of an Athenian fleet in those harbours would hand over to Athens all the Italian and Sicilian trade. She had at this time allies and friends in both countries, few but faithful. Sparta had to decide whether the western waters should be given up to Athens or not. It was almost impossible for Athens to withdraw: to check the expansion of her trade was to endanger the very existence of her empire. And lastly, Athens was aiming at complete control over the Chalcidian peninsula, which involved her in a prolonged contest with Potidaea. Potidaea, an ally of Athens but a colony of Corinth, was unwilling to part with her last scrap of independence and to become a member not of the Athenian confederation but of the Athenian Empire.

Sparta decided for war, though her prospect of victory was not very bright. It was a contest for mastery of the sea and demanded, above all, a fleet and money; and she, as an inland and agricultural power, possessed neither. Nor was the Corinthian fleet a match even for the fleet of Corcyra. Athens, on the other hand, had a fleet, a large reserve of money, control of the trade-routes, a great number of men for service in the fleet and army—the population of the empire reached two millions—and considerable wealth amassed by individual citizens. It is no wonder that Pericles insisted upon war. Still, Sparta did not act without definite grounds for her action. Her chief superiority lay in her army. If Athens decided to fight a pitched battle in defence of her territory, which the Greek cities generally did in their wars with one another, Sparta could easily defeat her on land; and such a defeat might naturally lead to disruption of the Athenian confederation and defection of the allies, in other words, to civil war within the empire. It is probable, too, that Sparta disbelieved in the strength of the Athenian democracy: on the eve of the Persian wars she had managed to interfere in the domestic affairs of Athens and had met with support in the city itself.

Beginning in 431 B.C., the war dragged on for twenty-eight years of almost continuous operations. Thucydides, a contemporary and himself an actor in the war—he was at one time in command of an Athenian force—has left us a description of it, which is one of the noblest monuments of the Greek genius in literature and art—a masterpiece both in detail and in its general survey of a period of primary importance. The course of the war is therefore known to us in all its particulars. The general outline is as follows. The first ten years are somewhat monotonous. The Spartan plan was to invade Attica year after year in harvest time, in order to reduce the population to despair and force the Athenians to fight a decisive battle. Sparta also endeavoured, without much success, to sow division among the subjects of the Athenian Empire. The policy of Athens was to abstain from an engagement on Attic soil, and on this account the population was withdrawn into the city. At the same time the Athenians took every means to seize the western sea-routes, i.e. the route through the Corinthian Gulf and round the Peloponnese. This was not easy, because most Greek cities in Italy and Sicily were hostile; many of them were Dorian colonies, and Syracuse, a purely Dorian colony, was more hostile than others. Further, it was imperatively necessary for Athens to keep full control over the northern and eastern waters; but this again was a difficult and complicated business. To secure the former of these objects it was not enough to hold the entrance of the Corinthian Gulf: it was necessary to have a maritime base and, if possible, more than one, on the coast of the Peloponnese itself.

Athens suffered a heavy blow when, in 430 B.C., at the very beginning of the war, a destructive plague broke out in the city and crippled her just at the very moment when the exercise of her full strength might have decided the war in her favour. The plague also carried off Pericles, whose genius had sketched out the main lines for conducting the war, and who held all the threads of it in his own hands. Yet, in spite of this incalculable calamity, the strength of Athens was so great that the course of events was, in general, favourable to her. But neither side was able to inflict a decisive blow upon the other. The western trade-route remained open, even after Athens had seized two points in or near the Peloponnese—Pylos and Cythera—and actually captured at Pylos a considerable Spartan force. It became clear that **to** control one end of this route was not enough, and that a powerful base at both ends was indispensable. As it was, the Peloponnese kept up connexion with Italy and Sicily and could not be forced to surrender. It must have surrendered, had it been possible for Athens to stop the importation of food, especially of grain, from Italy and Sicily.

But Sparta's plan of forcing the Athenian army to fight a decisive battle was a failure also. The devastation of Attica was ineffective, for the Athenian fleets retaliated by ravaging the Peloponnesian coast, and her control of the Black Sea route secured to Athens a supply of grain and fish for food and of raw materials for manufacture. Revolts among the allies were ruthlessly suppressed. The single success of Sparta was the seizure of Amphipolis in Macedonia and of Chalcidice ; but these places were not of vital importance to Athens. Meanwhile the strength of both antagonists was beginning to fail, and the peace party in both countries became prominent and importunate. After ten years of war, when Cleon, the chief of the war-like and imperialistic party, was killed in Thrace and predominating influence passed to Nicias, a man of small ability and a lover of peace, Sparta and Athens concluded a peace and even an alliance. This peace, which dates from 421 B. C., is called in history the Peace of Nicias.

Lasting this peace could not be. The Athenians were conscious of their strength and aware that the chance of victory was still, on the whole, on their side. Still the foundations of the Athenian Empire were shaking, and their confederation was threatened with gradual dissolution from within. The Persian spectre again raised its head in the East, and Persian gold found easy access to the pockets of orators who attacked Athens in the allied cities. Nothing but complete success could save Athens: a partial victory was little better than defeat. This point of view was expressed in set terms by Alcibiades, the nephew of Pericles, an able general and dexterous politician, and an incarnation of the virtues and vices which marked Athenian character in her time of empire. The military problem and the political problem were both clear to him. In Greece Sparta was invulnerable. Decisive success was attainable only by complete control at sea ; and, for this purpose, it was necessary that the Greeks in Italy and Sicily should be included in the Athenian confederation. Syracuse was the Athens of the

West; and it could not be expected that this Dorian rival should enter the alliance of her own free will. One course remained—to compel her to come in. This was the design of Alcibiades. If successful, it would bring speedy and certain victory; and failure was improbable, because no one expected such a step on the part of Athens.

The enterprise was planned and carried out on a great scale. In 415 B.C. a formidable expedition was suddenly sent westwards. The plan of campaign was carefully worked out, and all the threads of it were in the hands of Alcibiades, its author and the leader of the expedition. But at the very start a decisive blow was dealt to their design by the Athenians themselves. His political opponents first prosecuted Alcibiades on a frivolous charge, and then prevented an investigation while he was still on the spot; when he had started, they stirred up the people against him and condemned him in absence. This was a fatal blow to the whole enterprise. He fled to Sparta and revealed to the Spartans all the details of his plan. Nicias, his successor, had no plan of his own and was incompetent to devise one. For all this, the Athenian armament was so powerful that at first the capture of Syracuse seemed possible. But Nicias was slow and made mistake after mistake. Sparta had time to throw reinforcements into Syracuse under a competent general, who had got accurate information from Alcibiades concerning the resources of Athens and the weak points of the expedition. The affair ended with the complete destruction, in 413 B.C., of the Athenian army and navy.

So the stake was lost and the fate of the Athenian Empire settled. The chief assets of Athens, her fleet and her reserve, had perished at Syracuse; for nearly all the reserve had been spent in fitting out the expedition; and it was impossible to replace them. And yet the weakness and poverty of Sparta prolonged the agony for nearly ten years more. For victory Sparta needed a fleet, and for a fleet she needed money; but she and her partisans in Greece, already ruined by the war, could supply neither of these requisites. The Italian and Sicilian Greeks were never inclined to give her active and steady support, and now they were threatened with a fresh attack from Carthage. Persia was the one possible source from which funds might be got for continuing the war. Sparta did not hesitate: she even agreed to hand back the Greeks in Asia Minor to Persian rule. But Persia was slow to act. Each satrap in Asia Minor had a policy of his own to carry on, so that the affair took time. Also Sparta prolonged the negotiations, because she could not all at once make up her mind to betray the interests of Greece. The proposal was that Persia should send a Phoenician squadron to assist Sparta, and should provide pay for the crews of the Spartan ships.

Of this delay Athens took advantage. The general despair after the Sicilian disaster had enabled the oligarchs to seize control for a few months and to set up the Council of Four Hundred. But the democratic party soon turned them out and adopted as their watchword 'a fight to a finish', whereas the oligarchs were anxious to stop the war as soon as possible. In the restoration of democracy a leading part was played by the fleet; and the fleet also insisted that Alcibiades should be pardoned. The exile had quarrelled with Sparta and fled to Asia Minor, where he was now trying to hinder the negotiations between Sparta and the Persian magnates. Restoration from exile, a fresh outburst of patriotism at Athens, and the hesitations of Sparta, enabled Alcibiades to gain considerable successes during the next four years. In 410 B.C. he won a great naval victory off Cyzicus and began by degrees to bring pressure on the Spartans and Persians. But a trifling failure incurred by one of his subordinates at Notium in 407 B.C. gave a handle to his enemies at Athens, and they contrived to secure his condemnation in absence. He fled to the coast of Asia Minor and watched from there the course of the war. At the same time an energetic satrap made his appearance in Asia Minor, in the person of Cyrus, younger son of Darius II; and Sparta found in Lysander a skilful, brave, and ambitious general, not inferior in his aptitude for war to Alcibiades himself.

After the expulsion of Alcibiades the Athenians made one more great effort. The chief object of the Spartans and Persians was to seize the north-eastern waters and so to deprive Athens of food-supplies from the Black Sea; they had already driven her from the Anatolian coast and some of the chief Aegean islands. An Athenian fleet was now sent to defend the Hellespont and began with success: the Spartans were defeated at Arginusae in 406 B.C. But the battle was fought during a storm, and many Athenian sailors were drowned. The failure of the generals to rescue their drowning men caused an explosion of anger in the popular assembly at Athens. The generals were deprived of their command, and those of them who had come home were put to death. Such summary justice did not encourage their successors. To this cause among others the Athenians owed their final and decisive defeat, which took place at Aegospotami near the entrance of the Hellespont.

With the fleet the last hope of Athens perished. She was forced to accept the terms of peace dictated by Sparta in 404 B.C. The walls of the Piraeus were levelled, and also the walls connecting the fortifications of the Piraeus with those of Athens; the fleet, with the exception of twelve ships, was destroyed; and Athens was forced to join the Lacedaemonian league, in complete dependence upon Sparta. She continued, however, to exist as an independent state, in spite of the persistence with which Megara and Corinth demanded her complete destruction. Sparta even carried her magnanimous policy so far that she did not require Athens to retain the oligarchical government set up by Lysander, which was carried on by Critias and the rest of the Thirty Tyrants. When Thrasybulus overthrew the Thirty and restored the democracy, this revolution was quietly accepted by the Spartans.

The fundamental question of Greek politics was thus settled, and settled once for all. Local freedom and self-determination for each state had been bought; and the price paid was the collapse of the one attempt to consolidate Greece into a single political unit. It is true that this attempt was based on the ascendancy of one state over all the rest. We shall see later that Greece endeavoured to settle the question of national unity by resorting to federation. But by that time the existence of an independent Greek power, based upon an association of free city-states, was altogether out of the question.

XX

GREEK CIVILIZATION AND SOCIAL DEVELOPMENT FROM 500 TO 400 B. C.

AFTER the defeat of Persia by Athens and Sparta, Athens became the chief political power in the Greek world, especially in central Greece, the islands, and Asia Minor; and to her also fell the leadership in economic development and in culture. In these departments, Sparta had neither the power nor the wish to rival her, and Asia Minor, cut off from the Eastern markets, was entirely dependent upon her. Some independence was still kept by the Greeks in Italy and Sicily; but such outposts of Hellas had no important influence on the life of those Greeks who lived round the Aegean. Athens, on the other hand, had acquired not only great political influence but a still greater moral authority. Greece recognized that Athenian persistence and patriotism had saved her, when the whole nation was threatened with the fate of the Ionian Greeks. For this reason Athens and all her doings were now watched with intense interest by the whole nation.

Life at Athens itself underwent radical changes. The city had become the capital of Hellas, and the citizens were conscious of this. Perhaps the growth of the city itself is the most obvious proof of this change in the position of Athens. In the sixth century B. C. the city, though large, had grown up irregularly; its religious centre was on the Acropolis, which had once been occupied by the fortified palace of the kings and was now consecrated to Athena, the guardian goddess of Athens, and the site of her modest temple of local stone. Pisistratus did much for Athens. He built a large and convenient central market, improved the water-supply, erected a stately entrance to the Acropolis and a new central temple to Athena on the same hill. All this was swept away by the Persian invasion. When the city was recovered by its inhabitants, they found it in ruins. From 479 B. C. the work of making good the destruction went busily on. Cimon was conspicuous in this task; and one of his buildings is preserved—a superb temple at the base of the Acropolis, the so-called temple of Theseus, probably dedicated to Hephaestus. He also adorned the market-place, which served also as an exchange and a social club, and was the place where some political business was transacted. Beside the market-place he built the famous *Stoa Poecile*, or Painted Colonnade, whose walls were painted by a celebrated artist, Polygnotus. Of these frescoes some represented heroic actions belonging to the legendary past; but others depicted such recent achievements as the battle of Marathon.

The Acropolis, however, still lay in ruins. Pericles, the director and organizer of the Athenian Empire, undertook the task of restoring it. Millions were spent by Athens to turn the Acropolis into one of the most perfect of architectural productions, adorned with a whole museum of masterpieces in stone and in colour. The work was still going on during the Peloponnesian war, at the very time when the shipwreck of Athenian power was drawing near. In realizing his artistic design Pericles was assisted by the architect Ictinus, and by Phidias, the greatest of Greek sculptors. Their intention was to make the Acropolis a splendid dwelling-place for Athena, reigning above the city and symbolizing the power and might of Athens, both as an empire and as the heart of Greek civilization. It was still a fortress at the time of the Persian invasion, but it ceased now to be a fortress; the centre of Athens had no further need of fortifications. On its slopes there were no private houses and no shops; only a few shrines, including that of Asclepius, enlivened the steep sides of the hill. A stately staircase, ending in an elaborate entrance supported on pillars, led up from the plain below. In one wing of this entrance was a picture-gallery. Over the staircase, on the right-hand side as you went in, there rose on a high bastion the beautiful temple of Athena Nike, the guardian and defender of the Acropolis. The whole surface of the hill was converted into a level terrace, divided by the Sacred Way. Both sides of the Way were lined by a forest of votive offerings dedicated by Athenian citizens to their great goddess, and by the archives of the Athenian democracy —the most important decrees of the popular assembly, engraved on stone. To the right and left of this Way rose the two dwelling-places of Athena.

PLATE LXIX

ATHENS OF THE 5TH CENT. B.C.

1. RESTORATION OF THE BUILDINGS OF THE ACROPOLIS. In the centre the entrance gate (*Propylaea*), to which leads a sloping paved way. To the right before the entrance the temple of Nike (the goddess of Victory). On the Acropolis, to the right the Parthenon, to the left the Erechtheion. Behind the Propylaea the statue of Athena Promachos by Phidias. After Bohn.

2. VIEW OF THE RUINS OF THE PARTHENON, the grand creation of Pericles, Ictinos, and Phidias.

3. VIEW OF THE SO-CALLED TEMPLE OF THESEUS, perhaps dedicated to Hephaestus, the god of the Athenian craftsmen. It is one of the best-preserved ruins of the ancient world, a typical Doric temple of the 5th cent. B.C.

1. RESTORATION OF THE ACROPOLIS

2. THE RUINS OF THE PARTHENON

3. THE SO-CALLED TEMPLE OF THESEUS

LXIX. ATHENS OF THE Vth CENT. B.C.

To the right is the mighty Parthenon, the home of Athena Parthenos, a great Doric temple, with a gabled roof and columns all round it. The east of the building was occupied by the *cella*, the real temple, the dwelling of the goddess; here by the inner wall stood the ivory and gold statue of Athena; two rows of columns divided the *cella* into three aisles. Behind this was a chamber in which the treasures of Athena were kept. The rich sculpture which adorned the temple told the spectator the history of the relations between the goddess and the city. Over the columns, on their outer side, in the metopes (or spaces between the triglyphs) the struggle of civilization against the forces of primeval chaos was unrolled—the Lapithae, the oldest Greek inhabitants of Thessaly, conquering the Centaurs, half-men and half-horses; the Greeks conquering the East personified in the Amazons; and the gods conquering the giants. Of the pediments (or triangular gables at the ends of the temple) one represented the birth of Athena from the head of Zeus, the other the strife between Athena and Poseidon for possession of Athens. Lastly, the famous frieze which ran round the outer wall of the *cella* represents the Pan-Athenaic festival—the annual procession of Athenian citizens to the shrine of the goddess. In life-like groups they move towards the temple—priests and victims for sacrifice, magistrates, maidens carrying the garment newly woven for Athena by Athenian women, reverend elders leaning on their staves, and noble youths riding on thoroughbred horses. A group of gods looks on.

On the other side of the Sacred Way was the Erechtheum, one of the most refined and beautiful examples of the Ionic order of architecture. This second dwelling for Athena was built in the dark days of the Peloponnesian war; it was dedicated to Athena Polias, the protector of the city. This one building united the worship of Poseidon, god of the sea and sea-borne trade and formerly the protector of Athens, with that of Athena, the new mistress of the Athenian Empire, who brought with her the olive-tree to her city. Between the Parthenon and the Erechtheum stood a colossal bronze statue of Athena Promachos (the Champion), the golden gleam of whose spear-point could be seen by sailors approaching Athens from the sea.

Such was the centre of Athens as a great state, unrivalled in Greece. The rest of the city was mean and insignificant

PLATE LXX
GREEK SCULPTURE OF THE 5TH CENT. B.C.
THE GODS

1. PART OF THE MARBLE FRIEZE OF THE PARTHENON. The whole frieze is about one metre high and 160 metres long. It shows the procession of the Panathenaea, the chief festival of the Athenian calendar, in honour of Athena. The procession consists of young men on horseback (pl. LXXI) and in chariots, of old men, of musicians, of offering-bearers. The priest assisted by the priestess is busy folding the beautiful ' peplos ' (garment) of the goddess which has been woven by noble Athenian women. And finally the gods are watching the majestic procession. Our section of the frieze represents three of the group of the gods : Poseidon, Apollo, and Artemis. Whether the frieze was designed by Phidias and carved under his direction or not is a matter of controversy : certainly it breathes the spirit of Phidian art. About 440 B.C. Acropolis Museum, Athens.

2. MARBLE HEAD OF ZEUS. It has been thought that the sculptor of the statue to which this head belonged was influenced by the great statue of Zeus carved by Phidias for the temple of Olympia. The head bears a slight resemblance to those on coins of Elis, which reproduce the head of the Phidian Zeus. Museum of Fine Arts, Boston.

3. MARBLE RELIEF FOUND AT ATHENS, representing Athena leaning on her spear and looking at a stele. ' It is an attractive interpretation ', says Prof. Bury, ' that Athena is sadly engaged in reading the names of citizens who had recently fallen in defence of her city.' Middle of the 5th cent. B. C. National Museum, Athens.

1. PART OF THE MARBLE FRIEZE OF THE PARTHENON

2. MARBLE HEAD OF ZEUS

3. MARBLE RELIEF FROM ATHENS

LXX. GREEK SCULPTURE OF THE Vth CENT. B.C.

by comparison, with its narrow crooked streets, modest houses, shops and workshops, noise, dust, and mud. All the inhabitants lived in more or less identical conditions. Many of the citizens were rich, but they built themselves no luxurious palaces. It was a public scandal when Alcibiades broke the custom and adorned the walls of his house with painting. Athens was a democracy, and the rich were afraid to make themselves conspicuous by display and extravagance. Besides this, the men at Athens did not spend much of their time at home. The market-place; the Pnyx, where the popular assembly met; the law-courts and the council-chamber—these were the places where the higher classes passed their time. The lower classes worked in the docks and warehouses of the Piraeus, or in their shops and workshops. All classes alike devoted their spare time to bodily exercise and games, for the sake of health. For this purpose a number of gymnasiums, wrestling-schools, and paddocks surrounded by colonnades were constructed in the suburbs; and here all the population of Athens, young and old alike, practised running and wrestling, played ball, and threw the quoit and the javelin, and then plunged into the cold water of the pools which formed part of these establishments. Here, too, the education compulsory for every young Athenian was carried on. The boys were trained for war and for competition in the local and Pan-hellenic games; they also learned reading and writing, and elementary mathematics, but their chief study was music, singing, and the reading of literary masterpieces, especially the poems of Homer.

Women did not play that part in the life of Athens in the fifth century which they had played when Greece and Ionia were ruled by aristocracies, and which they still played in Sparta. The time of their political influence, of their importance in public life, and of their literary activity had gone by. As late as the beginning of the fifth century, Elpinice, the sister of Cimon, exercised considerable influence on Athenian politics; but in the age of Pericles, Aspasia, with her personal ascendancy over that great Athenian, was an exception. Democracy banished women from the street to the house: the kitchen and the nursery, and the *gynaeceum*, a special part of the house reserved for women and children, now became their sphere.

During this century the two unenfranchised classes, the

PLATE LXXI

THE FRIEZE OF THE PARTHENON

1-2. SLABS OF THE FRIEZE OF THE PARTHENON (see the description of pl. LXX) showing Athenian youths moving on their fiery horses towards the Acropolis in the religious procession. The beauty of the boys is only rivalled by the noble idealized forms of the horses. About 440 B.C. British Museum.

LXXI. THE FRIEZE OF THE PARTHENON

metoeci or resident aliens and the slaves, steadily increased in numbers and became more prominent in social life. The former class was deliberately attracted to the city by the political leaders. The citizens themselves were too busy with public affairs and war to give much time to trade and manufacture. Therefore the aliens, who had no other occupation or interest except commercial affairs, became the instrument which, more than anything else, created the extraordinary economic development of Athens in this century. They controlled the merchant-ships of Athens, the banks, now an important feature in financial life, and the large factories. They suffered under one disability : they might not own land within the bounds of Attica. They did not constitute a class by themselves : in society no distinction was made between an alien and a citizen.

Another notable feature of the time is the rise of slaves, if not in legal status, at least in social and economic importance. The industrial activity of an Athenian citizen was entirely based upon slave-labour. If he owned a factory, the power that ran it was his confidential slave who directed the workmen ; and some of the workmen also were slaves. If he was a trader, a slave was his right hand. If he owned a bank, all the business was managed by slaves and freedmen. There were, no doubt, other slaves of lower rank, mere outcasts and beasts of burden, like those who perished by hundreds in the silver-mines of Laureion, spending whole years in penal servitude. But such slaves were not visible at Athens. Those employed in trade and manufacture lived in the same way as the rest of the population. Many of these forced themselves to the front as dexterous men of business and eventually received their freedom. An Athenian conservative of this century, in the course of a malignant pamphlet directed against Athenian democracy, notes with good reason that it is impossible to distinguish slaves and aliens from citizens in the streets and squares of Athens, because all classes dress alike and live in the same way.

Such was the city of Athens, the pulse of Athenian life. But the city must not make us lose sight of the country ; for there the majority of Athenian citizens were to be found. After the time of Solon and Pisistratus the country came into favour again. In the demes of Attica, in farms scattered over hill and valley, in the forests that clothed the mountains,

PLATE LXXII

MYSTIC ELEMENTS IN GREEK RELIGION

1. RELIEF FOUND AT ELEUSIS, the great centre of the cult of Demeter and of the famous Eleusinian mysteries. The bas-relief shows the gods of the place: Demeter (to the left) gives Triptolemus the corn-ears that he may go out and teach; Kore, the daughter of Demeter, with the Eleusinian torch, puts a crown on the head of Triptolemus. The relief shows the typical features of the great art of Phidias. It is a little earlier than the frieze of the Parthenon (pls. LXX and LXXI). Middle of the 5th cent. B.C. National Museum, Athens.

2. RELIEF FOUND IN ITALY. Orpheus, the mythical hero of the Orphic mysteries, came down to Hades to rescue his bride Eurydice. Having charmed the rulers of Hades by his music, he received permission to take her back to life, on condition that he should lead her back without looking at her. He did not fulfil his promise, and Hermes is gently taking the poor young bride back to the nether world. The great mystery of life and death was the main point in the teaching of the Orphics. A copy, made in Roman times, of an Attic work of the late 5th cent. B.C. Naples Museum.

1. RELIEF FROM ELEUSIS. DEMETER, TRIPTOLEMUS, KORE

2. RELIEF FOUND IN ITALY. ORPHEUS AND EURYDICE

LXXII. MYSTIC ELEMENTS IN GREEK RELIGION

thousands of citizens spent their lives—small landowners, husbandmen, vine-dressers, olive-growers, shepherds, and charcoal-burners. They had no liking for the city and were a little afraid of it. But they were devoted with all their heart to their country, and came in their thousands, when they were needed, to the popular assembly. The existence of this class explains the fact that the Athenian state, in spite of its democratic constitution and boldness in speculation, never ceased to be, on the whole, conservative and devoted to the past.

But the most remarkable change at Athens in this century was in the region of the intellect. Among the poets and thinkers of the previous century Solon is the one Athenian citizen who finds a place. Now things are entirely different: the majority of prominent thinkers and writers are either Athenians or, if citizens of other states, live at Athens. In Asia Minor a few representatives of the fountain-head of Greek philosophy are still at work—Heraclitus, for instance, the first to understand and appreciate the importance of motion in the universe. But Anaxagoras, a native of Clazomenae in Asia Minor, lived and worked at Athens. In the West also a group of philosophers was busy; but Empedocles of Acragas, who carried on the Eleatic philosophy, invented the atomic theory, and taught the struggle for existence and the survival of the fittest, found no successors in his native country: it was at Athens that Leucippus, Democritus, and Anaxagoras supplemented the atomic theory by showing that the mechanical force of attraction creates all visible things out of atoms.

These examples show how quickly the intellectual centre of gravity was shifted to Athens. The conditions were favourable. Athens opened up opportunities, unequalled elsewhere, for original genius. Nowhere else was there such perfect freedom of thought and speech; nowhere else did men take such a keen interest in every novelty. The democracy, indeed, insisted on its right to dispose of the persons and lives of the citizens, when this was demanded by the interests of the state. A law passed in the popular assembly was all-powerful. Democracy feared too influential leaders of the strong minority as a possible source of revolutions; therefore it removed them by the device known as ostracism, and sentenced them to exile without disgrace. But with the

PLATE LXXIII

THE GREAT ATHENIAN DRAMATISTS

1. BUST OF ONE OF THE GREAT GREEK THINKERS OR ARTISTS OF THE 5TH CENT. B.C. It has been supposed to represent Aeschylus, but without reason. Copy, made in Roman times, of a work of about 400 B.C. Capitoline Museum, Rome.

2. HEAD OF EURIPIDES. Note the contrast between the sad sceptical look of Euripides and the serene and majestic expression of Sophocles. Copy, made in Roman times, of a contemporary portrait. Naples Museum.

3. THE FAMOUS STATUE OF SOPHOCLES. Probably a copy of the statue dedicated by Lycurgus, the well-known Athenian statesman, in 330 B.C. in the theatre of Dionysus at Athens. Lateran, Rome.

1. (?) AESCHYLUS

2. EURIPIDES

3. SOPHOCLES

LXXIII. THE GREAT ATHENIAN DRAMATISTS

private life and pursuits of the citizen, with his thoughts and words, democracy did not interfere but suffered each man to live as he chose.

In religious matters the Athenians were more conservative. While leaving men free to speak and think as they pleased, they were jealous in maintaining the ancient traditions in religion. Socrates, as we shall see later, fell a victim to this conservative feeling. Religion consisted chiefly in certain rites, and these rites were a special object of veneration to the Athenian citizen. Hence the people resented outspoken attacks on the gods and their worship; and Anaxagoras, the preacher of the atomic theory, had to leave his adopted country and depart into exile. But when attempts were made to spiritualize and purify religion, and when a tendency towards monotheism, such as we see in the plays of Aeschylus, began to develop, the popular reception of these changes was attentive and respectful. There is no doubt indeed that the drama raised the religious conceptions of the people to a much higher level. The Eleusinian Mysteries, also, rise higher and higher in reputation and just at this period become closely connected with Orphic rites.

Such were the surroundings of those marvellous achievements in intellect and art which permeated Athenian life of the fifth century B. C. and at once became standards of perfection for all Greeks. Tragedy ranks among the highest creations of Greek genius in this age. Aeschylus, as I have said already, was its creator. In the dialogue between the chorus and the narrator he introduced a second narrator, and this apparently trifling change in the mechanism of the drama, this introduction of a second actor, made it possible to convert the ritual acting at the festival of Dionysus into real drama and real tragedy, the same, in its essential features, as the tragedy of our own stage. The dialogue between the actors, divided up by songs from the chorus, enabled Aeschylus to thrill the spectator with pictures of the intense passions that fill the heart of man, while he supplemented these in the choric songs with his own feelings and reflections. The plots of his plays were almost all taken from mythology and not from actual life. But mythology offered such an endless variety of vivid stories in the lives of gods and heroes, that it was not difficult to get from these stories material for human drama. His plays, and those of his successors, were arranged in trilogies: that is, he produced three plays together on one subject, and also a satyr-play, a parody of tragedy, to end up with; but each of the three had to be complete in itself, while the connexion between them was maintained by the identity of the dramatis personae. Aeschylus wrote a great number of tragedies, perhaps as many as ninety. Seven have been preserved, and they include one trilogy, the *Oresteia*—the tremendous story of a son's vengeance on his mother for the murder of his father, and of the son's tortured conscience and final purification. The *Persians* is an exception to the rule: the subject was taken from recent history—from the Persian war, in which Aeschylus himself had taken an active part and fought in the ranks at Marathon. In the general opinion of antiquity, with which modern criticism entirely agrees, Aeschylus, from the artistic point of view, not merely created the tragic drama but also wrote tragedies whose perfection has never been surpassed either in ancient or in modern times.

Sophocles was a younger contemporary. The number of his plays was even greater—the titles of 111 are known to us —but only seven, with half of one satyr-drama, have been preserved. Three are connected by a common subject, being taken from the story of the royal house at Thebes—*Oedipus the King*, *Oedipus at Colonus*, and *Antigone*; but each of these is complete in itself and describes a separate series of events. Last comes Euripides, a younger contemporary and rival of Sophocles, and the author of 75 tragedies, of which 19 have survived. Though not enjoying much success in his lifetime, he became the idol of later generations and of Roman readers.

Athenian drama is astonishing for its literary perfection: the language is copious and richly coloured; the imagery is infinitely various, sublime, and beautiful; the metrical skill and the power of construction are altogether exceptional. But its chief importance is distinct from these excellences, and lies in this—that in it for the first time men saw their own hearts held up before them by the poet, and saw the process of conflict in that heart—conflict with itself, with circumstance, with society and government, with the laws of God and man. For all that, Athenian tragedy is practical and draws its inspiration from contemporary life and circumstances; it does not eschew politics, it takes a side in the settlement of many social problems. It is hard to convey in a few words all the wealth contained in Greek tragedy of the fifth century B. C., and no less hard to indicate the difference between the three equally great tragedians. For the historian of Athenian culture it is sufficient to point out that the appearance of this form of art gave rise to an entire revolution in the minds of those who first witnessed it : they carried with them from the theatre a whole world of new conceptions and ideas ; they learned to look deeper into their own hearts and to bear themselves differently towards the inner life of their neighbours.

Comedy also exercised a strong influence upon the Athenians. Later in development than tragedy, and owing much to tragedy, it was the work mainly of Eupolis, Cratinus, and Aristophanes. The last alone is known to us ; he lived during the Peloponnesian war and wrote forty-four comedies, of which eleven are preserved. Comedy did not touch mythological subjects, but drew its matter from the medley of passing events. It pays no attention to the experiences of the human heart. It passes judgement on topics of the day, or even of the hour, in a fanciful and highly comic spirit. The emancipation of women and their position, the teaching of Socrates and the Sophists, the question of war or peace, the personality of this or that statesman, theatrical innovations—such are the topics brought upon the stage for discussion and for mockery of the most merciless and outspoken nature. Comedy was a kind of chair for political and social deliverances, from which the author chats with the citizens and holds up to ridicule whatever seems to him to deserve laughter—laughter which is sometimes gay, sometimes sharp and even cruel, but always outspoken.

These same questions of morals, politics, and social life, which were raised by tragedy and comedy in a poetical and artistic form, were also forced upon the Athenians in their daily life. They passed laws in the popular assembly, they prepared bills in the council, they judged suits in the lawcourts. On the vote of any individual might hang the life or death of the foremost and best of his fellow-citizens. Each individual had to vote on complicated political issues—issues that often affected the very existence of the state. Each decision evoked criticism and ridicule, and often hatred and ill-feeling ; and no citizen could escape his share of responsibility. It is clear that the majority, in the assembly and the law-court, wished to vote according to their conscience. Often they were required to justify their opinion before an audience. But there was no preparatory training for these responsible duties. The professional politician was still unknown. Hence the average citizen sought guidance and felt the necessity of political education; he was often conscious of his own helplessness. He began to demand teachers who should instruct him how to reason, to think, and to speak. And such teachers were forthcoming.

Some of these were themselves seekers after truth and gave light to others merely by the way, while others made a profession of their teaching. The name of 'sophists' was given to both classes by the Athenians. The sophists were willing to teach all comers how to think and reason, how to speak and write. The most original thinkers, the most powerful reasoners, the most lucid and eloquent speakers, got the greatest reputation and attracted the largest classes. In natural sciences they took little interest: they concentrated their study on man, society, and the state; and they approached these topics with an open mind and with no ready-made solution of difficulties. 'Man', they said, 'is the measure of all things', meaning by 'man', human reason. That which seems to us to be truth and which convinces others is discovered by a process of logical reasoning; hence the most important thing is, to be able to think and argue logically, or, in a word, to convince others. Such was the general tendency of thought among the sophists; but it is hard to indicate any detailed instruction in which they all agreed. They were not a school of philosophers, though a succession of philosophic schools took rise later from their activities. One thing they had in common: they all sought plausible answers to troublesome questions. They sought these answers in different directions and by different paths; but these paths were always the paths of logic and dialectics, and the answers were never laid down as dogmas. And, lastly, their chief interest was in political and social questions; they deserve to be called the fathers of sociology and political science. We know that Protagoras, one of the most famous sophists, first discussed the origin of society and the state, and tried to settle the problem by logic. Another, Hippodamus of Miletus, was the first thinker who constructed a purely ideal state and society. He was a mathematician and engineer who invented a method of laying out a city in squares somewhat like the squares of a chessboard—a method which he put in practice when the Piraeus, the harbour of Athens, was rebuilt. Other sophists worked on similar lines: thus Thrasymachus preached that the strongest and best have a right to power, and there were also defenders of communism and anarchism. One fundamental notion pervaded all their teaching—that the part of human life determined by nature is natural and therefore indispensable, but the part created by man himself is conventional and transitory. This notion is very clearly expressed in the recently discovered fragments of a treatise *On Truth*, by the sophist Antiphon, a contemporary of Aristophanes, and the butt for many of his bitterest sarcasms; his philosophy, founded on the atheism of Democritus, was purely materialistic.

In the second half of the fifth century a figure of extraordinary originality and power towers over the sophists. This is Socrates. Socrates was not a professional teacher: he was a seeker after truth. Wherever Athenians gathered together, there he was to be found day after day, and there he started endless discussions on the main problems of life and conduct. He began by refuting with the edge of his logic the answers given to his questions by those present; and he prepared the ground for a reasonable and accurate solution by the way in which he raised each problem and by his preliminary objections. Thus he reached by degrees a position from which he could define the chief conceptions of the human mind: he asked, what is virtue? what is beauty? what is justice?—and so on. We do not know what his positive teaching really was: our sources are meagre and inconsistent. These sources are the *Memorabilia* of Xenophon and the series of *Dialogues* by Plato; both were pupils of Socrates. Xenophon was a man of moderate ability and slight philosophic training, Plato one of the greatest thinkers in the world's history; and it is difficult to reconcile their statements. There was much in the teaching of Socrates which Xenophon did not understand; and Plato may have attributed his own doctrines to his teacher. Still we must suppose that the immense influence of Socrates upon all later speculation, and the fact that all subsequent philosophic schools traced their descent from him, prove one thing—

PLATE LXXIV

THE GREAT MEN OF GREECE IN THE 5TH CENT. B.C.

1. HERM OF PERICLES. Copy of the head of the bronze statue by the sculptor Cresilas, dedicated on the Acropolis of Athens (the base has been found on the Acropolis). Pericles is represented as the great leader (*strategos*) of Athens in his prime. The portrait is probably idealized. The head is that of a great statesman and general. British Museum.

2. HERM OF THE GREAT HISTORIAN HERODOTUS. It is not a portrait. The bust was made after his death, perhaps long after it. Nevertheless it gives an excellent idea of the first historian, the father of history who knew so well how to tell a story and how to ask questions. Metropolitan Museum of Art, New York.

3. BUST OF THUCYDIDES, the first historian scholar, who wrote the history of the Peloponnesian war. The bust may be a copy of a real contemporary portrait of Thucydides. The face is individual, not typical. Holkham Hall, England.

4. A CHARMING STATUETTE OF THE GREAT PHILOSOPHER SOCRATES. The long beard, the nose and the square head are typical of the portraits of Socrates. The statuette is probably a work of the early Hellenistic period, inspired, of course, by earlier portraits. British Museum.

1. PERICLES 2. HERODOTUS

3. THUCYDIDES 4. SOCRATES

LXXIV. THE GREAT MEN OF GREECE IN THE Vth CENT. B.C.

that he imported some new element into philosophy which caught the attention of all contemporary thinkers. It appears that this novelty was partly the predominant importance which Socrates attached to man, and the soul and conscious self of man, and partly the enthusiasm with which he called on men to 'know themselves' and so to lead better lives both as individuals and members of associations, including the chief association, i. e. the state. Socrates had no definite political views and was not an opponent of democracy; but he saw its weaknesses clearly, especially its entire failure to train the citizens for the business of government; and he urged them to increase their knowledge and develop their reasoning faculties. Nor was he an atheist: he believed in the gods and habitually made offerings to them; and he felt the presence of a divine being, his *daimon*, within his own breast. His religious belief was, like that of Aeschylus, the belief in a superior being and ruler of the world. But there was something irritating and provoking in the mission of Socrates. There were few citizens to whom he had not proved how little they knew, how badly they reasoned, and how ill-founded were their most cherished opinions. It is therefore not surprising that the conservative Aristophanes attacked him fiercely in one of his comedies, and that an accuser named Anytus was found to prosecute him for 'disbelief in the gods recognized by the State, and for corrupting the young'. And we can understand how the Athenians were glad to rid themselves of this 'gadfly' and coolly condemned him to death, though he had honestly performed all the duties of a citizen.

Thirst for knowledge and pursuit of truth created also in men's minds a lively interest in the past. Every Athenian wished to know the events of the recent past and the Persian invasion, and to understand how Greece had been able to cope with that danger. We have seen that the Ionian thinkers took some interest in past history, and that some writers had already appeared in Asia Minor who collected facts about the history of the Anatolian Greeks and the Eastern nations who lived near them. No wonder then that Herodotus, one of those Asiatic Greeks and a native of Halicarnassus, a partly Carian and partly Dorian city, undertook to relate to the Athenians the history of the Persian wars. He had migrated to Athens and, as an Athenian citizen, took part with other

PLATE LXXV

GREEK SCULPTURE OF THE 5TH CENT. B.C.
STATUES

1. BRONZE STATUE FOUND AT DELPHI. It belonged originally to a group which, according to the inscription, was dedicated at Delphi by Polyzalos, the ruler of Gela in Sicily, brother of the rulers of Syracuse, Gelon and Hieron. The dedication took place probably in 474 B.C. in memory of a victory in racing. The group represented a chariot drawn by four horses. The statue is that of the charioteer. It is a magnificent piece of work, still a little archaic in its supreme simplicity. Probably a work of one of the sculptors of the Peloponnese or of Aegina. 474 B.C. Delphi Museum.

2. MARBLE STATUE OF A GODDESS (Demeter?) found at Cherchel in Northern Africa (Algeria). The statue is a copy of an original of the time of Phidias which was similar to the figure of Demeter on the bas-relief of Eleusis (pl. LXXII, 1). 5th cent. B.C. Cherchel Museum.

3. STATUE OF A DISCUS-THROWER. Copy of the famous bronze statue by the Athenian sculptor Myron. Many copies are in existence. Our photograph is taken from a cast which combines the head of the copy which is in the Palazzo Lancelotti (Rome) with the body in the Museum of the Terme (Rome), both copies in marble of a bronze original. The composition is daring. Such a position of the body cannot last for long. The short moment when the body is in full tension is represented in the statue. Middle of the 5th cent. B.C. Terme and Palazzo Lancelotti, Rome. After Arndt.

4. BRONZE STATUE OF A BOY VICTOR, the so-called 'Idolino'. The statue is probably an original Greek bronze, and may belong to the school of Argos. The most famous representative of this school was the great sculptor Polycleitus, whose reputation was as high as that of Phidias. His fame rested on his wonderful statues of athletes. About 440–430 B.C. Archaeological Museum, Florence.

1. CHARIOTEER   1. CHARIOTEER   2. GODDESS (DEMETER?)

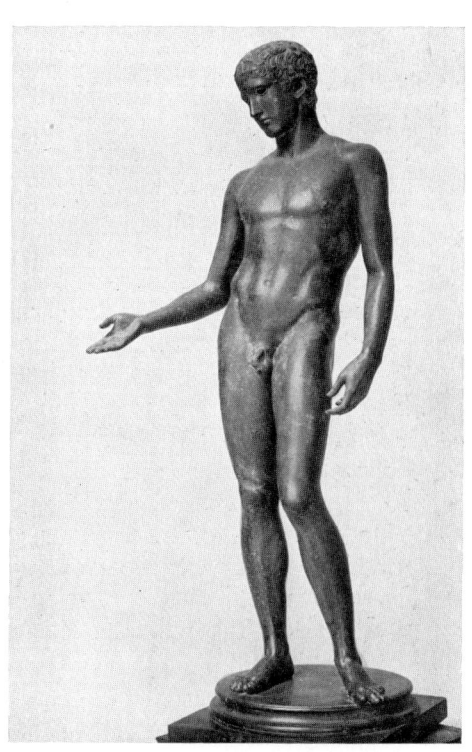

3. DISCUS-THROWER   4. 'IDOLINO'

LXXV. GREEK SCULPTURE OF THE Vth CENT. B.C.

Athenians in founding the colony of Thurii in Italy. Well read in the historical literature of the Ionians, he was himself a great traveller. He visited Egypt and Babylonia; he knew Asia Minor well; he may have paid a short visit to Olbia, at the mouths of the Dnieper and the Bug. In every country his unbounded curiosity led him to visit historic places with their monuments of hoary antiquity; he collected the tales told by the natives in explanation of these monuments; he had an eye for the manners and customs of the inhabitants and the characteristics of the country. With even greater enthusiasm he questioned at Athens those who had themselves taken an active share in the Persian wars, and those whose fathers and grandfathers had been concerned in the events which led up to the Persian invasion. He studied the monuments connected with that invasion, and collected the tales and legends that had grown up around them. He had especial pleasure in conversing with priests and drew much material from the lips of the priests at Delphi. And in this way his great work, his history of the Persian wars, was composed.

He was not content with a dry narrative of events. He wished, above all, to understand the past, and therefore prefixed to his history a sketch of those countries with which the history was in some way connected. His descriptions of Asia Minor, Persia, Babylonia, Egypt, and Scythia are of fascinating interest, although many of his notions concerning the history of those countries have turned out to be incomplete and inaccurate. When he proceeds to the story itself—to the gradual development of strife between Persians and Greeks, the general course of events is accurately stated throughout, though it is stated from the Athenian point of view, because Herodotus had become at Athens an eager partisan of the Athenians. Without Herodotus, the 'father of history', we should know as little of the Persian war as we do of the political history of Greece before that war and in the interval that divides it from the Peloponnesian war. His history was published in 430 B.C. He was the only writer who collected information about the war when those who fought in it were still living; and all later narratives by Greek historians make use of him as their main source.

In details, however, Herodotus is often inaccurate. He paid little attention to the exact chronology of events; he

PLATE LXXVI
GREEK SCULPTURE OF THE 5TH CENT. B.C.
RELIEFS

1-3. THREE MARBLE SLABS ADORNED WITH RELIEFS. Found in the Villa Ludovisi at Rome. It is still a question to what kind of structure the slabs belonged. Probably an altar. Equally controversial is the explanation of the figures. A young and beautiful woman is represented either in a crouching position or emerging from the soil or from the sea. Two other women are helping her. On the short sides we see a seated woman placing incense on a thurible, and a naked girl playing a double flute. Some scholars suggest that the central figure represents Aphrodite emerging from the sea, others think that it is Leto giving birth to the twins Apollo and Artemis as described in the Homeric hymn. Another related set of similar reliefs is in the Boston Museum of Fine Arts. The reliefs of the Villa Ludovisi are a fine product of Ionian sculpture of the early 5th century, soft and gracious. About 470 B.C. Museo delle Terme, Rome.

1, 2, 3. RELIEFS FROM VILLA LUDOVISI

LXXVI. GREEK SCULPTURE OF THE VTH CENT. B.C.

had little understanding of military matters; he describes many places which he had not himself seen. While we are aware of this, we are often unable to correct his errors owing to the lack of other authorities. Often he gives us a purely personal impression of incidents; and here, too, it is difficult to correct him. At times he lends too ready an ear to marvels and legends. But he generally recognizes how shaky the foundations of historical knowledge sometimes are. When he meets with different versions of the same incident, he is helpless; for the methods of historical criticism were unknown to him. But we are grateful to him for this, that in such cases he hands down all the versions known to him, leaving the reader to choose among them. A place of honour belongs to Herodotus in the history of mankind and of Greek civilization. He is truly the 'father of history'. He was the first to treat history, not as a collection of interesting stories about gods and men, but as the object of scientific investigation.

That the next Greek historian, Thucydides, should approach his task from a different standpoint is natural enough. An Athenian, born and brought up in the atmosphere of the fifth century at Athens, he had seen the tragedies of the three great dramatists on the stage, had listened to the sophists and may have met Socrates himself, had taken an active part in public life, and served as one of the generals in the Peloponnesian war. He witnessed that war from beginning to end, and survived it all with its successes and failures. On him, as on all the best Athenians, the defeat of Athens left a profound impression; and he laid upon himself the task of telling to present and future times the whole truth about the war, as he saw it and as he understood it. He possessed abundant and excellent material, which his knowledge of affairs and war enabled him to turn to account. When Amphipolis was seized by the Spartans in 424 B.C., he was in command in the north of Greece, and suffered banishment in consequence of his failure. But exile enabled him to become better acquainted with the antagonists of Athens, to understand their mental attitude, and to appreciate their points of superiority. Such was the material and such the experience he possessed, when he undertook the work of an historian, and determined, not merely to describe, but also to explain the Peloponnesian war.

For this purpose he had, first of all, to collect the ascertained facts in their exact chronological sequence. That was no easy task : passion burned too fiercely on each side, and the historical facts, framed in their proper environment, came home too closely to the hearts of both peoples. But Thucydides faced the problem of representing the facts in their reality, and of stripping off the wrappings in which they were disguised. And he did this with extraordinary precision, following scientific rule and applying all those methods which we call historical criticism. If he was not the father of history in general, he was at least the father of critical history and the first of all who have written the history of their own times. But even more must be said. In his eyes the facts were only a means ; the end was to throw light on them and explain them, and the explanation was not to be theological, like many of the explanations in Herodotus, but based upon rationalism and logic. To establish the causal connexion between events was the supreme object of Thucydides. His whole exposition aims at discovering causes —causes as distinct from motives—and proceeds by a strictly logical method, with no concessions to feeling or belief. While engaged in this work Thucydides realized the part played in history by personality, and also its occasional helplessness in the face of economic and social movements. He understood the 'psychology of the herd' and the mighty part it has played in history ; and he understood much else, reaching a height to which many modern historians aspire in vain. Thucydides was in history what Aeschylus was in tragedy. Once again Athens had produced a man who was not merely a pioneer in a new and important branch of human creation, but actually approached perfection in that sphere. The ancient world never produced a second historian of equal genius and scientific insight ; and he has few rivals among historians of our own day and of the recent past.

What we observe in the development of the drama, of historical inquiry and historical narrative, and in the sphere of philosophy and rhetoric, is equally noticeable in the history of the plastic arts, and especially of sculpture. The history of painting is more obscure, because we possess no direct copies of the great decorative and easel paintings, and can only judge of them by the imitations on purely decorative vases, where the artist has to take account of the nature and proportions of the object decorated, and, in general, to restrict himself to two colours, red and black; and we can learn something from the influence exercised by painting upon sculpture. It follows that Polygnotus and the other great painters of the fifth century are still to us mysterious figures. About sculpture we have much fuller information: in the Parthenon sculptures we possess a number of original works by great masters; we have also a multitude of later copies, more or less exact, taken from the great statues of

FIG. 32. *Red-figured cup found at Vulci (Italy). The picture represents an Athenian foundry. To the left the stove, to the right smiths working on a bronze statue, on the walls various instruments and the products of the shop. Attic work of about 480 B.C. Berlin Museum. After Furtwängler-Reichhold.*

the fifth century, and contemporary reproductions of those statues in small bronzes, terra-cottas, and coins.

By the end of the sixth century B.C., side by side with the Ionian schools of sculpture, independent schools were growing up in Greece proper and in Italy. The rapid development, technical and artistic, of sculpture is proved by many remains —from Aegina, from the temple of Zeus at Olympia, from the ornament of various treasuries of Greek states at Delphi, and from the decoration of Italian and Sicilian temples, especially at Selinus; step by step it cast off the conventionality that marks Ionian sculpture of the sixth century, and the heavy solidity of the archaic period in general. Nowhere was this

PLATE LXXVII

POTTERY OF THE 5TH CENT. B.C.

1. RED-FIGURED CUP BY THE PAINTER DURIS. It represents an Athenian school of the 5th cent. B.C. The boys are being taught music (lyre and flute), Greek literature, writing. Attic work of about 480 B.C. Berlin Museum. After Furtwängler-Reichhold.

2. RED-FIGURED CUP. On one side Dionysus is represented seated on a couch looking at a Satyr dancing. On the other Dionysus and Heracles, the god of ecstasy and the god of duty, are having a banquet together. Two Satyrs are acting as servants; one has just stolen a cake from the table. The picture illustrates the worship of the two great gods of the Greek religion who had originally been men. The painter has probably taken his inspiration from the so-called Satyr drama, a comic performance ridiculing divine beings. Attic work of about 470 B.C. British Museum.

1. RED-FIGURED CUP BY DURIS. ATHENIAN SCHOOL

2. RED-FIGURED CUP. HERACLES AND DIONYSUS

LXXVII. POTTERY OF THE Vth CENT. B.C.

development so rapid as in Athens after the Persian wars. Till then Athenian sculpture had been merely a branch of Ionian art; but now it discarded Ionian influence altogether, and the work of Athenian sculptors became free and independent. The advance went on with dizzy speed, and at the head of it stood Myron, with his statues of gods and athletes. It reached its zenith in the person of Phidias, the greatest sculptor of this century, who worked under the direction of Pericles and adorned Olympia and other centres of Greek civilization as well as Athens. His most famous statues were the Athena in the Parthenon and the Zeus at Olympia, both chryselephantine—that is, the head, hands, and feet, with the dress, were made of gold and ivory, and the remainder of wood. Polycleitus was a younger contemporary of Phidias; his statues of athletes, like the statues of gods by Phidias, set the standard at once; and his Hera at Argos was ranked with the Zeus at Olympia.

The essential features of this new Greek art are these: complete victory of the artist over his material and the technical difficulties which hampered him earlier; the endeavour to idealize the human body, not by copying nature nor by correcting it, but by searching out in nature that which is most perfect and nearest to the ideal which has formed itself in the artist's mind; and, lastly, the skill to embody in statuary ideas cherished by the artist, especially the idea of divine majesty and divine power. These sculptors are familiar with nature: they have studied it thoroughly; they have mastered the anatomy of the human body; they understand the beauty of drapery flowing down in various folds; they can harmonize the lines of the body with the lines of the drapery. But they do not copy nature slavishly. Their athletes, for example, are unsurpassed in the representation of the nude male body. The Discobolus of Myron embodies all the strength and beauty and life of the youthful frame at the moment of its most intense physical exertion. In the bronze charioteer from Delphi we admire the severe stateliness of the youth who stands at his ease, wearing the long garment that falls down in straight folds. Still more perfect is the sculpture on the pediments and frieze of the Parthenon. It may not have been carved by Phidias himself, but it was certainly carved under his direction and by his pupils.

Phidias surpassed himself in his representation of the

PLATE LXXVIII

GREEK PAINTING. POLYCHROME VASES OF THE 5TH AND 4TH CENTURIES

1. ONE OF THE MOST BEAUTIFUL 'LEKYTHOI' (grave-vases) with polychrome painting on white ground. The picture represents the grave-stele and the grave-tumulus (behind the stele) of a young Athenian. On the tumulus, green branches; on the stele, a 'taenia' (ribbon); on the steps of the base of the stele, offerings of wreaths and oil-flasks. Before the stele stands the deceased in the dress of an ephebus, while a girl brings grave-offerings in a basket. The style makes one think of Phidias. Attic work of about 440 B.C. National Museum, Athens. After Riezler.

2. AN ATHENIAN LEKYTHOS. The picture shows Charon, the ferryman of the nether world, receiving a dead woman from the hands of Hermes, 'the leader of the souls' (Psychopompus). The little winged beings in the air are souls. Attic work of about 450 B.C. National Museum, Athens. After Riezler.

3. A RED-FIGURED VASE ('lekanis'). The subject of the picture is the decking of a bride. The bride is represented among her girl-friends. She is receiving various gifts and being dressed for the wedding ceremony. Various religious rites preliminary to the wedding are being performed by her friends. Little Loves flying and running among the girls give the significance of the scene. Attic work of the middle of the 4th century B.C. Gold and white are extensively used. Museum of the Hermitage, Petrograd. After Furtwängler-Reichhold.

1. A POLYCHROME ATTIC LEKYTHOS. GRAVE OF AN EPHEBE

2. AN ATHENIAN LEKYTHOS. CHARON, HERMES, AND THE SOUL

3. RED-FIGURED VASE (LEKANIS). DECKING OF A BRIDE

LXXVIII. POLYCHROME VASES OF THE Vth AND IVth CENT. B.C.

supreme deities. We possess only poor copies of these statues, and must trust the judgement of the Greeks and Romans who saw the originals. Their evidence testifies to the ineffaceable impression, both artistic and religious, produced by these masterpieces. The Zeus of Phidias was the same omnipotent father of gods and men, terrible and also gracious, the same ruler of human destiny, whom we find in the poetry of Aeschylus. The head alone is poorly reproduced on coins of Elis; but even this conveys that impression of divinity which we feel also in reading the tragedies.

FIG. 33. *Red-figured water-pot (hydria) found at Ruvo in South Italy. The picture represents a potter's workshop with workmen (three boys and one girl) painting vases of various shapes. Athena is bringing a crown to the best painter. Victories are crowning the other two boys. The poor girl got no prize. Attic work of the middle of the 5th century B.C. Ruvo, Caputi Collection. After Perrot and Chipiez.*

As in the sixth century, art was not confined to the temples and public resorts of the city: it permeated the whole life of a Greek. This fact is proved to us most distinctly for that period by Greek vases. In that century the supremacy of Athens in the manufacture of pottery was virtually undisputed: her vases are found everywhere—in Egypt, Italy, Sicily, the south of France and Spain, the Black Sea coast, and even in the capital of the Persian Empire. Black figures on a red background had now given way to red figures on a black background. These vases represent the highest point ever attained in this branch of decorative art: many of them are really great artistic productions, for the grace and variety of their shapes, and for the decoration, in which the drawing is severe, exact, and extraordinarily rich, and the grouping of figures in scenes taken from the life of gods and men quite masterly. Like contemporary drama and contemporary sculpture, the vases reflect every phase of Athenian life. Even politics are not excluded: there are many drawings by the great vase-painters of this age which can only be explained thus; for instance, the marriage of Theseus with the sea typifies the maritime imperialism of Athens, and scenes from the life of Jason refer to Athenian aspirations in the region of the Black Sea.

A special group of Attic vases was not satisfied with the combination of two colours only, black and red. These are the *lekythoi*, tall, slim funereal vessels, and also some vases in the shape of men, animals, and mythical creatures. In the former, the figures, in rich combinations, are painted in natural colours on a white ground; while the vases shaped like the deities and mythical beings of the next world are covered all over with soft and brilliant colouring. From these vessels we get some idea of the painter's art in the fifth century, both in easel-pictures and in decorative work.

XXI

GREECE IN THE FOURTH CENTURY B.C.

THE Peloponnesian war ended in a victory for the decentralizing forces in Greece; but that victory was not complete or decisive. When Athens was crippled and the Athenian Empire destroyed, competitors for the succession put in an appearance, one after another; and even the Athenians themselves considered that their defeat was not final and that their dreams of restoring the empire might yet be realized. Though Sparta had issued from the war victorious, properly speaking, there was no real conqueror. All the partakers in the strife were weakened; all were confronted by sore points and difficult problems in domestic and foreign policy; and Sparta, in her new part as queen of the seas, had to face more trouble and responsibility than other states. Greece expected of her that she should restore order and tranquillity at sea as well as on land. But this needed men and money, because force alone could maintain order. She was obliged to adopt Athenian policy without possessing Athenian resources. During the war Persia had acted as paymaster; but her money was not given for nothing, and now she sent in the bill: she demanded the restoration of the cities in Asia Minor which had formerly belonged to her.

Persia was still a powerful, wealthy, and well organized empire. It is true that her reputation had suffered greatly from her failure in Greece. Further, a strong detachment of Greeks had fought for Cyrus in his struggle against his elder brother, Artaxerxes, for the succession in 401 B.C., and had succeeded in retreating from Babylonia after the defeat of Cyrus. This retreat was described by the Athenian, Xenophon; and the whole episode demonstrated afresh to the Greeks their superiority to the Persians in tactics and strategy. Yet the situation remained essentially unchanged. Greece was crippled and split up and torn by mutual hatred between the states; Persia was still a very rich country with a powerful army, and well acquainted with the state of affairs in Greece. In an armed conflict Greece would have no chance at all; but the Persians had changed their tactics since the time of Marathon and Salamis. They were convinced that a steady stream of their gold would break up Greece more and more, until any form of national union would be impossible, and Persia, without having recourse to a fresh campaign, would find it easy to reduce Greece to the position of a dependent vassal.

So Persia made her first move at the end of the Peloponnesian war. Sparta, constrained by public opinion and conscious that further demands from the same quarter were inevitable, was not inclined to surrender the Greek cities in Asia Minor. This made war certain, and war in Asia, not in Greece, offensive war on the side of Sparta, and defensive on the side of Persia. At one time, Sparta and especially Agesilaus, her able king and general, dreamed of a national war waged by all Greece against her old enemy, and of decisive victory in the struggle. But that dream remained a dream. Not even the ruthless measures taken by Lysander, when he kept garrisons and military governors in all the chief cities, could weld Greece together. Persian gold did its work, and when Sparta in 395–394 B.C. made the first serious effort to attack Persia, she was soon forced to give up operations in Asia for the defence of her own military supremacy in Greece. For at this time, 394–391 B.C., the Athenians rebuilt their walls and refortified their harbour, while the vassals of Sparta, profiting by the absence of her forces in Asia, were planning and carrying out new and, in some cases, very surprising alliances, which involved a rearrangement of forces among the city-states.

Sparta was obliged to make concessions which amounted to capitulation. Her supremacy in Greece was secured; but the price paid for that security was the freedom of the Greek cities in Asia Minor. It must be said that these cities shed few tears at their restoration to Persia, since it promised them great commercial advantages at the loss of political independence: they had never enjoyed either under Athens or under Sparta. The conditions of the treaty concluded with Persia in 386 B.C. by the Spartan ephor Antalcidas, are notable: the Persian king, like Flamininus the Roman general and the emperor Nero in later times, bestowed freedom on all Greek communities, except the cities in Asia, which became subject to

Persia, and except the islands of Lemnos, Imbros, and Scyros, which remained in the possession of Athens; rigorous war was declared against all who refused to submit to this settlement. The treaty did not touch the supremacy of Sparta; for it did not forbid pacts and alliances between individual states, such as formed the legal basis of that supremacy.

Meanwhile, Greece became more and more discontented with Spartan rule, and the difficulty of maintaining that rule became greater and greater. Persia and Syracuse, Sparta's allies, could not give her active assistance: the former was fighting hard against the process of disruption which had taken an acute form in her vast empire; and the latter was far away and entirely occupied with Sicilian and Italian affairs. Yet Sparta needed external support to control her empire, so large, so scattered, and so constantly disturbed. Constant wars had involved heavy loss of life, chiefly among the Spartiates, and the number of Spartan citizens with full rights was now dangerously reduced. On the other hand, the government of their foreign possessions was so profitable to the governors that the Spartiates took no steps to increase their numbers and treated every attempt in that direction as revolutionary. They preferred to ignore the transference of land, either allotted by the state or acquired, to the hands of women, rather than fill up their ranks by admitting Spartans without full rights, Perioeci, and Helots. Consequently, the Spartiates were too few to defend Sparta, to command the scattered garrisons of the empire, and to carry on foreign wars.

The rivals of Sparta meanwhile were gaining strength. A comparatively long peace had encouraged a renewal of Athenian trade. At the same time the former allies of Athens, oppressed by the Spartan garrisons and the *harmosts* who commanded them, sighed for the good old days of the Athenian confederation. The conditions seemed favourable for renewing that confederation on more equitable terms. Elsewhere, the power and influence of Boeotia and of her chief city, Thebes, were growing in central Greece; and hatred for the Spartan garrison which held the Cadmea, the acropolis of Thebes, was growing also.

For all this, the Greek world was surprised, first, by the news that a detachment of Spartan invincibles had been beaten by the Theban, Pelopidas, and later by the complete victory won by the Boeotian militia over a picked Spartan army at Leuctra in 371 B.C., when Sparta, backed by all Greece and confident of victory, was marching to suppress the obstinate Boeotians. The Thebans owed this victory entirely to the military genius of Epaminondas: he had reformed the tactics of Greek militia forces, won considerable victories, and inspired Boeotia to rise against the oppressors of Greece. The victory of Leuctra and the invasion of the Peloponnese led to the separation of Messenia from Sparta; and thus the military strength of Sparta was undermined; for many Spartiates had their allotments of land in Messenia, and could no longer maintain themselves and their families without them. The political state of Greece, bad enough already, was made worse by the collapse of Sparta. The last power which had tried, more or less successfully, to deal with the growing anarchy, now disappeared. Sparta ceased, and ceased for ever, to play the leading part in the life of Hellas.

There was no one to take her place. The second Athenian maritime alliance was formed on purpose to fight Sparta; but, when she lost political importance, the Athenians endeavoured to convert it into an empire by the same harsh measures which they had used before the Peloponnesian war. The result was resentment among the allies, war, and the dissolution of the alliance. The supremacy of Boeotia was bound to be short-lived and precarious: she had neither the historic past and the wealth and civilization which created the Athenian Empire, nor that excellent professional army of citizens which formed the strength of Sparta. The effect of her supremacy in Greece was purely destructive: she crushed the last attempt made in Greece to create the semblance of a national power with the resources of a single city-state.

When the Spartan league had fallen to pieces and Thebes was growing steadily weaker, the political condition of Greece can only be defined by the word 'anarchy'. The observers of that day, reflective and clear-sighted men of affairs, such as Xenophon and Isocrates, Plato and Aristotle, saw all the horror of this anarchy, but saw no way out of it. And indeed there was no way out for those whose political views could never rise above the limits of the Greek city-state, and its peculiar conception of freedom. For such men freedom meant simply the possession of certain political rights—rights strictly limited to the inhabitants of their native city and the limited territory belonging to it. The sovereignty of the city, its complete political independence, was an axiom in all Greek political science. Whatever interfered with that sovereignty seemed to a Greek intolerable slavery; and this is why Greece struggled so obstinately against Athens and against Sparta, choosing political anarchy rather than subjection to any one city-state.

Syracuse also, when she attempted to unite the western Greeks into one kingdom, was foiled by the same deeply rooted prejudice of the Greek mind. For a time the attempt was successful. Under the pressure of constant danger from Carthage and from the Italian peoples, the Greeks in Sicily and Italy endured the military dictatorship of Dionysius, tyrant of Syracuse and an able statesman. But when he died in 367 B.C., his empire in the island and on the mainland fell to pieces. Some decades later the same fate overtook the short-lived Syracusan Empire of Agathocles, another tyrant of Syracuse. Here also the failure was due to this—that the despotism of Dionysius and Agathocles was built up on the basis of a city-state, which, in its Greek form, was incapable of becoming the centre of a great national and political union.

Thus the Greek city-state, in the two centuries of its development, proved unable to create a national union of Greece, and reduced Greece to a condition of political anarchy, which must infallibly end in her subjection to stronger and more homogeneous governments. Apart from the tendency to separation innate in the Greek mind, the blame for this failure lies largely on the constitution of the city-states, and, most of all, on democracy, the most complete and progressive form of that constitution. Democracy in Greece proved unable to create a form of government which should reconcile the individualism characteristic of the nation with the conditions essential to the existence of a powerful state, namely, civic discipline and a preference of the general interest, even when it appeared to oppose the interest of particular persons or classes or even communities.

The fifth century B.C. was exceptionally favourable for the growth of individualism. The extension of trade, the great technical improvements in agriculture and industry, the supremacy of Greece in the world's markets, her production of oil, wine, manufactures, and luxuries for all those countries to which her colonists had penetrated—such conditions had enabled the Greeks to show their enterprise in the sphere of finance, and to abandon more primitive methods in favour of a capitalistic system and a production aimed at an unlimited market with a demand constantly increasing in amount. The rudiments of such a system are noticeable at Athens even earlier than this century. The transition to capitalism was made easier by the existence of slavery, as an institution everywhere recognized, whose necessity and normality no one questioned. The slave markets provided slave labour in abundance; and the growth of political anarchy only increased the supply of slaves and lowered the price of labour. But capitalistic enterprise was interfered with by the state: within the limits of small states it was difficult for the capitalist to go ahead: their territory was too small and the competition of neighbours too severe. And apart from this, within each state capital had to fight the socialist tendencies of the government and its inveterate jealousy of all who, either by wealth or intellectual and moral superiority, rose above the general level. Thus capitalism and individualism, growing irresistibly, came into constant conflict with democratic institutions; and the conflict led to utter instability, hindered the healthy development of capitalism, and turned it into speculative channels with which the state was powerless to interfere.

Among the characteristic peculiarities of Greek democracy is its view that the state is the property of the citizens—a view which includes the conviction that the state is bound, in case of necessity, to support its members, to pay them for performing their public duties, and to provide them with amusements. These expenses had to be defrayed by the state either out of the public funds, including its foreign possessions and the tribute paid by the allies, or, if these funds were insufficient, at the cost of the more wealthy citizens. In extreme cases the state resorted to confiscation and requisitioned, on various pretexts, the riches of the well-to-do. When the government sold corn and other food below the market price, or paid the citizens for attendance at the popular assembly and for serving as judges, members of the Council, and magistrates; when it gave them money to buy tickets for the theatre and fed them for nothing in times of dearth—in such cases the usual procedure was to squeeze the rich for the means: they were compelled either to lend money to the state, or to undertake, at their own cost, the management of certain public duties, for instance, the purchase and distribution or sale of corn. They were required also to fit out warships for service, and to pay and train choruses and actors for theatrical performances. Such public burdens were called *liturgiae*.

The same levelling tendency is shown by the state in every department of life. The equality of all citizens was a principle of democracy; and where it did not exist forcible measures were taken for reducing all alike to the average standard, if not to the standard of the lowest citizens. In public life all citizens might and must serve their country as magistrates; hence most of the magistrates were appointed by lot and the method of choice was abandoned. In private life, sumptuary laws aimed at the same object; and equality in morals was secured by laws which prescribed definite rules of conduct. And lastly, in order to preserve equality in matters of the intellect, thinkers and scholars, whose opinions appeared subversive of religion and government, were again and again prosecuted. I have already spoken of the fate of Anaxagoras and Socrates.

Democracy had good reason for prosecuting thinkers and men of learning. For they submitted the city-state to merciless criticism based upon a profound study of its essence. Some peculiar social institutions, such as slavery and the isolation of women, were repeatedly dealt with, from different points of view, by Euripides and Aristophanes. There is a remarkable review of Athenian democracy, witty, profound, and, in places, malicious, in an anonymous pamphlet of the fifth century; the writer is unknown, but was evidently an important figure in the politics of the day. But the heaviest blows suffered by this form of constitution were dealt by the sophists and by Socrates, of whom we have already spoken. Plato, the disciple of Socrates, and Aristotle, the disciple of Plato, summed up the results of this criticism and investigation: in their political writings they gave an excellent and detailed account of such a constitution in its development and practical working, classified all the possible forms which it might assume, and planned the formation of a new and more perfect city-state out of the elements actually existing in Greece.

Democracy was not the only form of government in Greece in the fourth century B.C.; and democracy in one state differed from democracy in another. It appeared in a moderate form at Athens. For Athens still possessed a numerous class of small landowners, an important element in the population of Attica. This essentially conservative class voted, at times of crisis, with the higher class of the city population, and so prevented the proletariat, who were mostly sailors or dock labourers in the Piraeus, from keeping power in their own hands for long. Economic conditions worked in the same direction: men who could earn good wages at Athens were not inclined to give up their earnings for the small sum paid to judges, councillors, and magistrates; so that in practice the business of government was generally left to the richer and more educated classes. And lastly, the ordinary citizen, who had not received the necessary education, felt himself lost in complicated political affairs, and gladly made them over to professional politicians to manage.

A serious danger to the city-state lurked in this tendency of most citizens to hold aloof from politics. Men lost the taste for public life; they felt that public duties, especially the duty of military service, were a grievous burden, and retired more and more into private life; they were thankful to any one who could govern in such a way as to relieve the citizens, as far as possible, from the current business of the state and the necessity of serving in the army. I said above, that democracy was not triumphant everywhere in Greece. Many states were ruled by an oligarchy, that is, by a small group of the richest and most influential men, others by a tyranny, in which one man, supported by hired soldiers, was supreme. Both these forms of government rested on a practice new in Greek life, and partly due to the distaste for public life already mentioned—I mean the gradual substitution of hired professional soldiers for an army composed of citizens.

From the earliest period of Greek history it was the custom of Eastern monarchs to base their military strength largely upon detachments of Greek mercenaries. The stormy politics of Greece were constantly pouring a stream of young and healthy men into the market, where they could be bought. They served in the armies of the Persian kings and satraps; and the vassals of Persia, the Carian kings, for instance, relied upon them. In the fourth century B.C. even the Greek city-states began to use mercenaries for foreign wars. Oligarchies employed them; and so did tyrants, in order to keep the power they had seized.

The case of Panticapaeum, the richest of the Greek colonies on the Black Sea, may serve as a typical example of the way in which the power of a tyrant was maintained for a long time by means of mercenary forces. Panticapaeum, a colony of Miletus, had become a tributary vassal of the Scythians; acting as middleman between Scythians and Greeks, it had grown rich by the export of grain and fish. In the second half of the fifth century B.C. it fell into the hands of tyrants. The decisive factor in this revolution was the hostility between two sections of the population in Panticapaeum and the other Greek cities on the straits of Kertch, which controlled a large part of the Crimea and all the Taman peninsula. The natives formed one section, and the Greek settlers the other; and the tyranny of Panticapaeum was established in order to reconcile the interests of both. It maintained itself for a long time and was converted into a hereditary monarchy, thanks to the strong mercenary army employed by the tyrants.

But if, in the sphere of politics, Greece of the fourth century B.C. presents a mournful picture of weakness and anarchy, we find a complete contrast in her economic condition. For the Greek world was never so rich as then, whether in Greece proper, Asia Minor, and the Black Sea, or in Italy, Sicily, Gaul, and Spain. There were many causes for this. In the first place, agriculture everywhere became more intensive and therefore more productive: old-fashioned methods were generally abandoned. Economic progress was powerfully aided by Greek science, which turned its attention to technical improvements. Specialists collected the results of private experiments, studied them and published them, and so created a science of agriculture. Evidence for this will be found in a short treatise by Xenophon, an Athenian citizen, the same who saw service with the younger Cyrus in Persia as one of his mercenary soldiers. Similarly the culture of the vine and the olive was placed on a scientific basis.

The expansion of Greek trade in this century was extraordinary. The export of wine and oil rose immensely, when the influence of Greek civilization had made these commodities, and also the productions of Greek workshops, familiar to the native inhabitants of Spain, Gaul, Italy, Sicily, Egypt, and the Black Sea coast. The graves of Scythian nobles contain quantities of great amphorae filled with wine and oil and quantities of Greek ornaments buried with the dead; the graves in Etruria and South Italy are as rich in the same objects; and both bear witness to the importance of exports from Greece. In exchange she imported from the countries above mentioned the raw materials required for her industries and food-stuffs to support the population of her cities— immense quantities of corn, salt fish, metals, hides, flax, hemp, and timber for shipbuilding; the forests of Greece, once productive, had now vanished utterly. The import of slaves was important also.

Such conditions naturally stimulated industry to intensive activity. The factory system, indeed, was never adopted— I have already pointed out how difficult it was for a sound capitalistic system to grow up in Greek cities; but workshops of moderate size with a score of workmen, partly free and partly slaves, abounded in every large city. The work done there was highly specialized, different shops turning out different parts of the same article. Thus, in the manufacture of candelabra, four sets of workmen might be employed in four different cities: the first would make the metal branches, the second the stem, the third the pedestal, and the fourth the lamps to be placed on the branches.

The development of trade and industry was facilitated by the abundance of monetary tokens, especially in silver, which were coined by each of the larger cities. Special repute was enjoyed by the Athenian 'owls', silver coins bearing the figure of an owl. Persian gold and the gold coins of Cyzicus and Lampsacus circulated everywhere. The increasing amount of money gave birth to the banking industry and set credit transactions on a firm footing. Banks at Athens in the fourth century B.C. did essentially the same business as our own do now: they received deposits and kept them, made payments on the order of the depositors, gave credit to merchants and traders, received real and personal property as security, and acted as brokers between capitalists and parties in need of credit. Improvements were made in commercial documents and civil law. International trade gradually created a civil law of nations, or rather, a law of cities.

The expansion of trade and, still more, of industry depended largely upon slave labour. The slaves at Athens were probably more numerous than the free population. But they were distributed in groups of moderate size over the different departments of industry. Great plantations and large factories, equipped with servile labour, were both unknown in Greece. The mines were the only exception to this rule. In outdoor and indoor work the slave was a member of a great family. In the fields he often worked side by side with his master, ate the same food, and slept under the same roof. In the workshop he rubbed shoulders with the free artisan, did the same work, and received approximately the same wages, i.e. a sum sufficient to cover the necessaries indispensable for a single man. In building the practice was the same: slaves and free citizens of Athens worked together to raise the Parthenon and Erechtheum. We may suppose that the same conditions held good in other parts of Greece.

XXII

MACEDONIA AND HER STRUGGLE WITH PERSIA

IN the middle of the fourth century B.C. the position of affairs within the Graeco-Oriental world may be described as follows. Greece was torn by political and social anarchy. The principle of autonomy for the different city-states had been victorious over the principle of unification, either in empires, like that of Athens, or in federations, like that of Boeotia; and this victory led to painful consequences in the foreign and domestic affairs of Greece. Of the eighty-five years that divide the beginning of the Peloponnesian war from the conquest of Greece by Macedonia, fifty-five were filled with wars waged by one state against another. Every considerable Greek city experienced at least one war or one internal revolution every ten years. Some cities, such as Corcyra, were perpetually under the strain of revolution, past, present, or future. These convulsions were social rather than political. Abolition of debt and redivision of land had become the programme of the popular party. At Athens the strife of parties was carried on without those atrocities which attended it at Argos, for instance, or Corcyra; yet the democracy, when restored after the Peloponnesian war, included in the jurors' oath a clause that no person taking the oath should demand abolition of debt or a redivision of land.

Anarchy in politics being thus complicated by social anarchy, Greece was filled with exiles from different cities, homeless adventurers, prepared to follow any leader and serve any cause for pay. In the cities the number of citizens with full rights grows smaller, and the unenfranchised, both freemen and slaves, become more important in society and in finance. The militia of citizens is no longer competent to bear the burden of foreign and domestic wars; patriotic feeling is less keen; every one tries to shirk military service by some means or other or to buy exemption. The citizen army of heavy-armed hoplites vanishes from the scene, and the new fashion is a mercenary force of light-armed peltasts. The same conditions prevailed in the fleet also.

What Greece had lost politically, Persia seemed to have gained. It looked as if a Persian conquest was imminent, and as if the enslavement of Greece was inevitable. From this point of view only is it possible to understand the fanciful notion represented by Isocrates—that there was no salvation for Greece, unless all Greeks would combine to attack Persia ; but who was to lead them remained uncertain. Nor were the fears of Greece exaggerated. It is true that the process of disruption was going on even in Persia. The more Asia Minor prospered in consequence of her active share in the international trade organized by Greece, the more stubbornly did the different parts of the country strive to cut themselves loose from the Persian monarchy. Asia Minor in the fourth century consisted virtually of a number of half-Greek monarchies which paid tribute to Persia. And the same tendency was shown by the satraps who represented Persian power in the country : each of them, if he had the chance, was ready enough to declare himself independent. Things were no better in Egypt. During this century she was constantly in revolt, and was brought back each time under the Great King's sceptre with difficulty and not for long. Phoenicia was less unruly : her competition with Greece in trade and finance strengthened her connexion with Persia. About the state of central Asia we are ill informed ; but there, too, the same process of disruption into separate kingdoms was going on.

For all this, Persia was still a mighty empire. Under Artaxerxes Ochus, a contemporary of Philip of Macedon, she showed her strength by dealing with the seceders and restoring the unity of the empire by harsh and cruel measures. But she was weakened partly by dynastic disputes, and partly by her stubborn conservatism in military matters. The war with Greece had proved the great superiority of the heavy-armed Greek infantry to the light-armed troops of Persia ; but still the Persians did not even attempt to improve their standing army, and ignored the mechanical skill, especially in siege operations, which the Greeks had attained. While recognizing Greek superiority they refused to reform their own army, and preferred to add to it detachments of Greek mercenaries, who were, of course, swamped in the heterogeneous mob that fought for Persia. And it must be remembered that each contingent sent to swell the Great King's army carried its own national weapons and fought in its own national manner. Yet, as I have already said, Persia was the only power in the civilized world of that day which had immense material resources and endless reserves of fighting men at its disposal. Disunited Greece was, beyond doubt, far weaker than Persia.

The position was very similar in the West. Carthage became more and more the predominant power. Her trade grew, her territory increased, she went on annexing African tribes who furnished her with good soldiers. She did not, indeed, score any decisive successes over the Sicilian Greeks; but she succeeded at least in establishing herself in the west of the island when the empire of Dionysius came to pieces. It was also an ominous presage that the Greek population in Italy was growing steadily weaker, as one city after another fell into the hands of their semi-Hellenized neighbours—the native clans of south and central Italy. We shall see later how this weakness of the Greeks encouraged the growth of one of these clans—the Latins with their capital of Rome in the centre of the peninsula, who had inherited from Etruria the ambition to unite Italy under one government.

More or less similar was the position of the Greeks in relation to the peoples inhabiting the north of the Balkan peninsula. On the borders of central Greece and strongly influenced by her civilization, three considerable powers were growing up which Greece could not disregard; these were Epirus with an Illyrian population, Thrace, and Macedonia. All three kept up constant relations with Greece; and in each there was a marked tendency to concentrate in the hands of a single dynasty the control over all the inter-related clans which made up the population. Instead of hindering this process Greece was more inclined to help it on. This patronage of upstart and more or less Hellenized nations we can trace with special clearness in the policy of Athens. To Athens all these countries, and especially Thrace and Macedonia, were very important from the point of view of commerce. Thrace was steadily becoming an agricultural country and increasing her export of corn to Greece. She had abundance of cattle and was one of the sources which furnished a constant stream of slaves. In all these ways her services to Greece and especially to Athens were like those of the distant kingdom of the Bosphorus, on the Kertch strait, which forwarded to Greece an immense quantity of grain, hides, fish, and slaves, supplied by the dwellers on the steppes of south Russia, subjects of the Scythians. In addition, Thrace and south Russia exported metals, especially gold, which was dug up in Thrace or carried from the Ural mountains through Scythia into Greece.

Macedonia was no less important to Athens and to all Greece. She possessed excellent timber, especially the pinewood required by Athens for shipbuilding. The only other sources for a supply of good timber were round Mount Ida in the north of Asia Minor and the mountains in south Asia Minor and Syria; but all these districts were included in the Persian Empire, and practically inaccessible to Athens and the rest of Greece. The pine forests of Macedonia also produced great quantities of the pitch and tar indispensable for building ships. Epirus, with its primitive and purely pastoral population, was of less importance to Greece.

In all these countries Athens found it more agreeable to deal with a single person in possession of executive power than with a number of petty tribes and rulers; and the productiveness of the land also was increased by political unity. For this reason Athens kept up friendly relations with the kingdom on the Bosphorus (see Chapter XXI), even after the tyranny of the semi-Hellenic Spartocidae had been established there; and in Thrace, when the Odrysian kings were able for a time to unite a number of Thracian clans under their rule, Athens showed them favour. Thus also there were ties of friendship between Athens and the kings of the Macedonian coast. Two of these, Archelaus, who reigned during the Peloponnesian war, and his successor, Amyntas, were Athenian allies in the north and highly valued by her. In those days no one at Athens dreamed that a strong Macedonia would ever be a danger to Greece.

But vast possibilities in the way of civilization and political development were now opening up before Macedonia. The origin of this people is still an unsettled question. Perhaps they were Greeks, just as the Aetolians and Acarnanians were; perhaps they belonged to the family of Illyrian or Thracian clans; or perhaps there gradually settled in Macedonia detachments from each of the three Indo-European stocks above mentioned, overspreading a non-Aryan population and gradually blending with it to form a new nation in many respects unlike the Greeks. But no certain conclusion is possible. The Greeks found their language difficult to understand, and ranked them as 'barbarians'. It is clear that the language was a dialect of Greek, with a strong infusion of foreign words, phrases, and expressions. For the future fortunes of Macedonia it was of more importance that the valleys on her coast, together with her mountainous district, including Paeonia, form one geographic and economic whole, divided by lofty mountains from Epirus, Illyria, and Thrace. These parts of the country are bound into one by three great rivers, which are quite large enough for navigation—the Haliacmon (now the Bistritza), the Axius (now the Vardar), and the Strymon (now the Strumnitza). The natural wealth of Macedonia was abundant and various—rich mines, excellent forests, extensive pastures, and wonderful cornfields. On the pasture lands horses were bred as well as sheep and oxen. The level land on the coast runs along two deeply indented bays—the gulfs of Therma and the Strymon; and these bays are divided by the peninsula of Chalcidice (now Mount Athos). There are good natural harbours in both bays, especially in the former, where Therma (afterwards Thessalonica and now Salonica) is still among the most important roadsteads of the Mediterranean. Greeks had long before this time settled on the coast of Macedonia and both the bays; Amphipolis had been built on the Strymonian gulf. Macedonia used the Greek cities for exporting her produce; and they served her also by introducing Greek civilization.

Under these conditions, Macedonia naturally grew rich in the palmy days of Greece, especially after the Persian wars, and her higher classes became more and more Hellenized. Nevertheless, the process of political unification, complicated by the continual intrigues of the chief Greek states and by the dynastic quarrels inevitable in monarchies, went on slowly in Macedonia, till the second half of the fourth century B.C., when the efforts of Archelaus and Amyntas pushed it forward with some success. In this way it became possible for Philip, who succeeded Amyntas on the throne in 360 B.C., to take as his task the complete unification of Macedonia; by this means he could create a powerful kingdom and begin extensive political activities in Greece, with the definite object of heading the Greek nation in a crusade against Persia. By long and persistent labour he succeeded in reforming the political and military system of the country.

Out of a feudal kingdom based upon clanship he made a powerful empire, ruled by a single head and depending on a standing army, well trained and well supplied. The nucleus of this force was supplied by small landowners, who served as infantry and formed the phalanx which later proved invincible. The large landowners, the former feudal aristocracy, now became the king's 'Comrades', and furnished the army with a force of heavy-armed cavalry superior to any then existing.

Philip introduced into his army all the latest improvements in Greek tactics, which he had learnt during his long residence at Thebes with Epaminondas, and also adopted all the Greek mechanical appliances for war. By means of this army he was able to check the disruptive tendencies of the country, to protect his frontiers against attack from their northern neighbours, to cripple the Odrysian kingdom of the Thracians, his most serious rival, and even to penetrate farther north and inflict some blows on the Scythian kingdom, which at this time was expanding southwards and westwards and seizing one part of the Balkan peninsula after another. At the same time he never relaxed his efforts to annex Thessaly and that strip of Macedonian coast which was occupied by Greeks. Without access to the sea, a wider political influence over the whole Greek world was out of the question. By degrees, and after a succession of wars, the Greek cities in Macedonia, Paeonia, and Chalcidice, became part of his kingdom.

I said above that in his youth, and before he ascended the throne, Philip spent a long time at Thebes while the Boeotian league was at the height of its power. There he became thoroughly familiar with the features of contemporary Greek politics; and there, probably, he conceived the plan of using the political and social anarchy of Greece, in order to unite that country under his own leadership, for the purpose of a common attack on Persia. He learnt the details of Greek politics even more thoroughly during the struggle for mastery on the Macedonian coast, which first brought him into collision with Athens. The Athenians were beginning to understand the greatness of the danger which threatened their political and commercial interests, if Macedonia were converted into a strong maritime empire.

Philip interfered in the complicated politics of Greece

herself, after he had finally annexed the Greek cities of Chalcidice and destroyed many of them, during 349 and 348 B.C. His pretext was a mournful business, typical of the time and place, which was transacted in northern Greece. A small alliance of Phocian cities had been at war with Boeotia from 356 B.C., when Boeotia declared a Sacred War against Phocis for laying hands on the property of the Delphian temple. The Phocians, taking advantage of their own proximity to Delphi and the weakness of Boeotia, had seized the temple with all the treasures amassed there, and used their spoils to create a strong army of mercenaries; they then proceeded to enlarge their territory at the expense of their neighbours, Boeotia and Thessaly. Thus they came into collision with Philip and were driven out of Thessaly by him. Just at this time Philip had overcome the Athenian defence of Chalcidice and had forced Athens to conclude a treaty of peace. He was now at liberty to interfere in the affairs of Greece. On the invitation of the Amphictyones, the official guardians of the Delphian temple, he undertook the command in the contest with the Phocians, defeated their army and destroyed their cities, and imposed on them an annual tribute to make good the losses suffered by the temple. The Phocians were expelled from the Amphictyonic assembly, and their place there was taken by Philip.

When Macedonia in this way became recognized as a member of the family of Greek states, Philip came forward with his plan of uniting Greece into one allied kingdom under the political and military direction of Macedonia. The statesman and soldier saw clearly that the question of his domination over Greece could not be settled in his favour without a decisive conflict against Persia. For, under the vigorous rule of Artaxerxes Ochus, Persia laid claim to Greece as her own property, and regarded her as the regular source of those mercenary troops which made it possible to maintain the unity of the monarchy. Hence the intention of Philip to unite all Greece was a serious threat to Persia; and her gold was actively employed in Greece to support hostility to Macedonia.

In the diplomatic strife between Macedonia and Persia, Greece had a hard part to play. She had early realized Philip's aspirations. There were a band of idealists in the country—the most important of them, Isocrates, has been mentioned already—who saw that the city-state was powerless to effect a union of the nation, and realized the Persian peril; they were therefore inclined to endure dependence on Macedonia, if only they could defy the Persian spectre and the yoke of the 'barbarian'. Macedonia they recognized as a Greek power; and in submission to Macedonia they saw the one possible solution, the only means of preserving for Greece her importance and her prominence in the political life and civilization of the world. One of the most active supporters of this policy at Athens was the eloquent orator, Aeschines.

But the majority in Greece took a different view; and they found a leader in Demosthenes, a forensic orator and statesman, a determined foe of Macedonia and a champion of old traditions. To Demosthenes and his followers the matter at issue was the freedom of Greece, which by them was identified with the city-state—its independence, its right to settle its own affairs, domestic and foreign, without interference from others. Opposed to this freedom was monarchy, in which they saw the mortal foe of the peculiar constitutional principles so dear to every Greek. It would not be just to describe Demosthenes and his party as opponents of national unity; but they were determined on one point: they would not buy national unity at the price of political freedom. Nor was there any reason to suppose that their dreams of a united but free Greece were merely fanciful. At the moment Greek freedom was menaced by two enemies, of whom Macedonia was the more immediate and Persia the more remote. Of two evils they chose what seemed to them the least. To be conquered by Macedonia meant immediate slavery; to conquer Macedonia, even with the help of Persian gold, did not necessarily mean slavery to Persia. A Persian conquest was a bugbear which few Greeks were frightened of. They had a lively remembrance of the previous wars, and were convinced that they could defend their country a second time from the invader, if he ever came. On the whole, the only immediate danger to freedom came from Macedonia; and from that danger Greece must, at all costs, be protected.

We may well wonder that the Greeks, in spite of their political anarchy, were able to struggle so long and so successfully in defence of their independence. Demosthenes contrived to bring together such irreconcilable rivals as Athens and Boeotia, to tear up the treaty concluded with Macedonia, and to bring matters to an open conflict between the two antagonists at Chaeronea in Boeotia in the year 338 B.C. The forces were equally matched, but Macedonia was victorious, thanks to the superior training of her army and the excellence of her cavalry. Sparta remained neutral in this contest; but she refused to recognize the leadership of Macedonia, even when that leadership was acknowledged at Corinth by a congress of representatives from the Greek states. At the same time a general alliance of Greeks was formed, in order to fight Persia under the direction of Macedonia.

The first Macedonian contingents had already reached the Asiatic shore of the Hellespont, when sudden death cut short the brilliant career of Philip, one of the world's greatest diplomatists and generals. In the autumn of 336 B.C. a marriage was to be celebrated at Aegae, the ancient capital of Macedonia—Pella became the capital later—between Philip's daughter, Cleopatra, and Alexander, King of Epirus; the purpose of this alliance was to strengthen the bond between the two countries. During the festival Philip fell by the hand of an assassin. He was only forty-seven years old. This accident had highly important political consequences. Who can tell what would have happened to Macedonia and Hellas if Persia had fallen a victim to the skilful diplomacy and ripe experience of Philip, and not to the assault of the young and romantic Alexander? The murderer was seized and killed on the spot by the king's guards. Whether the murder was merely a piece of personal revenge, or whether the injured and formidable figure of Olympias, Philip's rejected wife and mother of Alexander, stood behind the murderer, was never cleared up; but tradition, even when hostile to Alexander, has never charged him with parricide.

The devotion of the army to the young prince, who had been associated with it from his childhood and had even commanded a division at the battle of Chaeronea, saved Macedonia from the strife that usually attended the succession. The army at once acknowledged Alexander as king. His rivals were removed, and the danger of disturbance vanished. But Philip's death forced Alexander to postpone the campaign against Asia. The king was almost a boy, and no one believed in the capacity of this boy to continue his father's policy. The outskirts of his empire were in excitement; Greece was in a ferment, which rose to the highest pitch of intensity when Alexander disappeared from view in the mountains of Illyria and a rumour of his death spread abroad. Thebes, and then Athens for the second time, headed a movement of hostility to Macedonia. But Alexander, after a successful march to the Danube, and after assuring the safety of his rear, made a sudden appearance under the walls of Thebes. He took the city by assault and destroyed it; the inhabitants were either slain or sold into slavery. Greece calmed down after the settlement with Thebes. Alexander was acknowledged as leader in place of his father, and Corinth was again the place where the acknowledgement was made. He started at once for Asia, to continue the design planned by Philip. The fate of Greece was no longer to be decided in Greece itself, but in Asia Minor, Syria, Babylonia, and Persia. Greece was a spectator of the drama that followed, and there were Greeks fighting on either side.

During the two years from 336 to 334 B.C. Persia had done nothing to anticipate the Macedonian attack. The fate of Philip had fallen also on Artaxerxes Ochus, and Persia's hands were tied until the usual palace intrigues came to an end. In this way Alexander's antagonist was not the able and experienced monarch, Artaxerxes, but his successor, Darius III, surnamed Codomannus, who had given no proof of his quality before this conflict.

Alexander's task was not easy. The war, nominally waged by Macedonia and Greece, was in fact waged by Macedonia single-handed. The Greek contingents in Alexander's army were negligible; it was impossible to rely upon them or upon the Greek fleet. In resources and especially in money Macedonia was decidedly inferior to Persia. But she possessed the same advantages which had once enabled Persia to become a world-empire—a young and vigorous nation of soldiers, the best weapons then attainable and all the military appliances devised by Greek science, well organized communications, and a young, bold, and able leader, backed by a number of generals who had gained experience in the service of his father.

Nevertheless, it was difficult for a contemporary to foresee the issue of the struggle. One of the chief advantages of Persia was her powerful fleet and command of the seas. The maritime power of Macedonia and Greece was not, indeed, inferior to that of Persia; but Athens, stronger at sea than any other Greek state, showed no enthusiasm in the cause, and, without her active assistance, Persia ruled the waves. Alexander's task was first to weaken and then to destroy this superiority of the enemy. To attain this object, he had to seize by land the bases of the Persian fleet one after another, beginning with Asia Minor and proceeding to Syria and Phoenicia. His victory on the Granicus in the north of the country gave him access to the harbours of Asia Minor, and he took them all in turn. A second victory at Issus, at the entrance into Syria from Asia Minor, put the Phoenician coast in his power. Tyre alone held out, but was taken after a long siege in which Alexander's engineers showed their ability to master the most difficult problems of siege warfare.

Alexander was now able to march against Babylonia and Persia without exposing his rear to danger. But he directed his steps first to Egypt and established his authority there. This expedition was indispensable, to supplement his conquest of Phoenicia; for thus he deprived the Persian fleet of their only remaining base. He needed Egypt also in order to supply Greece with food-stuffs and to secure by this means her friendly neutrality. The decisive conflict between Alexander and Darius was fought at Gaugamela in Babylonia (331 B.C.). The huge Persian army was destroyed, and Darius fled to his satrapies in central Asia, and was there put to death. Alexander's subsequent campaign in Turkestan and India was intended to complete the conquest of all the satrapies belonging to Persia. This romantic enterprise, though it produced an immense impression at the time, was not of great historical importance: Greek institutions could not find a home in the heart of Asia.

By the victories of Alexander it was decided that Greeks should take the place of Iranians as rulers of the East; and by them also the future destiny of Greece was settled. The Greek cities lost for ever their political independence: in spite of repeated attempts to recover it, the city-state was forced to submit to a monarchy. Ceasing to exist as an independent political unit, it became part of a great monarchical kingdom, while retaining only a shadow of self-government. The Greek city-state had played its part in the history of the world, and Greek monarchy now held the stage.

XXIII

GREEK CIVILIZATION IN THE FOURTH CENTURY B.C.

IF the political development of Greece in the fourth century was based exclusively on the city-state, with its inherent belief in complete political independence, complete self-government, and, as far as possible, economic isolation from the rest of the world—and if this development was fundamentally hostile to any political union whatever to include all Greeks, yet Greek civilization tended more and more to transcend the narrow bounds of the city-state, until it became the common property first of all Hellas and then of all mankind. In the parts of Europe, Asia, and Africa which border on the Mediterranean, the conviction, which had long before been firmly held by the Greeks, now grew up in the minds of the majority, that there was only one civilization, that of the Greek city-state, and that everything outside of it was 'barbarism', i.e. a life under conditions which a Greek considered unworthy of a human being. It is interesting to note that modern historical thought has inherited this point of view from the Greeks. It is still a commonplace to contrast West with East—Greece, as the bearer of a true and unique civilization, with the East, as the possessor of a different civilization, lower than the first and not measurable by the same standards.

Nevertheless the Greeks, consciously in part and subconsciously in part, now impart to their production a more and more cosmopolitan character, leaving what is local and provincial and characteristic of a single city-state, and proceeding to a result accepted by all Greeks alike. This process is especially clear in art. The local schools, often referred to above, continue to exist; but local peculiarities become less important than the individual genius of the artist and his followers. In architecture, painting, and sculpture we cease to speak of the different schools, Peloponnesian or Ionian or Sicilian: we speak instead of Phidias, Praxiteles, Scopas,

Lysippus, Polygnotus, Apelles, and so on. Their statues and paintings appealed to the Greek eye and mind; and every community was eager to adorn its temples, open spaces, and museums with their works.

Applied art adapted itself with special ease to this change in the manner of artistic production. The clients and customers, for whom this industry was carried on, were in many cases not Greeks themselves, though they set a high value on the productions of Greek art. Their taste influenced the work produced, and the Greek artist adapted himself successfully to it. The two chief centres for the sale of Greek articles illustrate most clearly this process: these are Italy and Sicily in the West (and to some extent Gaul and Spain), and Thrace and Scythia in the North and East. In Etruria, Samnium, Campania, and Apulia on the one hand, and at Panticapaeum in the Bosporan kingdom on the other, local schools of Greek art-workers are formed—potters, jewellers, and workers in wood, leather, and metal. These men, while remaining Greeks, add a trifle of local tang which makes their work attractive to their customers, while at the same time it Hellenizes their taste. Thus the Greeks enter on a new path of great historical importance: their civilization attracts men who are not Greeks, and so becomes the common property of the world.

In Asia Minor, and even in Phoenicia and Egypt, the Greeks carry on the same work with remarkable success. Such Anatolian political communities as Lycia and Caria, arising out of satrapies of the decaying Persian kingdom, become more and more Greek in the external manifestations of their civilization. It is sufficient to mention the Lycian tombs, covered with reliefs and reproducing, in some cases, paintings of Polygnotus, and the famous Mausoleum of Halicarnassus. This was the monument erected over the grave of Mausolus, King of Caria, at Halicarnassus, a half-Greek city and the capital of the kingdom. The best Greek artists of the century worked at the adornment of this monument. For the political future of Greece, however, this peaceful conquest of foreign nations was disastrous. In Italy, in Asia Minor, in south Russia, the native inhabitants became more and more prominent in political affairs, and many Greek cities, lying on the outskirts of the Greek world, lost their purely national aspect; many of them were unable to cope with the forces which they themselves had called forth. And so the foundations were laid for the Hellenistic kingdoms of the future with their hybrid civilization.

Her place in the life of the countries bordering on the Mediterranean Greece owed to her sublime intellectual triumphs in the fourth century B.C. In this period also, in spite of political degradation, in spite of the fact that she was only one of many Greek states, equally feeble and equally incapable of uniting Hellas into a single nation, Athens is

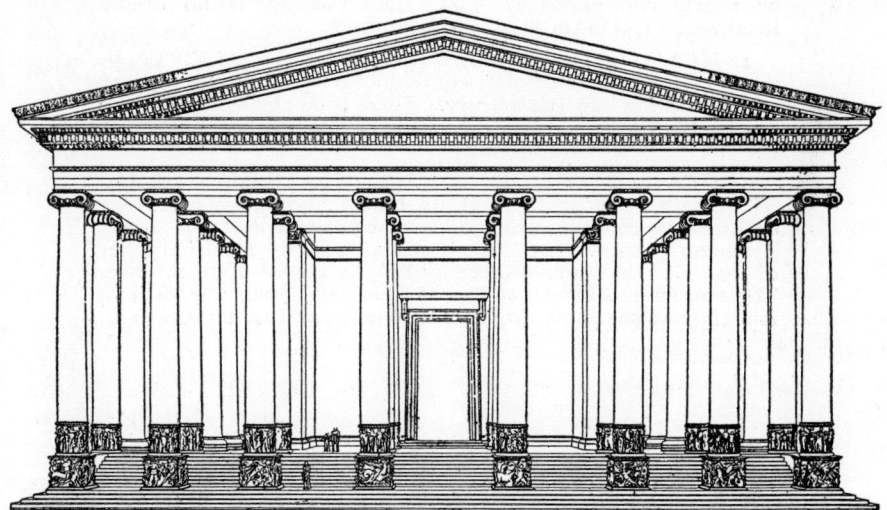

FIG. 34. *Restoration of the temple of Artemis at Ephesus after the fire of Herostratus. 4th cent. B.C. After Murray.*

still the foremost in the march of civilization. The dialect spoken and written by the Athenians of the fifth century becomes in the next century the language of every educated Greek, and banishes all other local dialects from literature and refined society. To speak Attic and to write Attic becomes obligatory for every man of education; and literature written in any other dialect has a merely local importance. The Attic dialect owed its position to the Athenian writers, who brought to perfection its expressiveness, its wealth of vocabulary, the pliancy of its syntax, and the harmony of its periods in prose and its strains in verse.

Some, indeed, of the literary forms invented by the Athenians had reached perfection in the fifth century. In these further development is impossible, and nothing is pro-

PLATE LXXIX
THE GREAT MEN OF GREECE OF THE 4TH CENT. B.C.

1. HEAD OF THE GREAT ATHENIAN PHILOSOPHER PLATO. It is a copy, made in Roman times, of a contemporary or nearly contemporary bust. The portrait is no doubt idealized. Holkham Hall, England.

2. HEAD OF THE PHILOSOPHER ARISTOTLE. Copy, made in Roman times, of a contemporary portrait by a great sculptor of the late 4th century. There is no idealization in the head. It is a true realistic portrait of the greatest scholar of the world. Vienna Museum.

3. HEAD OF THE ORATOR AND STATESMAN DEMOSTHENES, the great rival of Philip and Alexander, the enthusiastic champion of the Greek city-state and the ardent Athenian patriot. It is a real portrait slightly idealized, part of a copy of the bronze statue by Polyeuctus set up in 280 B.C. The famous full-length statue of Demosthenes in the Vatican is a copy of the same original. Ashmolean Museum, Oxford.

1. PLATO

2. ARISTOTLE

3. DEMOSTHENES

LXXIX. THE GREAT MEN OF GREECE OF THE IVth CENT. B.C.

duced that can rival the past. This is the case of tragedy and, to some extent, of comedy. But, on the other hand, new forms of literary creation appear and run their dazzling race. The most conspicuous of these are philosophy and rhetoric. Both were created by the sophists of the fifth century. In the person of Plato Greek philosophy reaches its highest point, alike in form and in substance. This is not the place to speak of what Plato did to deepen and widen Greek speculative thought. His Theory of Ideas, and his doctrine that reason makes the world and himself intelligible to man, laid a foundation for the development of philosophic speculation not only in antiquity but at the present day. For the history of Greek civilization it is important to note that Plato was the first definitely to concentrate his attention, as student and thinker, on man and not on the external world, and that he gave to ethics and politics, regarded by him as inseparable from one another, the precedence over other sciences.

The power to discover truth and understand justice is the first step towards the realization of justice; and this realization is the basis for the moral life of the individual and for the right ordering of government and society. Plato's theory of the state, of which we have already spoken, is founded entirely upon the conception of justice. Criticism of existing constitutions and (to some extent) of Athenian democracy is not for Plato an end in itself: it serves merely as the introduction to an elaborate and detailed scheme for a new political and social system, based upon the realization of abstract justice. That scheme is visionary and Utopian: it takes no account of historical development or human nature; but it remains a true statement of the essential goal, at which all later social reformers have aimed, even when their opinions were diametrically opposed to Plato's.

It is quite possible that Plato himself, especially after his repeated attempts to convert to his philosophy the younger Dionysius, tyrant of Syracuse, realized the Utopian character of his scheme. For he followed up his visionary *Republic* with a second political treatise called *The Laws*, in which he not only tried to show how a Greek city-state might be founded on a rational basis, but also brought together all the scientific conclusions which had been attained by Greeks in law and politics. We have here the first codification of

Greek law; and its influence upon the future has been very great.

Plato expounded his views to a scanty band of pupils in the form of lectures, which he delivered in the *Academeia*, a grove consecrated to the Attic hero, Academus. The lectures were not published, and we do not possess them. But, for the instruction of a wide circle of readers, Plato wrote and published his *Dialogues*, of which we possess a considerable part. Here in the form of conversations, carried on, as a rule, by Socrates, Plato's master, with some other person, Plato has expounded in a grand, brilliant, and copious style, his thoughts on various topics, and especially on ethics and politics. The *Dialogues* are admirable works of literature, in which the Greek language, while preserving all its simplicity and picturesqueness, was first adapted to express all the refinements of philosophic thought. Each dialogue is a finished work of art, and fascinates the reader from beginning to end.

Another pupil of Socrates and founder of a philosophic school was Antisthenes, an Athenian, who began his career as a rhetorician and sophist under the instruction of Gorgias. The business of this school was to define the relation of man to life, and to reconcile man with life and with himself. His preaching was founded on the conviction that earthly goods and the gains of civilization are vain. He called man to asceticism and the simple life; he bade them return to the laws of nature. The stability of mind thus acquired makes a man a king; he cares nothing for external things—food, drink, luxury, a fine dwelling, honour and glory; all such things are 'indifferent'. Social distinctions are meaningless: all men are brothers, and there is no difference between the slave and the freeman. He alone is free who is master of himself. Because Antisthenes taught in the gymnasium of Cynosarges, the name of Cynic was attached to the school. The most famous pupil of Antisthenes was Diogenes of Sinope, who lived in the time of Alexander the Great. Cynicism gave birth eventually to Stoicism, so called because its founder, Zeno, taught in the *Stoa Poecile* or Painted Colonnade.

Yet another pupil of Socrates offered a different solution of the same fundamental question. This was Aristippus of Cyrene. He, too, seeks happiness for man. Starting from a purely materialistic standpoint, the standpoint of Democritus and Antiphon, and insisting on the relativity of our knowledge, he calls on men to trust their feelings. That which procures happiness and pleasure is good. But happiness and pleasure must not be our masters. To conquer them and thus gain true freedom, man has the power of reason. The truly happy man is he who has learned truth and conquered feeling, who is the master of pleasure and not its slave. In these precepts there is no place for religion. It is probable that the gods exist; but they are outside the world and have no concern with it. The chief disciple of Aristippus was Epicurus, always sick and always suffering, but a cheerful sage, who taught his pupils in his 'Garden'.

Aristotle, a pupil of Plato, differs in much from his master. His works have come down to us almost complete : immediately after their appearance they became the companions of every educated man and were used in schools. Aristotle was not an Athenian. He was born in Macedonia, but spent nearly all his life at Athens, first as Plato's disciple, and then as head of his own school, which was called the Peripatetic school, because he preferred to walk about and not to sit while delivering his discourses. Three years he spent in Macedonia at the court of Philip, supervising the education of his son Alexander. He wrote *Dialogues*, but they have been lost. His lectures, however, which deal with almost every department of contemporary knowledge, have been preserved. As literature these do not rank with the *Dialogues* of Plato : they show little attention to form, and many of the works which pass under his name were not actually written by him : some are notes of his lectures, taken by his pupils ; others are the work of his pupils, written under his direction. In these lectures Aristotle and his pupils collected all that had been done previously in the different branches of knowledge, revised this matter, threw light upon it, and produced a finished picture of each separate science that was cultivated, more or less successfully, at the time. The sciences were divided by Aristotle into four groups : logic, metaphysics, natural history, and ethics. Rhetoric and politics he treated as a part of ethics ; and poetics, or the philosophy of art, had a section to itself. For the history of civilization his works on natural history and ethics are especially important. Under natural history he included physics, astronomy, psychology, zoology, botany, and mine-

PLATE LXXX

GREEK SCULPTURES OF THE 4TH CENT. B.C.
STATUES

1. HERMES, by Praxiteles, the greatest Athenian sculptor of the 4th century B.C. The statue was found at Olympia in the temple of Hera, where it was seen by the writer Pausanias, who, in the time of the emperor Marcus Aurelius, compiled a description of Greece. The statue represents Hermes playing with the infant Dionysus. It is one of the few original statues by great Greek masters which have remained to us. For the art of Praxiteles see the text. Olympia Museum.

2. STATUE OF DEMETER, found at Cnidus. The goddess is represented in all her majestic beauty The grieved expression of her face suggests that she is thinking of her ravished daughter Kore. An original of the 4th century B.C. British Museum.

3. COPY OF A STATUE BY LYSIPPUS. An athlete is ready to start and looks at his companions who are already in the field. He is taking off his sandals and will then join his companions. The whole body shows a kind of preparatory tension for the display of its youthful force. Lansdowne House, London.

4. SEA-GODDESS, from Ostia. Copy of an Hellenistic work inspired by the passionate art of the 4th-century sculptor Scopas. Ostia Museum.

1. HERMES OF PRAXITELES

2. DEMETER

3. ATHLETE

4. SEA-GODDESS

LXXX. GREEK SCULPTURES OF THE IVth CENT. B.C.

ralogy. In all this field the reasoning is based upon experiment, as far as experiment was possible without instruments of precision. Aristotle's work in zoology and botany is especially remarkable : indeed he was the creator of both sciences.

This experimental method was applied by Aristotle to politics as well. Before proceeding to describe in the *Politics* the normal or preferable forms of government, he made a thorough study of the constitution in 158 Greek and foreign city-states. Other types of community he considered unworthy of attention. But each considerable city was studied historically and systematically by him or one of his pupils, relying upon the best accessible sources. One of these treatises has been preserved—his investigation of the Athenian constitution, and it is the main authority for the constitutional history of Athens. For this work Aristotle used a digest of Athenian history compiled by Androtion from documents and the work of Herodotus. Aristotle's *Politics*, dealing with the city-state in general and the ideal form of constitution, is the fullest and most searching examination we possess of political conditions in Greece, and there is no modern work on the same subject which surpasses it.

The development at Athens of rhetoric, i. e. the art of speaking and writing with grace and ease, was as vigorous as that of philosophy. Practice went hand in hand with theory. The fourth century produced a number of excellent orators and publicists, whose forensic and political speeches were published in their lifetime, sometimes immediately after delivery, and served as models to the next generation of orators and advocates. A political speech was generally delivered by the writer himself in the popular assembly; but most forensic speeches were written for others to deliver, since the Athenian courts required every defendant to conduct his own defence. Some political speeches were never spoken, but merely published as occasional pamphlets. Isocrates, already mentioned, published most of his political works in this way, and may truly be called the earliest of European journalists.

Lysias and Isaeus must be considered as the most brilliant forensic orators of the century. Demosthenes and Aeschines are not only brilliant advocates but admirable political orators. Many of the speeches of Demosthenes are extant. They were recognized by contemporaries, and have since been recognized by later generations as perfect models of rhetorical

PLATE LXXXI

GREEK SCULPTURE OF THE LATE 5TH AND THE 4TH CENT. B.C. RELIEFS

1. ONE OF THE SLABS OF THE SCULPTURED FRIEZES ON THE MONUMENT OF MAUSOLUS OF CARIA (see pl. LXXXVI, 1). The two friezes which represent one, the fight of the Amazons and the Greeks, and the other the fight of the Centaurs and Lapiths, probably adorned the massive base of the monument, while a third frieze—a chariot race—ran above the columns. The sculptures were the work of the most famous Greek sculptors of the 4th century: Scopas and Leochares, Timotheus and Bryaxis. It is possible that the passionate fight of Greeks and Amazons on our slab is the work of Scopas. British Museum.

2. ONE OF THE MOST BEAUTIFUL OF THE GRAVE-STELAE FROM THE CEMETERY OF ATHENS. The deceased is a young athlete. To the right an old man is looking at him in sorrow and contemplation. A young boy has fallen asleep on the steps and a dog sniffs the ground. 4th century B.C. National Museum, Athens.

3. THE GRAVE-STELE OF A NOBLE ATHENIAN LADY, HEGESO. She is seated in all her Phidian beauty in a chair, before her is her maid with her jewel-box. Late 4th cent. B.C. Cemetery of the Ceramicus, Athens.

1. FIGHT BETWEEN AMAZONS AND GREEKS

2. GRAVE-STELE OF AN ATHLETE

3. GRAVE-STELE OF AN ATHENIAN LADY

LXXXI. GREEK SCULPTURE OF THE Vth AND IVth CENT. B.C.

art. They combine loftiness and complete sincerity with faultless logical construction ; and the marvellous beauty of each sentence and period often produces the impression of music itself. The speeches of Demosthenes show not only genius, but severe study and complete knowledge of the unalterable laws, laid down once for all by theorists of the subject, for musical speech. Apart from their artistic and literary merits, the speeches and political pamphlets of that age are priceless to the historian, because they are the chief source of information concerning the political events of the century, and also tell us of social and economic relations, of civil and criminal law. The first system of Greek law was compiled at Athens ; and by degrees Athenian law became the law of all Greeks.

Rhetoric, or the art of speech, spread its influence outside the domain of forensic and political oratory. Every branch of prose literature was affected by it, and history first of all and more than all. History in the fourth century loses the scientific character which Thucydides tried to impart to it, and becomes little more than a department of artistic prose. The chief business of the historian is not so much to collect, verify, and explain historical facts, as to set them forth in a beautiful and attractive form. This is the main object of Xenophon, the only historian of the time whose works have been preserved. Something has been said above of Xenophon. His *Hellenica* or Greek history is a continuation of Thucydides, brought down to the battle of Mantinea in 362 B.C. His *Anabasis* describes admirably the retreat of the Greek mercenaries from Babylonia to the Black Sea and thence to Greece·; the author himself took part in this retreat and was one of the leaders. The *Education of Cyrus* is partly a romance and partly a study of national characteristics, in which the writer has set forth his ideas about education, and has also communicated some interesting notices of contemporary life in Persia. In his *Recollections* he has drawn for us a portrait of his master, Socrates. Ephorus and Theopompus, whose works have been lost, were younger contemporaries of Xenophon. The former wrote a continuous history of Greece from the Dorian invasion to the end of his own life in 340 B.C. —the earliest attempt to write the history of a whole people ; the latter, like Xenophon, wrote contemporary history in two works—a *History of Greece* and a *History of Philip*.

The development of science and some kinds of literature during this century was rivalled by the development of the plastic arts and sculpture in particular. The great sculptors of the time make it their chief aim to study man in every phase of his bodily and spiritual life. Scopas, one of the greatest sculptors of antiquity, endeavours in his single figures and groups to convey the intense emotions felt by men or gods at a crisis in their lives—the intense exertion of all their physical powers in conflict, their sufferings of mind and body. We do not possess a single statue from his hand in the original; but we have a number of reproductions and a few figures, carved by him or his pupils, which adorned the pediments of Athena's temple at Tegea. The extant sculptures, also, which came from the monument of Mausolus at Halicarnassus, are strongly influenced by the dramatic and passionate quality imported into the art by Scopas. The scenes of battle between the Greeks and Amazons depicted on the walls of the Mausoleum are full of passion and movement.

Praxiteles, a younger contemporary of Scopas, took a different line. He enjoyed great fame in his lifetime, and had a strong influence upon the later development of sculpture. Our museums are crowded with reproductions and imitations of his work. And one of his works has survived in the original—a statue of Hermes carrying the infant Dionysus in his arms. It was made for the temple of Hera at Olympia. In all the statues of Praxiteles we note the endeavour to convey in marble the beauty of the human form, male and female—not the ideal superhuman beauty which the statues of Phidias represent, but a purely human beauty in its highest perfection. When one looks at his Hermes, one does not recognize a god in that nude figure, but one admires the perfection of form in the youthful body and the harmonious nobility of the face. His Aphrodite, made for the city of Cnidus, impresses the spectator by the harmonious lines of a faultlessly beautiful female form; and his Satyr conveys that careless enjoyment of life which is natural to a being that is half-man and half-beast.

The same love for the beauty of form in the human body gives life to all the works of Lysippus, a younger contemporary of Praxiteles, who devoted himself entirely to the figures of young athletes. He was also the creator of portrait sculpture.

Tradition reports that Alexander allowed no others than Lysippus and Apelles to carve and paint his likeness.

The same features are observable in painting. Large schemes of decoration give place by degrees to the production of single easel-pictures, intended for the adornment of public buildings or private houses. It is difficult, however, for us to judge of the painting, because not a single example from the hand of the great masters has been preserved even in a copy, while some specimens of the art, dating from this period, are the work of second-rate painters. In vase-painting, as the demand for Attic vases increased, the artistic quality fell off; and the vases do not convey, as precisely as they once did, the style and peculiar features of painting on a larger scale.

On the whole, the fourth century was a worthy successor of the fifth. The creative power of the Greek people was as strong as ever. It grew and flourished, conquering one new domain after another and attaining in some of them the same perfection that stamps the literature and art of the preceding century.

THE
HELLENISTIC PERIOD

THE
HELLENISTIC PERIOD

XXIV

THE WORLD-MONARCHY OF ALEXANDER THE GREAT, AND THE POLITICAL HISTORY OF THE GRAECO-ORIENTAL WORLD IN THE THIRD CENTURY B.C.

WHEN Alexander had conquered the Persian monarchy, he was faced by a further problem. What was to become of the huge empire, of which he found himself the supreme and absolute ruler? How he intended to organize these vast dominions, we do not know. Indeed, it is possible that he had no clear notions himself on the subject. Death came upon him at Babylon in 323 B.C., at a time when he considered his military problem, the problem of conquest, as still unfinished. On the eve of his sickness and death, which took him entirely by surprise, he was planning an expedition to Arabia. Perhaps the conquest of Arabia seemed to him necessary, partly to protect the frontier of his empire in Hither Asia, and partly that he might be able to continue the task of conquering India. And another scheme may have appealed to his adventurous nature, the scheme which had attracted Themistocles and Alcibiades and became later the object of Pyrrhus, King of Epirus. This was the annexation of the western Greeks to his empire. Had he done this, he must infallibly have come into collision with Carthage and with the Italian tribes, who had by this time formed more than one powerful state.

Hence it is not surprising that Alexander, who even in his lifetime was called Alexander the Great, gave less attention to organization than to purely military problems and matters affecting the basis of his own personal power. He governed his empire partly in accordance with the traditions of the Persian monarchy, and partly by means of temporary and purely military instruments—the generals commanding divisions of his army: it became their business to control the conquered countries and supply Alexander with the means for carrying out his further military enterprises.

PLATE LXXXII
PORTRAITS OF ALEXANDER AND HIS SUCCESSORS

1. PORTRAIT OF ALEXANDER, from Magnesia. An idealized portrait of the 3rd–2nd century B.C. Constantinople Museum.

2. BRONZE HEAD OF A HELLENISTIC RULER, probably Seleucus I Nicator. From Herculaneum. Roman copy of a contemporary portrait. Naples Museum.

3. PORTRAIT OF ATTALUS I, the great ruler of Pergamum. From Pergamum. 3rd century B.C. Berlin Museum.

4. A LARGE CAMEO, of sardonyx, in Vienna, probably made at Alexandria, and probably representing Alexander the Great and Olympias, in an idealized form. 3rd century B.C. Vienna Museum.

1. ALEXANDER

2. HELLENISTIC RULER

3. ATTALUS

4. (?) ALEXANDER AND OLYMPIAS

LXXXII. ALEXANDER AND HIS SUCCESSORS

He attached more importance to two questions. How was he to replenish the strength of his armies? And what source would supply him with additional staff-officers and coadjutors in the task of ruling the empire? As at the beginning of his campaigns, he placed little reliance upon the Greeks, whose political ideals were unchanged, and to whom Alexander and his power were an object of hatred rather than of attraction. There remained the Macedonians. But the resources of Macedonia were not inexhaustible, and a country of her size could only supply a limited number of men. The power of direction must, no doubt, be reserved for the Macedonians; but they must have help, and for this purpose other men must be found, as fit instruments as the Macedonians to carry out military and administrative business for their master.

It seemed to Alexander that the Iranians would answer his purpose. They were still a warlike and powerful nation, with the habit of war and the power to govern. He had learnt on the battle-field to respect their military capacity; and while governing the East he had seen their administrative powers and come to value their efficiency in organizing the Persian satrapies conquered by him. Thus impressed, Alexander set himself to bring together the Macedonians and Iranians, as the two most efficient elements of his empire; he even wished to blend them into one, at least in the army and in administration. The conversion of the army into a joint force of Macedonians and Iranians, the appointment of Iranians as military governors of provinces, his marriage with the Persian princess Roxana, and a number of similar mixed marriages between Persian women and generals, officers, and men of the Macedonian army—such were the first steps in that direction.

Alexander was anxious to be at once the Great King of Persia and the king of a small European people. This endeavour I should be inclined to regard as chimerical. To unite the dynasties of Macedonia and Persia was easy enough; but to establish the new dynasty upon an aristocracy and an army, which should be half Macedonian and half Iranian, was probably beyond the limits of what is possible for man. The difference was too great between the historical traditions of the two nations; and their mental attitude, the growth of ages, was too unlike. Yet the project itself is quite in keeping with Greek ideas of that time, and is entirely in the spirit of Plato's political fancies. To the speculative Greek mind no scheme seemed impossible, provided that the purely logical structure was harmonious and pleasing.

The second point that troubled Alexander was the nature of his own power. Philip, his father, had felt no anxiety about his position: he was the lawful King of Macedonia, inheriting his power from his ancestors and acknowledged by his people, while he ruled the Greeks because they had chosen him as their commander-in-chief. But for Alexander, a king of kings and ruler of a world-empire, more was needed. In the East kingly power was closely connected with religion, and to break that connexion would be a serious mistake. But there were many religions in Alexander's empire, and each had its own way of deciding whether kings were divine beings. How Alexander himself regarded this question, we do not know. He may, as a pupil of Aristotle, have taken the rationalistic view and treated it as a mere matter of politics; or the mystical side of the Greek mind, which saw no absolute distinction between the divine and the human and fully accepted the possibility of a divine incarnation, may have made itself audible in the conqueror's breast. We have no certain knowledge; but I am inclined to believe that Alexander ranked himself above ordinary mortals, not merely because he was a king and a distant descendant of Heracles. A man's thoughts are apt to take a mystical direction, when death threatens him every day, when his victories are checked by no limits, and when the flattery of those around him— flattery which in the ancient world, and especially in the East, took the shape of religious worship—went beyond all bounds.

The tendency of religious thought, both in the East and in the West, fell in with Alexander's own feeling. We saw in Chapter XI how the conception of divinity became more and more spiritualized at this time, losing its local impress and breaking free from national limits. We saw how religious bodies, unconnected with government and united only by a common belief and a common worship, came into existence again and again. The god of that period was not necessarily Zeus, or Ammon, or Oromazdes, or Jehovah; often he was simply God. Hence it was not difficult for Alexander to believe the oracles of Apollo at Didyma and Ammon in

Egypt, and at the same time to believe the priests of Babylon, when they assured him with one voice of his divine origin. It is certain that vast numbers of the people who inhabited his empire believed in his divinity. The legend of the 'divine Iskander' survives to this day in the Iranian world. The collapse of the Persian Monarchy at a single touch from the young King of Macedonia could not but seem a miracle to the mystical Oriental mind; and it could not fail to impress the Greeks also, especially the Anatolian Greeks, who had been inclined to pay divine honours even to Lysander and Agesilaus. To them Alexander's Indian campaign really seemed to be a repetition of the conquest of India by Dionysus. Thus it is natural enough that Alexander's power was formally pronounced to be divine; it became the custom everywhere to pay him divine honours, and this state of things was accepted by the inhabitants of his empire. Rationalists and sceptics in Greece might smile and return sarcastic answers when Alexander urged the recognition of his claim; but the divine nature of his power remained, for all that, a real and powerful factor in the life of his empire, even if we assume that he did not believe in it himself.

When Alexander died, leaving no legal heir of full age, it became an acute question whether the world-wide monarchy which he had left unfinished could still continue to exist. It was an artificial creation of a purely military kind, in which the disruptive forces were stronger than those which made for unity; and his personality was indispensable to its continuance. We have seen how strong a tendency there was in the Persian Monarchy, before the coming of Alexander, to dissolve into its component parts. Greece resented her submission as tantamount to slavery, and showed this feeling immediately after Alexander's death, till Macedonia was obliged once again to restore order by force. In fact, the only bond of union in the empire was the army, especially the Macedonian army with its hereditary devotion to the Macedonian dynasty. But this devotion of the soldiers to their lawful king could not maintain unity for ever, especially when the dynasty came to be represented by a feeble-minded youth and an infant.

Either Philip Aridaeus, Alexander's half-brother, or Alexander's posthumous son by Roxana, might be considered the lawful heir. But personal ambition and thirst

PLATE LXXXIII

HELLENISTIC SCULPTURE

1. MARBLE STATUETTE OF THE TYCHE (FORTUNE) OF ANTIOCH, the capital of the Seleucids. The original, of which this is a much reduced copy, was created in bronze by one of the pupils of Lysippus, Eutychides. It represented the 'Genius' (according to the Romans) or the Tyche, the personification of the city of Antioch. The beautiful majestic woman is seated on a rock, under her feet the river Orontes, on her head a mural crown, in her right hand a bunch of corn-ears. One of the earliest of the symbolical figures common in modern art. The head, and certain other parts, are modern. Early 3rd century B.C. Vatican, Rome.

2. RESTORATION OF THE NIKE OF SAMOTHRACE. After Falize and Cordonnier.

3. A VICTORY MONUMENT OF ONE OF THE HELLENISTIC RULERS OF THE 3RD CENT. B.C., dedicated on the island of Samothrace in memory of a naval victory (of Antigonus Gonatas of Macedonia?) and carved probably by a Rhodian sculptor in imitation of the victory monument of the same type dedicated by Demetrius Poliorcetes in 306 B.C. The goddess Nike walks half-flying on the beak of a warship; she probably held a wreath in her right hand, and in her left the 'stylis'—the ancient equivalent of the flag-staff. The statue is one of the finest creations of early Hellenistic art. 3rd century B.C. Louvre, Paris.

1. TYCHE OF ANTIOCH

2. RESTORATION OF NIKE OF SAMOTHRACE

3. NIKE OF SAMOTHRACE

LXXXIII. HELLENISTIC SCULPTURE

for power prevailed over devotion to the dynasty in the minds of Alexander's generals. A prolonged conflict ensued, in which the question of supporting one or other of the heirs to the succession sank by degrees out of sight, and another question came to the front—whether Alexander's empire should hold together or split up into separate kingdoms, ruled by those who had been his closest companions and coadjutors. In this confused struggle for power all Alexander's heirs and all the members of the ruling house perished one after another; each of them was removed by one or other of the generals, who wished to secure the succession for themselves and to rule that vast empire without a rival.

Not one of them, however, had sufficient ability or sufficient influence over the soldiers, to compel the obedience of the whole army and to force the other generals to admit his supremacy. Each pretender to power had to meet a strong coalition of his rivals who commanded divisions of Alexander's army stationed in the different parts of the empire; and nearly all of them died a violent death. In this way Perdiccas, Antipater, and Polyperchon disappeared one after another. Antigonus, surnamed The One-eyed, one of the ablest generals, who also possessed a capable assistant in his son, Demetrius Poliorcetes, came nearest to realizing the conception of an undivided empire under his personal rule. But even his authority was not recognized by the other generals who ruled separate provinces—Lysimachus in Thrace, Seleucus in Babylonia, Ptolemy in Egypt, and Cassander in Macedonia. They united to inflict a decisive blow on Antigonus in a battle at Ipsus in Asia Minor in 301 B.C., which cost Antigonus his life.

The battle of Ipsus settled the question: the undivided monarchy of Alexander ceased to exist. It split up into a number of component parts, of which the three most important were these: Syria, including all the eastern parts of Alexander's kingdom and some of Asia Minor; Egypt; and Macedonia. The Seleucidae, or dynasty of Seleucus, established themselves in Syria; the Ptolemies or Lagidae, descendants of Ptolemy Lagus, ruled Egypt; while Macedonia, of which Greece was still a dependency, became, after much strife and bloodshed, the kingdom of the Antigonidae, or descendants of Antigonus the One-eyed. In Egypt and Syria the 'kings', as they styled themselves after 307 B.C., based their power on the right of conquest, as successors of Alexander. Foreigners in the countries they ruled, they relied upon a mercenary army for support. The population submitted to them, as they had submitted to their predecessors, growing accustomed to them by degrees, until they settled down in the belief that it was impossible to resist their power and the power of the Greeks and Macedonians who came with them. In Macedonia the new dynasty of the Antigonidae considered themselves lawful successors of Philip's family, and acquired by degrees the confidence and support of the people. All three dynasties ruled over countries which had long been accustomed to absolute monarchy; and for this reason they were likely to last longer.

These powers are commonly called 'Hellenistic', a term which is applied also to the whole period between Alexander's death and the conquest of the East by Rome. Each of them, especially at the beginning of its independent existence, had aspirations to political supremacy and a restoration of the world-wide empire. But, apart from these pretensions, each had to face immediate problems, connected with the past history and economic needs of his realm. The situation led to constant wars between them; in consequence of war each was weakened, and a number of new independent kingdoms were formed by secession. These were mainly military monarchies, like the powers from which they seceded.

The first object of the Ptolemies was to secure the safety of Egypt, the country from which they derived all their political importance. Egypt was in constant danger, because the flat coast at the mouths of the Nile was at the mercy of any invader with a powerful fleet; and to conquer Egypt by land was easy for any enemy who controlled the Syrian and Phoenician coast. Thus to Egypt it was a matter of life and death, no less than in the age of the Pharaohs, to have a strong fleet and a good maritime base at home, and, as far as possible, to control the coast to the north. For the reasons that have been indicated, Alexandria, a Greek city founded by Alexander, became the key to Egypt and its capital. Alexandria had strong walls and a splendid harbour, partly artificial. Under Alexander and the Ptolemies Egypt turned definitely towards the sea and finally became one of the Mediterranean empires. Her wealth was based partly upon exports, and on the office discharged by the Nile as a cheap and convenient trade-route for Egypt and Central Africa. The wares of Arabia also were brought in caravans to the Nile from the Red Sea ports; and part of the trade between Hither Asia and India passed through the harbours of Arabia. Thus the chief anxiety of the Ptolemies was to develop and defend Alexandria, and to assure to Egyptian trade a free and wide market.

These objects brought Egypt in collision first of all with Syria, the empire of the Seleucidae, and formerly the Persian kingdom. It was as important to Syria as it had been to the Persian kings to command the coast-line of Palestine, Phoenicia, Syria, and Asia Minor: otherwise she would become an inland Asiatic power unconnected with the Greek world, and her kings would be unable to recruit her composite army with Greek and Macedonian mercenaries. The Iranian element in the population was never a support to the power of their new masters, and very soon seceded from Syria altogether. Hence the Seleucidae and the Ptolemies were constantly fighting for Palestine, Phoenicia, and south Syria; and the Anatolian coast was constantly passing from one rival to the other. The fortune of war was fickle, and neither combatant could claim a decisive victory. Their forces were approximately equal. The earlier Ptolemies—Soter, Philadelphus, Euergetes, and Philopator—succeeded in creating a great empire with a number of foreign possessions in Palestine, Phoenicia, south Syria, south and central Asia Minor, and on the coast of the Hellespont. But in the second century B. C. the Seleucidae had the advantage of the later Ptolemies—Epiphanes, Philometor, and Euergetes II—till Egypt was in danger of becoming a province of an Asiatic kingdom. The former struggle of Egypt in the Eighteenth Dynasty against Hither Asia, and later against the Assyrian and Persian kingdoms, was repeated again in its main features.

In fighting for supremacy at sea and control of the sea-routes, Egypt came into collision with the Greek city-states, especially Athens, and with the islands of the Archipelago. In disputing the command of the Aegean against Macedonia and Syria, the Ptolemies stuck to the former policy of Persia, which was afterwards adopted by the Romans also: they professed to defend the freedom of the Greek states, while within their own empire they demanded entire subservience from the Greek cities in Asia Minor and the islands. This policy brought against them the forces of the Macedonian kings. Antigonus Gonatas, son of Demetrius Poliorcetes, established himself as King of Macedonia in 283 B.C., and was followed by a line of active and able monarchs—Antigonus Doson, Demetrius, Philip V. To them control of Greece was highly important, because, without it, Macedonia would be exposed to attack by sea; and the master of Greece must also be master of the Aegean. Thus there was constant fighting between Macedonia and Egypt; the presidency over the league of Aegean islands was the prize for which they fought, and this presidency passed again and again from one rival to the other.

Constant warfare swallowed up the resources of the three great Hellenistic powers, drained their strength, and made them incapable of coping with the ever accelerating forces of internal disruption. Syria was the most heterogeneous of the three and suffered most from this cause. First to separate from her in 280 B.C. were Armenia, Cappadocia, Pontus, and Bithynia, formerly called satrapies of the Persian Empire, but, in fact, tributary kingdoms. Native kings with a veneer of Greek culture established themselves in all these countries, and tried to seize such Greek cities as lay within their domains; the form of government adopted was absolute monarchy of the type familiar in the East. The most civilized of these kingdoms was Bithynia, with its Thracian population and a whole row of ancient Greek cities on the Euxine and the Sea of Marmora.

The political life of Asia Minor was much complicated by the coming of the Celts (the Greeks called them Galatians), who crossed over about 278 B.C. from the Balkan peninsula, where the Macedonian Monarchy had been carrying on an obstinate struggle against them. They penetrated far into Asia Minor and established themselves on the plains of Phrygia, where they formed a strong alliance of several clans under the leadership of the clan-kings or princes. From this base they constantly threatened the peace of the country, bearing plunder, murder, and devastation in their train, and destroying the promising prospects of trade and industry. The Seleucidae were powerless to cope with the invaders, and therefore the inhabitants were forced themselves to undertake the task of defending their lands from these formidable barbarians. This state of affairs was the main reason which induced so large a part of Asia Minor to secede from the Seleucid monarchy and set up kingdoms of their own.

One of these independent powers was the kingdom of Pergamum. Pergamum was a fortified Greek city of moderate size which commanded the whole valley of the Caycus in Mysia; it had long been ruled by Greek tyrants who paid tribute to the Persian monarchy while it existed. When Alexander's generals were fighting against Antigonus the One-eyed, Lysimachus, who was one of them, adopted Pergamum as his base and entrusted the defence of it to one of his officers—Philetaerus, a Greek by one parent. The fort contained also a large sum of money, the general's war-chest. When Lysimachus fell in battle with Seleucus in 283 B. C., Philetaerus set up for himself and offered his aid to Seleucus. From that date Pergamum was a separate kingdom, at first tributary to Syria, but from the time of Eumenes I (263 B. C.) entirely independent.

This kingdom owed its stability to the bold and sagacious policy of Philetaerus and his successors, Eumenes I and Attalus I, who reigned from 241 to 197 B. C. They gained the attachment of the Greeks in the north-west of Asia Minor by their skill and courage in fighting the Galatians; they successfully defended against the invader not only their own domains but also the central and southern region of the country. At the same time they increased the prosperity of their kingdom by sensible and prudent management, and thus were able to maintain constantly a strong mercenary army and efficient fleet. This military strength made it possible to veer about at the right moment between Egypt, Syria, and Macedonia, and to increase their territory by degrees. They, too, were the first to realize the strength of Rome, relying upon whom they became in the second century B. C. masters of almost all central and southern Anatolia, by annexing the dominions which Syria and Egypt had held there.

Somewhat later than Asia Minor, central Asia also finally severed its connexion with Syria. Bactria, a half-Greek country, broke away in 250 B. C.; and in 248 the territory of the old Medo-Persian kingdom was conquered by the Parthians, a semi-nomadic people of Iranian stock. The Parthians founded in central Asia a strong state with a veneer of Greek civilization, which lasted for many centuries, terrify-

PLATE LXXXIV
COINS OF THE HELLENISTIC PERIOD

(*a*) TETRADRACHM OF PTOLEMY II PHILADELPHUS OF EGYPT. Head of Ptolemy I r. R. Eagle on thunderbolt l. Name of the king. 284–247 B.C.

(*b*) TETRADRACHM OF ANTIOCHUS II THEOS (the God). Head of the king r. R. Apollo seated on the 'omphalos' (the umbilicus, the centre of the earth) l. with arrow and bow. Name of the king. 261–246 B.C.

(*c*) TETRADRACHM OF EUMENES II OF PERGAMUM. Head of the founder of the dynasty Philetaerus r. R. Athena seated l. Name of Philetaerus. 197–159 B.C.

(*d*) TETRADRACHM OF PRUSIAS II OF BITHYNIA. Head of the king l. R. Zeus standing l. Name of the king. 180–149 B.C.

(*e*) TETRADRACHM OF PERSEUS OF MACEDONIA. Head of the king r. R. Eagle on thunderbolt in an oak-wreath. Name of the king. 178–168 B.C.

(*f*) TETRADRACHM OF EUTHYDEMUS OF BACTRIA. Head of the king. R. Heracles seated on a rock l. Name of the king. About 220 B.C.

(*g*) TETRADRACHM OF MITHRADATES I OF PARTHIA. Head of Arsaces, the founder of the dynasty r. R. Heracles walking l. Name of the king Arsaces. 171–138 B.C.

(*h*) SILVER CISTOPHORUS ($\frac{3}{4}$ of an Attic tetradrachm) OF EPHESUS. The cistophori were first issued by Ephesus at about 200 B.C. as a kind of federal coin for Asia Minor; they were adopted and spread by the kingdom of Pergamum and later by the Romans. Cista mystica (the mystic basket of the Dionysiac mysteries) with serpent issuing from it in an ivy wreath. R. Bow in bow-case between two serpents; r. the sacred stag of Artemis of Ephesus and l. the two first letters of the name of the city of Ephesus. 1st cent. B.C.

(*i*) TETRADRACHM OF ATHENS, struck by King Mithradates VI of Pontus and his factotum Aristion at Athens. Head of Athena. R. Owl on an olive-oil amphora Names of the city, of King Mithradates and of Aristion. In an olive wreath. 88 B.C.

All these coins are in the British Museum.

LXXXIV. COINS OF THE HELLENISTIC PERIOD

ing the eastern provinces of Syria and proving itself later the most powerful and formidable neighbour of the Roman Empire.

In Greece the forces of disruption never ceased working for a single moment. Macedonia tried every means to consolidate her authority and to convert the Greek city-states into administrative departments of the kingdom; but these attempts had no lasting results. Fresh revolts were constantly stirred up by the intrigues of Egypt and Syria. Sparta, which had never become a part of the Macedonian monarchy, played a conspicuous part in the struggle against Macedonia. Of special significance was her political action during the short period when two of her kings—Agis IV about 245 B.C., and then, with more success, Cleomenes from 235 to 219 B.C.—carried through a radical programme of economic and social reform. They divided up all the land among a large number of Lacedaemonians, and thus restored for a time the military strength of Sparta. Antigonus Doson, the Macedonian king, defeated Cleomenes in a decisive battle at Sellasia in 221 B.C.; but Sparta, even under the successors of Cleomenes, still preserved her political independence.

Athens was less successful in her attempts to recover freedom. During the Hellenistic Age she kept her democratic constitution and some of her foreign possessions, and enjoyed periods of marked commercial prosperity; but all her endeavours to regain complete political independence miscarried. Her most considerable effort was the so-called Chremonidean war (267 and 266 B.C.), when, having Sparta and Egypt for allies, she sought to shake off the Macedonian yoke; but the yoke only became tighter because of her action. At a later time, in the reigns of Antigonus Doson and Demetrius, Macedonia was content with friendly neutrality on the part of Athens; but this neutrality was hardly distinguishable from tributary dependence.

Macedonia found stronger and more serious opponents in two leagues of city-states which were formed in Greece at this time—the Achaean League in the north of the Peloponnese, and the Aetolian League in north-west Greece. The constitution of both was federal; that is, each state included in the league had a vote on all matters of business which was proportionate to its own size and military strength. Though these leagues were tough and long-lived institutions, yet they were never able to unite under their banner any considerable part of Greece. Their endeavours to gain additional territory led to frequent wars against individual states and between the two leagues; and Macedonia made skilful use of these quarrels, interfering now on one side and now on the other.

As a result of the unceasing strife between governments the island of Rhodes now asserted itself as an entirely independent power in the Hellenistic world and the Archipelago. Her favourable situation on the main trade-routes from the East to Greece, and from Italy to Greece and the East, made Rhodes one of the largest seaport towns in Hellas, more important even than Athens. Her fleet became by degrees one of the strongest in the Hellenistic world; and at the end of the third century B.C. and throughout the second, it fell to her, with the tacit consent of the three great powers, to fight against piracy and secure the safety of navigation in the Aegean. In this task she was guided by a law devised by Rhodes herself and recognized by all Hellenistic powers, great and small, for regulating international trade and shipping. Cyzicus and Byzantium, large cities and ports, discharged the same office in the Hellespont and the Sea of Marmora, patrolling the seas in defence of commerce; while the Bosporan kingdom, which had now become powerful both by land and sea, maintained peace and order on the Black Sea from its capital Panticapaeum, the modern Kertch.

Thus by degrees there grew up in the Hellenistic world a very complicated and confused political situation. There were a large number of independent and partly independent powers, each jealously watching the movements of its neighbours. The attempt of any single community to extend its territory and its power at the expense of others met with vigorous opposition, for coalitions were constantly being formed to suppress such land-grabbers. Something like a balance of power was reached, which made it impossible for any of the powers to keep the lead for long. The members of this Hellenistic family were as follows: three great powers —Egypt, Macedonia, Syria; about a dozen petty Greek and half-Greek monarchies—Epirus in the Balkan peninsula; Pergamum, Bithynia, Pontus, Armenia, Cappadocia, and Galatia, in Asia Minor; the Bosporan kingdom on the Black Sea; Parthia and Bactria in central Asia, Cyrene and the Nubian kingdom in Africa; and also a number of independent

Greek city-states, and the two Greek Leagues. Meanwhile, new states were growing up on the outskirts of the Greek world, and these began to pay some attention to Hellenistic affairs and the balance of power that ruled there. In the north of the Balkan peninsula a number of Thracian and Celtic states came into existence; in the steppes of south Russia a Scythian kingdom was followed by several kingdoms of Sarmatians. In the West the strongest powers were these: Carthage; the Sicilian Greeks, who had united again in the third century B. C. under the direction of Syracuse and her able ruler, Hiero II; various alliances of Italian clans, among which the league of Latin cities under the presidency of Rome was steadily growing in importance; and lastly, an alliance of Gallic or Celtic tribes in what is now France and in north Italy.

Thus the Greek world, even in the monarchical phase of its development, was reverting to the conditions of the fourth century B. C., that is, to extreme sub-division of political and military strength. Now, as then, war was the rule, not peace. Not a single one of the Hellenistic governments of this period possessed either a great extent of territory or a strong army. Egypt, under the weak and incompetent kings of the second century B. C., had lost nearly all her foreign possessions. Syria was crippled by constant internal commotions. Macedonia was perpetually at war with her Greek vassals and allies, especially with the Aetolian and Achaean Leagues. Nor did individual states enjoy peace at home. The strife of parties and classes was perhaps smothered in monarchies by the absolute power of the ruler, and came to the surface only in revolts of the natives against Greek rule; but it burned all the more fiercely in the Greek city-states. In most of them the same struggle of classes which marked the domestic politics of the fourth century B. C. was equally rife two centuries later.

XXV

THE GREEK WORLD AFTER ALEXANDER: POLITICS, SOCIETY, AND ECONOMICS

AFTER the death of Alexander the chief political powers in the Greek world were the so-called Hellenistic monarchies, which, with the exception of Macedonia, had once formed parts of the ancient kingdom of Persia. All these were ruled by kings of Macedonian birth and Greek culture, relying upon mercenary troops, who were either Macedonians or Greeks or Hellenized 'barbarians'. These men were recruited by agents in the great markets for mercenary soldiers in Greece and Macedonia, or among the Thracian and Celtic tribes which inhabited Asia Minor and the north of the Balkan peninsula. The kingdoms of Asia and Egypt found support also in the numbers of Greek settlers whom they attracted to their dominions, and who formed there the highest class of the population, comprising the well-to-do citizens and the numerous officials of the kingdom.

Though these upstart Eastern dynasties were entirely strange to the natives over whom they ruled, yet they had reason to believe that their position was secure. Their chief security was in the economic prosperity of their subjects: they made it possible to use the natural wealth of the country and the labour of the inhabitants, both natives and settlers, upon a wider scale and with more system. This methodical exploitation of natural resources increased the revenue and so made it possible for the king to maintain a large army and fleet, by means of which he could control his subjects at home and also stick fast to a foreign policy of his own. Hence, in the sphere of domestic affairs, the Hellenistic kings gave special attention to two points—the development of the country's resources and the taxable capacity of their subjects. In this matter they relied upon the tradition inherited by them from the Persian or native kings who had preceded them, and also upon the theory, created by themselves, of their own power.

This power they regarded as the power of a conqueror,

to whom, by right of conquest, the country and its population belonged. As the heirs of Alexander, whose worship had become official in all the Hellenistic kingdoms, they claimed divine origin also, and a supernatural sanction for their rule. They were assisted by finding a similar view of government and kingly power firmly believed by their subjects already. As we have seen before, throughout the East down to the time of the Macedonian conquest, government was based upon the unlimited and divine power of the king, who, in virtue of this power, had full right to dispose of the country and its inhabitants as he pleased. The Hellenistic kings of the different Eastern empires, following here also the example of Alexander, declared themselves the lawful successors of the native kings, and the heirs of their rights and privileges. Thus their power had a double aspect: to the Macedonians and Greeks they were successors of Alexander, but to the native populations they were the heirs of the extinct Eastern dynasties.

As master and owner of his kingdom the Hellenistic monarch exercised unlimited power in dealing with his own property, and considered the interests of the people as less important than those of the government, which he identified with his own personal interests and those of his dynasty. The prosperity of the people was a means, not an end, in his view. And this point of view concurs, in general, with the Greek feeling also about the state. That feeling required of the citizen complete submission to the state, unquestioning service, and sacrifice of his personal interests. The only difference was this—that in the monarchies the state was identified with a single person, whose will was law, whereas in a democracy a majority of the population belonging to a city-state were the government.

But in spite of this autocratic power, which was not contested by any one in the Hellenistic monarchies, the kings were forced to comply with tradition in their treatment both of the Hellenized settlers in their realms and of the native inhabitants. Their relations were different towards these two sections of the population. The latter section knew nothing of self-government and had no aspirations towards any form of it: they were accustomed to obey the officials appointed by the king. The Greeks, however, and other foreign settlers, such as the Jews, had their own idiosyncrasies

PLATE LXXXV

THE HELLENISTIC CITIES

1. RESTORATION OF THE LITTLE HELLENISTIC CITY OF PRIENE. A wall surrounds the city. On the slope near the wall is the beautiful and spacious gymnasium. The centre of the city is occupied by the market-place surrounded by temples and public buildings. The temple of Athena was the religious centre of the city, and a little theatre the centre of its intellectual life. The streets were all paved and cut the city into regular square blocks with many modest but comfortable houses in each. Outside the city is the cemetery, and on the top of the hill a fortress. After A. Zippelius.

2. RESTORATION OF THE ACROPOLIS OF PERGAMUM. The place of honour is occupied by the great altar, with its beautiful sculptures, now in the Berlin Museum; by the temple of Athena; and by the Library of Pergamum. On the top are buildings of the Roman period: the Traianeum and the temple of Caracalla. The lower parts are occupied by the market-place, the gymnasia, and the theatre. After Thiersch and Blaum.

1. RESTORATION OF THE CITY OF PRIENE

2. RESTORATION OF THE ACROPOLIS OF PERGAMUM

LXXXV. THE HELLENISTIC CITIES

and their own customs; and, above all, they were accustomed to a certain measure of self-government. This the monarchs were obliged to reckon with. For this reason, wherever a Hellenistic monarch, part of whose territory belonged to Greek city-states, was at the head of a government, he, like the Persian kings, respected the self-governing power of these communities; he merely deprived them of political independence and obliged them to pay part of their revenue into the royal treasury. Since a steady stream of Greek settlers quickened the economic life of the country and swelled the royal revenues, and since these settlers were a support to the power of the king, who secured to the Greeks financial prosperity in return, therefore the majority of the Hellenistic monarchs, especially the Seleucidae and the kings of Asia Minor, welcomed the appearance of new Greek cities in their dominions, and recognized their right of self-government.

The Ptolemies were an exception to this rule. Except Alexandria, founded by Alexander, and ancient Naucratis, and Ptolemais in south Egypt, founded by Ptolemy Soter, there were no cities in the whole kingdom which had Greek institutions and a predominantly Greek population. For the above-mentioned cities, however, the Ptolemies were forced to recognize the right of self-government; but this right was strictly controlled by the sovereign, and no new Greek cities were permitted. The Greeks who came to settle were distributed among the larger and smaller centres of the population. But there also the Greeks and other foreigners, especially the Jews and Persians, formed small associations, within which they led their peculiar life. The Ptolemies were forced to concede certain rights to them, and to recognize them as corporations possessing elective representatives and a limited measure of internal self-government.

In all these matters Macedonia differed from the Eastern monarchies. The position of the king was still just what it had been in Philip's time: he was a national monarch, recognized as such by the nation. The army consisted of soldiers recruited within the kingdom. The kings laid no claim to divinity, and abstained from introducing worship of themselves as part of the official religion; it is even doubtful whether worship of Alexander was recognized by the state. The Greek cities situated in Macedonia and Thessaly, while politically subject to the kings, kept their self-government.

The attitude of Macedonia to the cities of central Greece and the Peloponnese was determined from time to time by the actual strength of the rival parties; they were not permitted to have a foreign policy of their own, but their powers of self-government were seldom interfered with. Many of them, indeed, won by arms the power to pursue for a time their own foreign policy. In practice the Macedonian kings ruled only in those cities where they maintained a garrison of their own.

The economic conditions created by the Greek city-states were inherited by the Hellenistic monarchies. As early as the fourth century B.C. Greek trade predominated in the Mediterranean, and the Semitic traders of Carthage had to yield pride of place except to the west of Sicily. Even the Phoenician ports of Tyre and Sidon came by degrees under the influence of Greek traders, and dealt largely in wares produced in Greece. After the death of Alexander Greece is queen of the Mediterranean market and supplies nearly all the goods required by customers in the East and West in exchange for food-stuffs and raw material, and, to some extent, for luxuries, such as ivory, valuable woods, precious stones, and spices, imported from South Africa, Arabia, India, and China; but many of these luxuries were imported in the form of raw material to be manufactured in Greek workshops.

But Athens now loses her position as the chief market of the world; and Alexandria, as the port of transit for all Egyptian produce, such as grain, flax, glass, and papyrus, and for all produce exported from central Africa and the Red Sea harbours, becomes a centre, not only of trade on a great scale, but also of manufacture, where the native products and imported raw material are worked up with all the technical skill of the Egyptians. Alexandria becomes not only one of the chief markets which supply the world with grain, but also a great manufacturing centre, exporting throughout the Mediterranean a number of articles not produced elsewhere, such as paper, glass and flax, and also jewellery and cosmetics.

Side by side with Alexandria, some cities of Asia Minor are still important in commerce. Thus Miletus, Ephesus, and Pergamum take the lead in the production and exportation of woollen fabrics; while Cyzicus, Byzantium, Sinope, and especially Rhodes, become important as harbours of transit and vast exchanges, where the wares exposed are grain, hides, tar, hemp, building-wood, woollen materials, and slaves. These goods are supplied by the north coast of the Black Sea, with the Bosporan kingdom for a centre, by the Caucasus and Transcaucasia, by Asia Minor, Macedonia, Thrace, Syria, and Egypt. Delos, the island sacred to Apollo, rivals Rhodes as an international exchange. This importance of Rhodes and Delos is due to their geographical position: they lie on

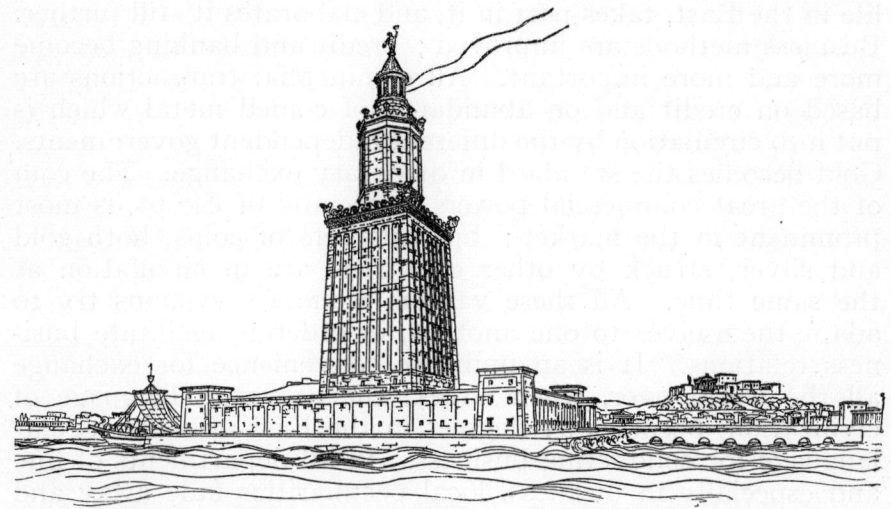

Fig. 35. *Restoration of the lighthouse of Alexandria (Pharos), built by Sostratos of Cnidus. 3rd cent. B.C. After Thiersch.*

the routes which connect the north and south-east with Greece and Italy.

Phoenicia and the Syrian coast continue to be important centres of export and import, and admit to the sea the great caravan routes which connect the Mediterranean with central Asia, India, and Arabia. The caravan trade with Arabia finds an important centre in Petra, and the trade with Hither and central Asia centres at Palmyra. The sea-route from India goes either to the Arabian ports and thence to Egypt through the ports of the Red Sea, or through the Persian Gulf to the mouth of the Tigris, where stands the great commercial city of Seleucia, or Ctesiphon, the successor of Babylon in commercial importance. Antioch, on the river Orontes, becomes the capital of the Seleucidae, and attains the position of a great industrial city, where the raw material imported from Asia and India is worked up into the finished article.

In short, the Hellenistic world becomes one great market controlled by the Greek or Hellenized merchant and the Greek manufacturer. The latter adopts and improves all the processes of skilled manufacture peculiar to the East, and adapts his wares to the taste of his customers. The Hellenistic trader becomes acquainted with the development of business life in the East, takes part in it, and elaborates it still further. Business methods are improved; credit and banking become more and more important. All commercial transactions are based on credit and on abundance of coined metal which is put into circulation by the different independent governments. Gold becomes the standard in monetary exchange. The coin of the great commercial powers, especially of Egypt, is most prominent in the market; but numbers of coins, both gold and silver, struck by other countries, are in circulation at the same time. All these various monetary systems try to adapt themselves to one another, in order to facilitate business relations. It is an immense convenience for exchange all the world over, when Greek, the universal language of civilization, becomes by degrees in the East also the regular language for conducting business. In all departments of life, and especially in business, local peculiarities fade away and acute angles become obtuse. Business life and life in general settle down everywhere on similar lines, familiar and customary all the world over, as free from local variations as the *koine*, the dialect spoken by all the Greeks of that age. But the Greek element is predominant in this new state of society: the Eastern world is Hellenized by degrees. In many places, no doubt, this Hellenism was superficial, and Hellenic culture no more than a thin veneer.

The growth of the old Greek cities in Greece proper, Macedonia, Asia Minor, and Syria, the foundation by the Hellenistic monarchs of new Greek cities in Macedonia, Asia Minor, Syria, and even in Egypt, and the great development, founded mainly on slave-labour, of trade and industry in these cities, led to an increase in the number of persons who were merely consumers, and not producers, of the means of subsistence. To these must be added the mercenary troops, the sailors who manned the fleets for war and commerce, and the steadily increasing swarm of government officials. Hence the problem of providing the cities with food, especially with bread, salt fish, cheese, wine, and vegetable oils, became more and more acute. In the fifth and fourth centuries B.C. it was possible for Athens to feed the subjects of her empire by importing provisions from south Russia and Thrace, and for most other Greeks to live on food-stuffs imported from Italy and Sicily; but this was possible no longer.

South Russia exported as before considerable quantities of corn, fish, hides, and other raw material, chiefly from part of the Crimea, the valley of the Kuban, the coast of the Sea of Azov, and the lower waters of the Don and Dnieper. But in the third century B.C., and especially in the second half of the century, the Scythian kingdom in the steppes of south Russia was broken up by the Sarmatians, a new Iranian stock coming from the East, and by Celtic and Thracian invaders from the West. A great part of south Russia thus became less productive: the area of cultivation and the head of cattle on the steppes went down steadily, and the fishing industry was disorganized. The situation was much the same in the north of the Balkan peninsula, where predatory tribes of Celts were making themselves at home.

Elsewhere, Italy and Sicily were passing through a difficult period, full of wars and acute conflict, while Rome was unifying the country under her own supremacy; and this period was followed by the prolonged warfare between Rome and Carthage. Thus the economic life of the West was crippled for a time, and the export of food-stuffs and raw material ceased almost entirely. The Greek world depended more and more on Egypt and Asia Minor for sustenance. The prominence of Egypt in politics and her influence on other parts of the Hellenistic world were due to this, that she had the largest supplies of grain to dispose of. The kingdom of Pergamum also began to play the same part, and was one of the chief sources of corn-supply at the end of the third century B.C. Then and in the second century the African corn, grown in the territory of Carthage and the Nubian kingdom, came into the market. Such conditions as these in the production of food-stuffs led to fluctuating prices and financial instability in the Greek cities; they also opened a field for speculation, and a class of capitalists who speculated on a great scale was created. In many cases the Hellenistic kings themselves

PLATE LXXXVI

HELLENISTIC ARCHITECTURE

1. RESTORATION OF THE TOMB OF MAUSOLUS AT HALICARNASSUS (the Mausoleum). The restoration is based on extant ruins and on the parts of the building which are now in the British Museum. 4th cent. B.C. After Pontremoli.

2. RESTORATION OF THE GREAT BANQUET-TENT OF PTOLEMY PHILADELPHUS. Of this tent we have a detailed description which had been compiled by a contemporary. The restoration is based on this description. 3rd cent. B.C. After Studniczka.

1. RESTORATION OF THE TOMB OF MAUSOLUS

2. RESTORATION OF THE BANQUET-TENT OF PTOLEMY PHILADELPHUS

LXXXVI. HELLENISTIC ARCHITECTURE

embarked on these speculations, making use of their economic advantages to gain political ends.

This state of things induced the kings of Egypt and Asia Minor and Hiero II in Sicily to give serious attention to the problem of increasing the productive powers of the lands over which they ruled. The systematic Greek genius came to their aid. Greek botany and Greek zoology now found a practical application in agriculture and stock-raising. Greek science collected the observations of practical farmers and breeders, combined them into a system, and made the first attempt to set the management of land on a scientific basis. Handbook after handbook on the subject appeared, dealing with the needs and peculiarities of different countries, and were regularly consulted by those landowners who managed their land on a capitalistic basis. It is a notable fact that among the authors of these manuals we find the kings of two of the monarchies mentioned above—Pergamum and Sicily. Another manual on the same subject written by Mago, a Carthaginian noble, was very famous.

This endeavour to increase the productiveness of the land shows itself also in new and improved methods applied to the cultivation of cereals; such were regular manuring of the soil, rotation of crops, and improvements in artificial irrigation. But special attention was paid to the scientific management of vineyards and olive trees; and novelties, in the way of fruit trees, vegetables, and grasses for fodder, were introduced into agriculture; while stock was improved by introducing new breeds and crossing them with the local strains. Improvements in agricultural science brought about a rapid transformation: primitive methods of tilling the soil gave place to a capitalistic system in which slave labour played a principal part. The same process is visible also in the domain of industry: here, too, kings set the example; here, too, slave labour and the large factory squeeze out more and more the independent artisan and domestic manufacture.

Connected with this is the extensive encouragement given by the kings to the enterprise of the Greeks settled in their dominions. We have seen already that trade was concentrated in Greek hands, and the same nation by degrees took the lead in agriculture and industry. The kings distributed large estates among their favourites, who were not owners but tenants under an obligation to introduce scientific methods of cultivation on these lands. A large amount of land belonging to the state was transferred to the hands of soldiers, who formed in Egypt a new class of foreign landholders, and created in Asia Minor and Syria new urban settlements. Great numbers of emigrants who were not soldiers were also attracted in order to develop the resources of the soil. Large territories in Asia Minor and Syria were allotted to settlers from Greece, and new Greek cities grew up there. In Egypt the settlers helped the king to organize the government of the country and its internal trade on the most satisfactory methods. The money which they gained these settlers invested chiefly in land.

In this way there grew up everywhere, both in town and country, a new middle class, containing both rich and poor. This class consisted, more often than not, of foreigners; and the native population were in general subservient to them and economically dependent upon them. Since all the territory of the realm belonged to the king, and the principle of private ownership applied only to districts bestowed upon Greeks and other settlers, and even in their case was limited, therefore the king could dispose of it all as he pleased. The native population, having cultivated the land from time immemorial, continued to cultivate it, not for themselves but for the king who owned it, and for those to whom the king had granted a part of it, together with its inhabitants, to enjoy for a term or in perpetuity. As before, the population remained bound to the soil, and their labour was exploited by the sovereign. Nor did the native population enjoy any more independence in their relation to the settlers. The latter seldom cultivated the lands bestowed on them: the usual practice was to leave the former tenants in possession and exact from them part of the produce. Wherever improvements in cultivation and reclamation of waste lands were undertaken by the king, or his favourites, or the settlers, this was carried out, almost invariably, by slaves or hirelings, and also by forced labour on the part of the native inhabitants.

Thus the immense majority of the natives in the Hellenistic monarchies were despised and impoverished; and this led to grave social and economic results. Wealth was concentrated in the cities. City dwellers, government officials, and the army, were almost the only customers for the products of industry. The rural population and the slaves, labouring for the benefit of others, have not the means to acquire anything whatever outside the limits of their most urgent needs. Whatever they must have, they try to produce for themselves. Hence industry is carried on to supply the needs of a comparatively small number; workshops are not converted into regular factories; ingenuity is not employed to discover means of mass production; machinery does not take the place of manual labour. And this depressed condition of the people gives rise to hostile relations between the higher and lower classes, both in town and country. This hostility takes the form of strikes, and bursts forth from time to time in revolts of the native populations—revolts often headed by priests. Such revolts were especially common in Egypt, but were, of course, put down by means of the mercenary troops.

This system by which the native population was exploited and ground down was carried through with exceptional thoroughness in Egypt. All the economic life of the country was based upon government control, which embraced all agriculture, all industry, and all trade. The middlemen between the toiling millions and the government were sometimes officials and sometimes tax-farmers, but generally both together. The tax-farmers, who collected the taxes, also directed the labour of the workshops and even domestic manufacture, which produced goods for sale, not for purposes of the household; and the same class had a monopoly in the sale of certain commodities in specified parts of the kingdom. Of course, all this business was done under the supervision, and with the assistance, of the officials, who included the police.

In Greece proper, the islands, and Asia Minor, where the Greek city-states still preserved their freedom fully or in part, economic life took a different line. They derived a great advance in prosperity from several causes—their share in the world's trade, the immense quantity of gold and silver thrown on the market by Alexander the Great after the conquest of Persia, the improvements in agriculture, and the development of industry. In all these cities, and also in the cities of the Hellenistic monarchies, there grew up a powerful and wealthy middle class, constantly growing in numbers and wealth, and engaged in agriculture, industry, and trade. On the other hand, the increasing number of slaves employed in the fields and workshops, and the falling price of the precious metals together with the rising price of commodities, especially of food, made the lot of the lower classes more and more difficult. While the price of necessaries rose, the demand for labour and the wages of labour fell, the capitalists employing slaves rather than their free fellow-citizens, because slave labour was cheaper and more constant. Part of the free population, therefore, enlisted in the armies of the Hellenistic kings, and part emigrated to the East; but many remained behind. Meanwhile the growth in the proletariate was irresistible, partly owing to natural increase, and partly to the spread of capitalism and the transference of many estates to the hands of large proprietors.

In the end the conditions of life became burdensome and unstable in almost all Greek cities. The rift between rich and poor, the *bourgeoisie* and the proletariate, grew wider. Division of land and cancellation of debt were still the war-cries of the popular party; and the strife was still carried on by political and social revolutions which ended in the victory of one class or the other and the extermination of their rivals, while the property of the vanquished was confiscated and distributed. The article which Athens inserted in her constitution after the Peloponnesian war, providing that no citizen should propose division of land or cancellation of debt, appeared now in the constitutions of many city-states. The Corinthian League of Greek communities, founded by Philip and renewed subsequently by Alexander, Demetrius Poliorcetes, and Antigonus Gonatas, was partly political and partly social in its aims; and one of its main objects was to suppress social revolution. But the League was unsuccessful; and the Achaean and Aetolian Leagues, the two largest in Greece, failed also, in spite of their rigid and systematic principles in favour of property. Social revolution burst out repeatedly, now here and now there, and steadily undermined the prosperity of Greece and the islands. The Hellenistic kings were powerless to cure this cancer of Greek life.

One episode of the kind is especially well known to us—the prolonged war of classes at Sparta. There the social question was exceptionally acute. We have seen how the predominance of Sparta after the Peloponnesian war brought wealth to the country and to many individual Spartans. On the other hand, the loss of Messenia, which followed on the blows inflicted by Boeotia, ruined a number of the Spartiates, while their failures in foreign policy and heavy casualties in war reduced to a minimum the number of Spartiates enjoying full rights. Thus there grew up among the Spartiates themselves, to say nothing of the Perioeci and Helots, a sharp division between the aristocracy and the proletariate, the rich and the poor. The growth of communistic and socialistic ideas, the conviction that Sparta had once been a land where the ideal of communism had been fully realized, and also an ardent patriotism which refused to put up with the political insignificance of the country—such were the motives which drove the young king, Agis IV, to enter on the path of social and economic reform. In 244 B.C. circumstances happened to be favourable, and he endeavoured to carry out his plan. All debts were to be cancelled; the land was to be confiscated and divided up among 4,500 Spartiates and 15,000 Perioeci. Some of the large landholders, whose property was mortgaged, supported the first item of this programme, and it was carried; but the endeavour to realize the second proved fatal to Agis. His opponents, led by the other king, Leonidas, put him to death.

Thirteen years later the attempt was renewed by Cleomenes III, the son of Leonidas. In order to carry out his designs Cleomenes did not stop short of violence. By banishing some and executing others he strengthened his personal position and apparently carried out the whole programme of Agis. Then at the head of a regenerated Sparta he tried to seize power in the Peloponnese and throughout Greece. At first he was supported by the proletariate in all the cities. But in the end, in order to preserve the existing system of society and to prevent the unification of Greece round Sparta, Antigonus Doson, king of Macedonia, declared war against Cleomenes and inflicted a decisive defeat on him at Sellasia. Thus the reforms of Cleomenes were brought to naught. The attempt was renewed once again in 207 B.C. by Nabis, who had seized power at Sparta. But by that time Rome was beginning to assert her authority in Greece. After the death of Nabis the Achaean League put an end, not only to his projects of social reform but also to the political importance of Sparta in general.

In consequence partly of the social disorder in Greece, from which Athens alone was free, and partly of the prosperity of the East, which had now become the centre of economic life, the marked progress which Greece had made at the beginning of the third century B.C. began to flag and fail more and more at the end of that century and in the next. Population and wealth began to leave Greece; and her ruin was completed by Rome.

XXVI

GREEK CIVILIZATION IN THE THIRD AND SECOND CENTURIES B.C.

IT is usual to regard the period which followed the death of Alexander as a period when the civilization of Greece mingled with that of the East, to form a new civilization which became the property of all men who were civilized at all. But this view is not supported by the facts. Above all, there was no real fusion of nationalities in the Graeco-Oriental monarchies ruled by Alexander's successors. Considerable numbers of Greeks or Hellenized barbarians were diffused over the surface of the Eastern world, collecting mainly in the cities, and admitted to their ranks certain members of the native population, preferring those who were highest in station. As I have pointed out already, these Greeks and Hellenized barbarians formed the highest class in the new Hellenistic kingdoms: they spoke Greek, and had a common manner of life, and shared the same interests and the same education and upbringing. But they remained merely a minority and foreigners to the great mass of the inhabitants. The latter continued to live their own life, to speak their native tongues, and to believe in their own gods. Greek culture found hardly any access to their midst. It remained an urban culture, and these Eastern cities were a mere superstructure, independent of the native population. To say nothing of India, central Asia, Syria, Palestine, and Arabia, even in Asia Minor and Egypt, where the connexion with Greece had existed for many centuries, the process of Hellenization was extremely slow; and even in the period of Roman domination, we have the express evidence of Paul the Apostle that the natives of Asia Minor still spoke Phrygian and Galatian.

Under such conditions it is difficult to suppose that the civilization of the East could exercise any strong influence upon the genius of Greece; and in fact we find hardly any trace of such an influence. Greek literature, Greek art, and Greek science remained Greek even after the death of Alexander. Some kinds of literature—the fairy tale, the novel, and apocalyptic literature—were slightly affected; and Eastern influence may be seen also in some local peculiarities of Greek art and some offshoots of Greek science, such as astrology and, perhaps, alchemy; but especially in the sphere of religion, where many Oriental ideas were assimilated by the Greek part of the population.

Thus the civilization of the so-called Hellenistic Age is really Greek civilization. In what then did its power consist, and what were its distinguishing marks? First of all, we must altogether discard the once fashionable notion, that this was a decadent civilization. We shall see later that the facts lend no support to this theory. The Greek genius was just as creative as it had been in earlier times; and it still shaped forth treasures not less precious than those of the fifth and fourth centuries B.C. It is true that the form of this civilization was altered; but the alteration followed the lines laid down in the fourth century. Athens in the fourth century aimed at creating a single civilization for all Greece, and was able to go far in that direction. In the third century the task was accomplished: Greek civilization actually spread over the world, and was shared by every one who, within the limits of the ancient world, lived a civilized or, in other words, an urban life.

At this time these dwellers in cities all spoke Greek, and the language was tacitly accepted as the only language for civilized people. The external conditions of life were the same for them all. Their cities had paved streets and squares, an excellent system of water-supply and drainage, hygienic markets, extensive school-buildings and libraries, stone theatres, athletic grounds and race-courses, elaborate temples and altars, and public buildings corresponding to the size of the city, where the town council and popular assembly held their meetings. In the provincial towns there were comfortable detached houses of moderate size, and in the capitals palaces on one hand and large lodging-houses on the other. And just these external conditions were reckoned as indispensable to the life of a civilized being.

Throughout the whole extent of the Hellenistic world this class read the same books, admired the same plays on

PLATE LXXXVII
HELLENISTIC PAINTING AND RELIEF

1. MENDICANT MUSICIANS. The woman's face and legs are modern. The little boy is either the audience or the collector of the coppers. Copy in mosaic, by Dioscurides of Samos (about 100 B.C.), of a Hellenistic picture. Naples Museum.

2. RELIEF REPRESENTING A COMIC POET, perhaps Menander, working in his room and looking at a mask. Roman copy of a Hellenistic work. Lateran, Rome.

1. MENDICANT MUSICIANS

2. COMIC POET AT WORK

LXXXVII. HELLENISTIC PAINTING AND RELIEF

the stage, and listened to the same musicians and actors who travelled from city to city. They all received a similar training and education in the wrestling-schools and gymnasiums, which exercised the body and educated the mind by music and letters—a combination characteristic of Greece. And again, unless he had undergone this Greek education, unless he could read Homer, Plato, and Sophocles, and enjoy the comedies of Menander and the refined music of the age, no one was counted a man of culture. All who stood outside this common culture were reckoned as barbarians, whether they lived outside or inside the circle of Hellenistic kingdoms. It is remarkable also that the Greeks did not force their civilization upon any man. To make proselytes by force never occurred to their minds. Their culture owed its worldwide recognition mainly to its perfection, and partly to the fact that it belonged to the dominating and ruling class of the population. One of the few attempts made to carry on propaganda by force was made by Antiochus IV in Judaea ; and it ended in utter failure ; for it provoked a violent reaction of nationality among the Jews, which led to almost complete isolation in religion and manners.

Under such conditions the creative genius of Greece finally lost its local limitations : it ceased to belong to separate Greek cities and became the common property of all Greeks. The poets of Alexandria or Athens no longer wrote for a restricted circle of fellow-citizens, but for every one, all the world over, who lived the Greek life and who thought and spoke in the Greek language. Long before, Greek philosophers had begun to speak of man in general ; and now authors, musicians, savants, and artists worked for the sake of this audience. Access to Hellenic civilization was freely granted to all who were able and willing to take part in it. The conception of a certain quality peculiar to a civilized being—the conception embodied in the Latin word *humanitas*—dates from this age, and so does the idea of a civilized world. The famous relief of Archelaus, a native of Priene in Asia Minor, which represents the crowning of Homer by the World and Time, clearly emphasizes the fundamental idea of Hellenistic humanity : Homer, the father of that humanity or, in other words, of Greek civilization, had created it for the sake of the whole world and to last for ever. The future proved that the pride of that age in its past and present was justified.

The power of the Greek genius did not show itself only in the creation of Greek civilization. It is manifest also in its infectious quality—in the fact that its influence extended far beyond the limits to which the Greek nation expanded. Hellenistic culture, though it was scarcely affected by Eastern influence, had a strong effect itself upon the future development of the East. It is true that this effect was not visible at once—the Greek leaven was slow in working—but it contributed largely to the renascence of Eastern civilization which took place under the Roman Empire and in the early Middle Ages : witness the Persian culture of the Sassanian era, the culture of north India at the beginning of the Roman Empire, and the renewal of culture in Armenia, Georgia, and finally Arabia in the early Middle Ages.

The infectious character of Greek civilization had also a powerful influence on the creation of Western European civilization, chiefly in Italy and, to some extent, in Gaul and Spain. The Latin culture of Italy and the West is one branch of the Greek culture of the third and later centuries—not a slavish copy, nor an imitation, but an independent national development of Greek ideas, Greek art, and Greek literature in the Latin West, a participation by the West in the city-life of the Hellenic East with all its external characteristics.

What new element did the Hellenistic Age add to the acquisitions of Greek civilization ? What gives us the right to call this age creative ? Let us, first of all, turn our attention to religion. What strikes us is the close connexion between religion and morality in this period. This was partly due to philosophy, especially Stoicism, to literature which discussed eagerly problems of public and private morals, and to the contact with the religions of the East. All this, taken together, prepared a soil for the growth of Christianity with its high moral and religious teaching. It is notable that at the same time the most prominent question in the sphere of religion concerns death and a future life ; and with this is bound up another question—a man's conduct in his lifetime in point of morality as well as of religion. The Eleusinian mysteries of Demeter, which, in combination with Orphism, had given a central position to these matters in their divine revelation, after the death of Alexander spread over the entire Greek world, penetrating Egypt, Italy, Sicily, and the remote colonies on the shores of the Black Sea. Gold plates inscribed with Orphic texts, which tell of what awaits man after death, have been found in south Italian graves belonging to the early Hellenistic Age, and also in Cretan tombs. Alexandria had an Eleusis of its own and a shrine of Demeter constructed on the Athenian pattern. An interesting document was lately found in Egypt—a roll, containing certain prayers commonly used in the mysteries, and an indication of what the believer may expect in a life beyond the grave. With these tendencies we may connect the diffusion over the whole Greek world of the cult of Sarapis, founded originally by the Ptolemies in Egypt and combining Greek and Egyptian beliefs, the Greek notions of a future life, and the ideas of Thracians and Anatolians concerning the same fundamental question.

This growing interest in the problem of a future life led to the gradual introduction of Eastern forms of worship into the Greek world. These cults were carried on by independent communities, which were not connected with any distinct country or nation. The Greeks were attracted by their mysterious and magnificent rites and the mystic meaning that they concealed, by the deep religious feeling of the worshippers, and by that opportunity of allegorical and philosophical interpretation which their tragical and edifying myths freely afforded. But at the same time the Greeks were repelled by the coarseness and sensuality of the Eastern mysteries. They sought, therefore, while accepting these forms of worship, to import into them their own religious and moral conceptions, and to mitigate the primitive rudeness of the ritual—in a word, to Hellenize them. In this connexion we may notice the rules of some Anatolian religious bodies, whose members united to celebrate the mysteries of the Great Goddess, and included in their requirements purity of heart as well as of body. These moral ideas they personified in a number of new divine figures, male and female, including Justice, Purity, and Virtuous Actions.

Greek religion thus becomes more and more spiritual and abstract, and at the same time loses its connexion with special city-states. In the mind of an educated Greek the idea of God in general, the idea of the divine, begins to take the place of particular deities; and the latter survive only in poetry and art and in the creeds of the uneducated. In the light of these new tendencies, which became more and more prevalent

PLATE LXXXVIII
HELLENISTIC SCULPTURE

1. A MARBLE COPY OF ONE OF A GROUP OF BRONZE STATUES dedicated by King Attalus I (241–197 B.C.) in the courtyard of the temple of Athena at Pergamum (see pl. LXXXV, 2) in memory of his brilliant victories over the Galatians. The statue represents a wounded Galatian dying. The pathos of death is rendered with mastery. The sculptor is not rejoicing over the death of a barbarian: he is full of sympathy with the brave fighter. 3rd cent. B.C. Capitoline Museum, Rome.

2. AN OLD PEASANT WOMAN WALKING WITH THE PRODUCE OF HER FARM (FOWL AND FRUIT) TO THE MARKET OF THE CITY. The age of the woman is finely expressed in all the details of her head and body and in the movement. The statue was probably part of a group: the woman is talking to somebody. Copy of a late Hellenistic work. Metropolitan Museum, New York.

3. BRONZE STATUE OF A HELLENISTIC RULER, probably one of the late Seleucids. The king is represented naked, as a hero, a demi-god. 2nd century B.C. Museo delle Terme, Rome.

4. BRONZE STATUETTE OF A NUBIAN BOY, singing and accompanying himself on a small stringed instrument, which is missing: found in Gaul (Chalon-sur-Saône). The movement of the body is carefully observed. The head is realistic but not ugly. The statue breathes the spirit of the mimes of Theocritus and Herondas. Late Hellenistic period. Cabinet des Médailles, Paris.

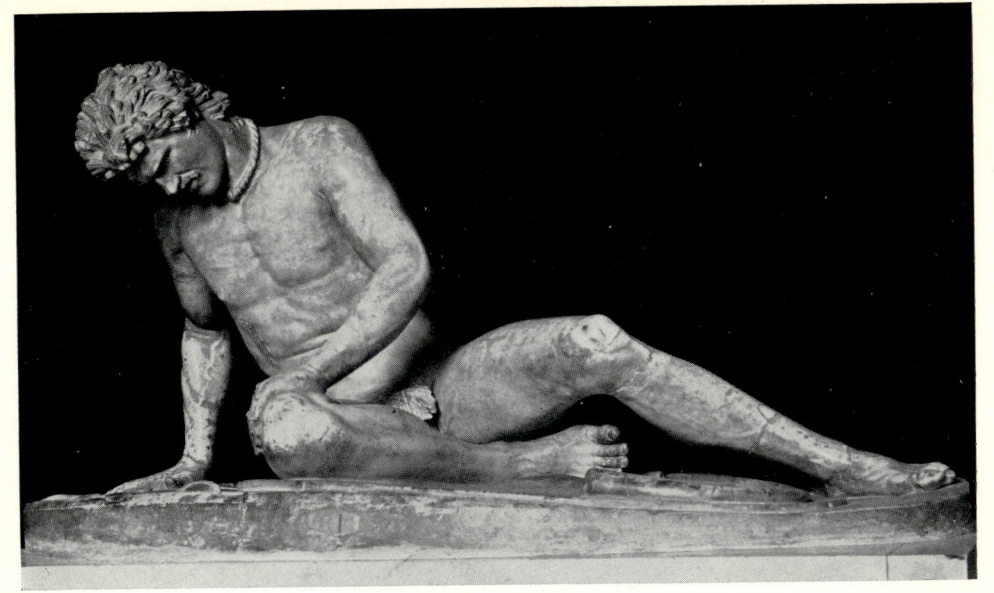

1. THE DYING GALATIAN

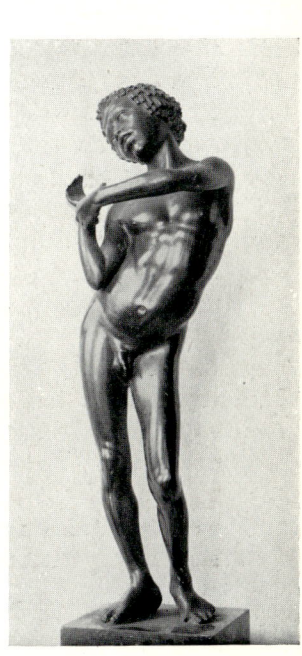

2. PEASANT WOMAN   3. HELLENISTIC RULER   4. NUBIAN BOY

LXXXVIII. HELLENISTIC SCULPTURE

both in Greece itself and among the Greeks of the Hellenistic monarchies, it is easier to understand the attempt of the Hellenistic kings to combine politics and religion in worship paid to the sovereign, to which we have referred in the preceding chapter. This worship, in so far as it entered into the life of their Greek or Hellenized subjects, had no connexion with the old Eastern king-worship which still persisted in its ancient forms among the native population of these countries. The worship of kings which became established by degrees in the Greek cities was quite different : it was intimately bound up with that conception of divinity mentioned above. To a Greek it was not at all astonishing that this divine element should, from time to time or continuously, be incarnated in leaders, saviours, and benefactors of mankind. Hence are derived the names under which the Hellenistic kings were worshipped—Soter, ' Saviour ' ; Theos, ' God ' ; Epiphanes, ' The Revealed One ' ; Euergetes, ' Benefactor ' ; New Dionysus, and New Heracles.

Side by side with religious mysticism, we find rationalism and materialism widely diffused in the society of the age. Agnosticism, which denies that man can know anything about God ; atheism, which disbelieves in God ; scepticism, and euhemerism, which explains away the supernatural part of religion—all these had plenty of partisans and followers, for whom religion was merely an artificial invention of the human mind. An instance of this tendency is the deification of Luck and Fortune—Tyché, *Fortuna*—powers whose worship was widely diffused throughout the whole Hellenistic world.

The inexhaustible power of Greek genius, even after the death of Alexander, is clearly shown in the domain of art and letters. New kinds of literature come to the front, created by the requirements and changed character of the age. Some of the old forms, tragedy for instance, die out by degrees, while others, such as epic poetry, change their aspect ; and new forms, closely allied to the old, flourish luxuriantly. Dramatic poetry is chiefly represented by the New Comedy, a comedy of character and idea and, in a less degree, of intrigue. It proceeds from the tragedy of Euripides and the philosophic study of human character in all its variety—a subject on which Theophrastus, the pupil of Aristotle, wrote a book. An Athenian, Menander, was the most famous writer of these comedies ; and some manuscripts of his plays have recently been discovered in the ruins of Egyptian towns and villages.

Akin to comedy are a number of new literary types, half realistic and half philosophical. Such are the mimes—scenes from common life, a distorting mirror which reproduces the low life of Greek cities. Sophron in the fifth century B.C. had been a skilful writer of mimes, and he was now followed by Herondas, a native of Cos. Together with the literary mime there were popular forms of it, full of lively humour and often frankly obscene. Partly sung and partly spoken, they parodied both comedy and tragedy ; they turned chiefly on love and the adventures of lovers. Very few specimens of this latter kind have been preserved : it did not reckon itself as literature and made no claim to permanence.

Another popular form of composition is the Diatribe, mainly Cynic in its origin. Written both in prose and verse, it fights a fierce battle against the conventionality, hypocrisy, frivolity, immorality, and injustice of the time. The most famous writer of Diatribe in prose was Bion, a native of Olbia on the Black Sea ; but from recent discoveries we know more of the Diatribes in verse, written by Crates of Thebes, Menippus of Gadara, Cercidas of Megalopolis, Phoenix of Colophon, and Timon of Phlius. The work of Cercidas is specially interesting, because it pictures so clearly the stormy politics and social life of the time.

In contrast with ludicrous and trifling scenes of town life, the Idyll, in which Theocritus, a Sicilian, reached the summit of perfection, depicts the life of shepherds and husbandmen— a life so remote and so desirable to the dwellers in great cities with their bustle and noise and pursuit of gain. The same idyllic note is imported into miniature epics, in which ancient legends are retold, and which, like the idyll, combine romantic description of the past with fine writing about lovers and, in some cases, delicate delineation of character. Callimachus is the chief writer of the little epic.

The wider horizon of the Hellenistic Greeks, their greater knowledge of other nations, and the stress laid by philosophers on humanity as distinct from nationality, made society take an interest in the so-called barbaric peoples—Scythians, Thracians, and Celts. The philosophers, followed by such historians as Ephorus, approach the study of these races from the moral point of view : their souls are vexed by the corruption of contemporary society, and they paint a somewhat imaginary picture of the noble savage, combining reality with fancy, and representing his life as an embodiment of personal and social morality. From the same sources the Romance of travel and adventure is developed after Eastern models; the author carries his hero and heroine from one unknown country to another, and finally unites them in the bonds of marriage. Of Eastern origin is the fairy tale also, which now, when written in Greek by Aesop, becomes a favourite both with adults and children.

Another highly popular form of literature is the Epigram —a brief rendering in verse of the most various impressions, a terse and witty summary of whatever excited the poet's interest. To the same category belong metrical epitaphs, which describe in brief the character of the dead man and the feelings of surviving relations and friends; and also inscriptions on consecrated objects. Hellenistic poetry lays more stress on love than on any other emotion. An infinite number of elegiac poems, with mortal men or immortal gods for heroes, were written at this time. As most of these poets had patrons among the powerful of this world and many of them were dependants of the kings, their verse often ministers to the pride of these personages—proclaiming the luxury of their palaces and parks, the splendour of their festivals, and the glory of their military exploits. Nevertheless, the poets are not blind to the seamy side of life. For instance, Lycophron in his *Alexandra* (another name for Cassandra, who declaims the whole tragedy as a monologue) in mysterious language, full of mystical and mythical presentiment, foretells the speedy ruin and destruction of those great Hellenistic monarchies which seemed so firmly established.

Finally, that local patriotism which, in spite of the dispersion of the Greeks, never ceased to burn in their hearts, and the consciousness that the city-state and its past glory were dying out by degrees, created a romantic interest in that half-legendary past not only among savants, but also among poets who were themselves savants and antiquarians. Thus there were produced such works as the *Aitia* of Callimachus, partly ethical and partly scientific, in which the learned poet parades before the reader's eyes a succession of far-fetched myths and forgotten legends, often dealing with unimportant and depopulated places. The same combination of science and poetry is found in attempts to expound in verse a treatise on some technical subject: Nicander's *Antidotes to Poisons* and *Snake-Bites*, and the versified Astronomy of Aratus are familiar instances.

In all the literary production of the Hellenistic Age one common feature is observable: apart from the interest of the subject, the reader demanded of the author excellence of form. And this excellence has been carried to the highest point in the best work. The vocabulary is copious, varied, and elegant; the style is refined and highly flexible, varying with the subject; the metres are handled with the utmost care on strictly scientific methods. Authorship had become a speciality requiring a long and laborious apprenticeship. A special class of writers by profession was now seen for the first time in Greek society.

These men did more than create a new literature: they guarded jealously and studied attentively all that had been done before their time. Most of them, whether poets or prose-writers, were scholars also, who gave a considerable part of their time to the study of the best productions belonging to that period which they also regarded as classical in the history of Greek literature; they published critical editions and commentaries on those productions. This interest in the past has borne fruit of the highest importance. For these learned authors first introduced past literature into schools, as an indispensable study for every educated man. They, too, saved for posterity the meagre information which we possess concerning the writers from the seventh to the third centuries B.C. They created literary biography and based on it the history of literature. Under their influence the first great public libraries were formed.

Under their influence also books made their way into private houses and families; and this promoted the trade in books and laid a foundation for the publishing business. The ubiquity of books in the life of the Hellenistic Greeks is clearly proved by the discoveries of books or scattered leaves in the private houses and tombs of Greeks who lived in the cities and even villages of Egypt. If a considerable part of Greek literature, and especially the classical, pre-Hellenistic part, has been preserved, we owe this to the scholars of the Hellenistic Age.

To study the past is the special province of history, which

is partly literature and partly science ; and it goes without saying that the historians of this age took a lively interest in the past, whether immediate or remote, of the Greeks themselves and of so-called 'barbarians' ; nor did they neglect the history of their own times. A number of writers, some of whom had taken part in the incidents they described, wrote the history of Alexander's reign. The Hellenistic monarchies and individual Greek cities had also their own historiographers. Others studied the history of the East. Recent archaeological discovery has thrown much light on the history of Egypt and Babylonia ; our previous knowledge, except that gained from Herodotus, was almost all derived from two Hellenized priests of this period, Manetho and Berosus, an Egyptian and a Babylonian. And other historians, notably Timaeus, undertook a new task, by collecting and arranging facts referring to the history of the West, especially of Italy. I may notice also that the religious books of the East were first translated at this time : the first translation of the Old Testament into Greek was made at Alexandria under the Ptolemies.

While the historian in literary form either described a single period in the development of the past or wrote a general history from the earliest times, there were also many historical specialists in the Hellenistic Age who collected materials for history in monographs or threw light upon disputed points. It should also be noticed that men were interested, not only in the records of political events, but also in the history of human civilization. The first general outline of civilization and its development in Greece was written by Dicaearchus, a pupil of Aristotle, and called *The Life of Hellas*. Unfortunately, hardly anything has been preserved out of the immense historical production of the Hellenistic Age. The Romans, who guarded jealously the classical literature of Greece, took little interest in Hellenistic history. So most of the historical works belonging to this period disappeared gradually from circulation and found no place in medieval libraries. And, indeed, the same fate befell the other writers and savants of the age : our knowledge of them is derived from sorry fragments or extracts preserved by later writers, under the Roman Republic or the Roman Empire.

Art in the Hellenistic Age, whether architecture or sculpture or painting, was still Greek. Architects gave their

PLATE LXXXIX
PAINTING AND SCULPTURE. 4TH CENT. B.C. TO 1ST CENT. A.D.

1. WALL-PAINTING IN A CHAPEL AT DOURA IN MESOPOTAMIA, representing Konon, a local Syro-Hellenic citizen of Doura, sacrificing to the gods. 1st century A.D. The style, like the life of the region, combines Greek and Oriental elements.

2. FUNERAL STELE OF A PHOENICIAN PRIEST BA'ALYATON BY NAME. The priest is shown praying to his god, with the right hand lifted and a libation patera in the left hand. Note the religious enthusiasm so strikingly rendered by the artist. Greco-Phoenician work of the late 4th century B.C. Found in Phoenicia. Kopenhagen, Glyptothek. (With the kind permission of the Direction of the Museum.)

3. RELIEF FROM THE TOMB OF PETOSIRIS, an Egyptian magnate at Hermupolis. Scenes from life on the estates of Petosiris. Men and women bringing gifts. The scenes repeat those of early Egyptian graves, but the style and the manner show unmistakable Greek influence. Note e.g. the baby in the arms of his mother, the head of the gazelle seen full face, &c. Greco-Egyptian art of the 4th century B.C. with some Persian influence. After Lefebvre.

1. WALL-PAINTING AT DOURA

2. FUNERAL STELE OF A PHOENICIAN PRIEST, BAʻALYATON BY NAME

3. RELIEF FROM TOMB OF PETOSIRIS

LXXXIX. PAINTING AND SCULPTURE, IVth CENT. B.C. TO 1st CENT. A.D.

attention chiefly to buildings for secular purposes. Temples, indeed, were still built in large numbers, remarkable for vast proportions and increasing elegance of detail; and immense altars surrounded by colonnades, like the altar of Zeus at Pergamum, were constructed; but no new architectural ideas or forms were employed in these works. Secular architecture, on the other hand, was rich in invention. Royal palaces, parks and gardens to surround them, pavilions and lakes in the parks, royal country residences—all these were planned and built in rapid succession at Alexandria, Antioch, Pergamum, and Pella. Construction of this kind offered new problems to the architects of the day. Though they could learn much from their Eastern predecessors, it is certain that they solved many of their difficulties independently; for one thing, they employed for their new objects the colonnades and pillars which had been first freely used for Greek temples. Unfortunately, not a single Hellenistic palace has been preserved, except that of Pergamum, which was built in Roman times. But it is very probable that the Palatine residence and Italian villas of the Roman emperors were copied from the palaces and villas of the Hellenistic monarchs.

About their methods of town-building we have much fuller information. A number of cities, which were either founded or entirely rebuilt in this age, have been investigated in recent times: such are Pergamum, Miletus, Priene, Assus, Magnesia on the Maeander, in Asia Minor; Pompeii in Italy; and others in Sicily, Syria, and Egypt. Everywhere we see the skill with which the town has been planned, the regularity with which the separate districts have been laid out, the care with which the sites for public buildings and open spaces were chosen. The haphazard arrangement of houses which had before been normal now gave place to a regular system. Types of public buildings were definitely fixed for the first time and constantly repeated—halls for the city council, the civil courts, and the body of citizens; theatres and concert-rooms; markets and exchanges; lighthouses; gymnasiums and wrestling-grounds; fields for athletics and race-courses. Lastly, now and not till now, architecture stoops to the construction of convenient and beautiful private houses, with entrances, courts, and enclosed gardens.

Another architectural novelty which belongs to this period is the rapid erection of temporary buildings, purely decorative, and large and beautiful, for the festivals and gaieties of the Hellenistic kings. Thus an immense pavilion was constructed in a few days at Babylon by Alexander's orders, on the occasion of a splendid banquet given to his soldiers when by his command they were marrying Persian brides; and another pavilion, of great size and richly adorned, was put up at Alexandria by the architects of Ptolemy Philadelphus as a banqueting-room on a great occasion. Among the triumphs of architecture some Hellenistic writers mention huge floating palaces built for the kings of Egypt, and a luxurious vessel for passengers and cargo built in Sicily by the orders of Hiero II.

In sculpture and painting Hellenistic art repeats the subjects of the classical period, or imitates the simplicity and severity of the ancients in what are called archaistic statues and pictures; and also it seeks new paths of its own. The novelties of their art resemble the novelties of their literature. Some attempt to realize the colossal and the grandiose, as in the statue of Helios at Rhodes; or, as in the altar of Pergamum, to represent superhuman suffering and the limits of bodily and mental effort; others delight in the idyllic and romantic, or in realism carried to the point of caricature and oddity. The altar of Pergamum shows an accumulation of contending figures in the battle of gods and giants; the Laocoon depicts the suffering of a man dying in ineffable torments; and the mosaic found at Pompeii represents Alexander and his Macedonians fighting Darius and his Persians. But sculpture and painting depict other scenes as well—the noble knight saving a tender maid from a terrible dragon; Dionysus, finding Ariadne sleeping, when she was deserted by her faithless lover, Theseus; the young and old Centaurs in the power of mischievous Eros; a group of shepherds with their sheep and goats beside a rustic shrine; a peasant driving his cow to market; a fisherman returning from his toil; a lioness with her cubs, a ewe with her lambs, a flock of pigeons on the edge of a vessel of water; a tipsy old woman holding a bottle; a little slave asleep beside a lantern; scenes from the life of barbarian nations. In fact, there is no limit to the subjects chosen by painters and sculptors.

Apart from this variety of subject and treatment, the Hellenistic sculptors, led by Lysimachus, attacked and finally solved one of the hardest problems of sculpture in general—the problem of movement. In the Hellenistic statues movement is expressed, not only by the position of the separate limbs, but by every muscle of the body: each muscle is affected by the violent or slow motion of the figure.

Painting now attained absolute mastery of technique. Perspective was carefully studied, and foreshortening correctly practised; the problem of representing bodies in space was dealt with; serious attention was paid for the first time to

FIG. 36. *Restoration of the pleasure-ship of Ptolemy IV built for his trips on the Nile. Late 3rd cent. B.C. After F. Caspari.*

landscape, which involved such difficulties as the grouping of figures and the conveying of light and shade.

Perhaps the most remarkable achievements of the Alexandrian Age were performed in the domain of science. Philosophy at this time became detached from science and occupied a special position of its own. It was entirely devoted to the study of humanity, and preferred the psychological point of view to the physiological. The Academy, founded by Plato, continued to discuss the theory of knowledge which their master had been the first to open up; but the final result of inquiry was to convert Plato's idealism into a dull and barren scepticism. Far greater influence was enjoyed by other Socratic schools founded in the fourth century B.C. The Peripatetics, or followers of Aristotle, now definitely devoted themselves to the exact sciences and the social sciences. The Cynics, Stoics, and Epicureans take just the opposite view: they assert their complete independence of science. And all three schools have a further point in common. When the civic ideal set by the city-state had collapsed, the more reflective inhabitants of the Hellenistic states sought feverishly for a meaning of life, an ideal, and rules of conduct. A few could draw consolation from religion; but the purely rationalistic education given by philosophy in the past had produced its effect, and the majority sought an answer to their doubts, not from God but from reason. And that answer came from the Cynics, Stoics, and Epicureans. The schools all start with the same idea: a man can find satisfaction nowhere but in himself and his own inner world. Tranquillity of mind (*ataraxia*) is a thing inside us; to the sage the external world is a matter of indifference. ' It is possible', said the Stoics, ' to adapt yourself to that world, and to work in it and for it honestly and actively; but you must not sacrifice your own peace of mind.' ' You may fight with it and show it up', said the Cynics, ' and put on a warlike aspect in relation to it.' ' You may look at it with a pitying sneer', said the Epicureans, ' and take from it the best it has to give; but this is of small account compared with that peace of mind which turns a slave into a free man and a king.' A man has duties towards his fellow men, but his chief duty is towards himself; and that alone can save him from a life of petty anxiety and moral insignificance.

This theory of indifference, however, had little practical effect upon men's actions. They continued to work and to create, especially in the domain of science. Of the social sciences I have already spoken. Still more was accomplished in what are called the exact or experimental sciences. We are still quite unable to estimate the progress made in these by the Greeks of the third and second centuries B.C. Their treatises are lost, and we have to piece them together from selections or later work in the same field. This is a difficult and complicated process, for which a knowledge of languages and ancient history is needed, and also a knowledge of the stage reached at a given period by this or that branch of exact science. But even now it is becoming clear that the capital discoveries of the nineteenth century were, in respect of their principle, anticipated by the savants of the Hellenistic Age. Few know how marvellous were the anatomical and physiological discoveries of Herophilus. By a series of experiments he explained the functions of the brain, studied the nervous system, and mastered the main principles of the circulation of the blood. Aristarchus of Samos, a contemporary of Ptolemy II, proved by science and mathematics the existence of the solar system, and his discoveries were carried farther by his pupil, Seleucus of Babylon. Diels and Heiberg have shown in recent investigations the extraordinary attainments of Archimedes in mathematics and mechanics, and have pointed out the continuous development of mathematical science from ancient times to our own. We must not forget that the manual of geometry commonly used in our schools till a few years ago was compiled by Euclid, a Hellenistic Greek. What Euclid did for geometry was done for trigonometry by Apollonius of Perga. The foundations of mathematical geography were laid by Eratosthenes. Nor would it be difficult to add many more names to this list.

It is typical also of the Hellenistic Age that learning and the importance of learning were then for the first time recognized and appreciated by the state. The private philosophic schools still went on; but side by side with them rose the first public establishments for the encouragement of literature and science. The Museum (or 'Home of the Muses') at Alexandria was the first learned society maintained by the state. It was a society of savants and men of letters who devoted their whole lives to science and literature. A great library was placed at their service, and also other appliances for study, for instance, a zoological garden. Pergamum could boast of a similar institution, and so sought to rival Alexandria in this field also.

PLATE XC
GREEK LIFE IN HELLENISTIC TIMES

1. BRONZE FIGURINE OF A NEGRO FOUND IN EGYPT. A negro slave with his arms bound behind his back. The expression of his face is arrogant. He has probably done something bad and is going to be punished. 3rd cent. B.C. Paris, Louvre.

2. FRAGMENT OF A CLAY STATUETTE FROM ALEXANDRIA. The statuette represents a lamplighter of Alexandria carrying a lantern and a ladder. The statuette shows that at night time the streets and the public buildings, e. g. temples, were not dark. At Pompeii a painted election inscription says: 'lamplighter, hold the ladder'. The painter of this inscription probably employed the services of a public lamplighter. 3rd to 2nd cent. B.C. Paris, Cabinet des Médailles.

3. CLAY STATUETTE FROM ASIA MINOR. A slave walks down the street. He has been at the market and is going home with the daily supply of provisions. 3rd to 2nd cent. B.C. Paris, Louvre.

4. CLAY STATUETTE FROM ASIA MINOR. Old nurse with the baby in her lap. 2nd to 1st cent. B.C. Paris, Louvre.

5. CLAY STATUETTE OF A WAR ELEPHANT FROM ASIA MINOR. An Indian war elephant carrying a tower adorned with circular shields tramples with his feet and beats with his trunk a dying Gaul. The terra-cotta no doubt reproduces a statue which was set up in memory of one of the victories of the Hellenistic kings over the Galatians in Asia Minor. 3rd to 2nd cent. B.C. Paris, Louvre.

1. FIGURINE FOUND IN EGYPT

2. STATUETTE FROM ALEXANDRIA

3. STATUETTE FROM ASIA MINOR

4. STATUETTE FROM ASIA MINOR

5. STATUETTE FROM ASIA MINOR

XC. GREEK LIFE IN HELLENISTIC TIMES

CHRONOLOGY

BABYLONIA

	B.C.
Process of unification of cities in Sumer and Akkad	end of fifth millennium
First historical dynasties of Kish, Uruk, and Ur	beginning of the fourth millennium
King Mesilim of Kish	end of the fourth millennium
Third dynasty of Kish	about the end of the fourth millennium
Dynasty of Lagash	about 3100
Ur-Nina, king of Lagash	about 3100
Eannatum, king of Lagash	about 3000
Lugal-zaggizi, king of Uruk and Umma	after 2900
Sargon I, king of Akkad (union of Sumer and Akkad)	about 2800
Naram-Sin, king of Akkad	about 2730
Gudea, patesi of Lagash	about 2600 or 2550
Gutian dynasty	about 2597–2472
Utukhegal, king of Uruk	after 2472
Ur-engur, king of Ur (union of Sumer and Akkad)	about 2465
Dungi, king of Ur	about 2447
Semitic dynasties of Larsa and Isin	till 2131
Dynasty of Babylon	after 2129
Hammurabi, king of Babylon	2123–2081
Hittites seized Babylonia	at the beginning of the second millennium
Kassite dynasty in Babylon	1746–1169
New Babylonian kingdom	625–539
Capture of Jerusalem by Nebuchadnezzar	597
Conquest of Babylon by the Persians	539

EGYPT

Beginning of the historical epoch in Egypt	fifth millennium
Introduction of a correct calendar	4241 or 4238
Dynasty of Hieraconpolis in Southern Egypt	second half of the fifth millennium
United Egypt (Dynasties I to VI)	end of the fourth millennium to the beginning of the third
Fourth, Fifth, and Sixth Dynasties	3100–2700
Feudal period in Egyptian history (Dynasties VII to XI)	third millennium
Eleventh and Twelfth Dynasties (attempts of the Theban Pharaohs to reunite feudal Egypt, foreign campaigns, extension of sea power)	end of third millennium
Senusret III	2099–2061
Amenemhet III	2061–2013
Invasion of Egypt by the Hyksos	1800
Expulsion of the Hyksos from Egypt	about 1600
Eighteenth Dynasty (Imperialistic policy of Egypt)	1580–1346
Thutmose I	1545–1514
Hatshepsut	1501–1479
Thutmose III	1479–1447
Amenhotep II	1447–1420
Thutmose IV	1420–1412

Note.—The exact chronology of the Oriental world is controversial. In the few dates given here I follow for Sumer and Babylonia the dates of S. Langdon, and for Egypt the dates of H. R. Hall.

	B.C.
Amenhotep III	1412–1376
Amenhotep IV (Ikhnaton)	1376–1362
Tutankhamen	1360–1350
Nineteenth Dynasty	1346–1210
Ramses II	1321–1234
Treaty between Ramses II and Hattushil III, king of the Hittites	1272
Downhill trend of Egypt . . end of the second and beginning of the first millennium	
Conquest of Egypt by Esarhaddon, king of Assyria	671
Saitic Dynasty	663–525
Conquest of Egypt by Cambyses, king of Persia	525

HITTITES, ASSYRIA, PERSIA

Iranian civilization (Elam)	third and second millennium
Formation of new centres of culture around Egypt and Babylonia	first half of second millennium
Rise of the kingdom of the Hittites	first half of second millennium
Rise of the kingdom of Mitanni	second millennium
Summit of development of the Hittites	about 1500
Shubbiluliuma, 'Sun-King' of the Hittites	about 1385
Code of Hittite law	about 1300
Treaty between Hattushil III and Ramses II, king of Egypt	1272
Beginning of the downfall of the Hittite Empire	about 1200
Rise of the kingdom of Van, rival of Assyria	end of the second millennium
Appearance of Jews in Palestine	end of the second millennium
Creation of an independent Jewish kingdom	beginning of the first millennium
Foundation of the Philistine kingdom	end of second millennium
Foundation of Phoenician colonies on the shores of the Mediterranean (Africa, Spain, Gaul, Italy)	beginning of first millennium
Assyrian code	about 1500
Assyria forming an independent kingdom	end of second millennium
Tiglath-pileser I	1110–1100
Ashur-nazir-pal III	884–860
Shalmaneser II	860–825
Tiglath-pileser IV	747–727
Sargon	722–705
Sennacherib	705–681
Esarhaddon (conquest of Egypt)	681–668
Ashur-bani-pal (conquest of Elam)	668–624
Rise of the Medes	VIIth cent.
Destruction of Ashur and Nineveh by the Medes	614 and 612
Conquest of the Median kingdom by the Persians	555
Conquest of Lydia by the Persians	546
Conquest of Babylon by the Persians	539
Conquest of Egypt by the Persians	525

GREECE

Cretan civilization	third and second millennium
Fortified Aegean towns in Asia Minor and Greece	beginning of second millennium
Rise of the Aegeans	second millennium
Destruction of the palaces of Cnossus and Phaestus	about 1600
Palmy days of Crete	XVIth cent.
End of the maritime empire of Crete	about 1400
Decay of Aegean culture	end of the second and beginning of the first millennium

Chronology 399

B. C.

Greco-Aegean culture	end of the second and beginning of the first millennium
Trojan war	end of the second millennium
Thracian Cimmerian Empire on the northern shores of the Black Sea and in Asia Minor	end of second millennium
Redistribution of population in Greece (migratory epoch)	end of second and beginning of first millennium
Etruscans appear in Italy	beginning of the first millennium
Advance of the Thracians to the boundaries of Assyria	VIIIth cent.
Formation of the *Iliad* and *Odyssey*	IXth—VIIIth cent.
Greek colonization	VIIIth—VIth cent.
Formation of a powerful Scythian kingdom in South Russia	800–700
Invasion of Cimmerians into Asia Minor	VIIth cent.
Phrygian kingdom broken by Cimmerians	VIIth cent.
Lydian hegemony in Asia Minor	end of VIIth cent.
Introduction of coined money in Asia Minor	VIIth cent.
Wars between Sparta and Messene	VIIIth—VIIth cent.
Lacedaemonian military league	VIth cent.
Unification of Attica under Athens	VIIIth cent.
Loss of political power by the king at Athens	about 650
Social revolutions in Greece (age of revolution and tyranny)	VIIth—VIth cent.
Solon elected archon	594
Pisistratus tyrant	561
Restoration of Pisistratus	540
Death of Pisistratus	528
Conquest of Asia Minor by the Persians	546
Hippias and Hipparchus	528–510
First European Expedition of Darius	512
Constitution of Cleisthenes	502
Ionian revolt	499
Expedition of Mardonius	492
Marathon	490
Artemisium, Thermopylae, Salamis	480
Plataea	479
Confederacy of Delos	478
Eurymedon	468
Ostracism of Cimon	461
Athenian Expedition to Egypt	459
Failure of the Egyptian expedition	457
Treasury of the Athenian league transferred to Athens	454
Death of Cimon	450
Peace with Persia	448
Thirty years' peace between Athens and Sparta	446
Peloponnesian war. First period	431–421
Peace of Nicias	421
Athenian expedition to Sicily	415
Decelea occupied by the Spartans	413
Battle of Arginusae	406
Battle of Aegospotami	405
Dionysius, tyrant of Syracuse	405
Surrender of Athens	404
Expedition of Cyrus	401
Agesilaus in Asia	396
Peace of Antalcidas	387
Second Athenian League	378
Battle of Leuctra	371
Philip of Macedonia	359–336
Battle of Chaeronea	338

	B.C.
Alexander the Great	336–323
Alexander's Expedition to Asia. Granicus	334
Battle of Issus	333
Battle of Gaugamela	331
Death of Darius	330
Partition of Alexander's Empire	311
The Diadochs take the title of king	306
Battle of Ipsus	301
The Ptolemies in Egypt	323–30
The Seleucidae in Syria	312(301)–63
The Antigonids in Macedonia	283–148
The invasion of the Celts	279–278
Establishment of the Pergamene kingdom	263
The Attalids in Pergamum	263–133
Bactria independent	about 250
Establishment of the Parthian kingdom	248
Reform of Agis IV in Sparta	245
Reform of Cleomenes	235–219
Fall of Sparta. Battle of Sellasia	221
Battle of Cynoscephalae	197
Battle of Pydna	168
Destruction of Corinth	146

BIBLIOGRAPHY

I. GENERAL WORKS ON ANCIENT HISTORY

1. *The Cambridge Ancient History*, ed. by J. B. Bury, S. A. Cook, F. E. Adcock. Vol. i (1923) and following.
2. J. H. Breasted, *Ancient Times*, 1914 and later.
3. H. Berr, *L'Evolution de l'Humanité (Bibliothèque de Synthèse historique)*. In progress. English translation with some additional volumes in progress.
4. E. Cavaignac, *Histoire de l'Antiquité*, vols. i–iii, 1913–20.
5. A. Gercke und Norden, *Einleitung in die Altertumswissenschaft*, 2nd ed.
6. M. Hartmann, *Weltgeschichte in gemeinverständlicher Darstellung*. In progress.
7. P. Hinneberg, *Die Kultur der Gegenwart*, 3rd ed.
8. E. Meyer, *Geschichte des Altertums*, vol. i, 1 and 2 (5th ed.) and supplement to vol. i, vol. ii, 1 (2nd ed.) ; vols. iii–v (1st ed.).
9. Iw. Müller, *Handbuch der klassischen Altertumswissenschaft* (last edition).
10. Pauly-Wissowa–Kroll, *Real-Encyclopädie der classischen Altertumswissenschaft*, 1893 ff. In progress.
11. G. Perrot and Ch. Chipiez, *History of Art in Egypt, Babylonia, &c.* (or the French original which contains also the Art of Greece).
11a. A. Springer, *Handbuch der Kunstgeschichte I. Das Altertum* (last, 12th ed., 1923).
12. Barclay V. Head, *Historia Numorum*, 2nd ed., 1911.
13. G. F. Hill, *A Handbook of Greek and Roman Coins*, 1889.

II. THE ANCIENT ORIENT

A. GENERAL WORKS ON THE HISTORY OF THE ORIENT

1. H. R. Hall, *The Ancient History of the Near East. From the earliest times to the battle of Salamis*, 5th ed., 1920.
2. G. Maspero, *Histoire ancienne des peuples de l'Orient classique*, 6th ed., 1904.
3. Id., *The Dawn of Civilization : Egypt and Chaldaea*, 5th ed., 1910.
4. Id., *The Struggle of the Nations*, 2nd ed., 1910.
5. Id., *The Passing of the Empires : 850–330 B.C.*, 1900.
6. J. L. Myres, *The Dawn of History*, 1918.
7. *Sacred Books and the Early Literature of the East*, 1917 ff., vol. i, foll.
8. E. Cuq, *Etudes sur le droit babylonien, les lois assyriennes et les lois hittites*, 1929.

B. EGYPT

1. J. H. Breasted, *History of Egypt*, 2nd ed., 1909.
2. Id., *A History of the Ancient Egyptians*, 1920.
3. A. Moret, *The Nile and Egyptian Civilization*, 1927.
4. Sir E. A. W. Budge, *History of the Egyptian People*, 1914.
5. A. Erman, *Aegypten*, 2nd ed., by Ranke, 1922–4 (English translation of the 1st ed. : *Life in Ancient Egypt*, 1894).
6. A. Wiedemann, *Das alte Aegypten*, 1920.
7. J. H. Breasted, *Development of Religion and Thought in Ancient Egypt*, 1st ed., 1912.
8. W. Wrezinski, *Atlas zur altägyptischen Kultur*.
9. J. H. Breasted, *Ancient Records of Egypt*, vols. i–v.
10. J. Capart, *Egyptian Art*, 1922.
11. Id., *Lectures on Egyptian Art*, 1928.
12. G. Maspero, *Art of Egypt*, 1921.
13. Id., *Manual of Egyptian Archaeology*, 1914.
14. Sir W. M. Flinders Petrie, *Arts and Crafts of Ancient Egypt*, 1923.
15. Id., *Social Life in Ancient Egypt*, 1923.
16. H. Carter and A. C. Mace, *The Tomb of Tut-ankh-Amen*, 1924.

C. BABYLONIA AND ASSYRIA

1. L. W. King, *A History of Sumer and Akkad*, 1910.
2. Id., *A History of Babylon*, 1915.
3. C. L. Woolley, *The Sumerians*, 1928.
4. C. J. Gadd, *History and Monuments of Ur*, 1929
5. C. H. W. Johns, *Ancient Babylonia*, 1913.
6. R. W. Rogers, *A History of Babylonia and Assyria*, 1915.
7. L. J. Delaporte, *Mesopotamia : the Babylonian and Assyrian Civilization*, 1925.
8. B. Meissner, *Babylonien und Assyrien*, vols. i, ii, 1920-4.
9. M. Jastrow, *The Civilization of Babylonia and Assyria*, 1915.
10. Id., *Religious Beliefs in Babylonia and Assyria*, 1911.
11. R. F. Harper, *Assyrian and Babylonian Literature*, 1901.
12. Id., *Code of Hamurabi*, 1904.
13. A. T. Olmstead, *History of Assyria*, 1923.
14. P. S. Handcock, *Mesopotamian Archaeology*, 1912.
15. G. Contenau, *Manuel d'archéologie Orientale*, 1927-.

D. THE HITTITES

1. A. Cowley, *The Hittites*, 1918.
2. J. Garstang, *The Hittite Empire*, 1929.
3. A. Götze, *Das Hittiterreich (Der alte Orient 27)*, 1928.
4. E. Meyer, *Reich und Kultur der Chetiter*, 1914.
5. F. Hrozny, *Code Hittite*, 1922.
6. F. D. H. Zimmern, *Hethitische Gesetze (Der alte Orient 23, 2)*, 1922.
7. E. Pottier, *L'Art Hittite*, in *Syria*, vol. i and foll. (and separately 1926).
8. P. Westhein, *Hethitische Kunst*, 1921.
9. O. Weber, *Die Kunst der Hethiter (Orbis pictus* series, vol. ix).

E. THE JEWS

1. G. A. Barton, *A Sketch of Semitic Origins, Social and Religious*, 1902.
2. Id., *Archaeology and the Bible*, 1916.
3. A Bertholet, *Kulturgeschichte Israels*, 1919.
4. A. T. Clay, *The Empire of the Amorites*, 1919.
5. S. A. Cook, *The Religion of Ancient Palestine in the Second Millennium B.C.*, 1908.
6. P. S. Handcock, *The Archaeology of the Holy Land*, 1916.
7. R. Kittel, *Geschichte des Volkes Israel*, vol. i and foll. (1922-3).
8. L. B. Paton, *Early History of Syria and Palestine*, 1902.
9. Id., *Jerusalem in Bible Times*, 1908.

OLD TESTAMENT CRITICISM

10. J. Wellhausen, *Prolegomena to the History of Israel*, 1885.
11. W. R. Smith, *The Old Testament in the Jewish Church*, 2nd ed., 1892.
12. S. R. Driver, *An Introduction to the Literature of the Old Testament*, 9th ed., 1913.
13. Lyman-Abbot, *The Life and Literature of the Ancient Hebrews*, 1901.
14. C. A. Briggs, *General Introduction to the Study of Holy Scripture*, 1899.
15. A. S. Peake, *The Bible*, 1913.

F. MINOAN CIVILIZATION

1. R. Burrows, *The Discoveries in Crete*, 2nd ed., 1908.
2. C. H. and H. Hawes, *Crete the Forerunner of Greece*, 1909.
3. G. Glotz, *The Aegean Civilization*, 1925.
4. R. Dussaud, *Les civilisations préhélleniques*, 2nd ed., 1914.
5. D. Fimmen, *Die kretisch-mykenische Kultur*, 1921.
6. Sir A. Evans, *Palace of Minos*, vol. i, 1921 ; vol. ii, 1 and 2, 1928.
7. Maraghiannis, Karo, Pernice, *Antiquités Crétoises*, 1912 ff.
8. H. R. Hall, *Aegean Archaeology*, 1915.
9. Id., *The Civilization of Greece in the Bronze-Age*, 1928.
10. H. T. Bossert, *Altkreta*, 2nd ed., 1923.

G. PERSIA

1. G. Rawlinson, *The Five Great Monarchies of the Ancient Eastern World*, 1871.
2. Prasek, *Geschichte der Meder und Perser*, vols. i–ii, 1906–9.
3. C. Huart, *Ancient Persia and Iranian Civilization*, 1927.
4. F. Sarre, *Die Kunst des Alten Persien*, 1923 (also in French).

H. SCYTHIA

1. M. Rostovtzeff, *Iranians and Greeks in South Russia*, 1922.
2. Ellis H. Minns, *Scythians and Greeks in South Russia*, 1913.

I. LYDIA

1. G. Radet, *La Lydie et le Monde Grec aux temps des Mermnades*, 1893.
2. D. G. Hogarth, *Ionia and the East*, 1909.

K. PHOENICIA

1. C. Autran, *Les Phéniciens*, 1920.
2. V. Berard, *Les Phéniciens et l'Odyssée*, 1902–3.

III. GREECE IN THE ARCHAIC AND CLASSICAL PERIOD

A. GENERAL WORKS ON THE HISTORY OF GREECE

1. J. Beloch, *Griechische Geschichte*, 2nd ed., 1912 and foll.
2. J. B. Bury, *History of Greece*, 1922.
3. G. W. Botsford, *Hellenic History*, 1923.
4. G. Busolt, *Griechische Geschichte*, vols. i–iii, 2nd ed., 1893–1904.
5. E. Curtius, *History of Greece*, vols. i–v, 1886.
6. G. Glotz, *Histoire de la Grèce, des origines aux guerres Médiques*, 1926.
7. Id., *La cité grecque*, 1928.
8. G. Grote, *History of Greece*, vols. i–xii, 1849–53.
9. P. Roussel, *La Grèce et l'Orient des Guerres Médiques à la Conquête romaine*, 1928.
10. U. Wilcken, *Griechische Geschichte*, 1924.
11. L. Whibley, *Cambridge Companion to Greek Studies*, 3rd ed., 1916.
12. Daremberg et Saglio, *Dictionnaire des Antiquités grecques et romaines*, 1877–1918 (complete).

B. CONSTITUTION

1. G. Busolt, *Griechische Staatskunde*, 1920.
2. W. W. Fowler, *City-State of the Greeks and Romans*, 1895.
3. Fustel de Coulanges, *La cité antique*, 1893.
4. A. H. J. Greenidge, *A Handbook of Greek Constitutional History*, 1902.
5. G. Gilbert, *Constitutional Antiquities of Sparta and Athens*, 1895.
6. W. R. Halliday, *The Growth of the City-State*, 1923.
7. P. Vinogradoff, *Outlines of Historical Jurisprudence*; vol. ii, *The Jurisprudence of the Greek City*, 1922.
8. A. Zimmern, *Greek Commonwealth*, 4th ed., 1924.
9. T. R. Glover, *Democracy in the Ancient World*, 1927.

C. SOCIAL AND ECONOMIC LIFE

1. P. Guiraud, *La propriété foncière en Grèce*, 1893
2. Id., *Études économiques sur l'Antiquité*, 1895.
3. H. Francotte, *L'Industrie dans la Grèce Ancienne*, vols. i–ii, 1900–1.
4. E. Meyer, *Die wirthschaftliche Entwicklung des Altertums*.
5. Id., *Die Sklaverei im Altertum* (both in *Kleine Schriften*, 2nd ed., 1924).
6. R. Pöhlmann, *Geschichte der Sozialen Frage und des Sozialismus der antiken Welt*, vols. i–ii, 1912.
7. G. Glotz, *Ancient Greece at Work*, 1926.
8. G. M. Calhoun, *The Business Life of Ancient Athens*, 1926.

D. CIVILIZATION AND LIFE

1. G. W. Botsford and E. G. Sihler, *Hellenic Civilization*, 1915.
2. Ch. B. Gulick, *The Life of the Ancient Greeks*, 1909.
3. *The Legacy of Greece* (Clarendon Press), 1922.
4. T. G. Tucker, *Life in Ancient Athens*, 1906.
5. L. Whibley, *Cambridge Companion to Greek Studies*, 3rd ed., 1916.
6. E. N. Gardiner, *Greek Athletic Sports and Festivals*, 1910.

E. RELIGION

1. G. Murray, *Five Stages of Greek Religion*, 1925.
2. M. P. Nilsson, *Greek Religion*, 1925.
3. Th. Zielinski, *Religion of Greece*, 1926.
4. F. C. Cornford, *Greek Religious Thought from Homer to the Age of Alexander*, 1923.
5. L. R. Farnell, *The Cults of Greek States*, vols. i–v, 1896–1909.
6. Id., *The Higher Aspects of Greek Religion*, 1912.
7. Id., *Outline History of Greek Religion*, 1921.
8. C. H. Moore, *The Religious Thought of the Greeks from Homer to the Triumph of Christianity*, 1916.

F. ART AND ARCHAEOLOGY

1. E. A. Gardner, *A Handbook of Greek Sculpture*, 1915.
2. Id., *Six Greek Sculptors*, 1910.
3. G. M. A. Richter, *The Sculpture and Sculptors of the Greeks*, 1929.
4. P. Gardner, *New Chapters in Greek Art*, 1926.
5. E. Buschor, *Greek Vase-painting*, 1921.
6. H. B. Walters, *History of Greek Pottery*. 1905.
7. E. Pfuhl, *Malerei und Zeichnung der Griechen*, vols. i–iii, 1923.
8. H. N. Fowler and J. R. Wheeler, *Handbook of Greek Archaeology*, 1909.
9. P. Gardner, *A History of Ancient Coinage, 700–300 B.C.*, 1918.
10. G. F. Hill, *Historical Greek Coins*, 1916.
11. B. V. Head, *Historia Numorum*, 2nd ed., 1911.
12. E. A. Gardner, *Ancient Athens*, 1902.
13. M. L. D'Ooge, *The Acropolis at Athens*, 1908.
14. C. H. Weller, *Athens and its Monuments*, 1913.
15. E. N. Gardiner, *Olympia, its History and Remains*, 1925.
16. F. Poulsen, *Delphi*, 1920.

G. LITERATURE

1. J. B. Bury, *The Ancient Greek Historians*, 1909.
2. A. and M. Croiset, *Histoire de la littérature grecque*, vols. i–v.
3. H. N. Fowler, *A History of Ancient Greek Literature*, 1902.
4. E. Capps, *From Homer to Theocritus*, 1901.
5. E. G. Sihler, *Testimonium animae*, 1918.
6. R. W. Livingstone, *The Greek Genius and its meaning to us*, 2nd ed., 1915.
7. J. A. Symonds, *Studies of the Greek Poets*, vols. i–ii, 1893. Compare the monographs on the Greek writers in the series : G. D. Hadzsits and D. M. Robinson, *Our Debt to Greece and Rome*.

H. PHILOSOPHY AND SCIENCE

1. Th. Gomperz, *Greek Thinkers : a History of Ancient Philosophy*, vols. i–iv, 1901–12.
2. A. Windelband, *History of Ancient Philosophy*, 1899 (the last edition of this work, that of 1912, has not been translated).
3. J. Burnet, *Early Greek Philosophy*, 3rd ed., 1920.
4. Id., *Greek Philosophy*, Part I, 1914.
5. E. Barker, *Greek Political Theory*, 1917.
6. W. Th. Sedgwick and H. W. Tyler, *A Short History of Science*, 1917.

Bibliography

I. MONOGRAPHS ON VARIOUS PERIODS

a. Homer and History

1. T. W. Allen, *The Homeric Catalogue of Ships*, 1921.
2. H. M. Chadwick, *The Heroic Age*, 1912.
3. D. G. Hogarth, *The Ancient East*, 1914.
4. A. Lang, *Homer and his Age*, 1906.
5. Id., *The World of Homer*, 1910.
6. W. Leaf, *Troy*, 1912.
7. Id., *Homer and History*, 1915.
8. H. J. Rose, *Primitive Culture in Greece*, 1925.
9. T. D. Seymour, *Life in Homeric Age*, 1907.
10. J. A. Scott, *The Unity of Homer*, 1921.
11. F. M. Stawell, *Homer and the Iliad*, 1909.
12. U. von Wilamowitz-Mollendorff, *Die Ilias und Homer*, 1916.

b. Archaic Period

1. P. N. Ure, *The Origin of Tyranny*, 1922.
2. C. T. Seltman, *Athens, its History and Coinage*, 1924.
3. L. Whibley, *Greek Oligarchies, their Character and Organization*, 1896.

c. Greeks in Foreign Lands

1. F. Bilabel, *Die Ionische Kolonisation*, 1920.
2. E. A. Freeman, *History of Sicily*, 1891–4.
3. E. Pais, *Ancient Italy*, 1908.
4. E. H. Minns, *Scythians and Greeks in South Russia*, 1913.
5. M. Rostovtzeff, *Iranians and Greeks in South Russia*, 1922.

d. Persian and Peloponnesian Wars

1. G. B. Grundy, *Great Persian War*, 1901.
2. Ev. Abbot, *Pericles and the Golden Age of Athens*, 1897.
3. T. R. Glover, *From Pericles to Philip*, 3rd ed., 1919.
4. G. B. Grundy, *Thucydides and the History of his Age*, 1911.
5. L. Whibley, *Political Parties in Athens during the Peloponnesian Wars*, 2nd ed., 1889.
6. M. Croiset, *Aristophanes and the Political Parties at Athens*, 1909.
7. A. W. Pickard-Cambridge, *Demosthenes and the Last Days of Greek Freedom*, 1914.

IV. HELLENISTIC PERIOD

A. GENERAL WORKS

1. J. G. Droysen, *Geschichte des Hellenismus*, 1877.
2. J. Kaerst, *Geschichte des Hellenismus*, 2nd ed., vols. i–ii, 1917.
3. B. Niese, *Geschichte der Griechischen und Makedonischen Staaten*, vols. i–iii, 1893–1903.
4. *The Hellenistic Age*, Cambridge, 1924.
5. W. S. Ferguson, *Greek Imperialism*, 1913.
6. P. Jouguet, *Macedonian Imperialism and the Hellenization of the East*, 1928.
7. W. W Tarn, *Hellenistic Civilization*, 1927.

B. MONOGRAPHS

1. J. P. Mahaffy, *Alexander's Empire*, 1902.
2. D. G. Hogarth, *Philip and Alexander of Macedon*, 1897.
3. B. I. Wheeler, *Alexander the Great*, 1900.
4. E. R. Bevan, *The House of Seleucus*, 1902.
5. Th. A. Bouché-Leclercq, *Histoire des Seleucides*, 1913.
6. Id., *Histoire des Lagides*, vols. i–iii.

7. J. P. Mahaffy, *A History of Egypt under the Ptolemaic Dynasty*, 1899.
8. W. Schubart, *Aegypten von Alexander bis Mohammed*, 1924.
9. W. Tarn, *Antigonos Gonatas*, 1915.
10. G. Cardinali, *Il regno di Pergamo*, 1906.
11. W. Tilyard, *Agathocles*, 1908.
12. E. A. Freeman, *History of Federal Government in Greece*, 2nd ed., 1893.
13. W. S. Ferguson, *Hellenistic Athens*, 1911.

C. CIVILIZATION, SOCIAL AND ECONOMIC CONDITIONS

1. J. P. Mahaffy, *Greek Life and Thought from the Age of Alexander, &c.*, 2nd ed., 1896.
2. F. Baumgarten, F. Poland, and R. Wagner, *Hellenistisch-Römische Kultur*, 1913.
3. G. Dickins, *Hellenistic Sculpture*, 1920.
4. U. Wilcken and L. Mitteis, *Grundzüge und Chrestomathie der Papyruskunde*, 1912.
5. W. Schubart, *Einführung in die Papyruskunde*, 1918.
6. M. Rostovtzeff, *A Large Estate in Egypt*, 1922.
7. Id., 'The Foundations of Social and Economic Life in Egypt in Hellenistic Times,' in *Journal of Egyptian Archaeology*, vol. vi, 1920.

INDEX

Abdu, *see* Abydos.
Abraham, 70.
Abu-simbel, 97, 107, 152.
Abusir, 150; pyramids, 48.
Abydos (Abdu), 32, 33, 46, 97, 107, 154.
Academus, 338.
Acarnanians, 205, 325.
Achaean League, 361, 363, 376, 377.
Achaeans, 109.
Achaia, 201.
Achilles, 72, 246, 254, 274.
— his mother, 215.
Acragas, 201, 241, 249, 291.
Adad, 124, 165.
Admetus, 233.
Adriatic Sea, 203.
Aegae, 330.
Aegean civilization, 8, 85–95, 129, 177.
— islands 65, 70, 156, 194, 231, 280, 358.
— kingdoms, 105 sqq.; and Greece, 177–88.
— Sea, 70, 71, 79, 121, 262, 263, 265, 266, 268, 358, 362.
Aegeans, 70, 73, 179, 195.
Aegina, 196, 201, 207, 213, 249, 255, 256, 257, 258, 269, 305.
Aegospotami, 281.
Aeolian-Achaean dialect, 182.
Aeschines, 329, 341.
Aeschylus, 243, 292, 293, 299, 304, 309; *Oresteia*, 294; *Persians*, 254, 294.
Aesop, 387.
Aetolian League, 361, 363, 376.
Aetolians, 182, 205, 325.
Africa, 16, 31, 37, 70, 73, 132, 260, 261, 362, 368; central, 20, 357; north, 14, 111.
Agesilaus, 312, 353.
Agiadae, 209.
Agis IV, 361, 377.
Ahiram, 129, 130.
Ahmose, 75.
Ahuramazda, 116, 118, 136, 170.
Akkad, 25, 27, 28, 29, 31, 66, 77.
Akkadian language, 114; religion, 163, 165.
Alcaeus, 241, 242.
Alcibiades, 278, 279, 280, 287, 349.
Alcmaeonid family, 224.
Aleppo, 69.

Alexander, king of Epirus, 330.
Alexander, king of Macedonia, 259.
Alexander the Great, 10, 92, 156, 172, 196, 330, 331, 332, 336, 338, 339, 345, 389, 392; and his successors, 349–77.
Alexandria, 350, 356, 357, 367, 368, 381, 383, 389, 391, 392, 395, 396; pharos of, 369.
Alyattes, 251.
Amasis, 123, 126.
Amathus, 130, 168.
Amazons, 254, 285, 342, 344.
Amenemhet III, 37, 38.
Amenhotep II, 77.
Amenhotep III, 76, 77, 92, 97, 100, 105, 146.
Amenhotep IV (Ikhnaton), 77, 78, 105.
Amenirtis, 122.
America, 16.
Amisus, 203.
Amon (Ra-Amon), 37, 76, 97, 153, 154, 162, 352; *see also* Karnak.
Amorites, 70, 76, 110.
Amos, 111.
Amphictyones, 328.
Amphipolis, 278, 303, 326.
Amphitrite, 264.
Amrith, 168.
Amyclae, 227.
Amyntas, 325, 326.
Anacreon, 242.
Anatolia, 250, 275, 280, 357, 359.
Anatolian Greece, 189–204.
— kingdoms, 155.
— religion, 172.
Anatolians, 123, 179, 283.
Anaxagoras, 291, 293, 317.
Anaximander, 240, 242.
Anaximenes, 240.
Andromache, 274.
Androtion, 341.
Angra-Mainu, *see* Ariman.
Ankhesenamen, 103.
Antalcidas, 312.
Antigonidae, 355, 356.
Antigonus Doson, 358, 361, 377.
Antigonus Gonatus, 358, 376.
Antigonus the One-eyed, 355, 359.
Anti-lebanon, 69.
Antioch, 354, 369, 391.
Antiochus II Theos, 360.

Antiochus IV, 381.
Antipater, 355.
Antiphon, 297, 339.
Antisthenes, 338.
Anu, 165.
Anu-Adad, 167.
Anubis, 33, 97.
Apate, 254.
Apelles, 334, 345.
Aphrodite, 232, 243, 245, 302, 344.
Apollo, 193, 227–47 *passim*, 254, 274, 286, 302, 352, 360, 369.
Apollonia, 203.
Apollonius, 395.
Apries, 123.
Apuki, 146.
Apulia, 334.
Arabia, 21, 349, 357, 368, 369, 378, 382 ; deserts of, 19.
Arabian powers, 9.
Arabs, 70.
Aradus, 69.
Aramaeans, 70, 78, 132, 153.
Aramaic cities, 111.
— tribes, 114, 115.
— writing, 129.
Ararat, Mount, 117.
Aratus, 388.
Arcadia, 205, 212, 270.
Arcadian dialect, 182.
Arcesilas, 246.
Archelaus, 325, 326, 381.
Archilochus, 242.
Archimedes, 395.
Ardys, 251.
Ares, 232.
Arginusae, 280.
Argishti I, 117.
Argishti II, 117.
Argo, 264.
Argolis, 109, 212, 238.
Argos, 73, 182, 206, 212, 236, 238, 270, 300, 307, 322.
Ariadne, 392.
Ariman (Angra-Mainu), 173.
Aristarchus, 395.
Aristeas, 242.
Aristides, 265.
Aristion, 360.
Aristippus, 338, 339.
Aristogiton, 224.
Aristophanes, 295, 297, 317.
Aristotle, 11, 314, 317, 336, 339, 341, 352, 385, 389, 394 ; *Dialogues*, 339 ; *Politics*, 341.
Armenia, 17, 67, 123, 358, 362, 382.
Armenians, 117.
Arsaces, 360.
Artaxerxes, 311.
Artaxerxes III, 139.

Artaxerxes Ochus, 323, 328, 331.
Artemis, 191, 192, 193, 247, 254, 286, 302 ; of Ephesus, 335, 360 ; Orthia, 192.
Aryans (Iranians), 39, 67, 69.
Asclepius, 235, 283.
Ashur, 67, 112, 113, 123, 133, 135, 151, 161, 165, 167, 169.
Ashur-bani-pal, 112–14, 119, 123, 132.
Ashur-nazir-pal III, 108, 113, 138, 151.
Asia, 9, 16, 36, 262, 369, 370.
— Central, 8, 9, 79, 243, 252, 378.
— Hither, 14, 17, 20, 21, 27, 37, 43, 45, 66, 69, 73, 110, 111, 113, 115, 125, 132, 148, 194, 349, 357, 369.
— Iranian, 66.
Asia Minor, 27 *et passim*.
Aspasia, 287.
Assus, 391.
Assyria, 8, 29, 43, 45, 66, 67, 70, 77, 78, 111, 131, 132, 133, 144, 250.
Assyrian code, 28, 81, 114, 138, 162.
— Empire, 113 sqq.
— kingdoms, 357.
— language, 114.
— religion, 158, 161, 167, 171.
Assyrians, 115.
Astyanax, 274.
Athena, 196, 237, 245, 246, 254, 264, 282, 283, 286, 307, 344, 360.
Athena Nike, 283.
Athena Parthenos, 285.
Athena Polias, 285.
Athena Promachos, 284, 285.
Athens, civilization and political and economic development, 73, 109, 182, 206, 213–28, 238, 249, 282, 289, 307, 311–21, 357, 361, 368, 376, 377, 379 ; from 800 to 600 B.C., 213–28 ; during the Persian Wars, 253–9 ; the Athenian Empire, 262–72, 273–81, 322 ; in fourth century B.C., 311–21, 339–43, 379 ; and Macedonia, 325, 329, 331, 332.
— art, 309, 310 ; drama, 303, 304 ; law, 343 ; learning, 291, 301, 304, 339, 341, 381 ; trade and industry, 199, 368.
— Acropolis, 282, 283, 284, 288, 298.
— Cemetery of the Ceramicus, 342.
— Coin of, 196.
— Dipylon gate, 186.
— Erechtheum, 284, 285, 321.
— Parthenon, 32, 284, 285, 286, 288, 290, 305 ; statue of Athena, 307.
— Piraeus harbour, 214, 263, 265, 275, 281, 297, 318.
— Pnyx, 287.
— Pottery of, 309.
— Propylaea, 284.

Athens, Statue of Athena Promachos, 285.
— Temple of Athena, 237.
— Temple of Athena Nike, 283, 284.
— Temple of Athena Parthenos, 285.
— Temple of Athena Polias, 285.
— Temple of Theseus, 283, 284.
— Wall of Themistocles, 244.
Athos, Mount, 253; *see* Chalcidice peninsula.
Aton, 78, 103, 163.
Attalus I, 350, 359, 384.
Attica, 109, 238, 263; language, 182; social conditions, 182, 184, 199, 289, 318; religion, 243; from 800 to 600 B.C., 213-28; during Persian Wars, 255, 258, 259, 260; and the Peloponnesian War, 277, 278.
Augustus, 11.
Aura-Mazda, *see* Ormuzd.
Australia, 16.
Axius (Vardar), river, 326.
Azov, Sea of, 371.

Ba'alu, 102.
Ba'alyation, 390.
Babel, tower of, 57, 63, 166.
Babylon, 8, 9, 39, 153, 369, 389; art, 93; language, 118; political, &c., organization, 143 sqq.; religion, 158, 161, 162, 169.
— 4th and 3rd mill. B.C., 29, 31.
— 3rd mill. B.C., 40-64.
— 2nd mill. B.C., 65-104.
— 2nd and 1st mill. B.C., 119, 123, 125.
— 1st mill. B.C., 111, 113 sqq., 127 sqq.
— 4th cent. B.C., 311, 331, 343.
— and Persia, 251.
— Alexander in, 332, 349, 353, 392.
— Herodotus in, 301.
— Ishtar gate, 128.
— Temple of Marduk, 124.
Babylon, New, 138, 145 sqq., 165, 167, 171.
Bacchylides, 264.
Bactria, 359, 360, 362.
Bactrians, 120.
Balkan peninsula, 8, 9, 109, 156, 179, 198, 203, 224, 251, 252, 253, 262, 265, 324, 327, 358, 362, 363, 364, 371.
Bathycles, 227.
Bedouin, 135, 137.
Behistun, 116, 118, 142.
Berosus, 389.
Bible, the, 111, 389.
Bion, 386.
Bistritza, *see* Haliacmon.
Bithynia, 358, 360, 362.
Biton, 236.
Black Sea, 22, 27, 65 *et passim*.

Boeotia, 109, 182, 184, 199, 206, 213, 214, 223, 238, 242, 255, 259, 260, 269, 313, 314, 322, 328, 330, 376.
Boghaz-Keui, *see* Hatti.
Borsippa, 165.
Bosphorus, 203, 224, 324, 325.
Bosporan kingdom, 362, 369.
Britain, 132, 197.
Bryaxis, 342.
Brygos, 274.
Bubastite dynasty, 122.
Bug, river, 198, 203, 301.
Busiris, 202.
Buto, 33.
Byblos, 160.
Byblus, 69, 71, 111, 129, 130.
Byzantine Empire, 9.
Byzantium, 203, 270, 362, 368.

Cabeiros, 196.
Caere, 202, 264.
Caicus, river, 189, 359.
Calah, *see* Nimrûd.
Calauria, temple of Poseidon, 237.
Callimachus, 386; *Aitia*, 387.
Cambyses, 123, 126, 153.
Campania, 334.
Canaanites, the, 70, 110.
Canusium, 254.
Cappadocia, 29, 67, 123, 358, 362.
Caracalla, 366.
Carchemish, 74, 81, 82, 107, 164.
Caria, 213, 334, 342.
Carian kings, 318.
Carians, 195.
Carthage, 111, 156, 197, 203, 249, 260, 261, 279, 315, 324, 349, 363, 368, 371.
Carthaginians, 234.
Cassander, 355.
Cassandra, 387.
Caucasian coast, 203.
Caucasus, 9, 65, 67, 79, 264, 369.
Celtic states, 363.
Celtic tribes, 364.
Celts, 9, 203, 358, 371, 386.
Centaur, 186.
Centaurs, 285, 392.
Ceos, 242.
Cephissus, river, 213.
Cercidas, 386.
Cercinites, 203.
Chabiru, 76.
Chaeronea, 330.
Chalcedon, 203.
Chalcidian peninsula, 276.
Chalcidice, 224, 278, 327, 328.
— peninsula, 203, 326.
Chalcis, 201, 207, 249.
Chalybes, 195.

Charon, 308.
Cherchel, 300.
Chersonesus, 203.
Chersonnese, Thracian, 224.
China, 368.
Chios, 182, 194, 270.
Chremonidean war, 361.
Christ, 3, 11.
Chrysafa, 244.
Cilicia, 69, 73, 153.
Cimmeria, 121.
Cimmerian Bosphorus, 203.
— Empire, 110, 203, 204.
Cimmerians, 193, 250.
Cimon, 266, 268, 269, 287.
Clazomenae, 201, 291.
Cleisthenes, 224, 225, 228, 265.
Cleobis, 236.
Cleomenes III, 361, 377.
Cleon, 278.
Cleopatra, 330.
Cnidus, 340, 344, 369.
Cnossus, 71, 84, 86, 88, 90, 91, 109, 160, 180.
Codomannius, *see* Darius III.
Colchis, 264.
Colophon, 386.
Corcyra, 275, 276, 322.
Corinth, 182, 196, 199, 201, 202, 206, 212, 214, 219, 237, 248, 249, 258, 269, 275, 276, 281, 330, 331.
— Gulf of, 213, 277.
— Isthmus of, 213, 258, 259, 269.
— Temple of Poseidon, 235.
Corinthian League, 376.
Cos, 386.
Crates, 386.
Cratinus, 295.
Cresilas, 298.
Cretans, 88, 184.
Crete, 37, 65, 68, 70, 71, 73, 75, 77, 85, 86, 93, 105, 109, 134, 177, 179, 182, 199, 207, 230, 383.
Crimea, 203, 270, 319, 371.
Critias, 281.
Croesus, 196, 251, 254.
Croton, 201, 235, 249.
Ctesiphon, *see* Seleucia.
Cumae, 201.
Cyaxares, 123.
Cyclopes, 178.
Cyme, 201.
Cynics, 394.
Cynosarges, 338.
Cynuria, 212.
Cyprus, 27, 37, 65, 70, 71, 73, 75, 77, 109, 130, 132, 160, 182, 268, 269.
Cyrene, 246, 338, 362.
Cyrus, 45, 125, 134, 194, 251, 254, 280, 311, 319.

Cythera, 277.
Cyzicus, 156, 196, 203, 280, 320, 362, 368.

Daedalus, 230, 239.
Dalmatia, 203.
Damascus, 69, 111, 115.
Danube, river, 179, 198, 253, 331.
Darius, 116, 118, 126, 134, 139, 142, 170, 253, 254, 255, 256, 332, 392.
Darius II, 280.
Darius III (Codomannus), 331.
Daskylion, 120.
David, 111, 131.
Deir-el-Bahari, 76, 94.
Delos, 265, 270, 369.
— Temple of Apollo, 233, 235, 238.
Delphi, 182, 206, 224, 236, 250, 300, 301, 305, 307, 328.
— Temple of Apollo, 230, 232, 233, 235, 247, 328.
Demeter, 196, 233, 235, 243, 290, 300, 340, 382, 383.
Demetrius, 358, 361.
Demetrius Poliorcetes, 354, 355, 358, 376.
Democritus, 291, 297, 338.
Demosthenes, 329, 336, 341, 343.
Den, *see* Semti.
Dicaearchus, *Life of Hellas*, 389.
Didyma, 352.
— Temple of Apollo, 233, 235.
Diogenes, 338.
Dionysius, 315, 324.
Dionysius, the younger, 337.
Dionysus, 233, 235, 243, 292, 306, 340, 344, 353, 385, 392.
— Festival of, 293.
Dionysus-Iacchus, 235.
Dioscorides, 380.
Dioscurias, 203.
Dnieper, river, 198, 203, 301, 371.
Dniester, river, 198, 203, 253.
Dodona, temple of Zeus, 235.
Don, river, 198, 203, 371.
Dorian colonies, 277.
Dorians, 180, 181, 183, 207, 208, 214.
Doura, 390.
Draco, 219.
Dudu, 24.
Dungi, 29, 43, 67.
Dur Sharrukin, 113, 133.
Duris, 264, 274, 306.

Ea, 165.
Eannatum, 25, 26, 59.
Ecbatana, 118.
Edfu, 132.
Egypt: earliest history, 8, 9, 13–21; feudal age, 49, 53, 75; pyramid age,

Egypt (*cont.*)
   51, 53; art, 122, 195, 309, 319; political, &c., organization, 144, 145; religion, 161 sqq., 382, 383; 'Nomes', 161.
— 4th and 3rd mill. B.C., 22–39.
— 3rd mill. B.C., 40–64.
— 2nd mill. B.C., 65–104.
— 2nd and 1st mill. B.C., 105–26.
— 1st mill. B.C., 127 sqq.
— 4th cent. B.C., 323, 334, 355.
— 3rd and 2nd cents. B.C., 362, 363, 378; religion and literature, 382, 383, 388; architecture, 391, 392.
— and Hittite Empire, 179.
— and Persia, 251, 252, 256, 266.
— and Athenian Empire, 268, 269.
— Herodotus in, 301.
— Alexander in, 332, 353.
— and the Ptolemies, 356, 357.
— and Macedonia, 358, 361.
— and Pergamum, 359.
— after Alexander, 369, 370, 371, 373, 374, 375.
Elam (Susa), 27, 29, 64, 66, 113, 114, 119, 125.
Elamites, 31, 144, 153.
Elea, 201, 240.
Eleusinian mysteries, 235, 290, 293, 382.
Eleusis, 213, 235, 290, 300, 383.
— Temple of Demeter, 233.
Elijah, 111.
Elis, 212, 270, 286; coin of, 309.
Elisha, 111.
Elpinice, 287.
Empedocles, 291.
Enlil, 165.
Ennead (Nine Gods), 162.
Entemena, 60.
Eos, 246.
Epaminondas, 314, 327.
Ephesus, 182, 249, 360, 368.
— Temple of Artemis, 191, 192, 193, 247, 335.
Ephialtes, 267.
Ephorus, 262, 343, 386.
Epicureans, 394.
Epicurus, 339.
Epiphanes 357, 385.
Epirus, 205, 235, 324, 325, 326, 349, 362.
Eratosthenes, 395.
Eretria, 207, 249, 253, 255.
Eridu, 25.
Eros, 392.
Esarhaddon, 112, 113, 115, 123, 169.
Etana, 64, 169.
Etruria, 202, 249, 320, 324, 334.
Etruscan cities, 249.
Etruscans, 165, 177, 179, 197, 201, 203.

Euboea, 182, 201, 207, 255.
Euclid, 395.
Euergetes, 357, 385.
Euergetes II, 357.
Eumenes I, 359.
Eumenes II of Pergamum, 360.
Euphrates, river, 17–20, 22, 25, 27, 39, 40, 43, 65, 69, 74, 82.
Euphronius, 264.
Eupolis, 295.
Euripides, 292, 294, 317.
Europe, 3, 8, 9, 10, 14, 16, 40, 61, 83, 129.
Eurotas, river, 207, 211.
Eurydice, 290.
Eurymedon, river, 266.
Eurypontidae, 209.
Euthydemus of Bactria, 360.
Eutychides, 354.
Euxine, 224, 358.
Exekias, 246.
Ezekiel, 123.

Fayum, 37, 100.
France, 309, 363.

Gadara, 386.
Galatia, 362.
Galatians (Celts, q.v.), 359, 384.
Gaugamela, 332.
Gaul, 111, 203, 260, 268, 319, 334, 382, 384.
Gaumata, 118.
Gaza, 69.
Ge, 231.
Gela, 201, 249, 261, 300.
Gelon, 261, 300.
Georgia, 382.
Georgians, 117.
Gilgamesh, 60, 64, 169.
Gizeh, 150; pyramids of, 34, 48–51; Sphinx, 48, 51.
Gorgias, 338.
Gournia, 89.
Graeco-Roman civilization, 10.
Granicus, river, 189, 332.
Greece, 8, 9, 83, 93, 115, 128; art, &c., 85, 230, 234, 236, 244, 246, 254, 264, 274, 286; religion, 290, 293.
— 2nd mill. B.C., 70, 71, 73, 79.
— 2nd and 1st mill. B.C., 109, 113.
— 1st mill. B.C., 132.
— and Aegean kingdoms, 177–88.
— Anatolian, 189–204, 250, 251, 252.
— 7th and 6th cents. B.C., 229–48.
— 6th and 5th cents. B.C., 282–310.
— 4th cent. B.C., 311–21; civilization, 333–45.
— after Alexander, 364–77.
— 3rd and 2nd cents. B.C., 378–95.

Greeks, 3, 5, 9, 11, 61, 121, 123, 127, 137, 138, 155, 156, 172.
— Anatolian, 153, 156, 251, 253, 299, 353.
— Ionian, 253, 282.
— Italian, 279.
— Sicilian, 260, 279, 324, 363.
Gudea, 24, 29, 60.
Gutian dynasty, 29.
Gutium, 29.

Hadad, 164.
Hades, 290.
Hagia Triada, 68, 86, 160.
Haldia and Haldians, 111, 114, 117, 119, 121, 125, 131.
Haliacmon (Bistritza), river, 326.
Halicarnassus, 299, 334, 344; tomb of Mausolus, 372.
Hamath, 111.
Hammurabi, 29, 31, 104, 145.
— Code of, 28, 114, 138, 162.
Hanigalhat, 39.
Harmodius, 224.
Harran, 111.
Hathor, 30, 97, 152.
Hatshepsut, 75, 76, 94, 97.
Hatti (Boghaz-Keui), 67, 74, 77, 81, 83.
Hattushil III, 107.
Hawara, 38.
Hebe, 246.
Hebrews, 78.
Hecataeus, 243.
Hector, 72.
Hegeso, 342.
Helen, 207.
Heliopolis, 33, 37, 162.
Helios, 392.
Hellas, 193.
Hellespont, 189, 197, 198, 203, 224, 253, 265, 280, 281, 330, 357, 362.
Hephaestus, 232, 283, 284.
Hera, 232, 236, 247, 254, 307, 340.
Heraclea, 203.
Heracleopolis, 37.
Heracles, 196, 232, 246, 274, 306, 352, 360, 385.
Heraclitus, 291.
Herculaneum, 350.
Hermes, 232, 290, 308, 340, 344.
Hermupolis, 390.
Hermus, river, 189.
Herodotus, 123, 243, 262, 298, 301, 303, 304, 341, 389; *Histories*, 254; *Persian Wars*, 301.
Herondas, 384, 386.
Herophilus, 395.
Herostratus, 335.
Hesiod, 199.
Hieraconpolis, 30, 32, 33, 34, 46.

Hiero II, 363, 373, 392.
Hieron, 300.
Himera, 261.
Hipparchus, 222, 224.
Hippias, 222, 224, 255.
Hippodamus, 296.
Hittite art, 142.
— Civilization, 129, 131.
— Empire, 79, 81, 109, 155, 161, 179, 190, 193, 195, 249.
— Kingdom, 105 sqq.
— Kings, 177.
— Law, code of, 81.
— Religion, 164.
Hittites, 31, 39, 67, 69, 135, 139.
Homer, 190, 207, 232, 287, 381; *Iliad*, 72, 85, 109, 183, 231; *Odyssey*, 85, 109, 183, 231.
Homeric poems, 231, 241.
Horemheb, 76, 100, 105.
Horus, 30, 34, 35, 154, 162, 163.
Husein Kuh, 170.
Hyacinthus, 227.
Hyksos, 38, 39, 65, 66, 69, 73, 75, 105, 107, 145, 171.
Hystaspes, 126.

Ialu, fields of, 162.
Iberians, 203.
Ibi-sin, 29.
Ictinus, 283, 284.
Ida, Mount, 325.
Idolino, 300.
Ikhnaton, 96, 101, 102, 103, 105, 163; family of, 100, 101; *see* Amenhotep IV.
Ilissus, river, 213.
Illyria, 326, 331.
Illyrians, 179, 203, 325.
Imbrus, 182, 313.
India, 252, 332, 353, 368, 369, 370, 378, 382.
Ionia, 73, 202, 213, 253, 255, 287.
Ionian art, 245, 247; cities, 269; dialect, 182; islands, 201.
Ionians, 182, 214, 233, 301.
Ipsus, 355.
Ipuwer, *Admonitions*, 36.
Irania, 66, 79, 114.
Iranians, 9, 117, 119, 121, 125, 135, 138, 171, 204, 332, 351, 357; *see also* Aryans.
Isaeus, 341.
Isaiah, 111.
Ishpu-na, 117.
Ishtar, 28, 62, 64, 163, 169.
Ishtar Gate, *see* Babylon.
Isin, dynasty of, 29.
Isis, 68, 146, 154, 162, 172.
Isocrates, 314, 323, 328, 341.

Index 413

Isopata, 86.
Issus, 332.
Ister, 203.
Italy, 8, 9, 70, 109, 111, 132, 177, 179, 187, 197, 198, 201, 203, 219, 233, 234, 247, 249, 260, 268, 269, 275, 277, 278, 282, 290, 305, 309, 315, 319, 320, 324, 334, 362, 363, 369, 371, 382, 383, 389, 391.
Itoba'al, 129.

Jacob, 70.
Jason, 264, 310.
Jehovah (Yahweh), 111, 169, 171, 352.
Jeremiah, 111, 121.
Jerusalem, 69; Solomon's Temple, 131.
Jewish religion, 11.
Jews, 70, 110, 151, 153, 167, 169, 171, 172, 365, 367, 381.
Jordan, river, 69.
Judaea, 111, 115, 131, 381.

Kadesh, 69, 102.
Kalhu, 113, 133.
Karnak (Thebes), 37, 75, 78, 80, 92, 94, 97, 106, 122, 127 sqq., 162.
— Temple of Amon, 80, 92, 95, 97, 98, 99.
Karomama, 122.
Kassites, 31, 39, 65, 66, 67, 69, 114, 144, 145, 158.
Kertch, 362; straits of, 319, 324.
Khafre (Khefren), 34, 35, 48, 51, 150.
Kharri, the, 67, 69.
Khefren, *see* Khafre.
Kheops, *see* Khufu.
Khufu (Kheops), King, 35, 36, 48.
Khorsabad, 133.
Kish, 25, 42, 62, 64.
Konon, 390.
Kore, 235, 290, 340.
Kuban, 67, 371.
Kuyundshik, *see* Nineveh.

Labarnis, 67.
Lacedaemon, 207, 212.
Lacedaemonians, 361.
Laconia, 207, 208, 211.
Laertes, 185.
Lagash, 25, 26, 29, 42, 47, 60, 61, 64.
Lahun, 38, 54.
Lampsacus, 196, 320.
Laocoon, 392.
Lapithae, 285.
Larissa, 182.
Larsa, dynasty of, 29.
Laureium silver mines, 257, 289.
Lebanon, 69.
Lemnos, 182, 313.
Leochares, 342.
Leonidas, 258, 377.

Lesbos, 194, 242, 249, 270.
Leto, 231, 302.
Leucippus, 291.
Leuctra, 314.
Libyan coast, 20.
Libyans, 76, 105.
Ligurians, 203.
Lisht, 38.
Locri, Epizephyrian, 201.
Lot, 70.
Lugal-zaggizi, 25, 27, 33.
Luxor, 92, 97.
Lycia, 73, 109, 110, 153, 250, 334.
Lycians, 109.
Lycophron, *Alexandra*, 387.
Lycurgus, 208, 214, 292.
Lydia, 79, 110, 117, 125, 129, 153, 193, 194, 196, 197, 250, 251.
Lydian Empire, 250.
Lydians, 195.
Lysander, 280, 281, 312, 353.
Lysias, 341.
Lysimachus, 355, 359, 392.
Lysippus, 334, 340, 344, 345, 354.

Macedonia, 224, 250, 255, 268, 339, 351, 352, 353, 355, 358, 359, 362, 363, 367, 368, 369, 370, 377.
— and Persia, 322–32.
Macedonians, 392.
Maeander, river, 189, 391.
Magnesia, 350, 391.
Mago, 373.
Malatia, 107.
Mallia, 71.
Manetho, 389.
Mannai, 117, 123.
Marathon, 256, 260, 264, 265, 283, 312.
Marcus Aurelius, 340.
Mardonius, 255, 259, 260.
Marduk, 28, 62, 124, 153, 161, 165, 166, 167, 169.
Marmora, Sea of, 189, 196, 197, 198, 203, 265, 358, 362.
Massilia, 203.
Mausolus, 334, 342, 344, 372.
Medes, 117, 123, 144, 251.
Median dynasty, 125.
Medinet Habu, 102.
'Mediterranean civilization', 9.
Mediterranean Sea, 19, 20, 25, 27, 37, 110, 115, 197, 201, 204, 266, 268, 326, 333, 335, 356, 368, 369.
Megalopolis, 386.
Megara, 182, 201, 206, 214, 219, 221, 222, 242, 269, 275, 281.
Mehenkwetre, 52.
Memnon, 97, 246.
Memphis, 33, 35, 37.
— Temple of Ptah, 100.

Menander, 380, 381, 385.
Menelaus, 207.
Menes, 33.
Menippus, 386.
Menkaure (Mycerinus), 35, 51.
Mentuhotep III, 94.
Merenpta, 107, 109.
Merpeba, 33.
Mesembria, 203.
Mesilim, 25, 64.
Mesopotamia, 8, 12–39, 61, 114, 119, 163, 195, 390.
Messana, 201.
Messene, 206, 207.
Messenia, 208, 212, 314.
Messenian wars, 208.
Midas, 193.
Miletus, 182, 193, 196, 201, 204, 233, 243, 249, 253, 296, 319, 368, 391.
Miltiades, 256, 266.
Minaean kingdom, 70.
Minoan religion, 160.
Minoans, 69.
Minos, 264.
Mitanni, 67, 77, 107.
Mithra, 172.
Mithradates I, 360.
Mithradates VI, 360.
Moeris, lake, 37, 38.
Montesupis, 34.
Moses, 110, 169, 171.
Mummius 312.
Murshilish II, 107.
Mussulman creed, 11.
— powers, 9.
Mutallu, 107.
Mycale, 260, 262.
Mycenae, 68, 72, 87, 88, 109, 160, 177, 178.
— Palace of, 180.
Mycenean culture, 179.
— Empire, 109.
— Greece, 178.
— pottery, 186.
Mycerinus, *see* Menkaure.
Myron, 300, 307.
Mysia, 359.
Mysians, 107.

Nabis, 377.
Nabonid, 125.
Nabopallasar, 123.
Nabu, 165.
Nahum, 111, 123.
Nakht, 140, 141.
Naples, 201.
Naram-Sin, 27, 28, 29, 35, 61, 65.
Narmer, 30.
Naucratis, 127, 367.
Nausicaa, 185.

Naxos, 182, 222.
Nebamun, 146.
Neb-Siny, 58.
Nebuchadnezzar I, 158.
Nebuchadnezzar II, 108, 124, 128.
Necho, 123.
Neferrohu, 36.
Nefertiti, 96.
Nekhebet, 102.
Neo-Babylonia, 124.
Neoptolemos, 274.
Ne-ouser-ra, 150.
Nero, 312.
Nicander, *Antidotes, to Poisons*, 388; *Snake-Bites*, 388.
Nicias, 278, 279; peace of, 278.
Nicosthenes, 246.
Nike, 196, 254, 284.
Nike of Paeonius, 238.
Nike of Samothrace, 354.
Nile, river, 20, 21, 22, 31, 40, 46, 48, 49, 50, 53, 97, 150, 356, 357; Delta, 19, 20; Upper, 20.
Nimrûd (Calah), 108.
Nineveh (Kuyundshik), 67, 112, 113, 123, 133, 138.
Ningirsu, 24, 26.
Nippur, 25.
Nisaea, 222.
Notium, 280.
Nubia, 20, 36, 37, 65, 77, 78, 97, 104.
Nubian boy, 384.
Nubian kingdom, 362, 371.
Nubians, 31.

Odrysian kingdom, 327.
Odrysian kings, 325.
Odysseus, 185, 223.
Oedipus, 264.
Olbia, 196, 203, 301, 386.
Olympia, 182, 206, 237, 238, 307.
— Altis, 238, 239.
— Statue of Zeus, 307.
— Temple of Hera, 340, 344.
— Temple of Zeus, 233, 235, 236, 247, 286, 305.
Olympias, 330, 350.
Olympus, Mount, 232, 245, 246.
Orchomenus, 73, 109.
Ormuzd (Aura-Mazda), 173.
Oromazdes, 352.
Orontes, river, 65, 69, 354, 369.
Orpheus, 235, 290.
Orphic mysteries, 290, 293.
Orphism, 382.
Osiris, 146, 154, 162, 172.
Ostia, 340.

Paeonia, 326, 327.
Paestum, *see* Poseidonia.

Palestine, 20, 179, 357; culture, 131; religion, 171, 172.
— 4th and 3rd mill. B.C., 35, 36, 37, 39.
— 3rd and 2nd cents. B.C., 378.
— 2nd mill. B.C., 65, 66, 69, 70, 75, 77.
— 2nd and 1st mill. B.C., 109, 110, 113, 115, 121, 123.
— Persians in, 266.
— Philistines in, 177.
Palmyra, 369.
Pamphylia, 109.
Panticapaeum, 196, 203, 319, 334, 362.
Paphlagonia, 130.
Paphos, 160.
Paros, 242.
Parthia, 360, 362.
Parthians, 359.
Pasargadae, 134.
Pasinisu, 146.
Paul, the apostle, 378.
Pausanias, 227, 259, 260, 340.
Pegasus, 196.
Pella, 330, 391.
Pelopidas, 313.
Peloponnese, 180, 182, 201, 205, 206.
— Language and peoples, 182.
Peloponnesian War, 262, 268, 273–81, 283, 285, 295, 298, 301, 303, 311, 312, 314, 322, 325, 376.
Penelope, 185.
Pentelicus, mountain, 213.
Penthesilea, 254.
Pepi I, 34, 35.
Perdiccas, 355.
Perga, 395.
Pergamum, 350, 359, 360, 362, 366, 368, 373, 395.
— Altar of Zeus, 391, 392.
— Temple of Athena, 366, 384.
Pericles, 267, 268, 270, 271, 275–8, 283, 284, 287, 298, 307.
Persepolis, 116, 120, 132, 134, 139, 142, 170.
Perseus of Macedonia, 360.
Persia: Art, 120, 136, 138.
— Civilization and culture, 8, 9, 27, 65, 79, 132, 382.
— Cion of, 196.
— Greek mercenaries in, 318.
— Peoples, 204.
— Persian wars, 247, 249–61, 267, 271, 301, 307, 326.
— Political, &c., organization, 144 sqq., 367.
— Religion, 170–3.
— World Empire, 116, 123, 144, 197, 262, 309, 349, 357, 358, 364.
— and Alexander, 351, 353, 375, 392.
— Cyrus in, 125.

Persia, and Greece, 194, 214, 265, 268–70, 278–80, 282, 326, 328.
— and Herodotus, 301.
— and Macedonia, 322–32.
— after Peloponnesian War, 311–13.
— Themistocles in, 266.
— and Thucydides, 343.
Persian Gulf, 17, 25, 65, 369.
Pesto, see Poseidonia.
Petosiris, 390.
Petra, 369.
Phaestus, 68, 71, 88, 91.
Phalerum, 214.
Phanagoria, 203.
Pharos of Alexandria, 369.
Phasis, 203.
Phidias, 283, 284, 286, 290, 300, 307, 308, 309, 333, 344.
Philetaerus, 359, 360.
Philip of Macedonia, 196, 323, 326, 327, 328, 331, 336, 339, 352, 356, 367, 376.
Philip Aridaeus, 353.
Philip V, 358.
Philistines, 109, 177, 179.
Philometor, 357.
Philopator, 357.
Phlius, 386.
Phocis, 182, 206, 328.
Phoenicia, 4th and 3rd mill. B.C., 35, 36, 37.
— 2nd mill. B.C., 65, 69, 70, 71, 73, 75, 77.
— 2nd and 1st mill. B.C., 105, 107, 109, 110, 111, 115.
— after Alexander, 369.
— and Greece, 179, 187, 195, 268, 269, 323, 334.
— and Persia, 266.
— Ptolemies in, 356.
— and Syria, 357.
— Art and culture, 130, 131.
— Colonies, 260.
— Government, 155, 156.
— Language and writing, 129, 153.
— Religion, 161, 168.
Phoenicians, 127, 132, 197, 203, 250, 252, 268.
Phoenix, 386.
Phrygia, 79, 110, 129, 153, 193, 250, 358.
Phrygians, 107.
Piankhi, 122.
Pindar, 233, 242.
Piraeus, see Athens.
Pirithous, 236.
Pisistratus, 222–5, 243, 244, 264, 282, 289.
Plataea, 259, 260, 262–5.
Plataeans, 256.

Plato, 11, 314, 317, 336–9, 352, 381, 393; *Dialogues*, 297, 338, 339; *Laws*, 337; *Republic*, 337.
Polycleitus, 300, 307.
Polyeuktos, 336.
Polygnotus, 283, 305, 334.
Polymedes, 236.
Polyperchon, 355.
Polyzalos, 300.
Pompeii, 391, 392, 396.
Pontus, 358, 360, 362.
Poseidon, 200, 232, 235, 237, 243, 264, 285, 286.
Poseidonia (modern Pesto, Latin Paestum), 234.
Potidaea, 276.
Praxiteles, 333, 340, 344.
Priam, 79, 274.
Priene, 366, 381, 391.
— Temple of Athena, 366.
Prinias, 230.
Prometheus, 239.
Protagoras, 296.
Prusias II of Bithynia, 360.
Psammetichus I, 123.
Psammetichus II, 123, 152.
Psammetichus III, 126.
Pseira, 86.
Ptah, 33, 100.
Ptahotep, 50.
Ptolemais, 367.
Ptolemies (Lagidae), 355–7, 367, 383, 389.
Ptolemy I (Lagus or Soter), 355, 357, 360, 367.
Ptolemy II (Philadelphus), 357, 360, 372, 392, 395.
Ptolemy III (Euergetes), 357.
Ptolemy IV (Philopator), 397.
Ptolemy V (Epiphanes), 357.
Ptolemy VI (Philometor), 357.
Ptolemy VII (Euergetes II), 357.
Punic War, first, 234.
Punt (Somaliland), 20, 65, 76, 94, 97.
Pylus, 73, 277.
Pyrrhus, 349.
Pythagoras, 235, 240.
Python, 232, 233.

Ra, 33, 35, 37, 150, 162, 163.
Ramses I, 105, 154.
Ramses II, 97, 102, 105, 107, 152.
Ramses III, 102, 107, 109.
Red Sea, 20, 37, 65, 357, 368, 369.
Rhegium, 201.
Rhodes, 182, 248, 362, 368, 369, 392.
Ritti-Marduk, 158.
Roman emperors, 156, 391.
Roman Empire, 9, 10, 137, 361, 382, 389.
Roman Republic, 389.
Romans, 61, 172, 357, 360, 389.
Rome, 10, 127, 165, 302, 324, 356, 359, 363, 371, 377.
Roxana, 351, 353.
Rusa I, 117.
Rusa III, 117.
Ruvo, 309.

Sabaean kingdom, 70.
Sadyattes, 251.
Sais, 33, 123.
Sais period, 127.
Sakkarah, 50.
Sakkari, 109.
Salamis, 219, 221, 222, 258, 259, 264, 265, 312.
Salonica, *see* Therma.
Samal (Zenjirli), 74, 81, 107, 112.
Samnium, 334.
Samos, 182, 194, 249, 260, 270, 380, 395.
— Temple of Hera, 247.
Samothrace, 354.
Sappho, 241, 242.
Sarapis, 383.
Sardis, 129, 251.
Sardur I, 117.
Sardur II, 117.
Sardur III, 117.
Sargon, 25, 27, 29, 33, 35, 37, 43, 65, 67, 113, 121, 133, 138.
Sarmatians, 363, 371.
Saronic gulf, 213.
Sassanian era, 382.
Sat-hathor-iunut, 54.
Saul, 111.
Scamander, river, 189.
Scopas, 333, 340, 342, 344.
Scorpion, 46.
Scyros, 313.
Scythia, 253, 301, 334.
Scythian campaign, 256.
Scythian Empire, 252.
Scythian kingdom, 224, 327, 363, 371.
Scythian-Iranian kingdom, 138.
Scythians, 121, 204, 243, 250, 319, 320, 325, 386.
Seleucia (Ctesiphon), 369.
Seleucidae, 354, 357, 358, 359, 367, 369, 384.
Seleucus, 355, 359, 395.
Seleucus I Nicator, 350.
Selinus, 234, 305.
Sellasia, 361, 377.
Semites, 9, 19, 27, 43, 69, 70, 77, 78, 115, 144, 168.
— Arabian, 11.
Semti (Den), 46.
Sennacherib, 113, 131, 138.
Senusret I, 38, 70.

Index 417

Senusret II, 54.
Senusret (Sesostris) III, 37, 38.
Sesostris, *see* Senusret III.
Sestos, 262.
Set, 162, 163.
Seti I, 97, 105, 107, 154.
Shalmaneser II, 113, 167.
Shamash, 165.
Sheikh-abd-el-Gurna, 80, 140, 141, 146.
Sheshonk, 122.
Shub-ad, 60.
Shubbiluliuma, 105, 107.
Sicilian temples, 305.
Sicily, 70, 109, 111, 132, 179, 197, 198, 201, 203, 234, 242, 247, 249, 260, 261, 269, 275, 277, 278, 282, 309, 315, 319, 334, 368, 371, 373, 382, 391, 392.
Sicyon, 201, 202, 206, 212, 214, 219, 249, 275.
Sidon, 69, 71, 111, 368.
Sigeum, 224.
Simonides, 242.
Sin, 165.
Sinai, Mount, 20, 22, 35, 36, 110, 171.
Sinope, 203, 338, 368.
Sinuhe, 70.
Slavonic kingdoms, 9.
Smyrna, 182.
Snefru, 36.
Socrates, 293, 295, 297, 298, 299, 303, 317, 338, 343, 394.
Solomon, 111, 131.
Solon, 219–22, 224, 225, 242, 289, 291.
Somaliland, *see* Punt.
Sophists, 295.
Sophocles, 292, 294, 381 ; *Oedipus the King*, 294 ; *Oedipus at Colonus*, 294 ; *Antigone*, 294.
Sophron, 386.
Sostratus, 369.
Soter, 357, 385.
Spain, 70, 111, 132, 197, 203, 268, 309, 319, 334, 382.
Sparta, civilization, 182, 238, 248.
— Social and economic conditions, &c., 184, 199, 205–14, 219, 376.
— after Alexander, 377.
— and Athens, 223, 224, 228, 262, 263, 266, 268–70, 272, 275, 276, 311.
— and Attica, 222.
— and Greece in 4th cent. B.C., 313–15.
— and Persia, 251, 255–9, 282, 312, 313.
— and Macedonia, 330, 361.
— Sanctuary of Artemis, 192.
Stesichorus, 242.
Stoics, 394.
Stoicism, 382.
Strumnitza, *see* Strymon.
Strymon, gulf, 326.
Strymon (Strumnitza), river, 326.

Sumer, 25, 27, 29, 31, 43, 44, 45, 59, 61, 64, 67, 77, 161.
Sumerian civilization, 104.
— language, 114.
— Religion, 158, 163, 165.
Sumerians, 9, 19, 27, 31, 42, 43, 57, 144.
Susa (Elam), 28, 29, 116, 119, 132, 136, 139.
Sybaris, 196, 201, 249.
Syracuse, 201, 249, 261, 277, 278, 279, 300, 313, 315, 337, 363.
Syria, culture, 27, 109 ; religion, 161.
— 2nd and 1st mill. B.C., 105, 107, 110, 111, 115, 121, 123.
— 2nd mill. B.C., 65, 66, 67, 69, 70, 71, 75, 76, 77, 81.
— 1st mill. B.C., 132.
— and Alexander, 332.
— after Alexander, 355–63, 369, 370, 374, 378, 391.
— and Egypt, 35, 36, 37, 61, 105, 107, 357.
— and Greece, 179, 325, 331.
— and the Parthians, 361.
— and Pergamum, 359.
— and Persia, 266.
Syrophoenicia, 113.

Taanach, 77.
Taharka, 112.
Taman peninsula, 319.
Tammuz, 64.
Tanais, 203.
Tanis, 38.
Tarentum, 201.
Tarsus in Cilicia, 69.
Tartessus, 197.
Tauromenium, 201.
Taurus, mountains, 78.
Tegea, Temple of Athena, 344.
Tell-el-Amarna, 77, 96, 100.
Tell-el-Obeid, 44, 158.
Tempe, 257.
Teos, 242.
Terpander, 242.
Teshub, 161, 164.
Thales, 240.
Theban dynasty, 37
Thebes (Egypt), *see* Karnak.
Thebes (Greece), 73, 109, 182, 206, 238, 294, 313, 314, 327, 331, 386.
Themistocles, 244, 257, 258, 265, 266, 349.
Theocritus, 384, 386.
Theodosia, 203.
Theognis, 204, 242.
Theophrastus, 385.
Theopompus, 262, 343 ; *History of Greece*, 343 ; *History of Philip*, 343.
Theos, 385.

Theozotos, 199.
Therma (Thessalonica, now Salonica), 326.
Therma, gulf, 326.
Thermopylae, 257, 258.
Theseus, 214, 219, 236, 264, 283, 284, 310, 392.
Thessalians, 184, 222.
Thessalonica, see Therma.
Thessaly, 182, 199, 207, 223, 257, 259, 260, 285, 327, 328, 367.
Thetis, palace of, 215.
Thinis, 33.
Thisbe, 73.
Thrace, 224, 233, 253, 255, 256, 263, 268, 270, 278, 324, 325, 326, 334, 355, 369, 371.
Thracian states, 363.
Thracian tribes, 364.
Thracians, 107, 110, 117, 121, 179, 204, 327, 383, 386.
Thrasybulus, 281.
Thrasymachus, 297.
Thucydides, 262, 277, 298, 303, 304, 343.
Thurii, 301.
Thutmose I, 75, 96, 97.
Thutmose III, 75, 77, 78, 80, 95.
Thutmose IV, 77.
Ti, 50.
Tiamat, 167.
Tiberius, 11.
Tiglath-pileser I, 113.
Tiglath-pileser IV, 108, 113.
Tigris, 17–19, 27, 28, 29, 40, 43, 65–7, 113, 114, 369.
Timaeus, 389.
Timon, 386.
Timotheos, 342.
Tiryns, 73, 88, 177, 178, 181.
Titans, 233.
Tityos, 231.
Tiy, 100.
Tomi, 203.
Tortose, 168.
Transcaucasia, 27, 67, 110, 117, 369.
Transcaucasian mountains, 22.
Trapezus, 203.
Triptolemus, 290.
Triton, 264.
Trojan War, 207, 246.

Troy, 71, 79, 109, 177, 183, 190, 274.
Turkestan, 65, 79, 332.
Turkish powers, 9.
Turushpa (Tushpash), see Van.
Tutankhamen, 76, 78, 100, 101, 102, 103; his wife, 103.
Tyche, of Antioch, 354.
Tylissos, 71.
Tyras, 203.
Tyre (Phoenicia), 69, 71, 111, 112, 332, 368.
Tyrtaeus, 202, 207, 242.

Umma, 25, 26, 64.
Ur, 25, 29, 42, 44, 57, 60, 158.
Ur-engur, 29, 67.
Ur-Nina, 24, 25.
Ural, mountains, 325.
Urartu, 117.
Urmia, lake of, 117.
Uruk, 25, 29.
Urukagina, 47.
Utica, 111, 197.
Utukhegal, 29.

Van, city (Turushpa or Tushpash), 117, 131.
Van, kingdom, 67, 110, 195.
Van, lake, 67, 117.
Vardar, see Axius.
Venus, 169.
Vulci, 305.

Xenophanes, 240.
Xenophon, 311, 314, 319; *Anabasis*, 192, 343; *Education of Cyrus*, 343; *Hellenica*, 343; *Memorabilia*, 297; *Recollections*, 343.
Xerxes, 120, 134, 139, 170, 256, 257, 258.

Yahweh, see Jehovah.
Yasili-Kaia, 83.

Zagros, mountains, 28.
Zenjirli, see Samal.
Zephaniah, 111, 123.
Zeus, 188, 193, 196, 232, 233, 235, 236, 238, 243, 245, 247, 254, 285, 286, 305, 307, 309, 338, 352, 391.
Zoroaster, 126, 171, 172, 173.

PRINTED IN GREAT BRITAIN AT THE UNIVERSITY PRESS, OXFORD
BY JOHN JOHNSON, PRINTER TO THE UNIVERSITY